D0500307

THE CHILL

VERTIGO CRIME

WRITER
JASON STARR

ART
MICK BERTILORENZI

LETTERS
CLEM ROBINS

THE
CHILL

Karen Berger SVP – Executive Editor
Will Dennis Editor
Mark Doyle Associate Editor
Robbin Brosterman Design Director – Books
Louis Prandi Art Director

DC COMICS
Paul Levitz President & Publisher
Richard Bruning SVP – Creative Director
Patrick Caldon EVP – Finance & Operations
Amy Genkins SVP – Business & Legal Affairs
Jim Lee Editorial Director – WildStorm
Gregory Noveck SVP – Creative Affairs
Steve Rotterdam SVP – Sales & Marketing
Cheryl Rubin SVP – Brand Management

Special Thanks to Alberto Bontempi.

THE CHILL
VERTIGO CRIME

THE CHILL Published by DC Comics, 1700 Broadway, New York, NY 10019.

Printed in Canada. First Printing. DC Comics, a Warner Bros. Entertainment Company.

HC ISBN: 978-1-4012-1286-5 SC ISBN: 978-1-4012-2546-9

SUSTAINABLE FORESTRY INITIATIVE
Certified Chain of Custody
90% Certified Fiber Sourcing and 40% Post-Consumer Recycled
www.sfiprogram.org

NSF-SFICOC-C0001801

This label applies to the text stock

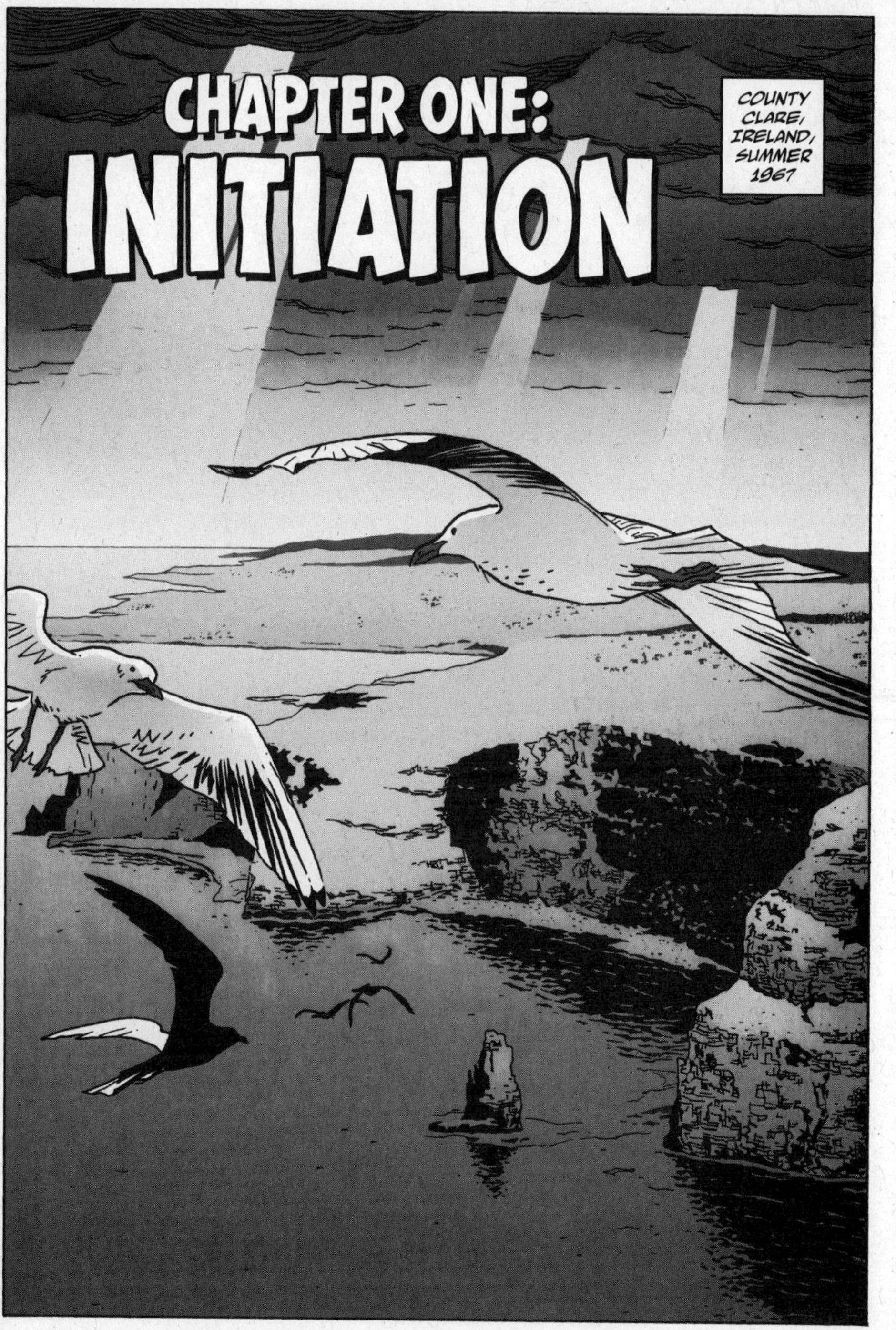
CHAPTER ONE:
INITIATION
COUNTY CLARE, IRELAND, SUMMER 1967

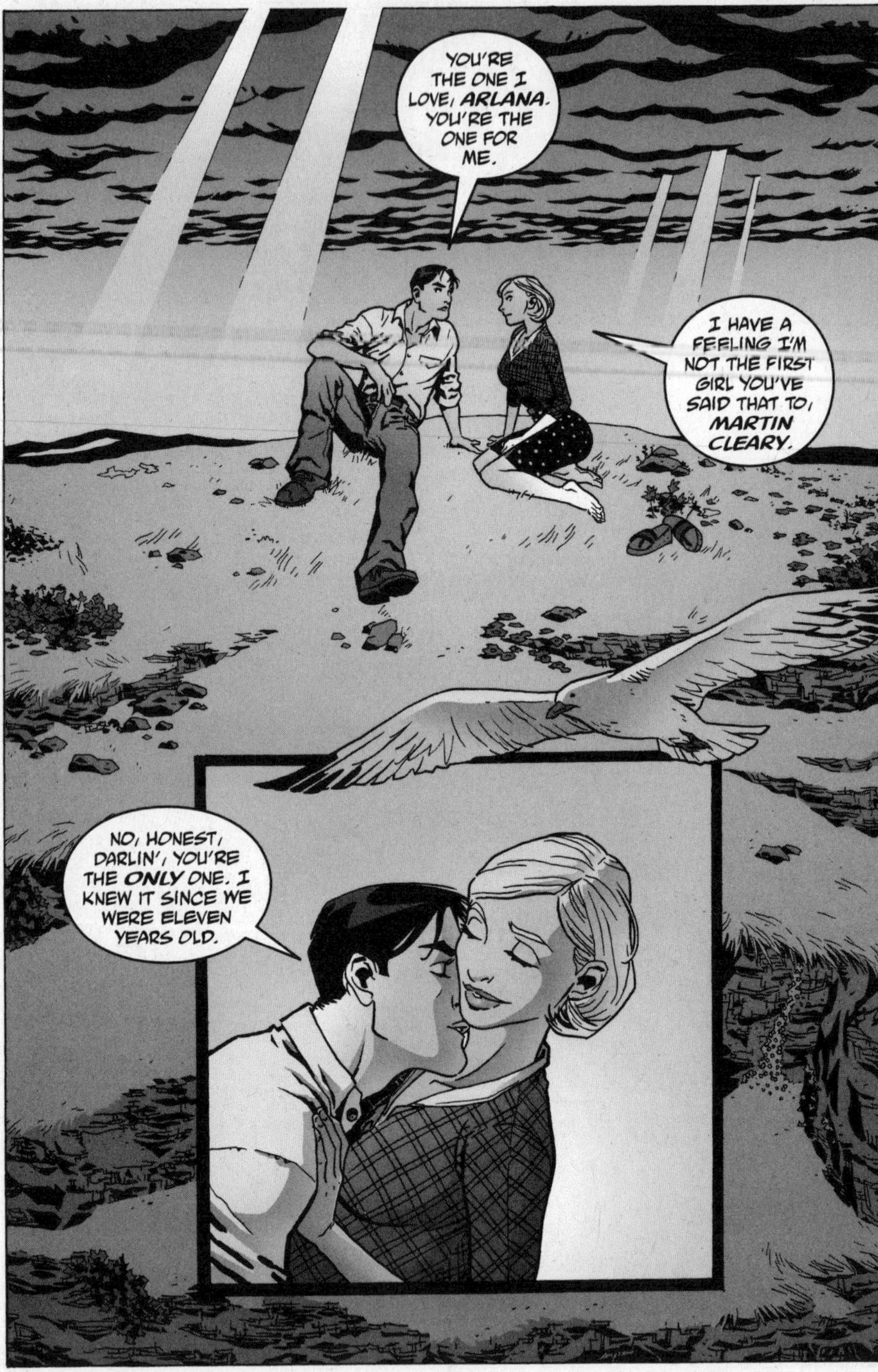
YOU'RE THE ONE I LOVE, ARLANA. YOU'RE THE ONE FOR ME.
I HAVE A FEELING I'M NOT THE FIRST GIRL YOU'VE SAID THAT TO, MARTIN CLEARY.
NO, HONEST, DARLIN', YOU'RE THE ONLY ONE. I KNEW IT SINCE WE WERE ELEVEN YEARS OLD.

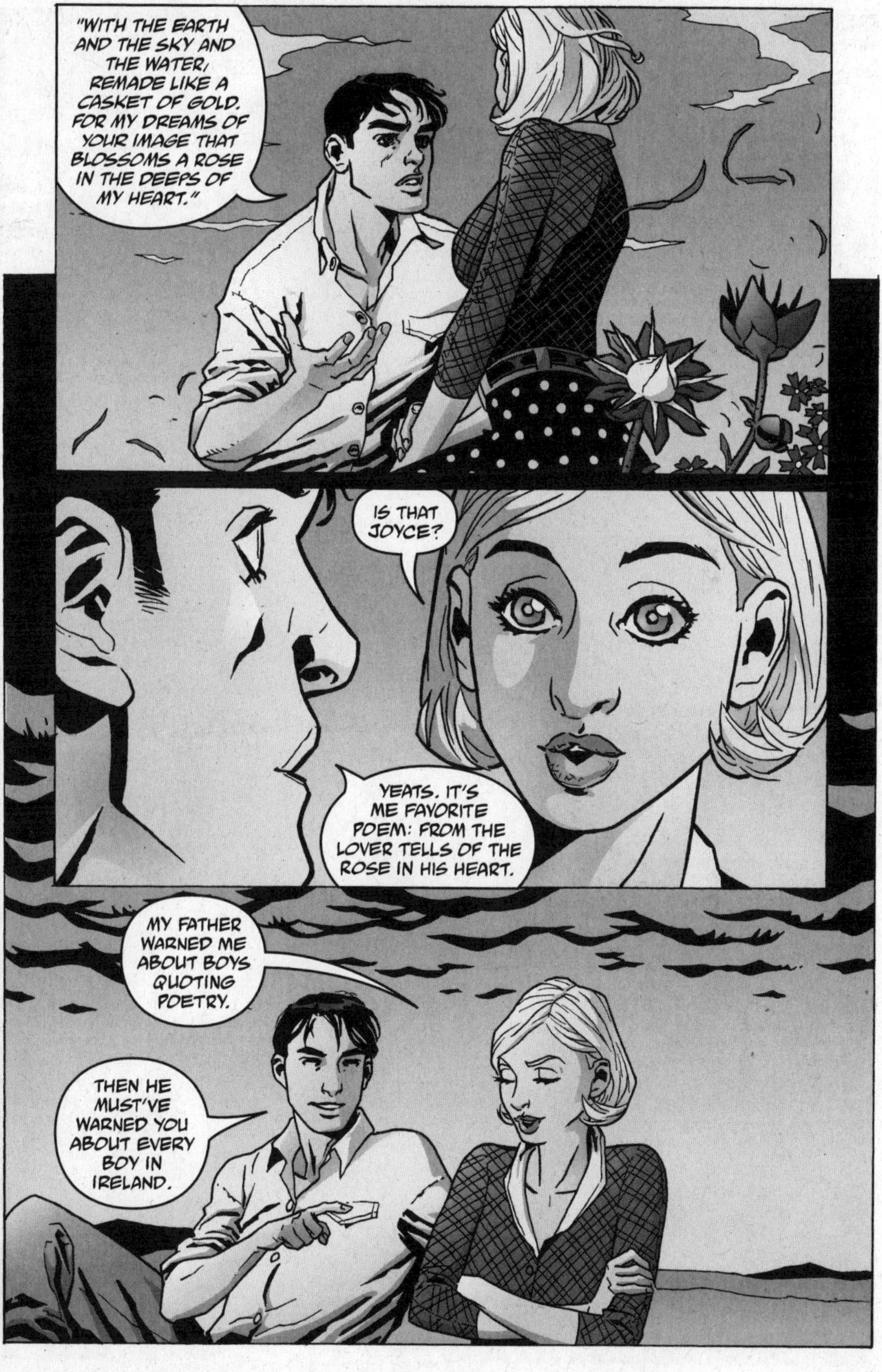
"WITH THE EARTH AND THE SKY AND THE WATER, REMADE LIKE A CASKET OF GOLD. FOR MY DREAMS OF YOUR IMAGE THAT BLOSSOMS A ROSE IN THE DEEPS OF MY HEART."
IS THAT JOYCE?
YEATS. IT'S ME FAVORITE POEM: FROM THE LOVER TELLS OF THE ROSE IN HIS HEART.
MY FATHER WARNED ME ABOUT BOYS QUOTING POETRY.
THEN HE MUST'VE WARNED YOU ABOUT EVERY BOY IN IRELAND.

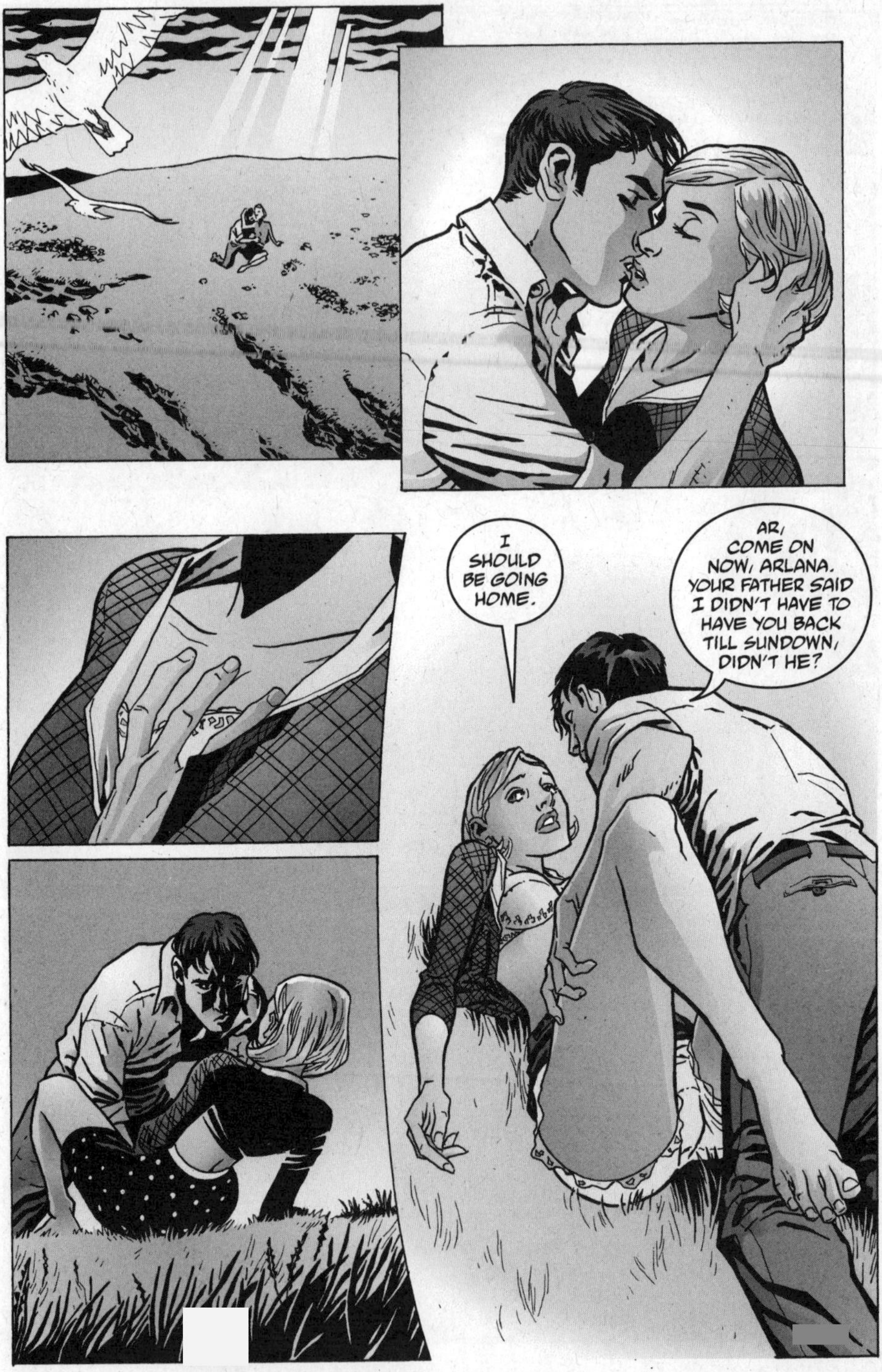
I SHOULD BE GOING HOME.
AR, COME ON NOW, ARLANA. YOUR FATHER SAID I DIDN'T HAVE TO HAVE YOU BACK TILL SUNDOWN, DIDN'T HE?

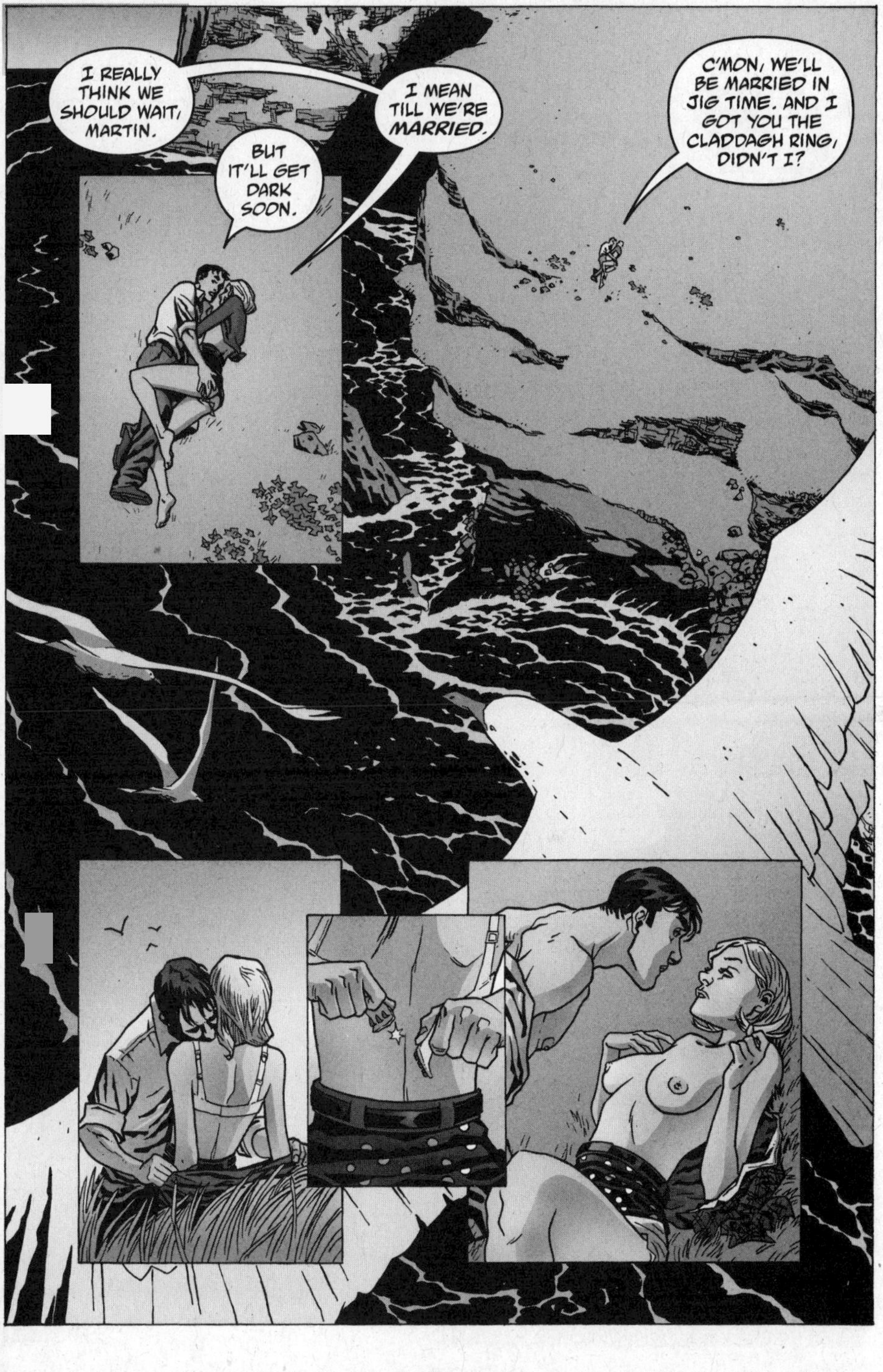
I REALLY THINK WE SHOULD WAIT, MARTIN.
BUT IT'LL GET DARK SOON.
I MEAN TILL WE'RE MARRIED.
C'MON, WE'LL BE MARRIED IN JIG TIME. AND I GOT YOU THE CLADDAGH RING, DIDN'T I?

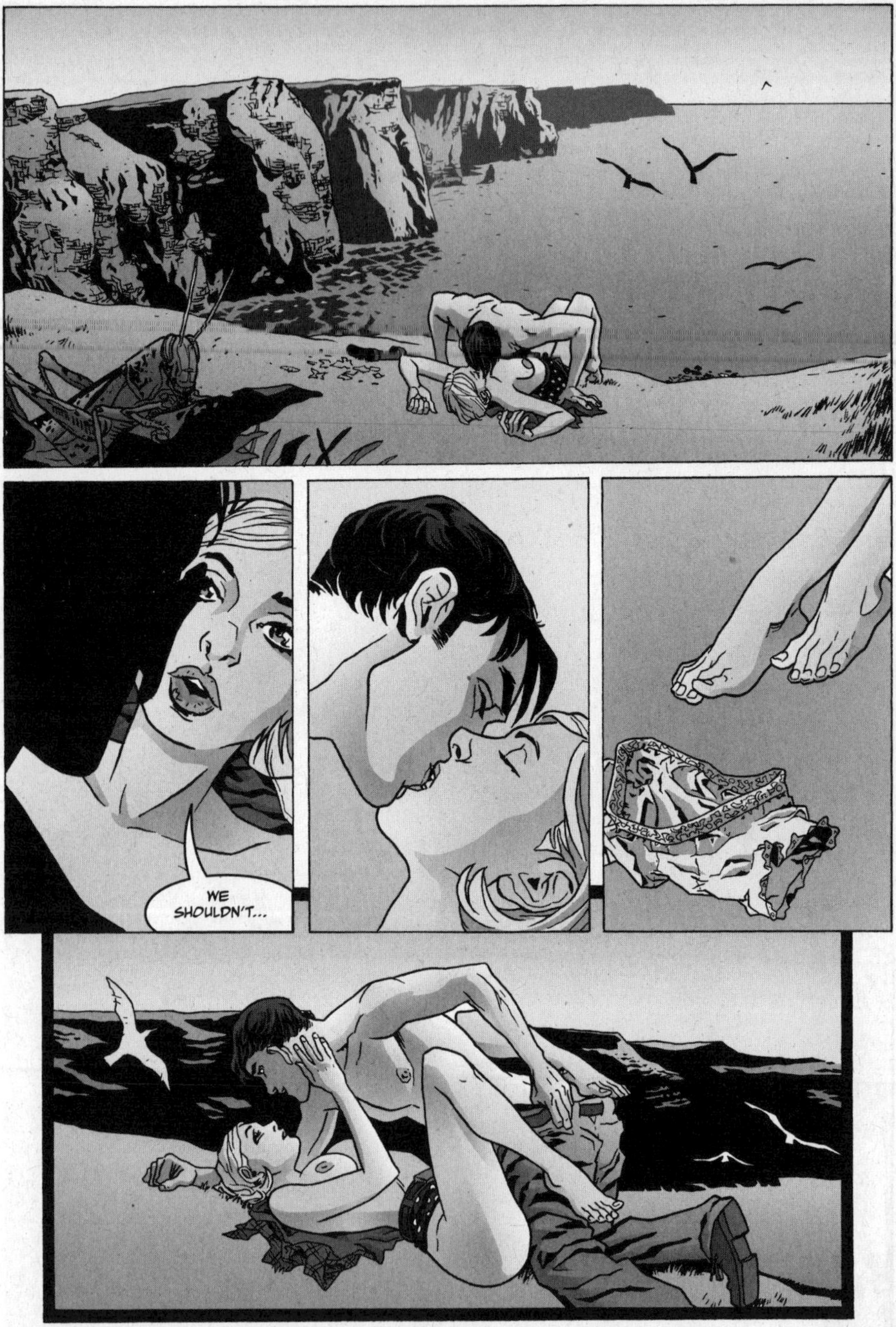
WE SHOULDN'T...

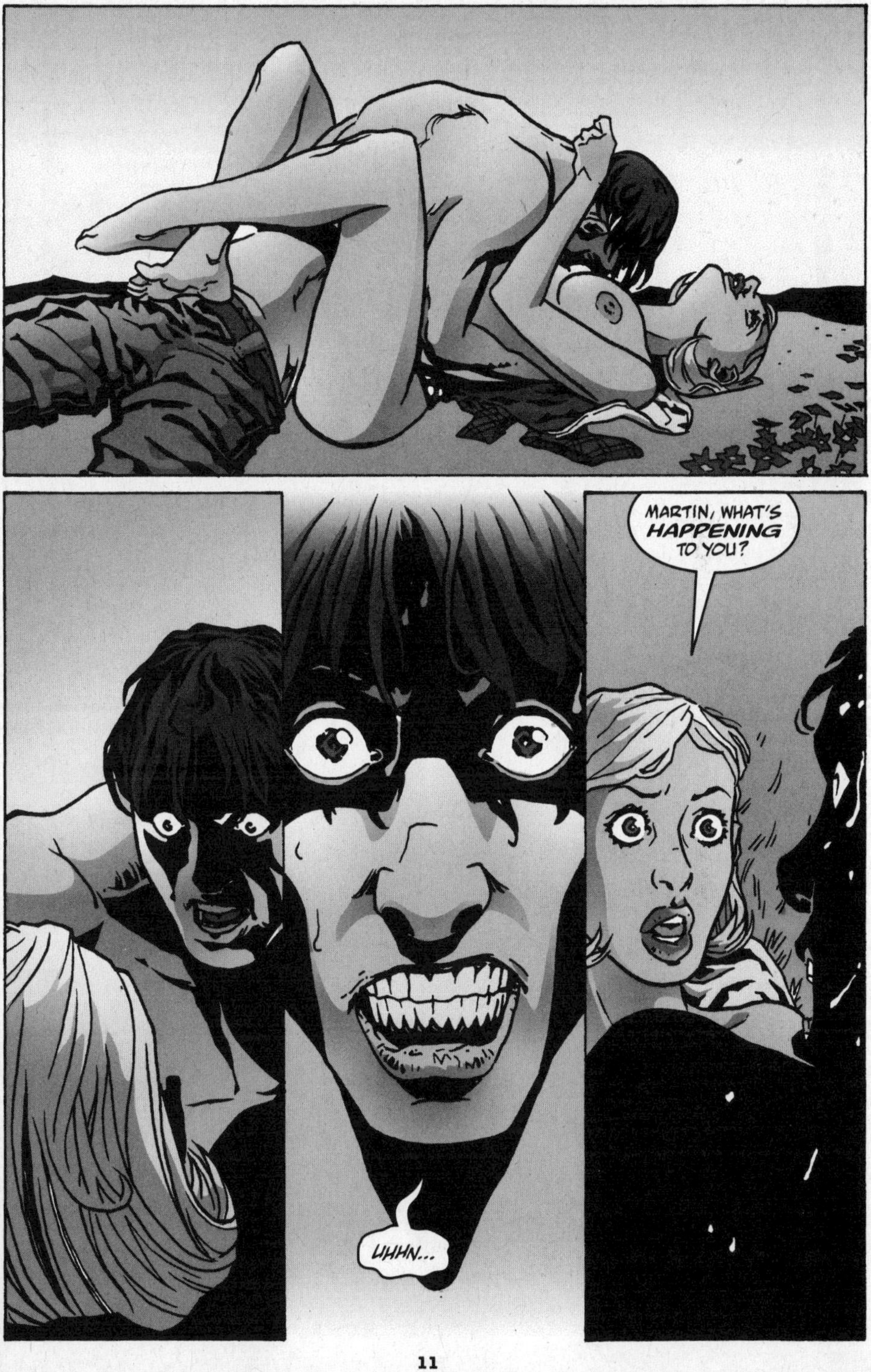
MARTIN, WHAT'S HAPPENING TO YOU?
UHHN...

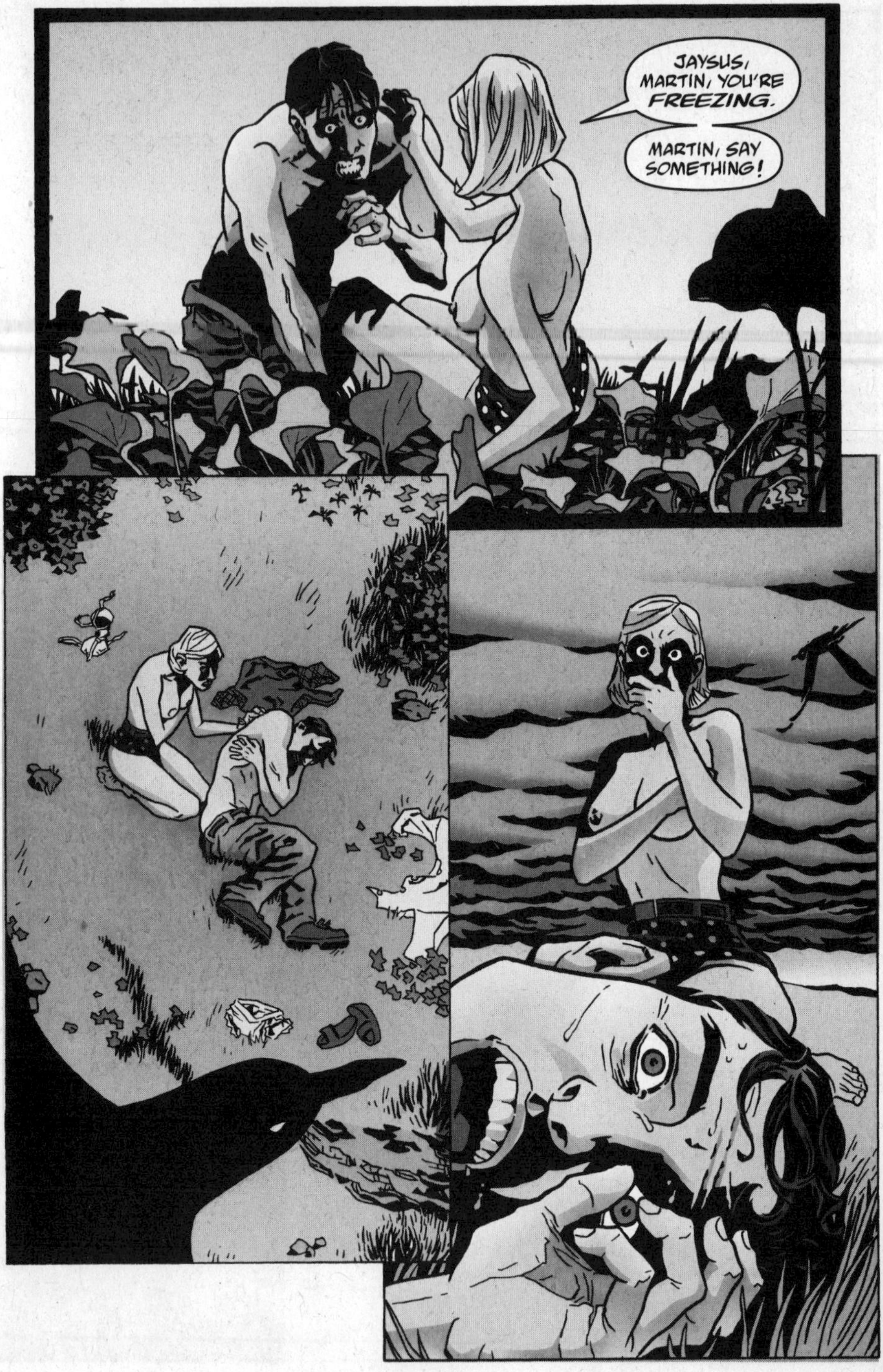
JAYSUS, MARTIN, YOU'RE FREEZING.
MARTIN, SAY SOMETHING!

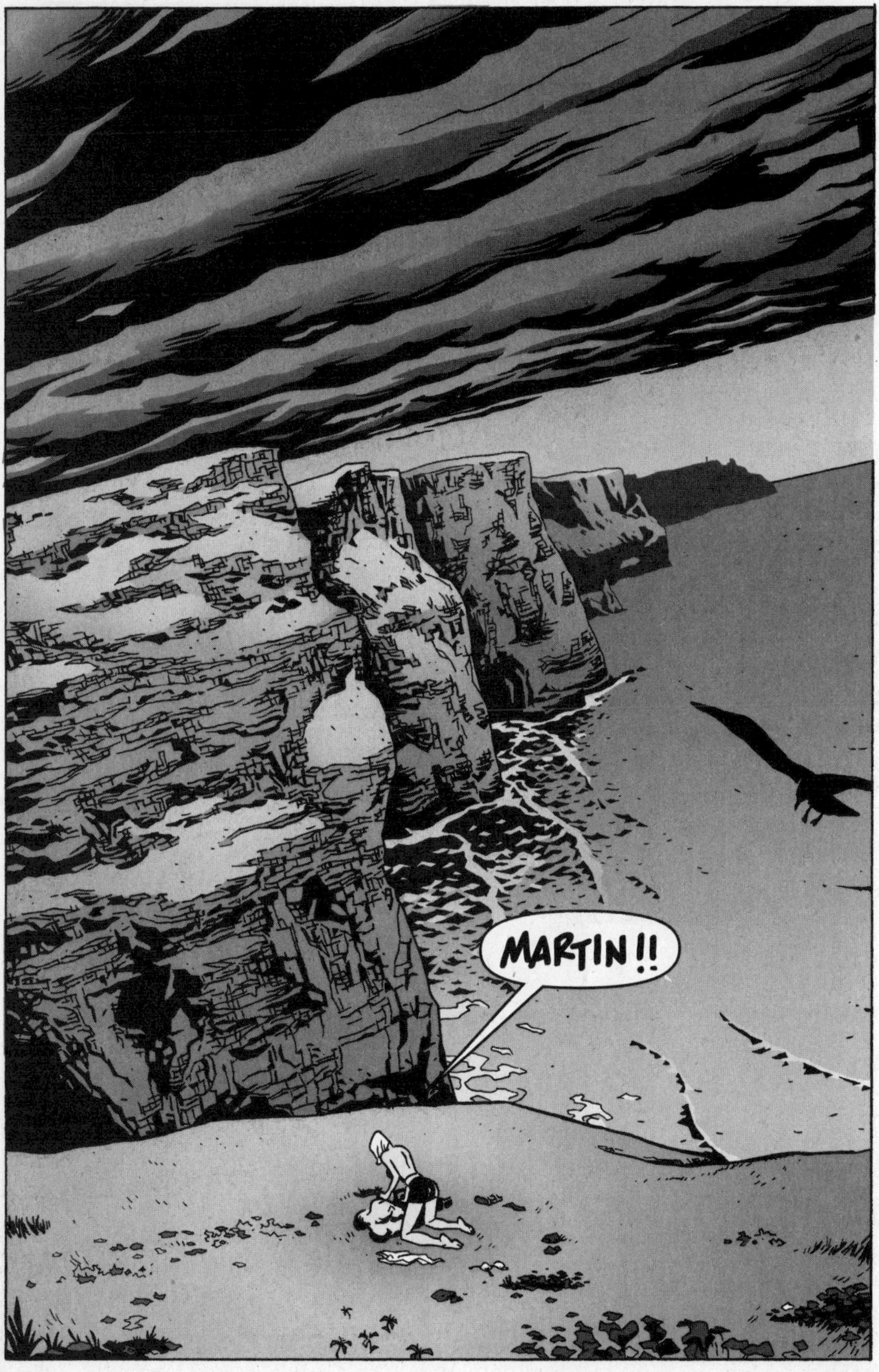
MARTIN!!

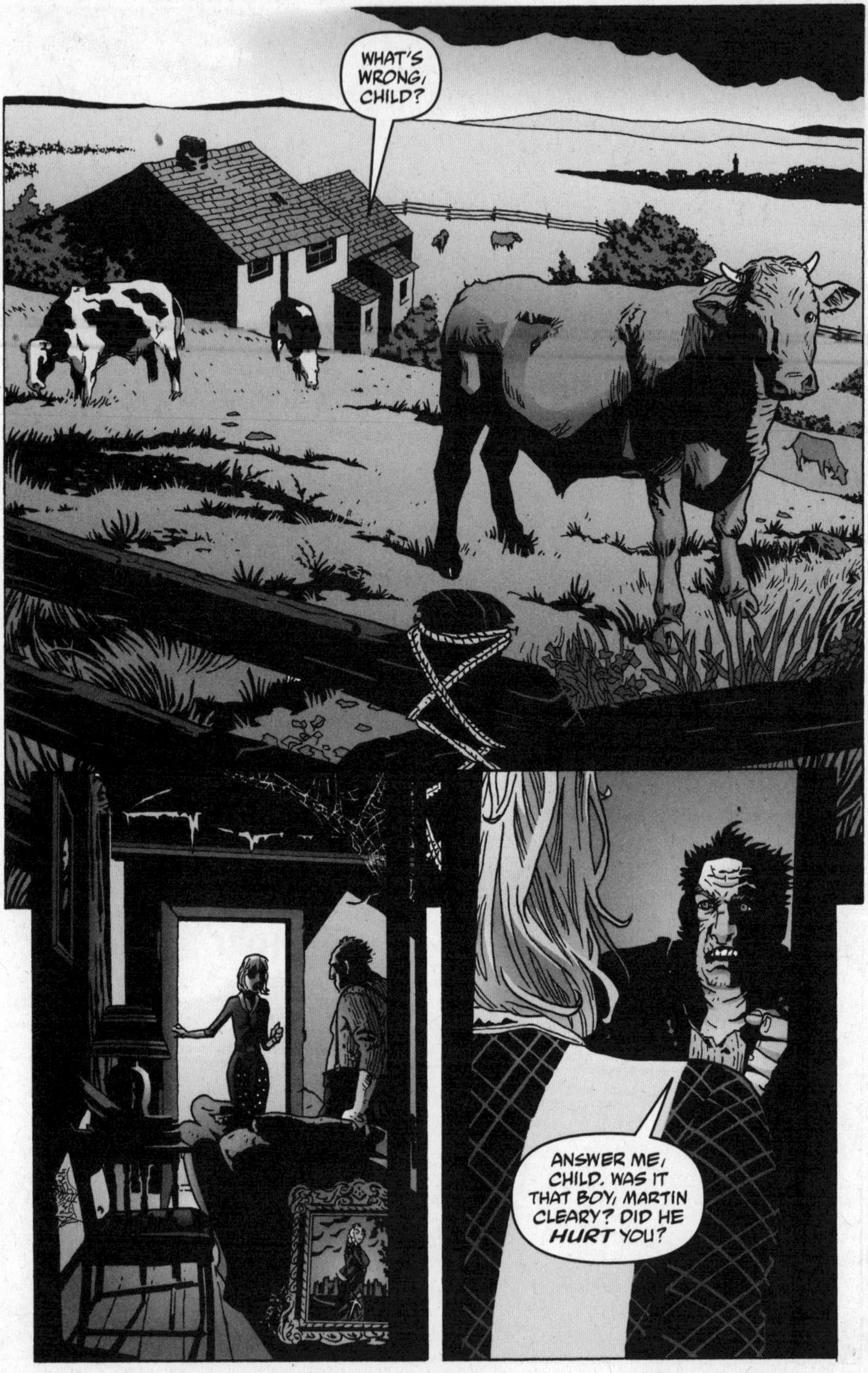
WHAT'S WRONG, CHILD?
ANSWER ME, CHILD. WAS IT THAT BOY, MARTIN CLEARY? DID HE HURT YOU?

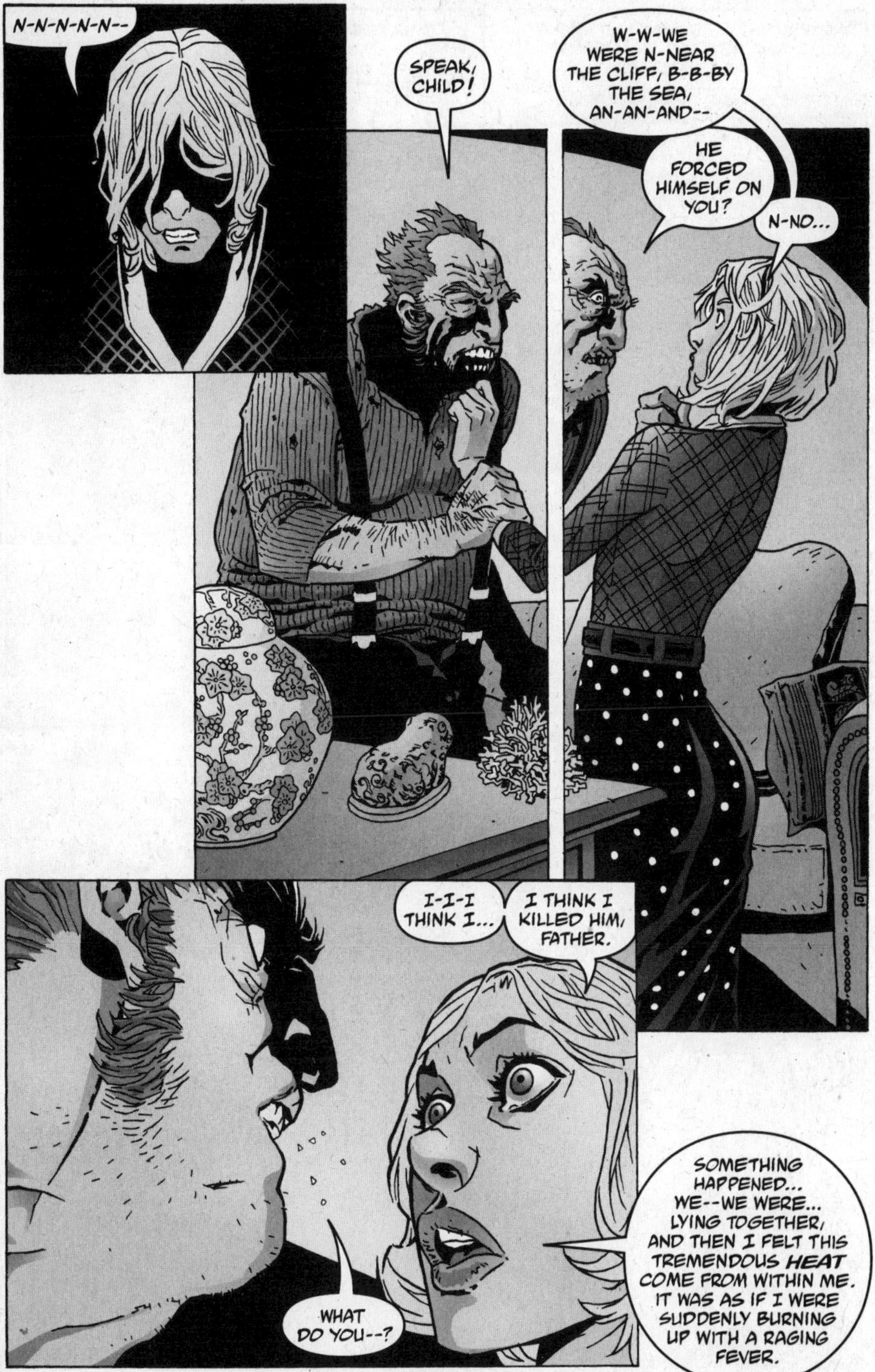
N-N-N-N-N--
SPEAK, CHILD!
W-W-WE WERE N-NEAR THE CLIFF, B-B-BY THE SEA, AN-AN-AND--
HE FORCED HIMSELF ON YOU?
N-NO...
I-I-I THINK I...
I THINK I KILLED HIM, FATHER.
WHAT DO YOU--?
SOMETHING HAPPENED... WE--WE WERE... LYING TOGETHER, AND THEN I FELT THIS TREMENDOUS HEAT COME FROM WITHIN ME. IT WAS AS IF I WERE SUDDENLY BURNING UP WITH A RAGING FEVER.

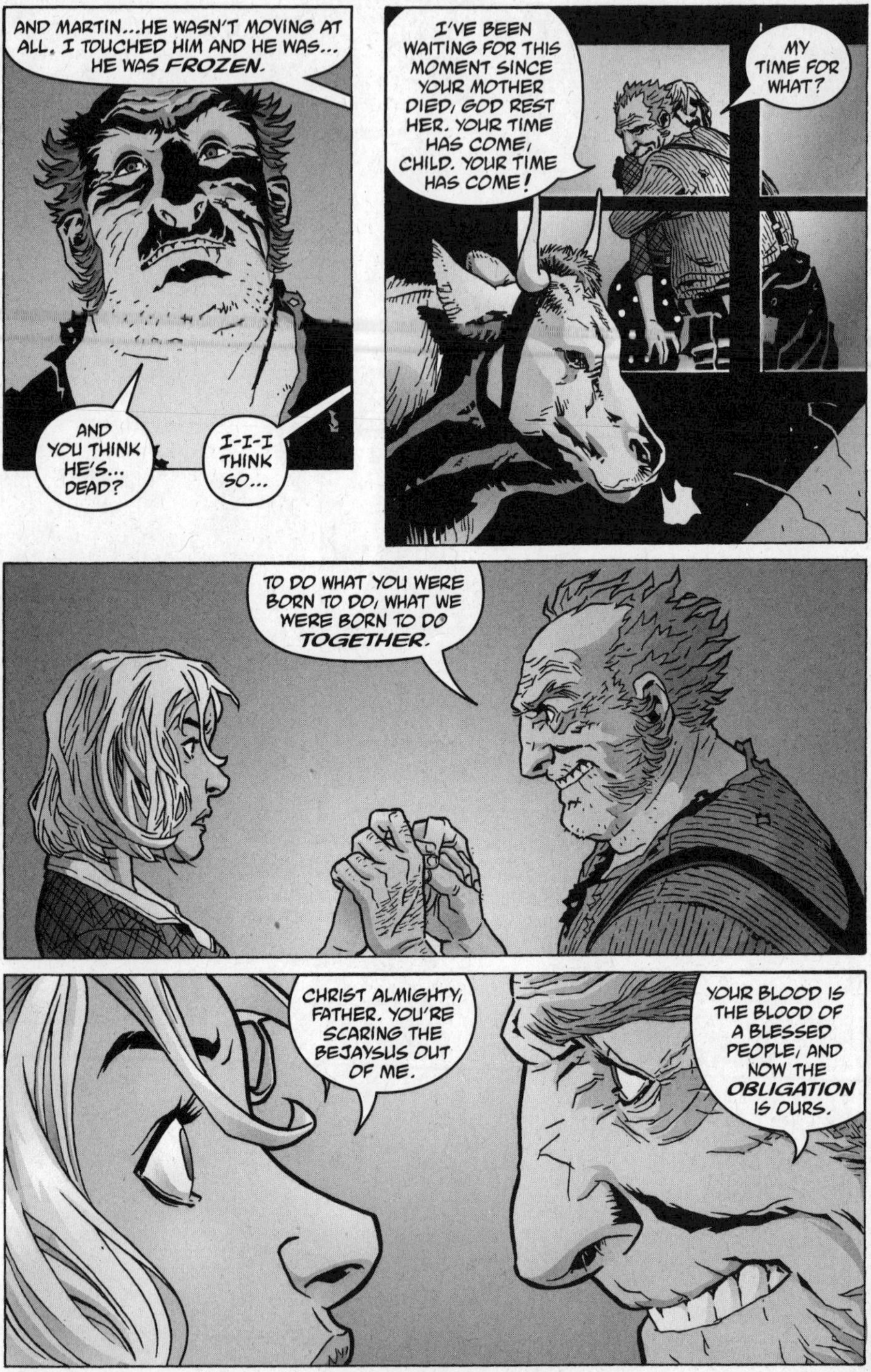
AND MARTIN...HE WASN'T MOVING AT ALL. I TOUCHED HIM AND HE WAS... HE WAS FROZEN.
AND YOU THINK HE'S... DEAD?
I-I-I THINK SO...
I'VE BEEN WAITING FOR THIS MOMENT SINCE YOUR MOTHER DIED, GOD REST HER. YOUR TIME HAS COME, CHILD. YOUR TIME HAS COME!
MY TIME FOR WHAT?
TO DO WHAT YOU WERE BORN TO DO, WHAT WE WERE BORN TO DO TOGETHER.
CHRIST ALMIGHTY, FATHER. YOU'RE SCARING THE BEJAYSUS OUT OF ME.
YOUR BLOOD IS THE BLOOD OF A BLESSED PEOPLE, AND NOW THE OBLIGATION IS OURS.

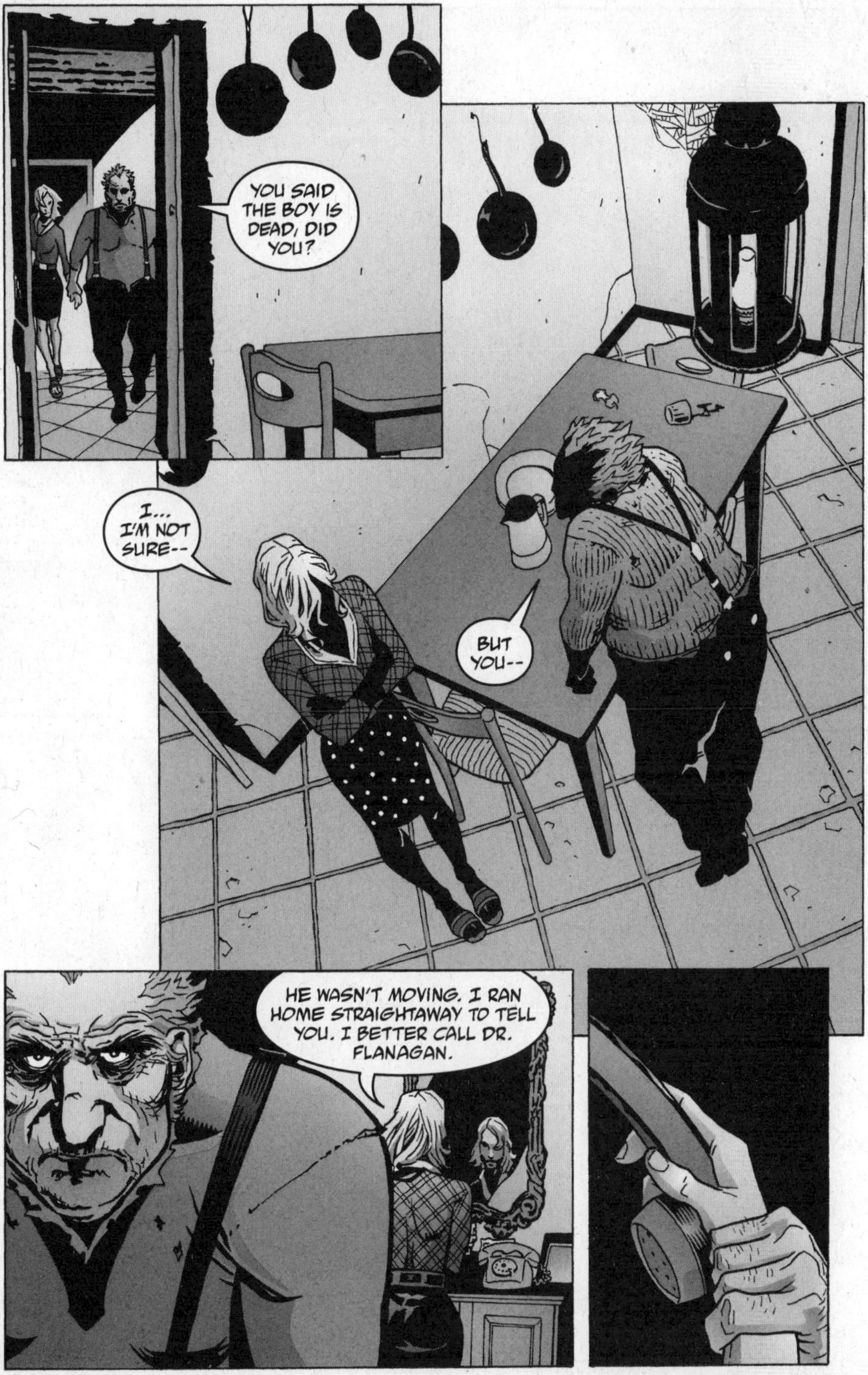
YOU SAID THE BOY IS DEAD, DID YOU?
I... I'M NOT SURE--
BUT YOU--
HE WASN'T MOVING. I RAN HOME STRAIGHTAWAY TO TELL YOU. I BETTER CALL DR. FLANAGAN.

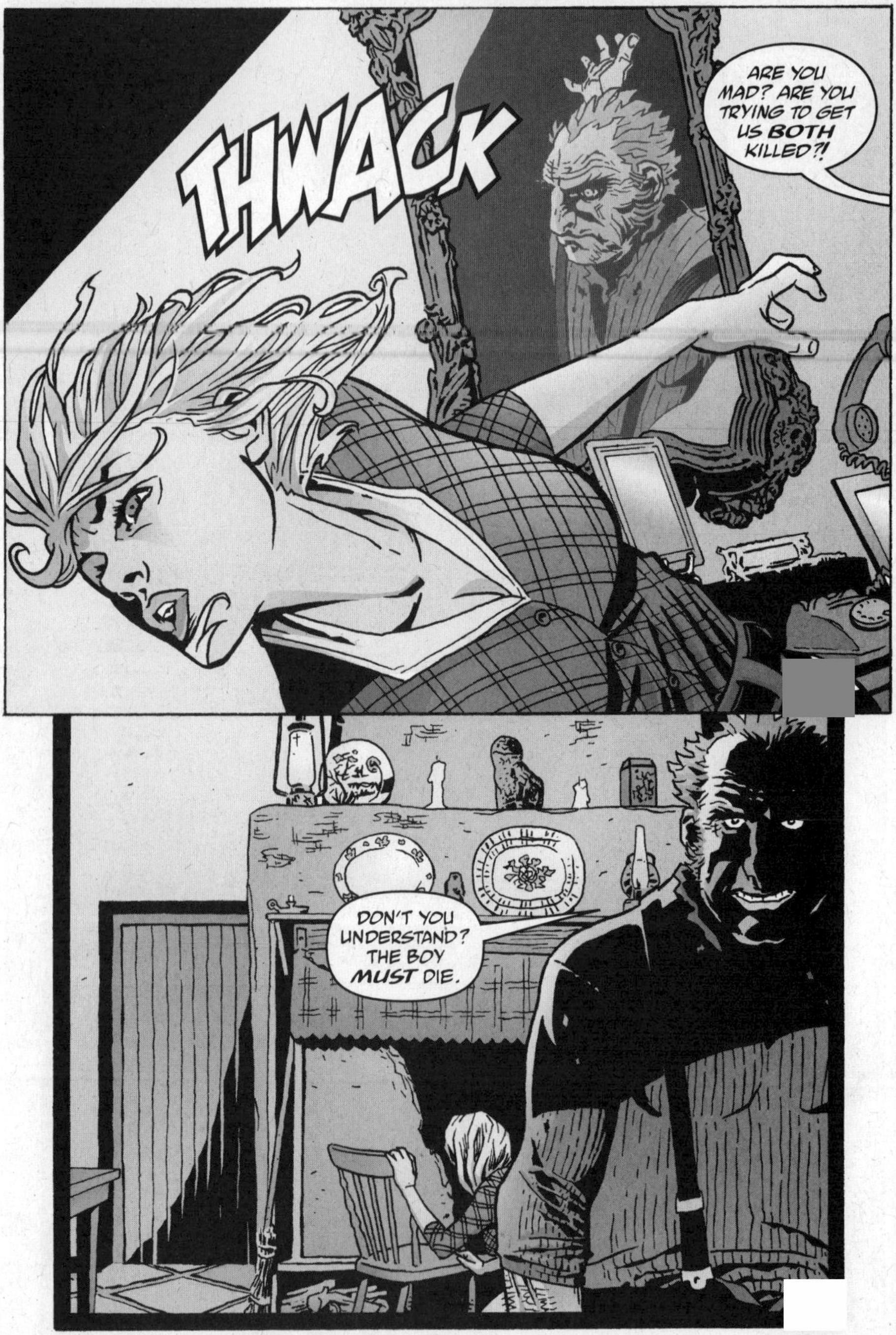
THWACK
ARE YOU MAD? ARE YOU TRYING TO GET US BOTH KILLED?!
DON'T YOU UNDERSTAND? THE BOY MUST DIE.

IF HE'S NOT STILL THERE, WE MUST FIND HIM.

THE SACRIFICE MUST BE DONE THE WAY IT HAS *ALWAYS* BEEN DONE.

YOU WILL LIE WITH HIM AGAIN.

THE CHILL WILL EXTINGUISH THE TOXIC FIRE THAT IS WITHIN HIM AND THEN WE WILL FEAST ON THE SPIRIT OF THE *DEVOTED ONE*.

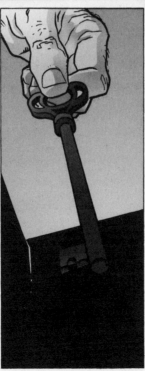

WE MUST TAKE WHAT BELONGS TO THE SKY UNTO OURSELVES...

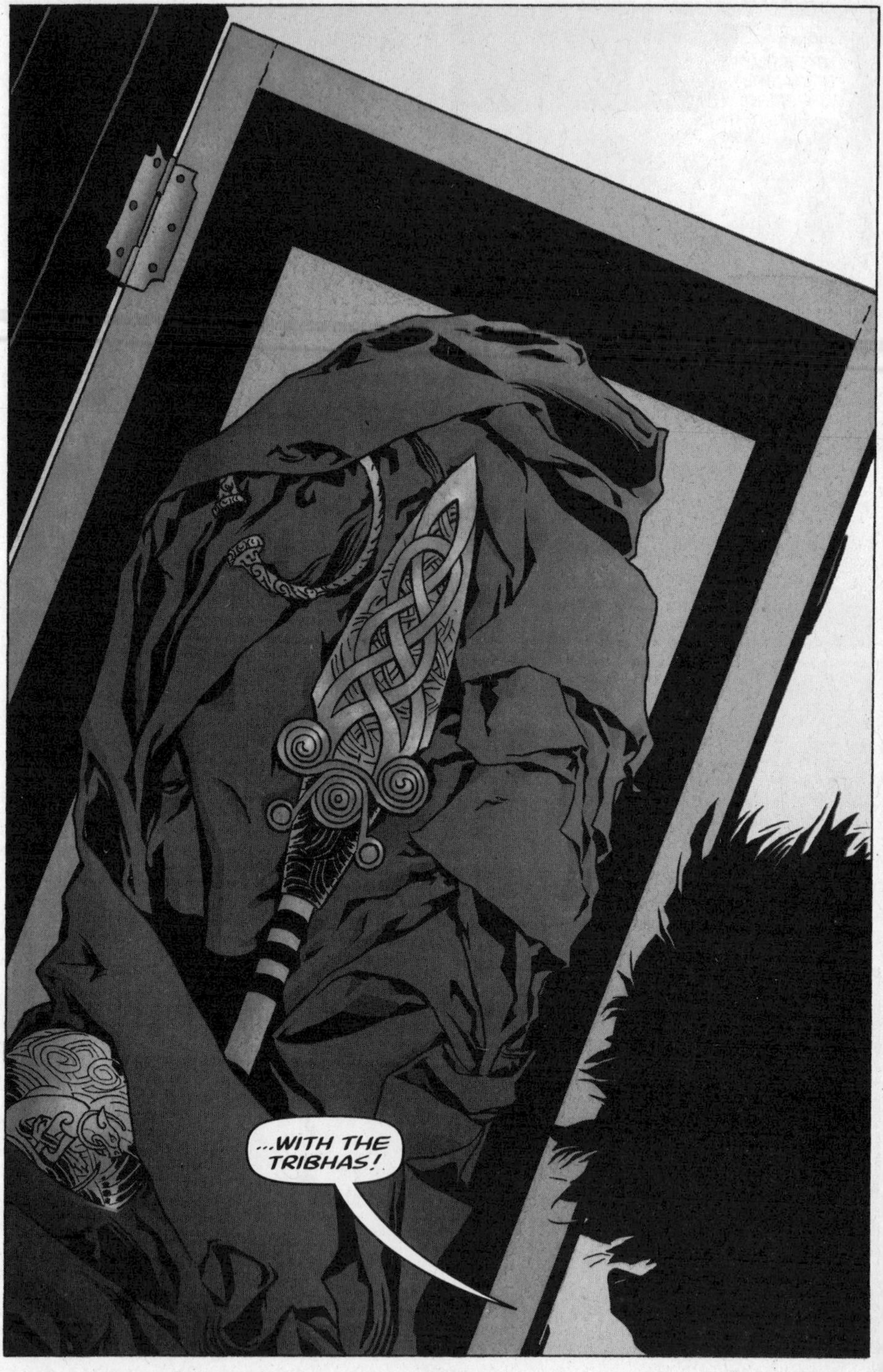
...WITH THE TRIBHAS!

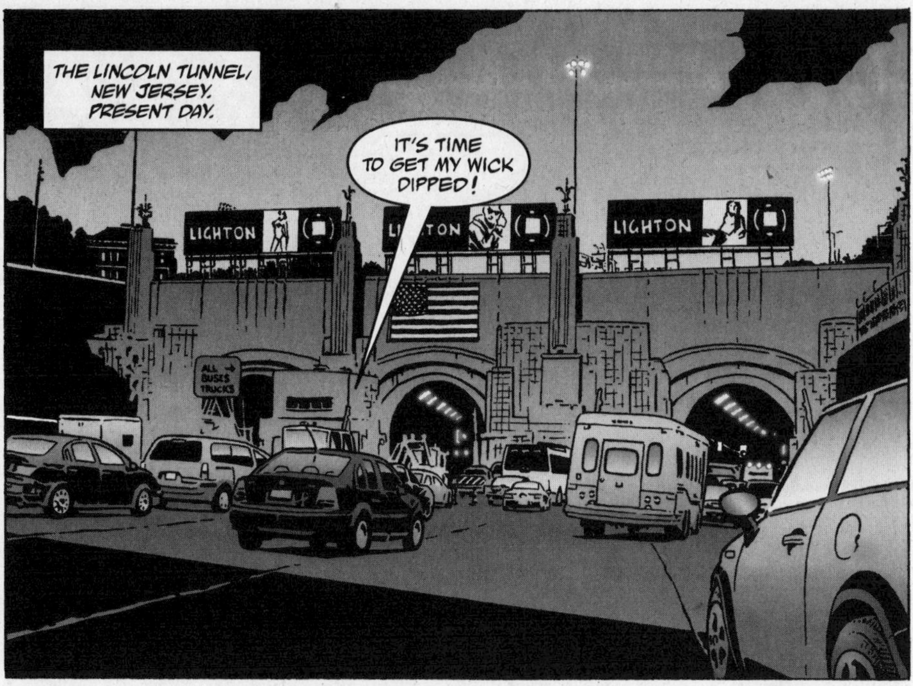
THE LINCOLN TUNNEL, NEW JERSEY. PRESENT DAY.
IT'S TIME TO GET MY WICK DIPPED!
LIGHTON
LIGHTON
ALL BUSES TRUCKS

CHAPTER TWO: HAVOC

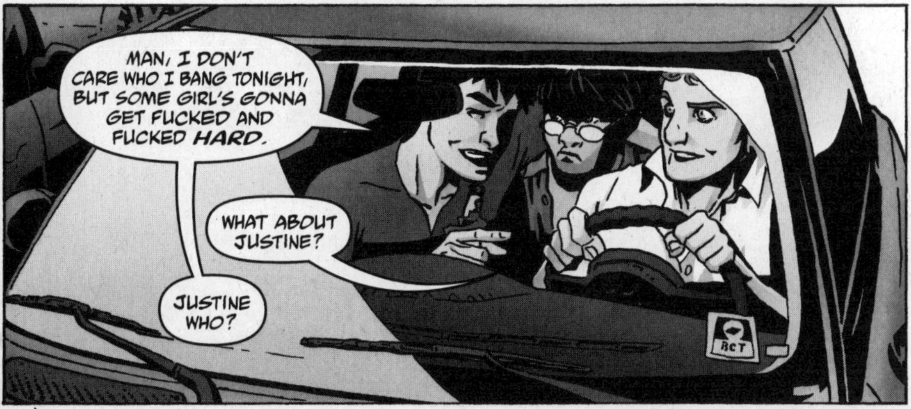
MAN, I DON'T CARE WHO I BANG TONIGHT, BUT SOME GIRL'S GONNA GET FUCKED AND FUCKED *HARD*.
WHAT ABOUT JUSTINE?
JUSTINE WHO?

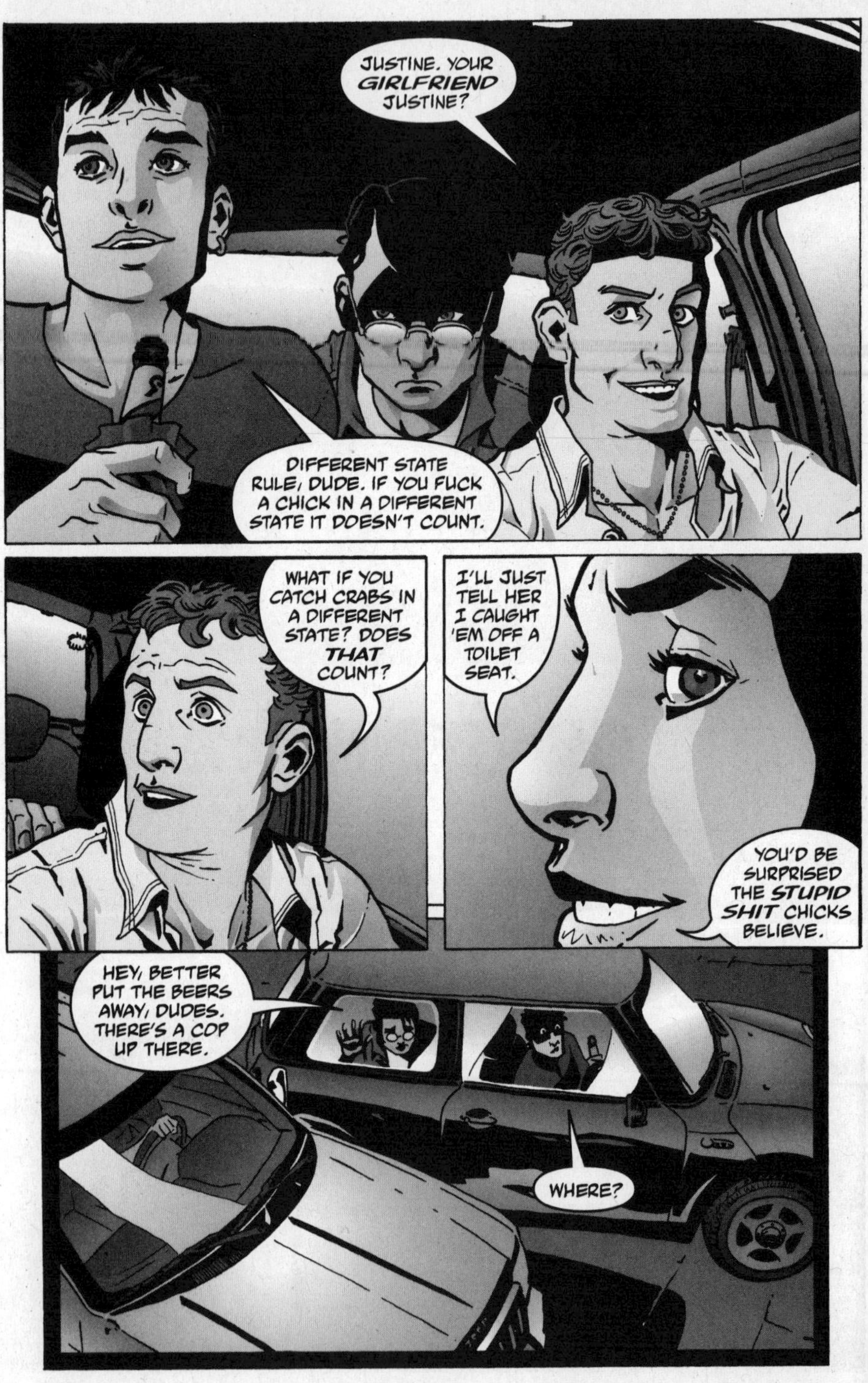
JUSTINE. YOUR GIRLFRIEND JUSTINE?
DIFFERENT STATE RULE, DUDE. IF YOU FUCK A CHICK IN A DIFFERENT STATE IT DOESN'T COUNT.
WHAT IF YOU CATCH CRABS IN A DIFFERENT STATE? DOES THAT COUNT?
I'LL JUST TELL HER I CAUGHT 'EM OFF A TOILET SEAT.
YOU'D BE SURPRISED THE STUPID SHIT CHICKS BELIEVE.
HEY, BETTER PUT THE BEERS AWAY, DUDES. THERE'S A COP UP THERE.
WHERE?

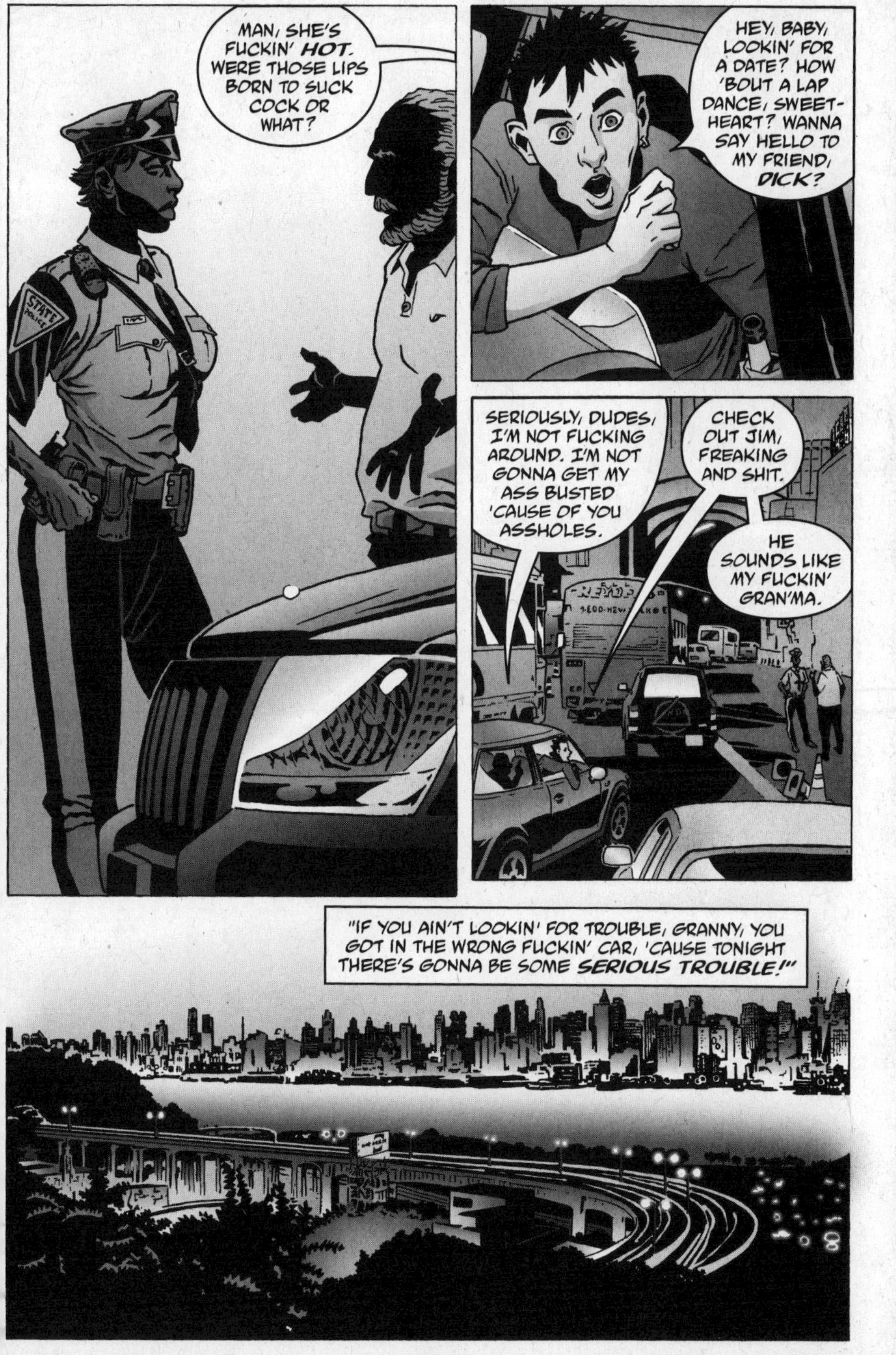
MAN, SHE'S FUCKIN' HOT. WERE THOSE LIPS BORN TO SUCK COCK OR WHAT?
HEY, BABY, LOOKIN' FOR A DATE? HOW 'BOUT A LAP DANCE, SWEET-HEART? WANNA SAY HELLO TO MY FRIEND, DICK?
SERIOUSLY, DUDES, I'M NOT FUCKING AROUND. I'M NOT GONNA GET MY ASS BUSTED 'CAUSE OF YOU ASSHOLES.
CHECK OUT JIM, FREAKING AND SHIT.
HE SOUNDS LIKE MY FUCKIN' GRAN'MA.
"IF YOU AIN'T LOOKIN' FOR TROUBLE, GRANNY, YOU GOT IN THE WRONG FUCKIN' CAR, 'CAUSE TONIGHT THERE'S GONNA BE SOME SERIOUS TROUBLE!"

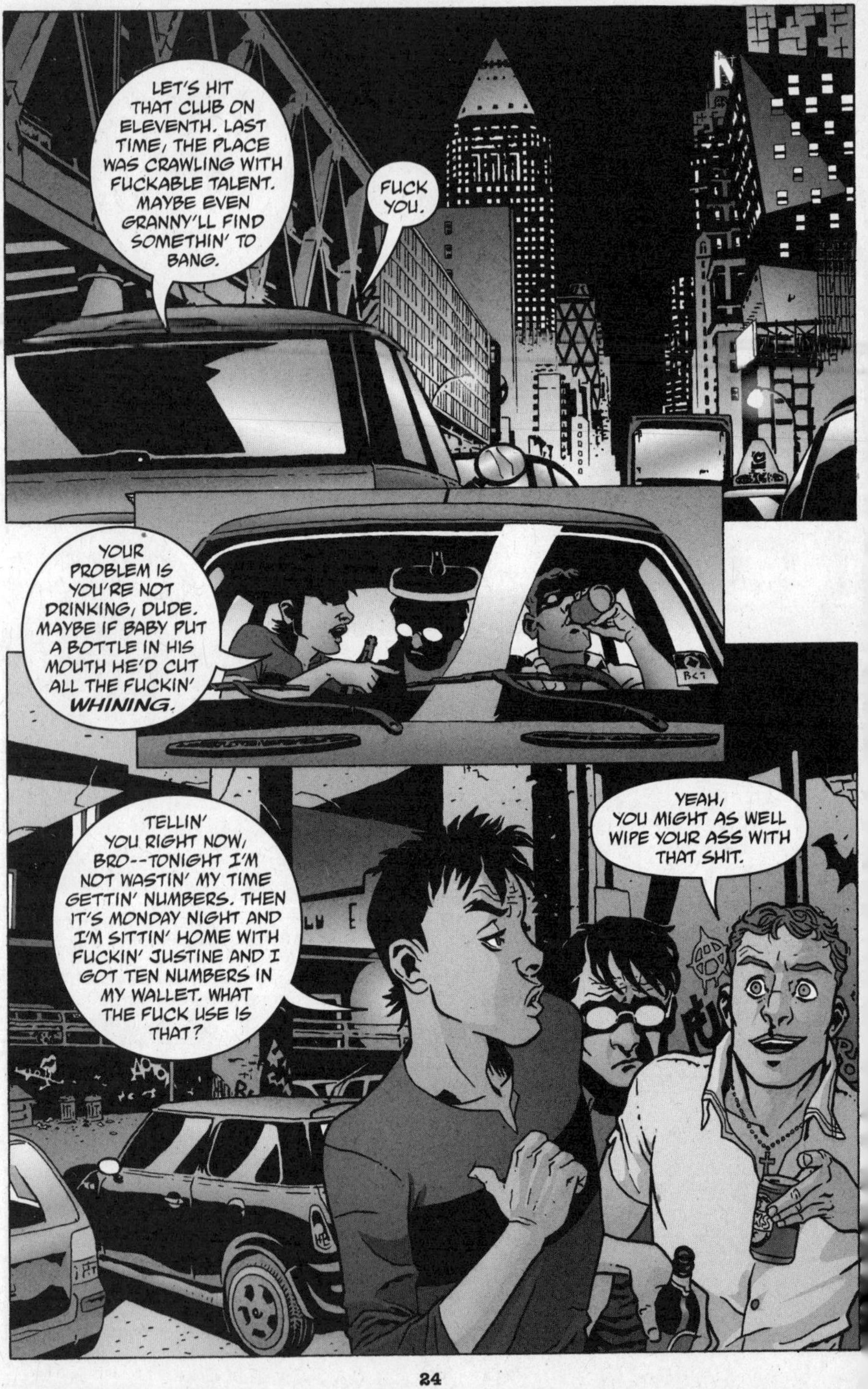
LET'S HIT THAT CLUB ON ELEVENTH. LAST TIME, THE PLACE WAS CRAWLING WITH FUCKABLE TALENT. MAYBE EVEN GRANNY'LL FIND SOMETHIN' TO BANG.
FUCK YOU.
YOUR PROBLEM IS YOU'RE NOT DRINKING, DUDE. MAYBE IF BABY PUT A BOTTLE IN HIS MOUTH HE'D CUT ALL THE FUCKIN' **WHINING**.
TELLIN' YOU RIGHT NOW, BRO--TONIGHT I'M NOT WASTIN' MY TIME GETTIN' NUMBERS. THEN IT'S MONDAY NIGHT AND I'M SITTIN' HOME WITH FUCKIN' JUSTINE AND I GOT TEN NUMBERS IN MY WALLET. WHAT THE FUCK USE IS THAT?
YEAH, YOU MIGHT AS WELL WIPE YOUR ASS WITH THAT SHIT.

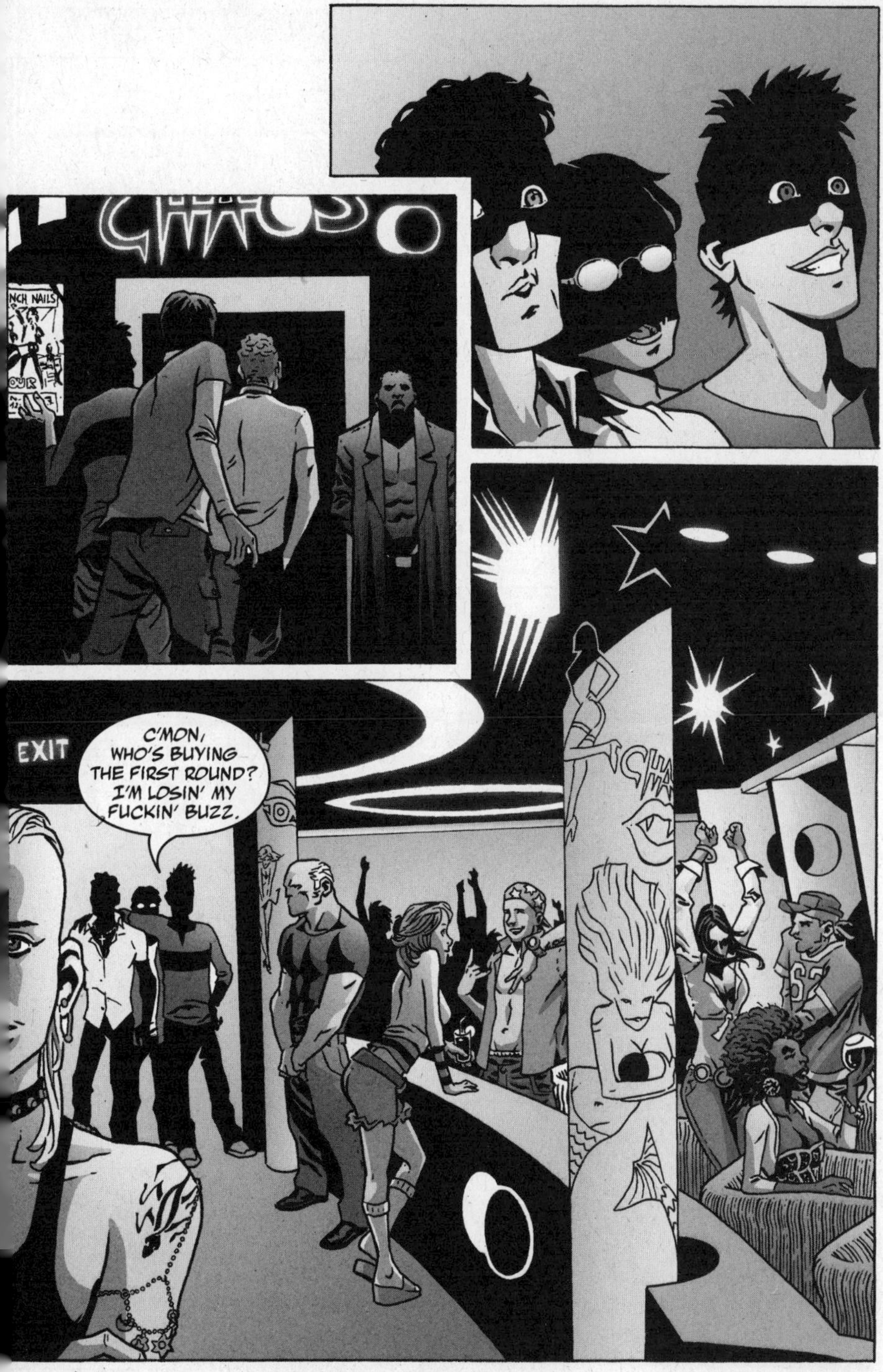
CHAOS
NCH NAILS
EXIT
C'MON, WHO'S BUYING THE FIRST ROUND? I'M LOSIN' MY FUCKIN' BUZZ.
CHA

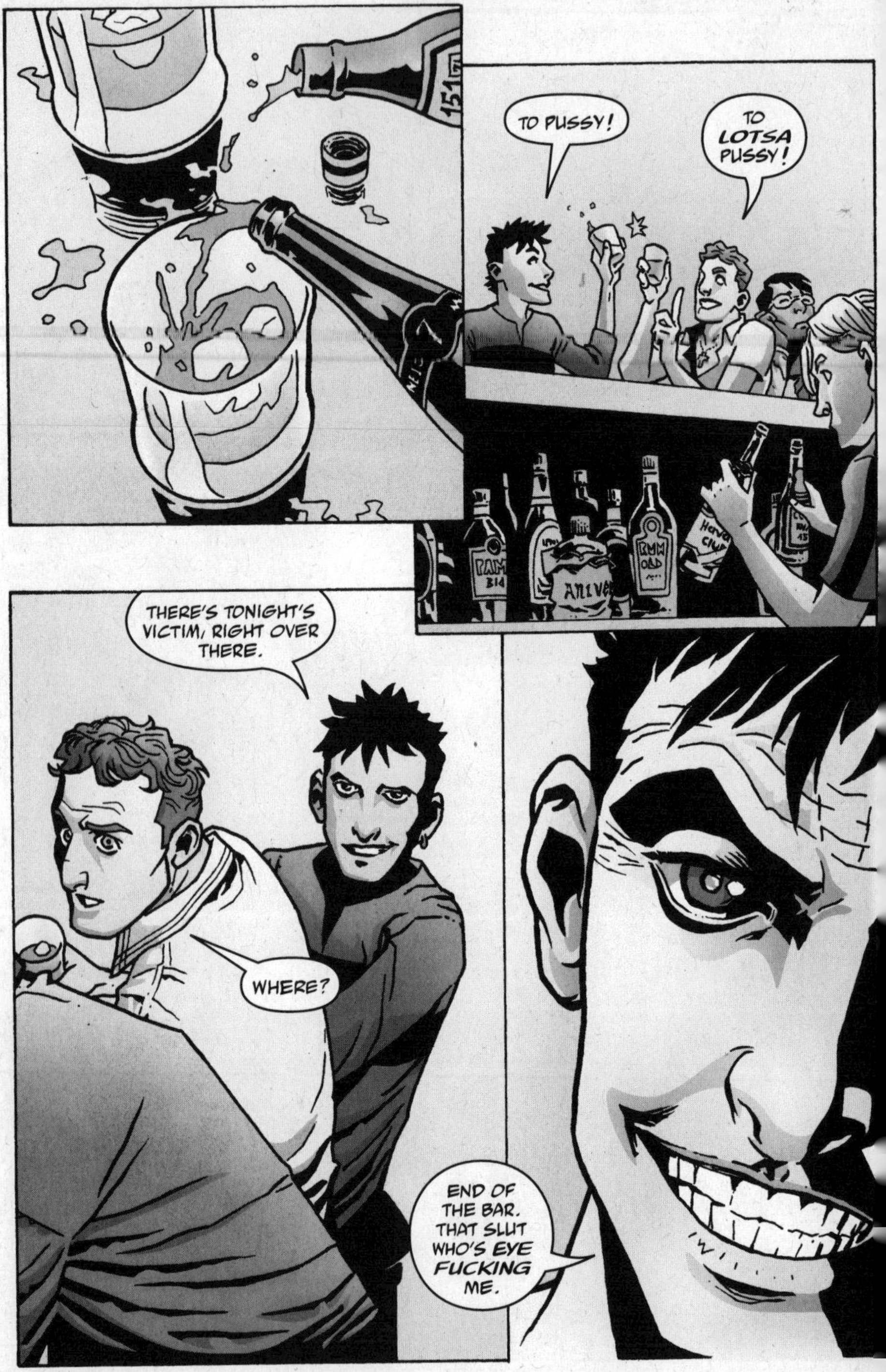
TO PUSSY!
TO LOTSA PUSSY!
THERE'S TONIGHT'S VICTIM, RIGHT OVER THERE.
WHERE?
END OF THE BAR. THAT SLUT WHO'S EYE FUCKING ME.

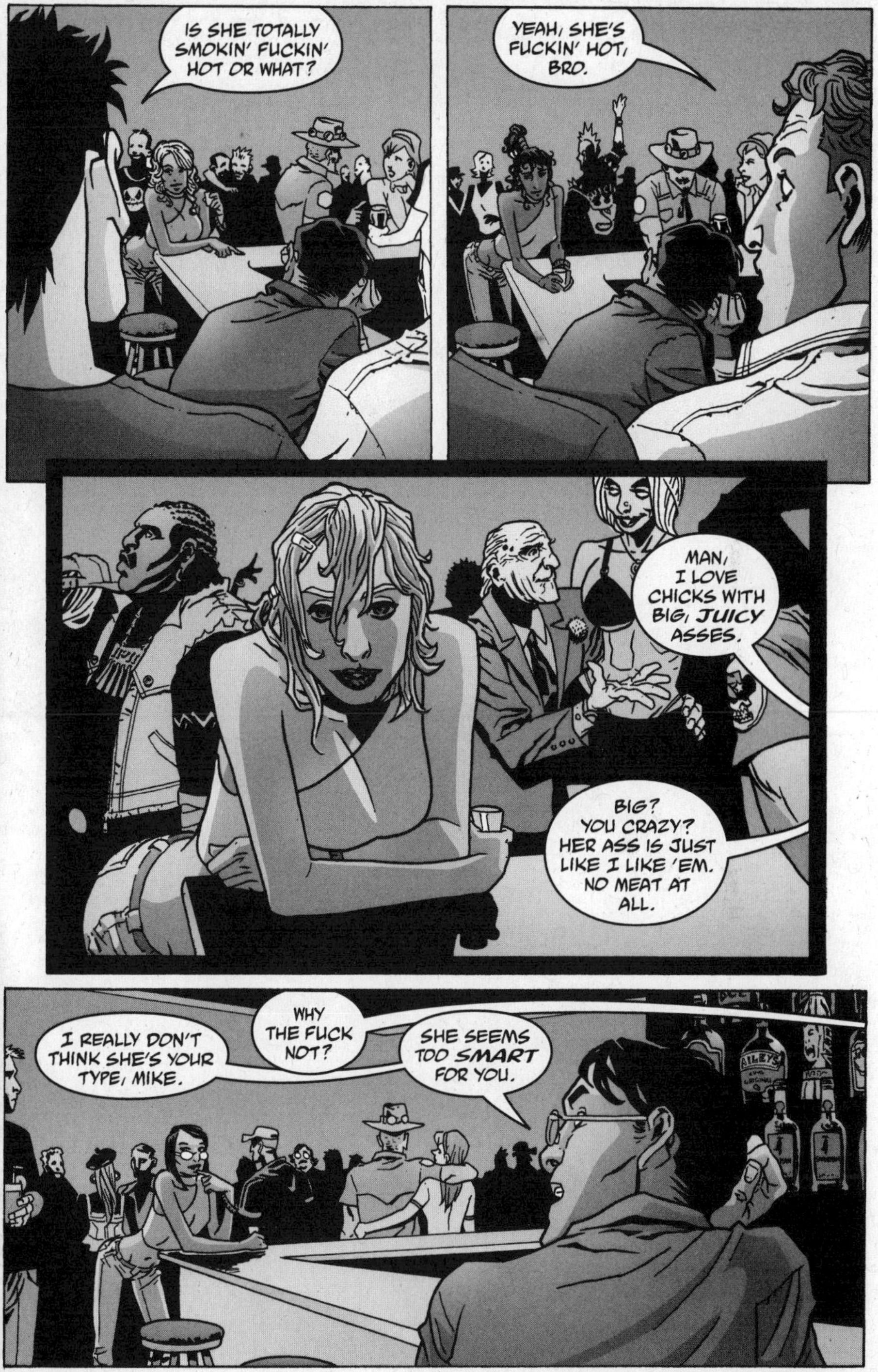
IS SHE TOTALLY SMOKIN' FUCKIN' HOT OR WHAT?
YEAH, SHE'S FUCKIN' HOT, BRO.
MAN, I LOVE CHICKS WITH BIG, JUICY ASSES.
BIG? YOU CRAZY? HER ASS IS JUST LIKE I LIKE 'EM. NO MEAT AT ALL.
I REALLY DON'T THINK SHE'S YOUR TYPE, MIKE.
WHY THE FUCK NOT?
SHE SEEMS TOO SMART FOR YOU.

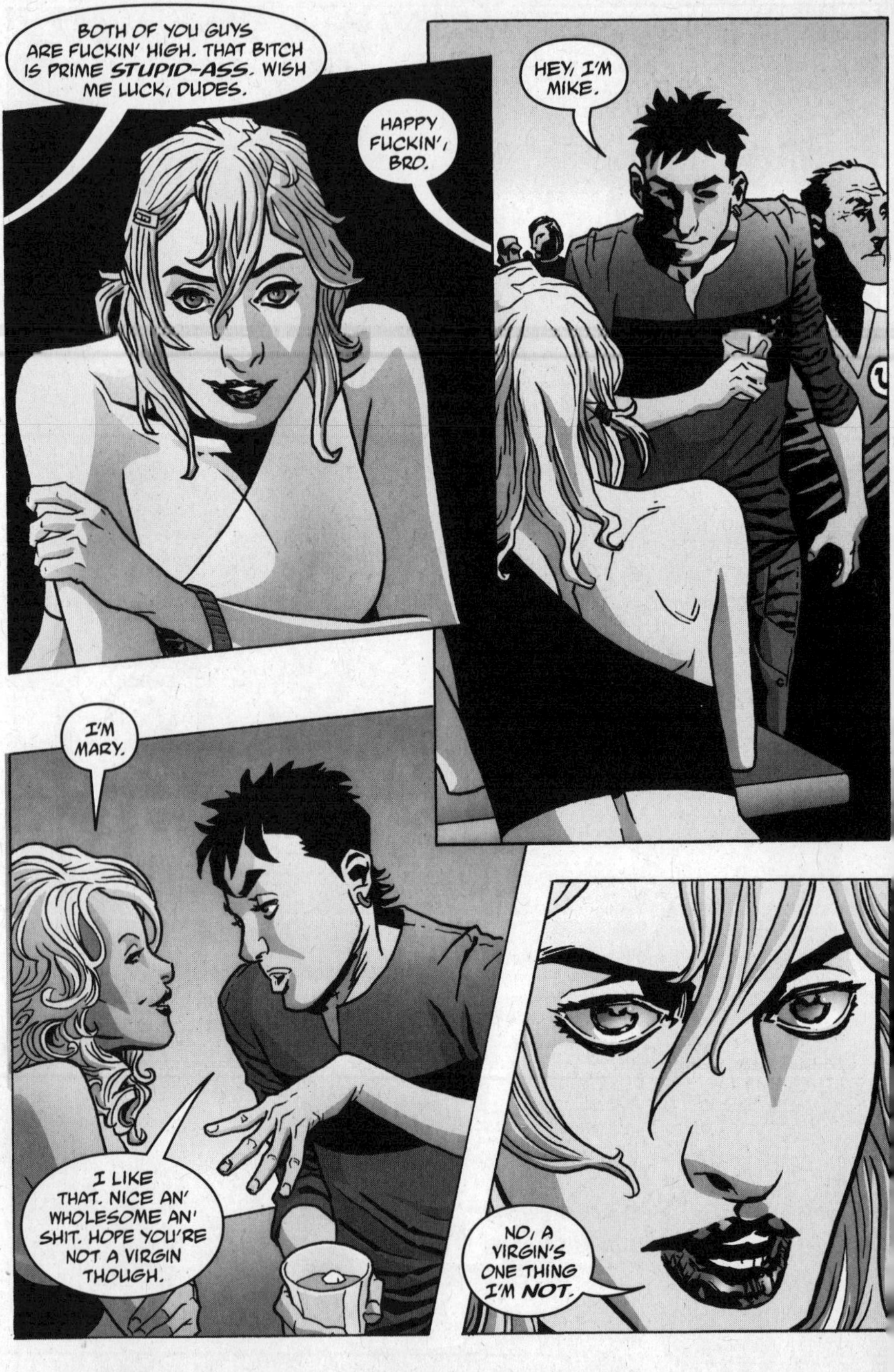
BOTH OF YOU GUYS ARE FUCKIN' HIGH. THAT BITCH IS PRIME STUPID-ASS. WISH ME LUCK, DUDES.
HAPPY FUCKIN', BRO.
HEY, I'M MIKE.
I'M MARY.
I LIKE THAT. NICE AN' WHOLESOME AN' SHIT. HOPE YOU'RE NOT A VIRGIN THOUGH.
NO, A VIRGIN'S ONE THING I'M NOT.

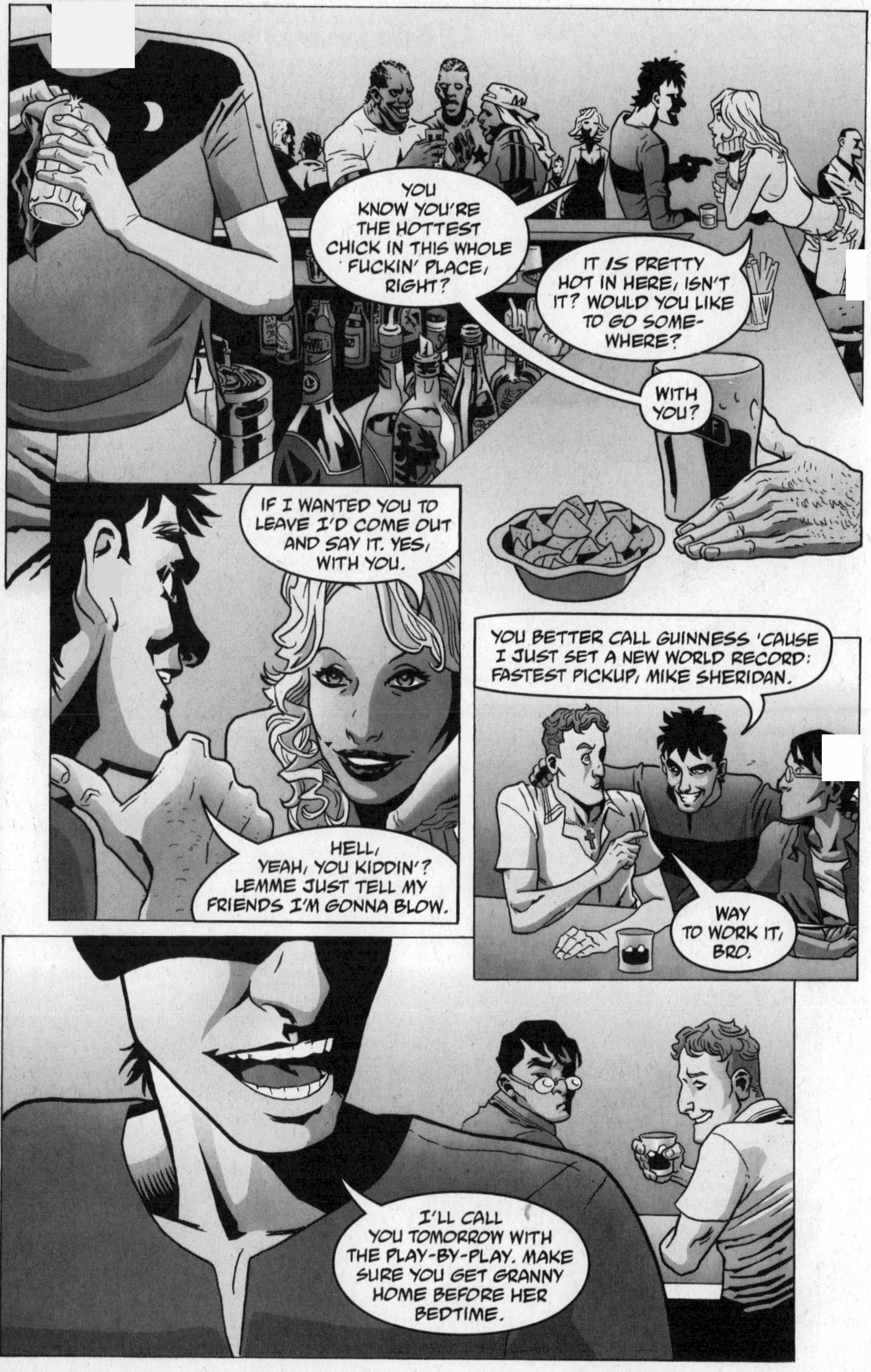
YOU KNOW YOU'RE THE HOTTEST CHICK IN THIS WHOLE FUCKIN' PLACE, RIGHT?
IT IS PRETTY HOT IN HERE, ISN'T IT? WOULD YOU LIKE TO GO SOMEWHERE?
WITH YOU?
IF I WANTED YOU TO LEAVE I'D COME OUT AND SAY IT. YES, WITH YOU.
HELL, YEAH, YOU KIDDIN'? LEMME JUST TELL MY FRIENDS I'M GONNA BLOW.
YOU BETTER CALL GUINNESS 'CAUSE I JUST SET A NEW WORLD RECORD: FASTEST PICKUP, MIKE SHERIDAN.
WAY TO WORK IT, BRO.
I'LL CALL YOU TOMORROW WITH THE PLAY-BY-PLAY. MAKE SURE YOU GET GRANNY HOME BEFORE HER BEDTIME.

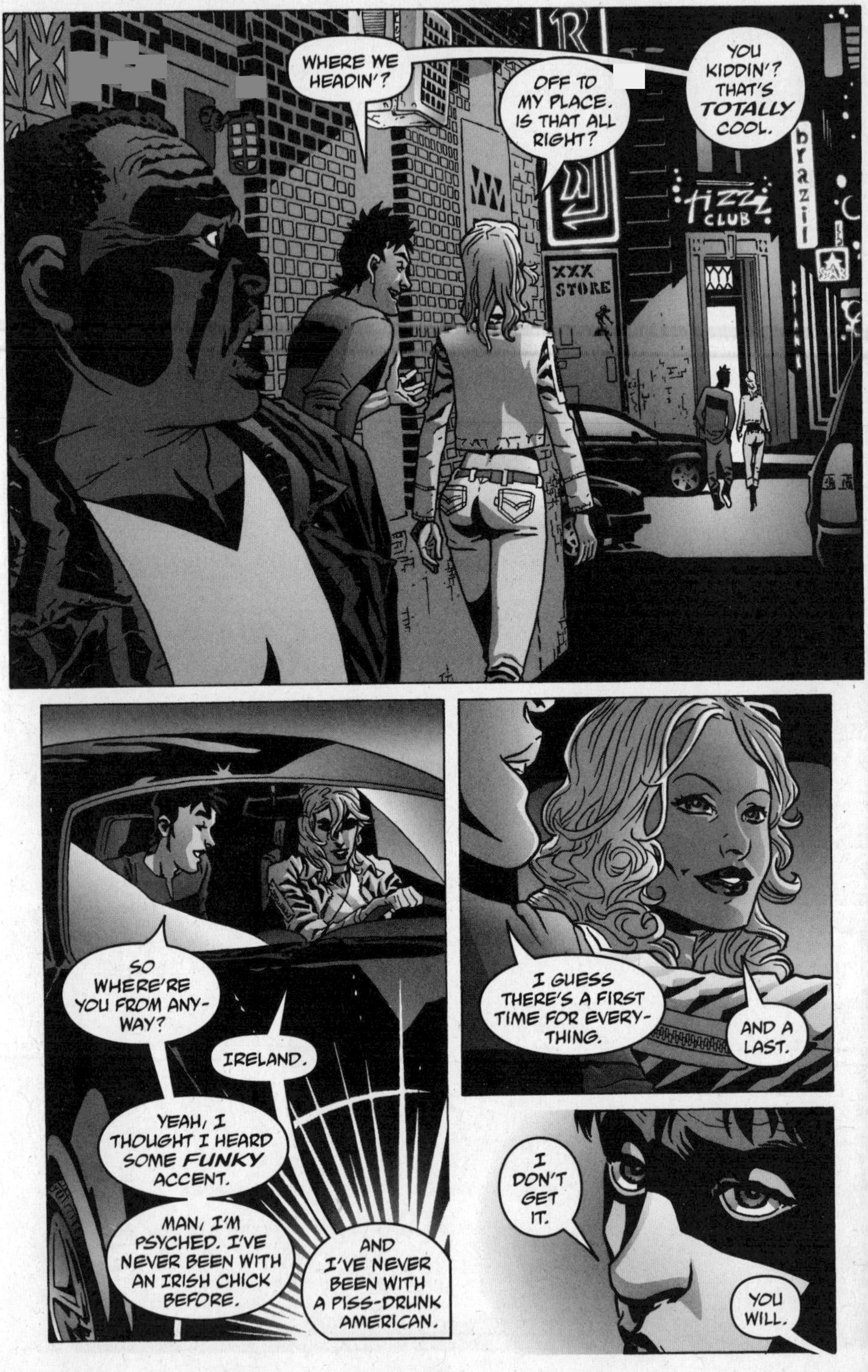
WHERE WE HEADIN'?
OFF TO MY PLACE. IS THAT ALL RIGHT?
YOU KIDDIN'? THAT'S *TOTALLY* COOL.
XXX STORE
fizz CLUB
brazil
SO WHERE'RE YOU FROM ANY-WAY?
IRELAND.
YEAH, I THOUGHT I HEARD SOME *FUNKY* ACCENT.
MAN, I'M PSYCHED. I'VE NEVER BEEN WITH AN IRISH CHICK BEFORE.
AND I'VE NEVER BEEN WITH A PISS-DRUNK AMERICAN.
I GUESS THERE'S A FIRST TIME FOR EVERY-THING.
AND A LAST.
I DON'T GET IT.
YOU WILL.

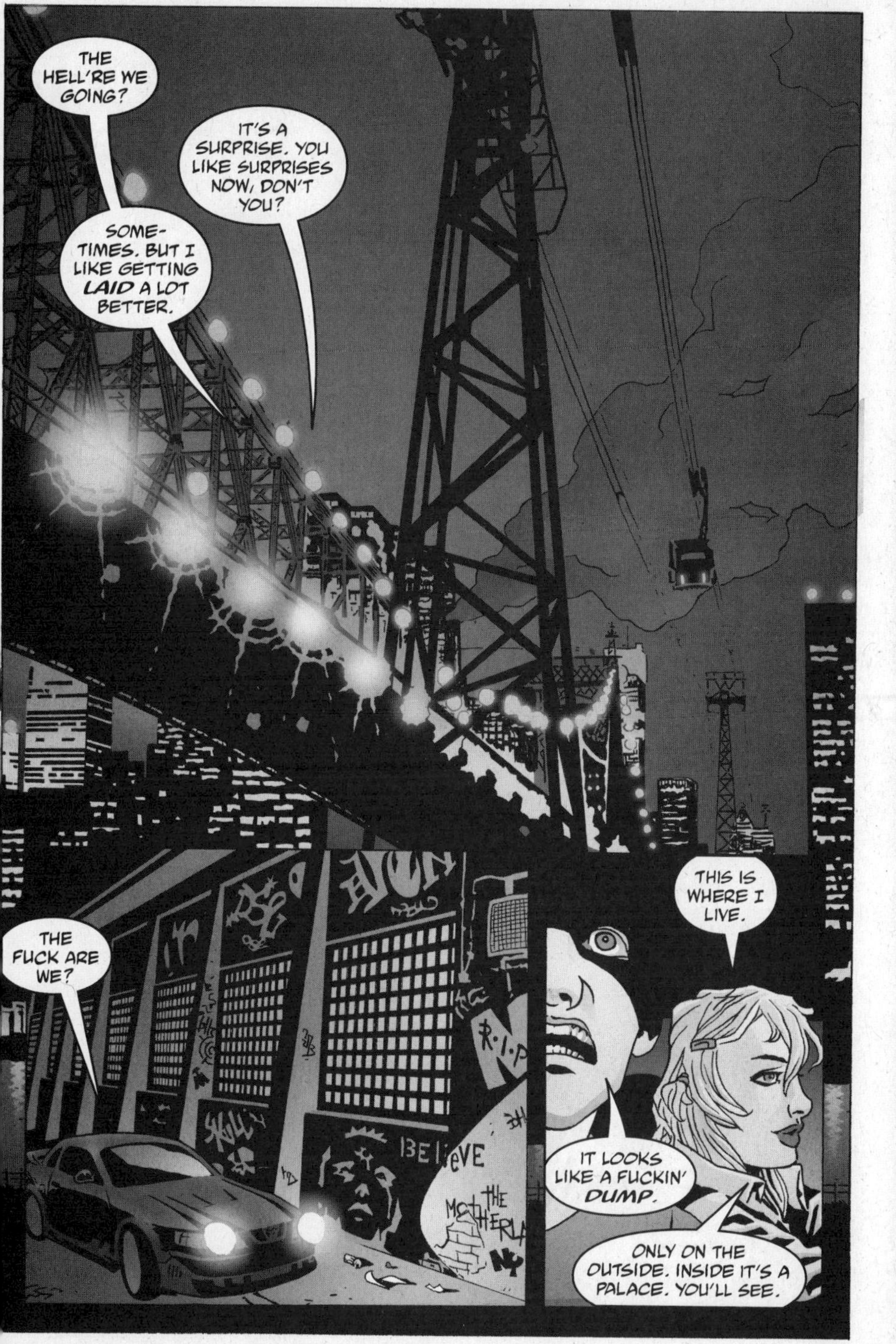
THE HELL'RE WE GOING?
IT'S A SURPRISE. YOU LIKE SURPRISES NOW, DON'T YOU?
SOME-TIMES. BUT I LIKE GETTING **LAID** A LOT BETTER.
THE FUCK ARE WE?
BELIEVE
THE MOTHERLA
NY
R.I.P
THIS IS WHERE I LIVE.
IT LOOKS LIKE A FUCKIN' **DUMP**.
ONLY ON THE OUTSIDE. INSIDE IT'S A PALACE. YOU'LL SEE.

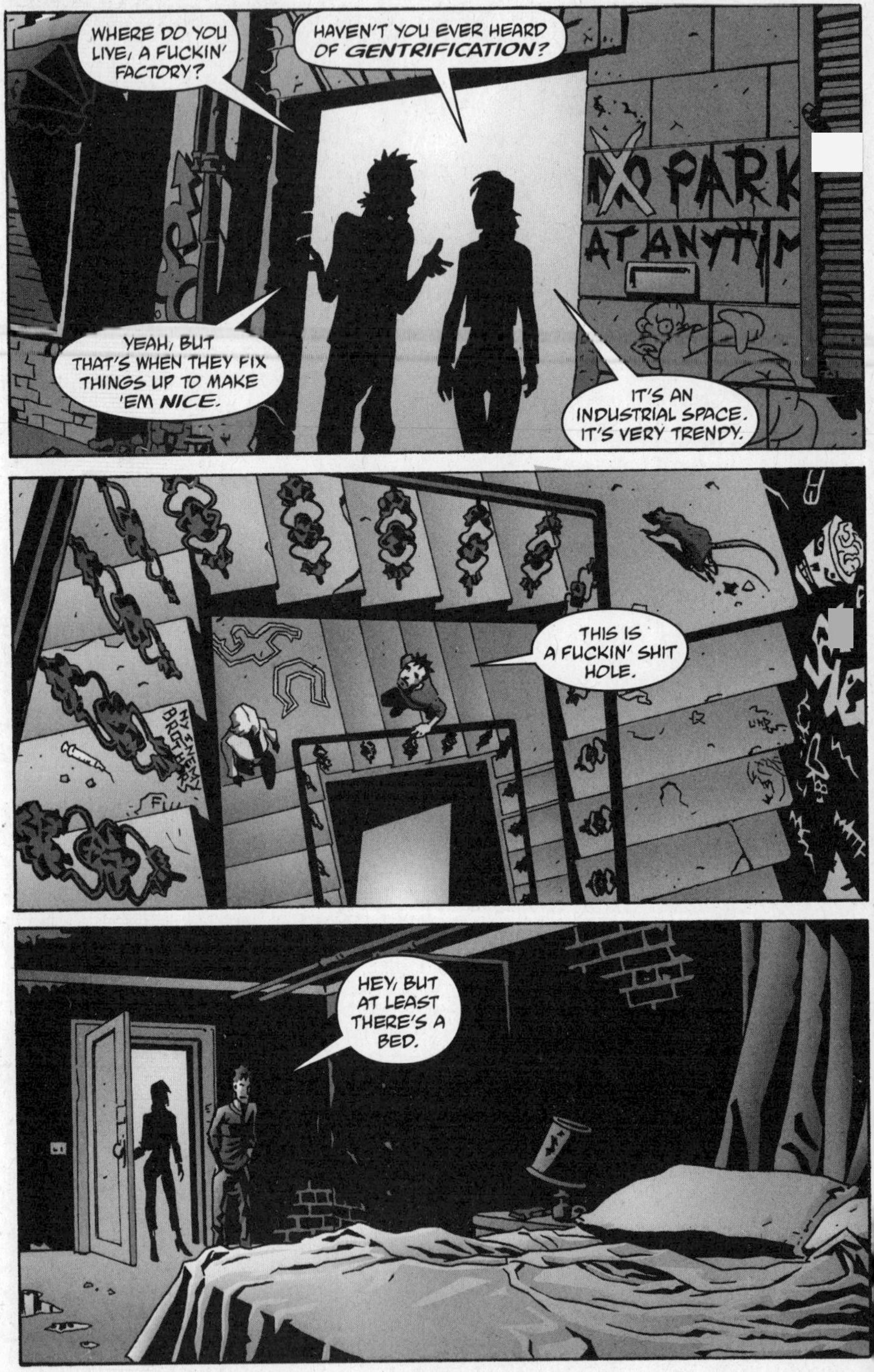
WHERE DO YOU LIVE, A FUCKIN' FACTORY?
HAVEN'T YOU EVER HEARD OF ***GENTRIFICATION?***
NO PARK
AT ANYTIM
YEAH, BUT THAT'S WHEN THEY FIX THINGS UP TO MAKE 'EM ***NICE.***
IT'S AN INDUSTRIAL SPACE. IT'S VERY TRENDY.
THIS IS A FUCKIN' SHIT HOLE.
HEY, BUT AT LEAST THERE'S A BED.

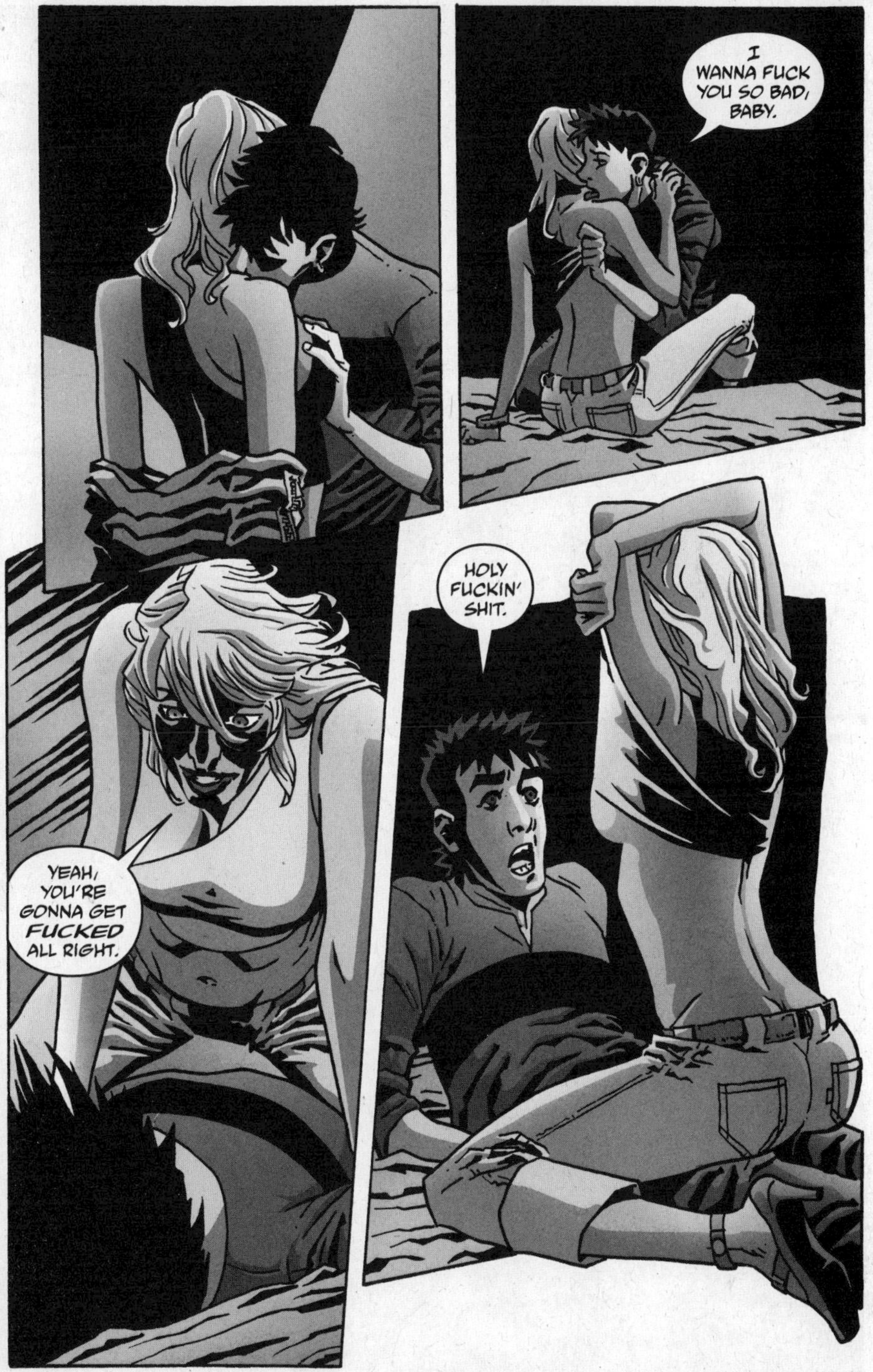
I WANNA FUCK YOU SO BAD, BABY.
YEAH, YOU'RE GONNA GET FUCKED ALL RIGHT.
HOLY FUCKIN' SHIT.

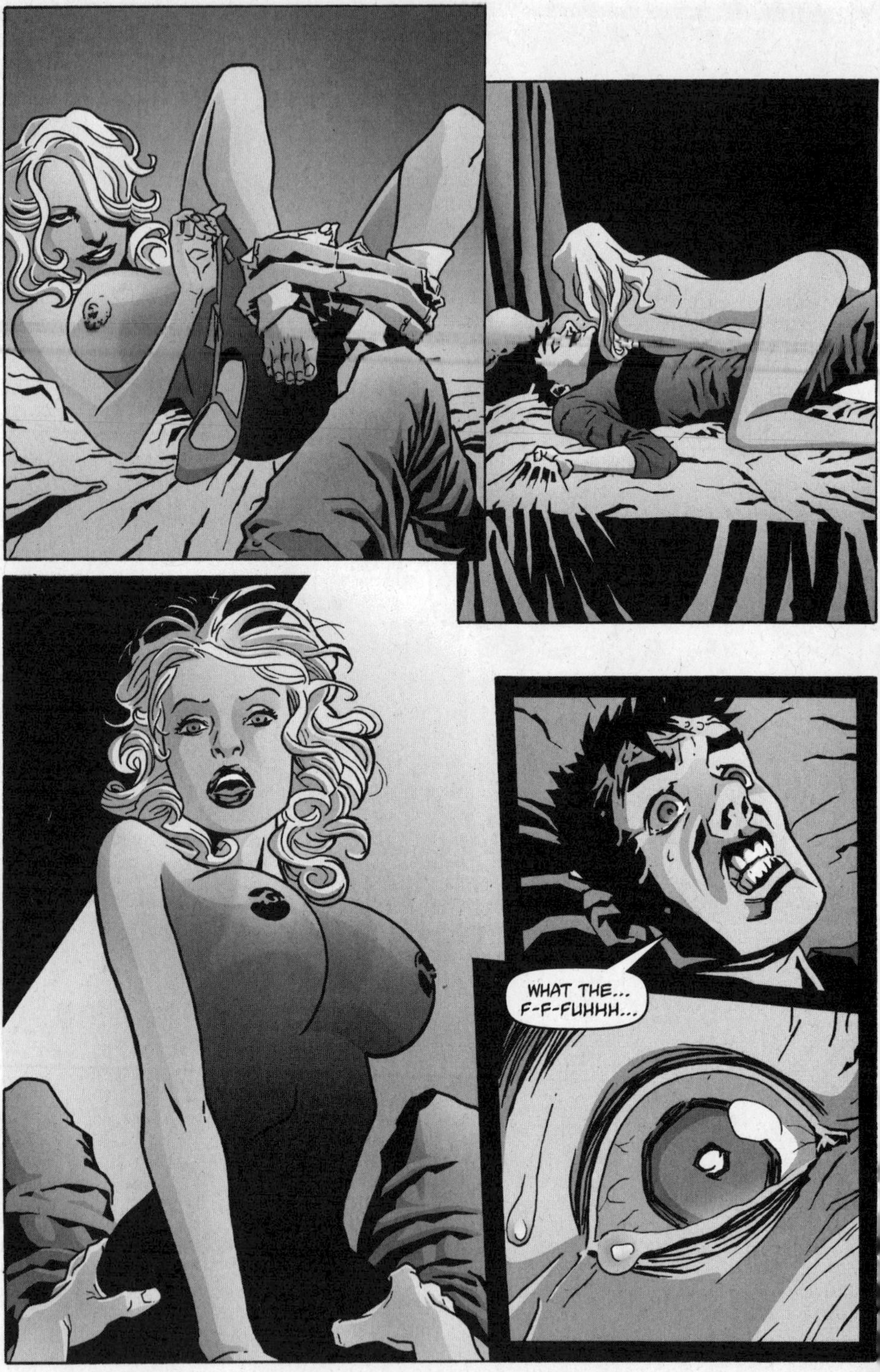
WHAT THE... F-F-FUHHH...

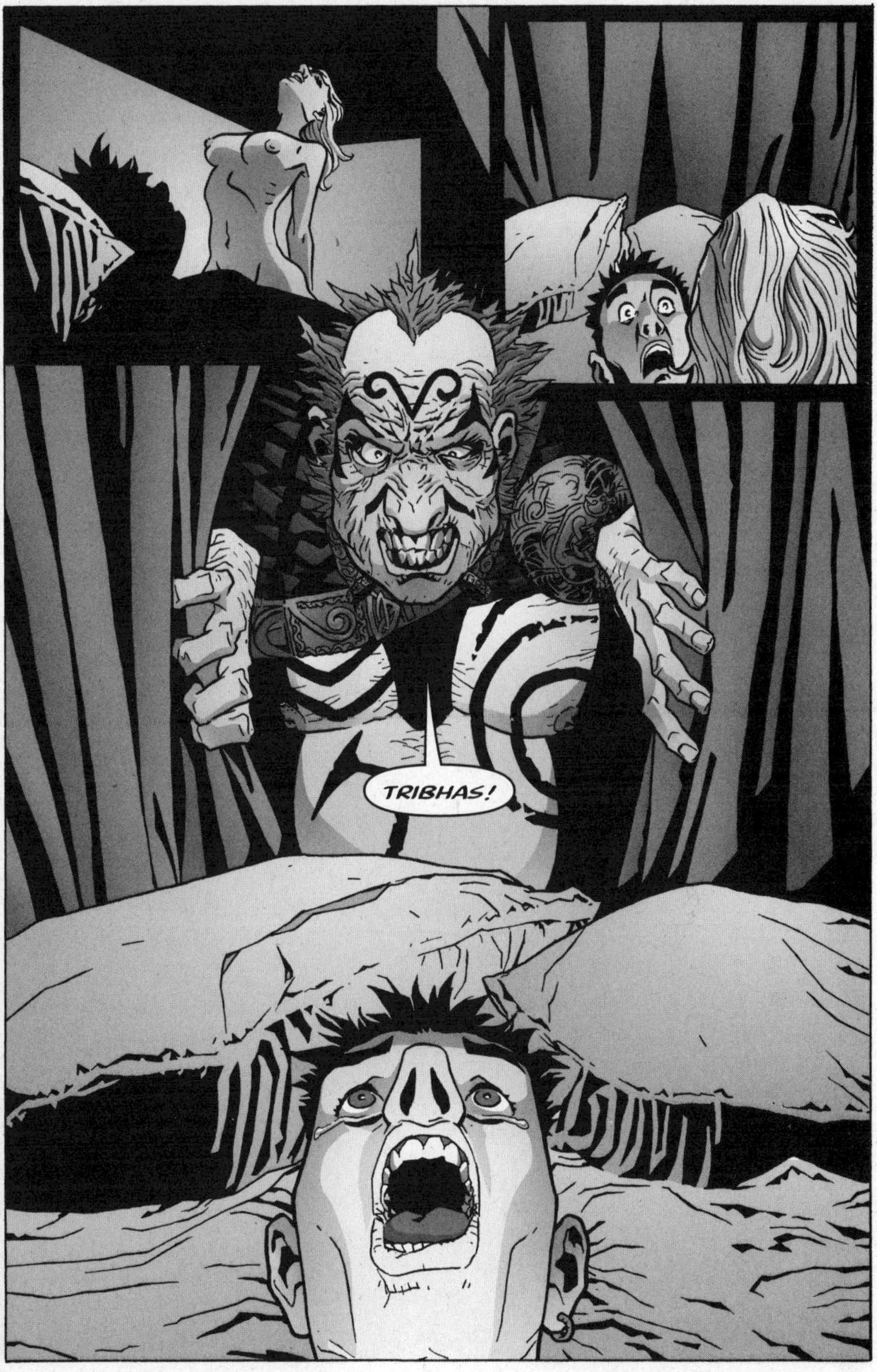
TRIBHAS!

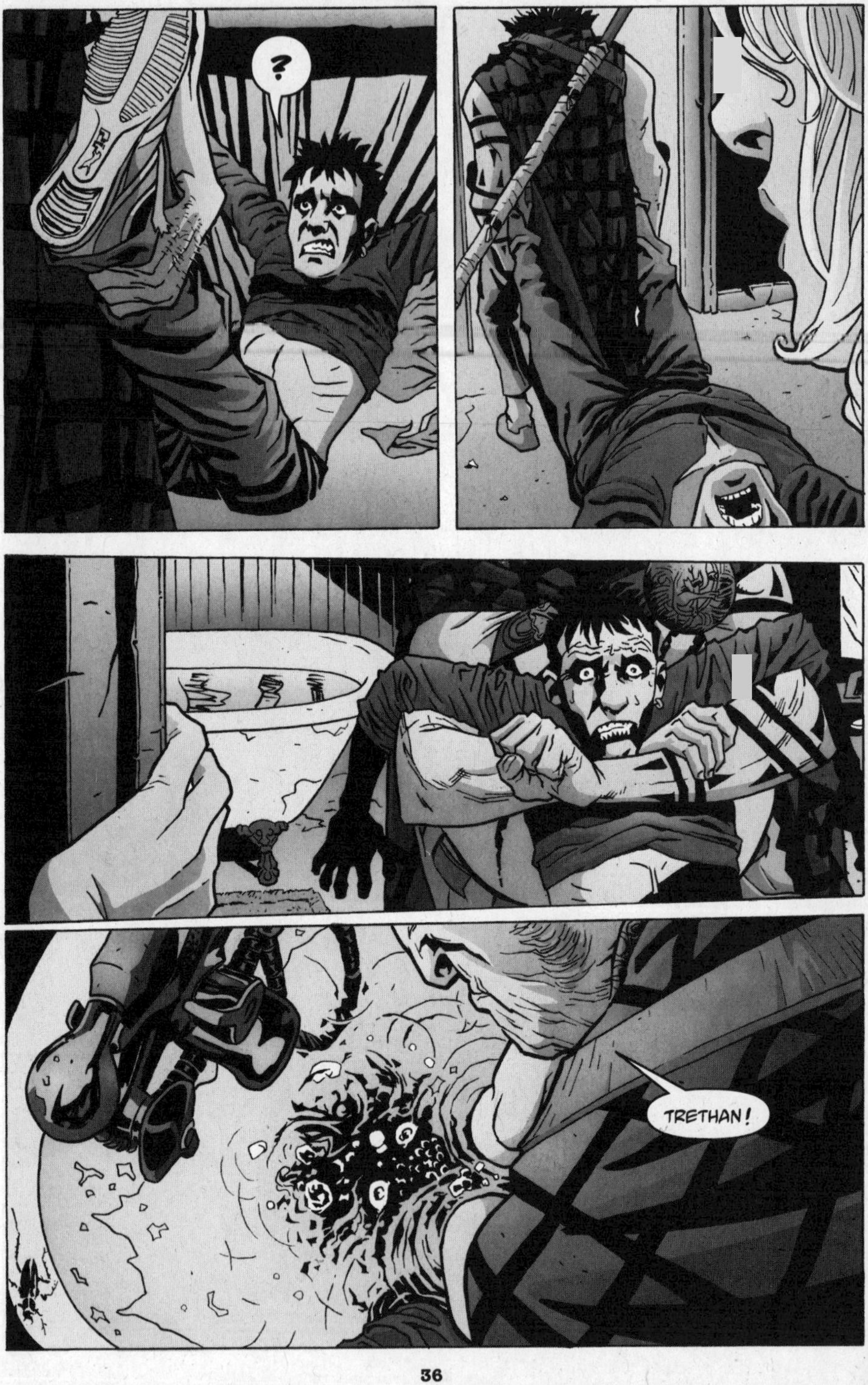
?
TRETHAN!

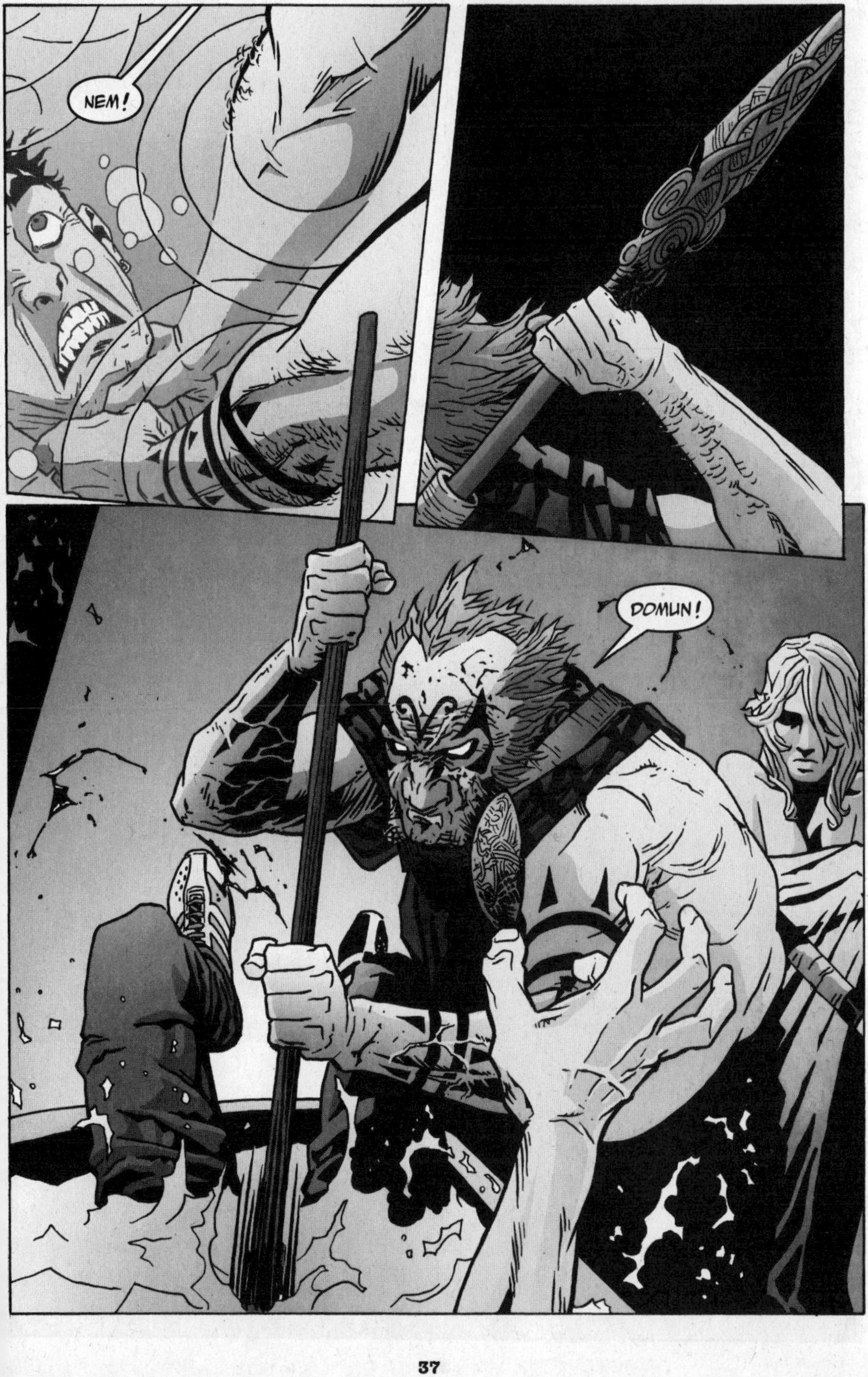
NEM!
DOMUN!

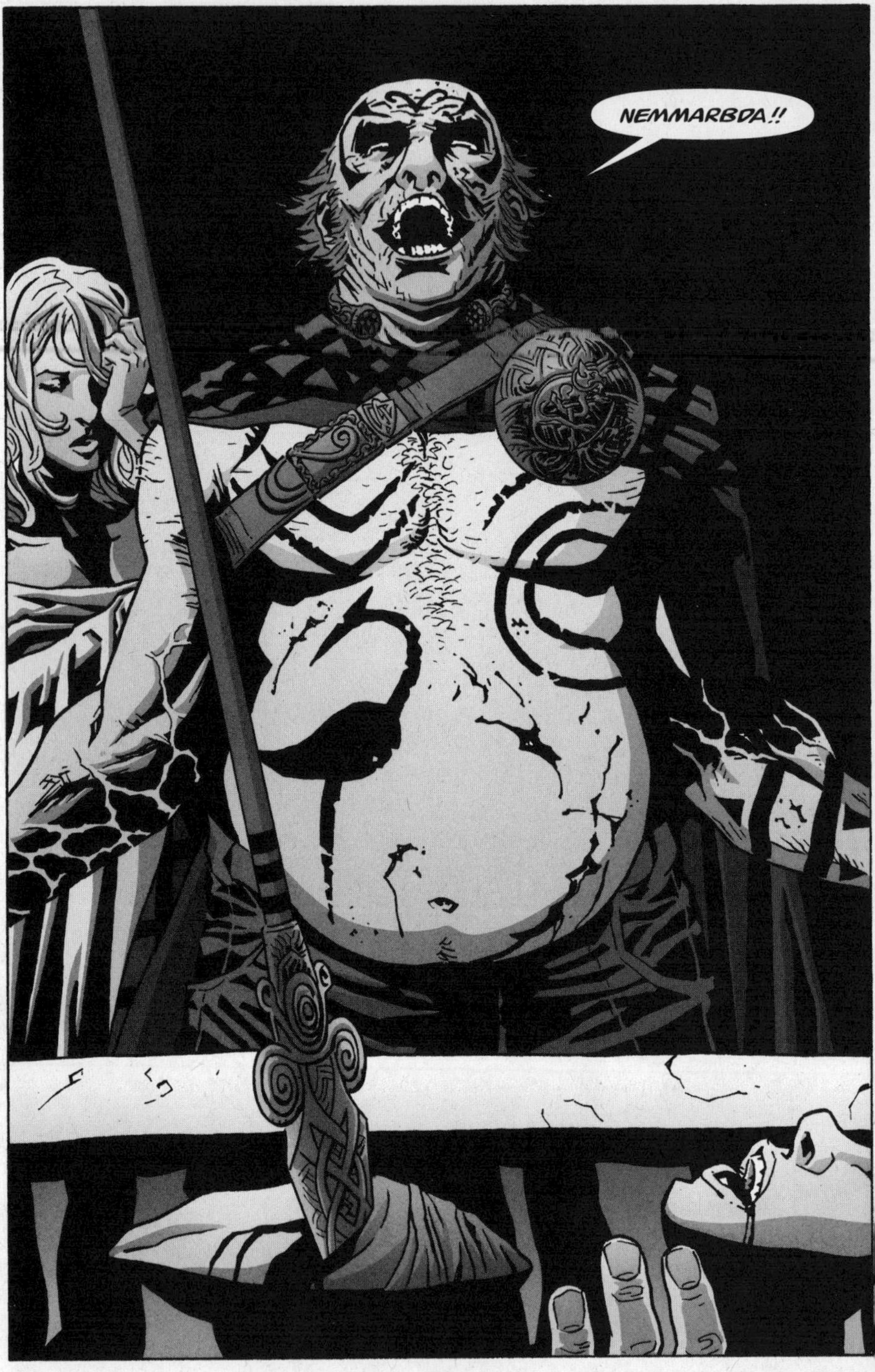
NEMMARBDA!!

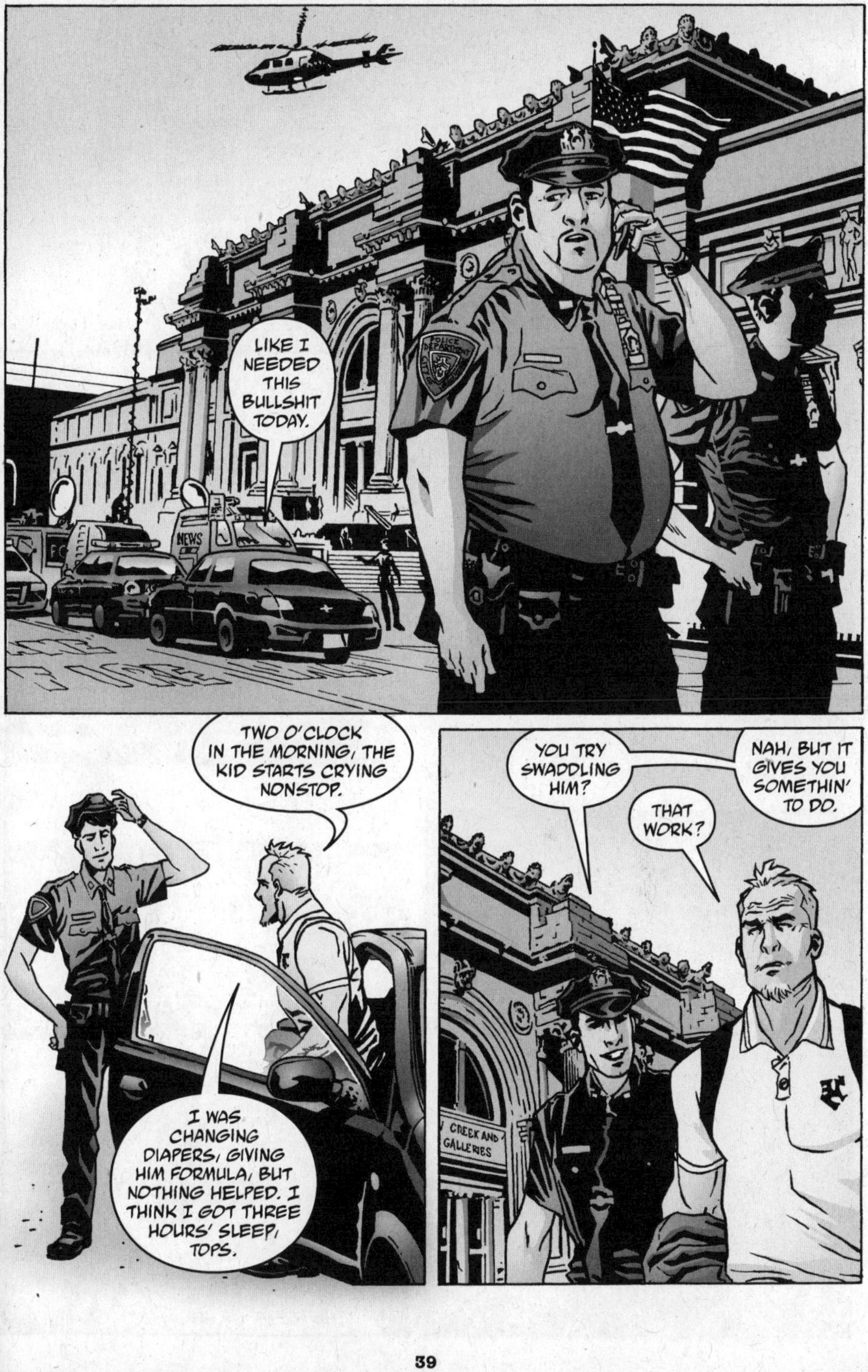
LIKE I NEEDED THIS BULLSHIT TODAY.
NEWS
TWO O'CLOCK IN THE MORNING, THE KID STARTS CRYING NONSTOP.
I WAS CHANGING DIAPERS, GIVING HIM FORMULA, BUT NOTHING HELPED. I THINK I GOT THREE HOURS' SLEEP, TOPS.
YOU TRY SWADDLING HIM?
THAT WORK?
NAH, BUT IT GIVES YOU SOMETHIN' TO DO.
GREEK AND GALLERIES

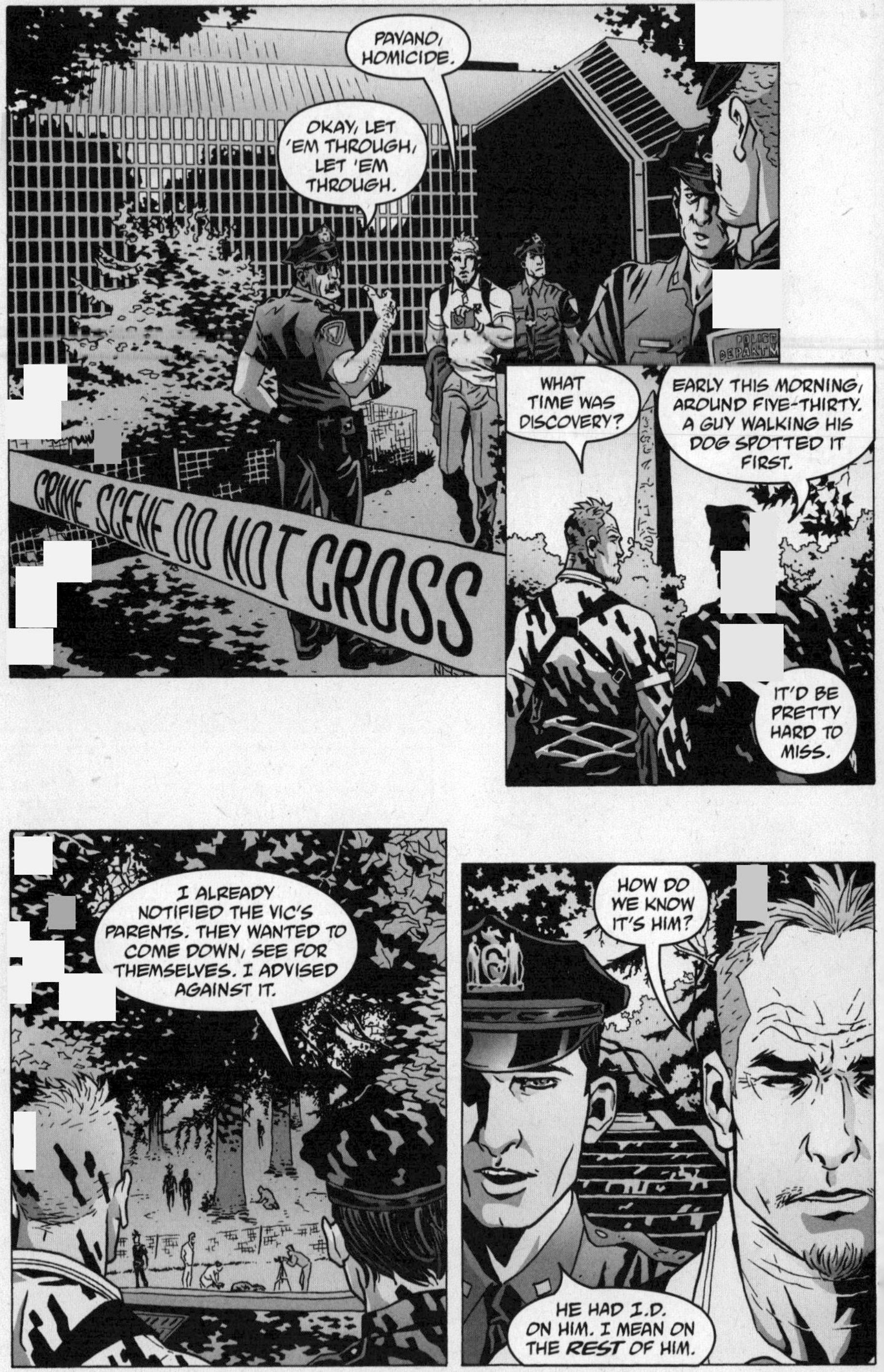
PAYANO, HOMICIDE.
OKAY, LET 'EM THROUGH, LET 'EM THROUGH.
CRIME SCENE DO NOT CROSS
WHAT TIME WAS DISCOVERY?
EARLY THIS MORNING, AROUND FIVE-THIRTY. A GUY WALKING HIS DOG SPOTTED IT FIRST.
IT'D BE PRETTY HARD TO MISS.
I ALREADY NOTIFIED THE VIC'S PARENTS. THEY WANTED TO COME DOWN, SEE FOR THEMSELVES. I ADVISED AGAINST IT.
HOW DO WE KNOW IT'S HIM?
HE HAD I.D. ON HIM. I MEAN ON THE *REST* OF HIM.

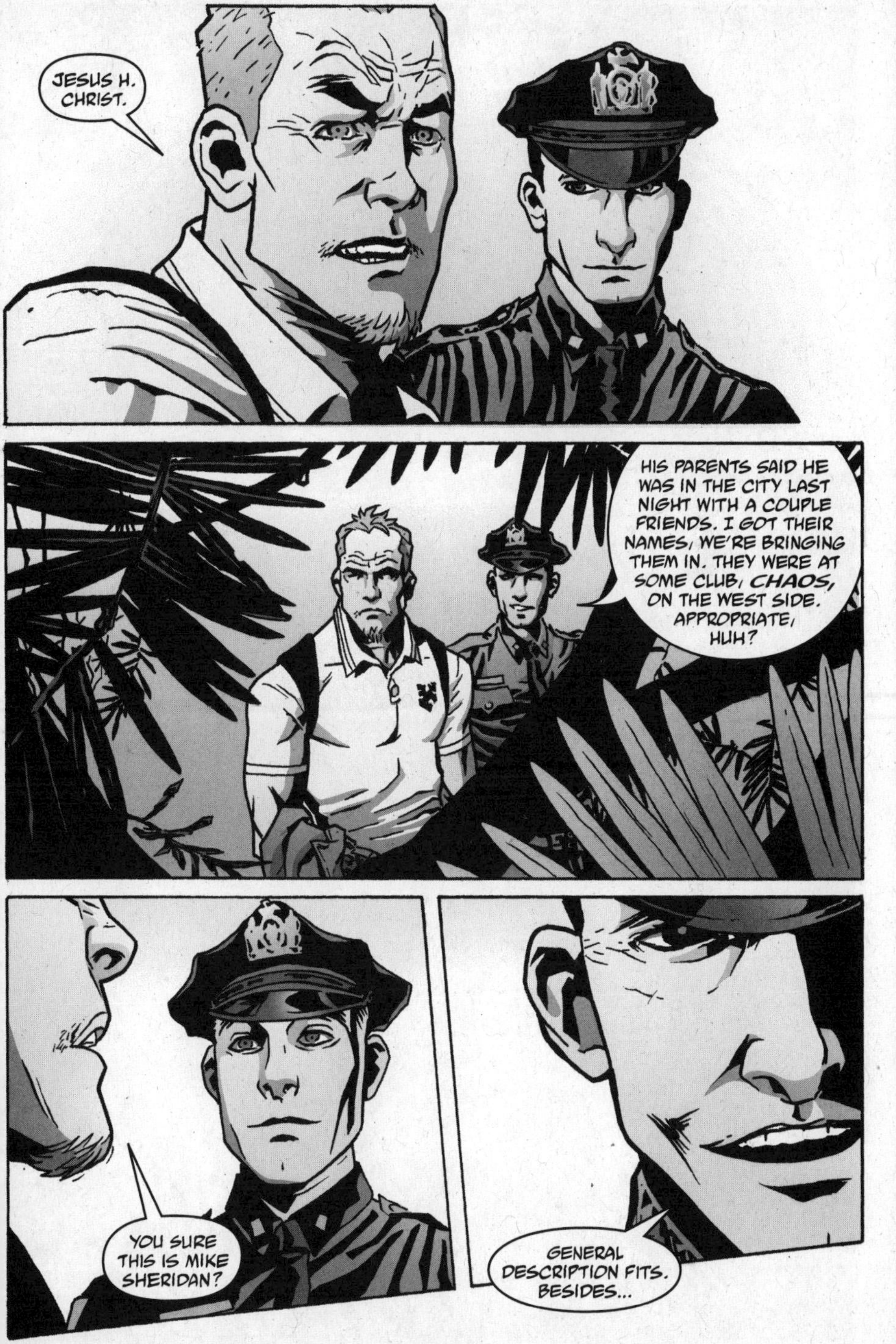
JESUS H. CHRIST.
HIS PARENTS SAID HE WAS IN THE CITY LAST NIGHT WITH A COUPLE FRIENDS. I GOT THEIR NAMES, WE'RE BRINGING THEM IN. THEY WERE AT SOME CLUB, CHAOS, ON THE WEST SIDE. APPROPRIATE, HUH?
YOU SURE THIS IS MIKE SHERIDAN?
GENERAL DESCRIPTION FITS. BESIDES...

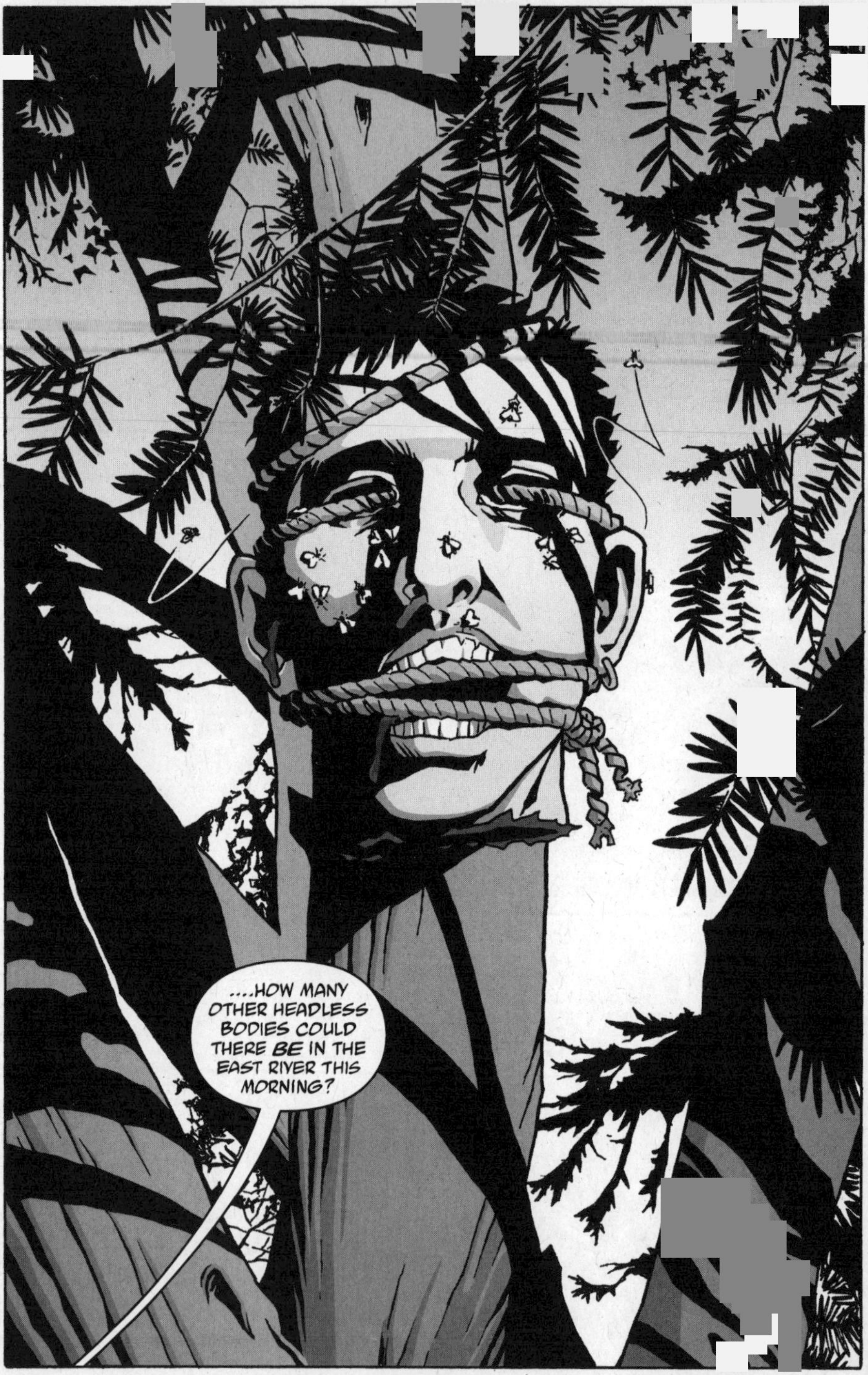
....HOW MANY OTHER HEADLESS BODIES COULD THERE *BE* IN THE EAST RIVER THIS MORNING?

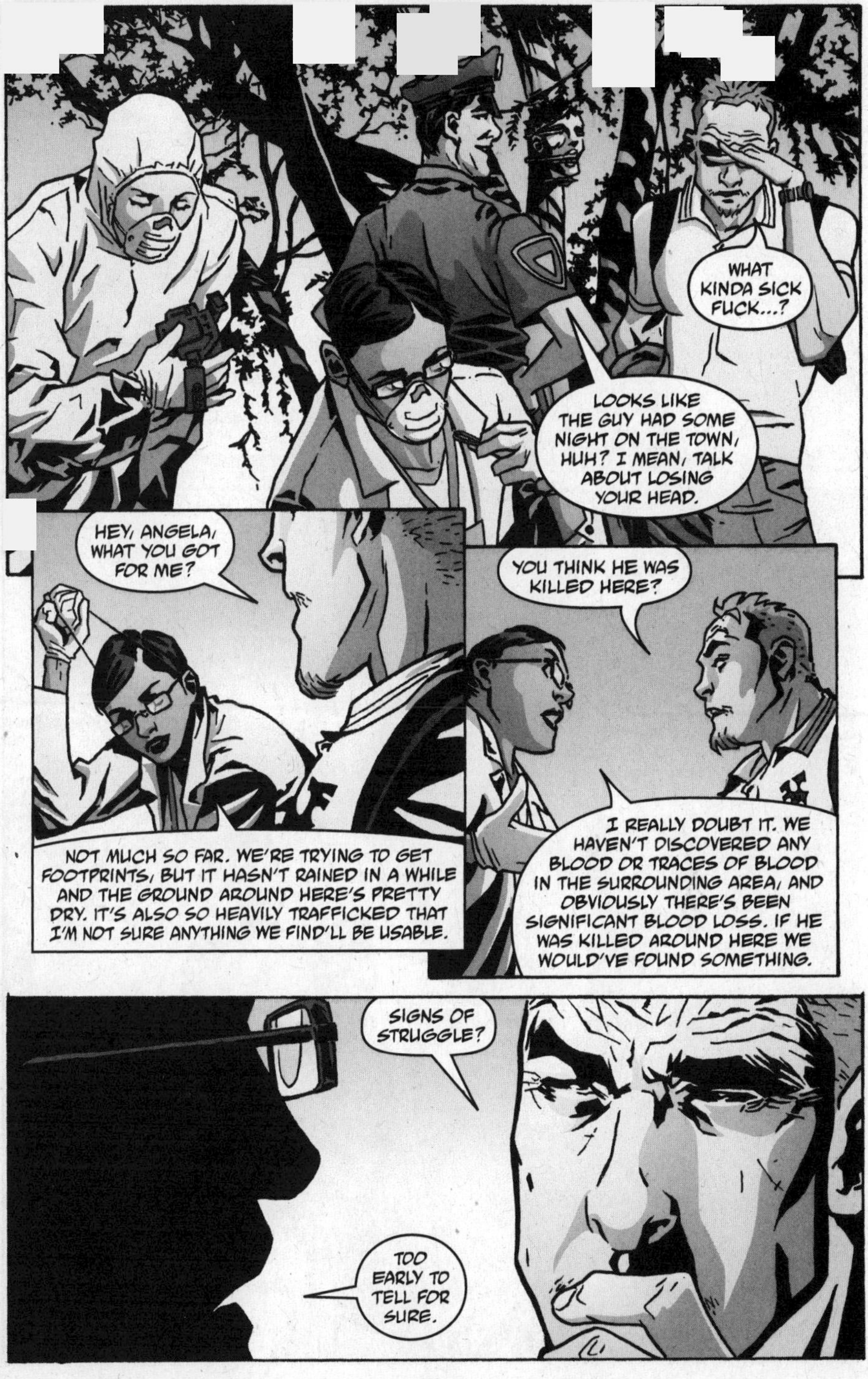
WHAT KINDA SICK FUCK...?
LOOKS LIKE THE GUY HAD SOME NIGHT ON THE TOWN, HUH? I MEAN, TALK ABOUT LOSING YOUR HEAD.
HEY, ANGELA, WHAT YOU GOT FOR ME?
NOT MUCH SO FAR. WE'RE TRYING TO GET FOOTPRINTS, BUT IT HASN'T RAINED IN A WHILE AND THE GROUND AROUND HERE'S PRETTY DRY. IT'S ALSO SO HEAVILY TRAFFICKED THAT I'M NOT SURE ANYTHING WE FIND'LL BE USABLE.
YOU THINK HE WAS KILLED HERE?
I REALLY DOUBT IT. WE HAVEN'T DISCOVERED ANY BLOOD OR TRACES OF BLOOD IN THE SURROUNDING AREA, AND OBVIOUSLY THERE'S BEEN SIGNIFICANT BLOOD LOSS. IF HE WAS KILLED AROUND HERE WE WOULD'VE FOUND SOMETHING.
SIGNS OF STRUGGLE?
TOO EARLY TO TELL FOR SURE.

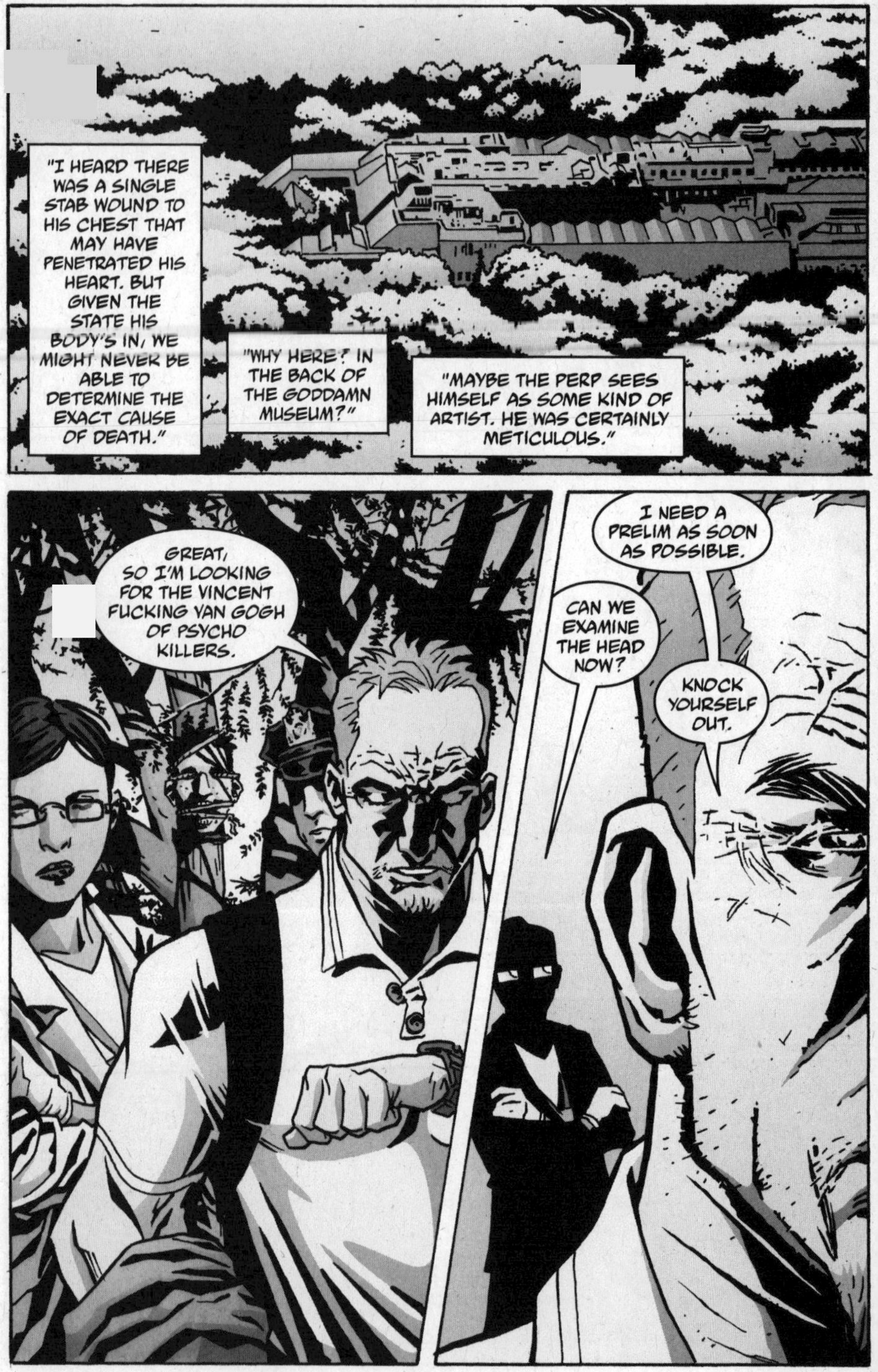
"I HEARD THERE WAS A SINGLE STAB WOUND TO HIS CHEST THAT MAY HAVE PENETRATED HIS HEART. BUT GIVEN THE STATE HIS BODY'S IN, WE MIGHT NEVER BE ABLE TO DETERMINE THE EXACT CAUSE OF DEATH."
"WHY HERE? IN THE BACK OF THE GODDAMN MUSEUM?"
"MAYBE THE PERP SEES HIMSELF AS SOME KIND OF ARTIST. HE WAS CERTAINLY METICULOUS."
GREAT, SO I'M LOOKING FOR THE VINCENT FUCKING VAN GOGH OF PSYCHO KILLERS.
I NEED A PRELIM AS SOON AS POSSIBLE.
CAN WE EXAMINE THE HEAD NOW?
KNOCK YOURSELF OUT.

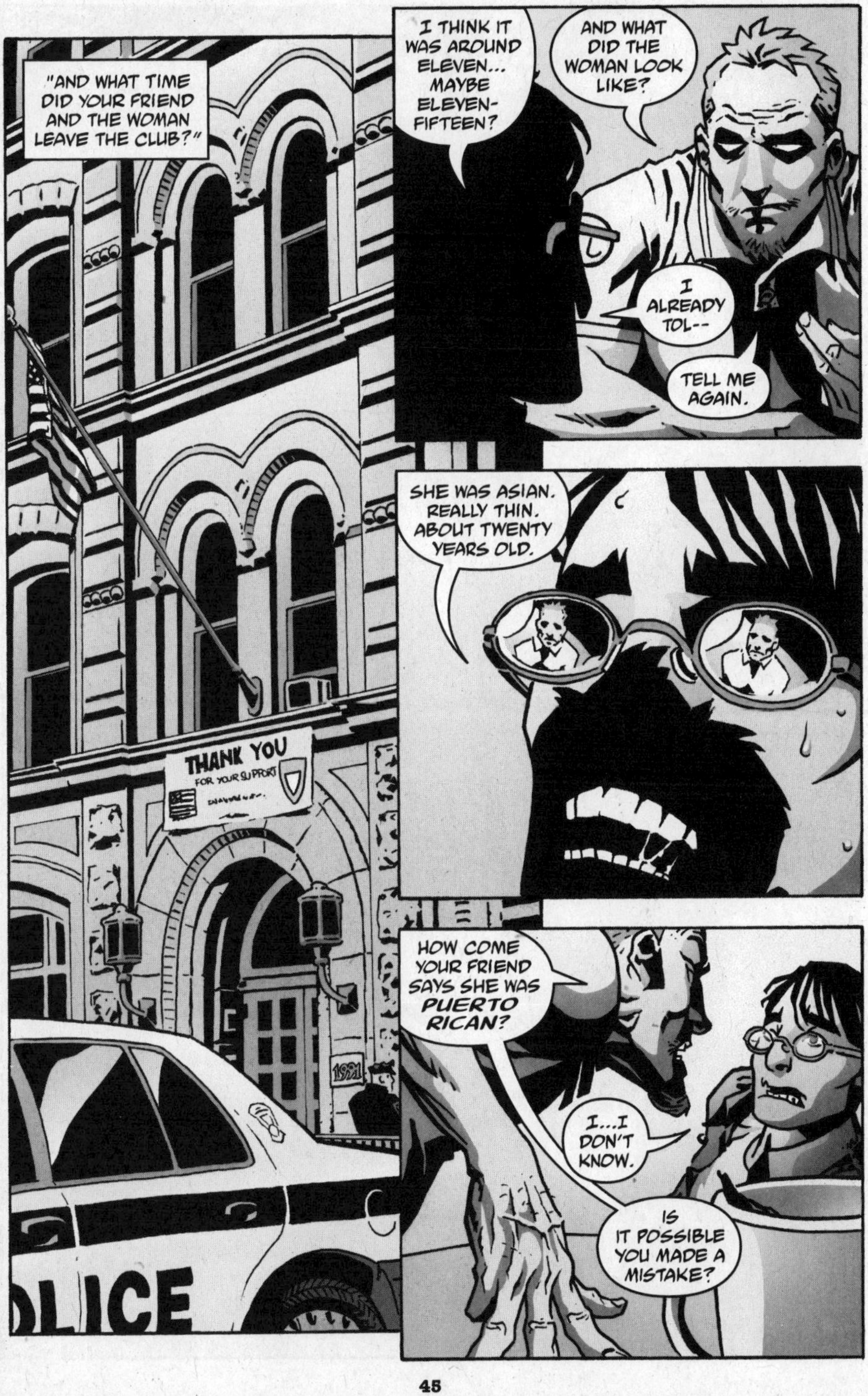
"AND WHAT TIME DID YOUR FRIEND AND THE WOMAN LEAVE THE CLUB?"
THANK YOU
FOR YOUR SUPPORT
1991
OLICE
I THINK IT WAS AROUND ELEVEN... MAYBE ELEVEN-FIFTEEN?
AND WHAT DID THE WOMAN LOOK LIKE?
I ALREADY TOL--
TELL ME AGAIN.
SHE WAS ASIAN. REALLY THIN. ABOUT TWENTY YEARS OLD.
HOW COME YOUR FRIEND SAYS SHE WAS *PUERTO RICAN?*
I...I DON'T KNOW.
IS IT POSSIBLE YOU MADE A MISTAKE?

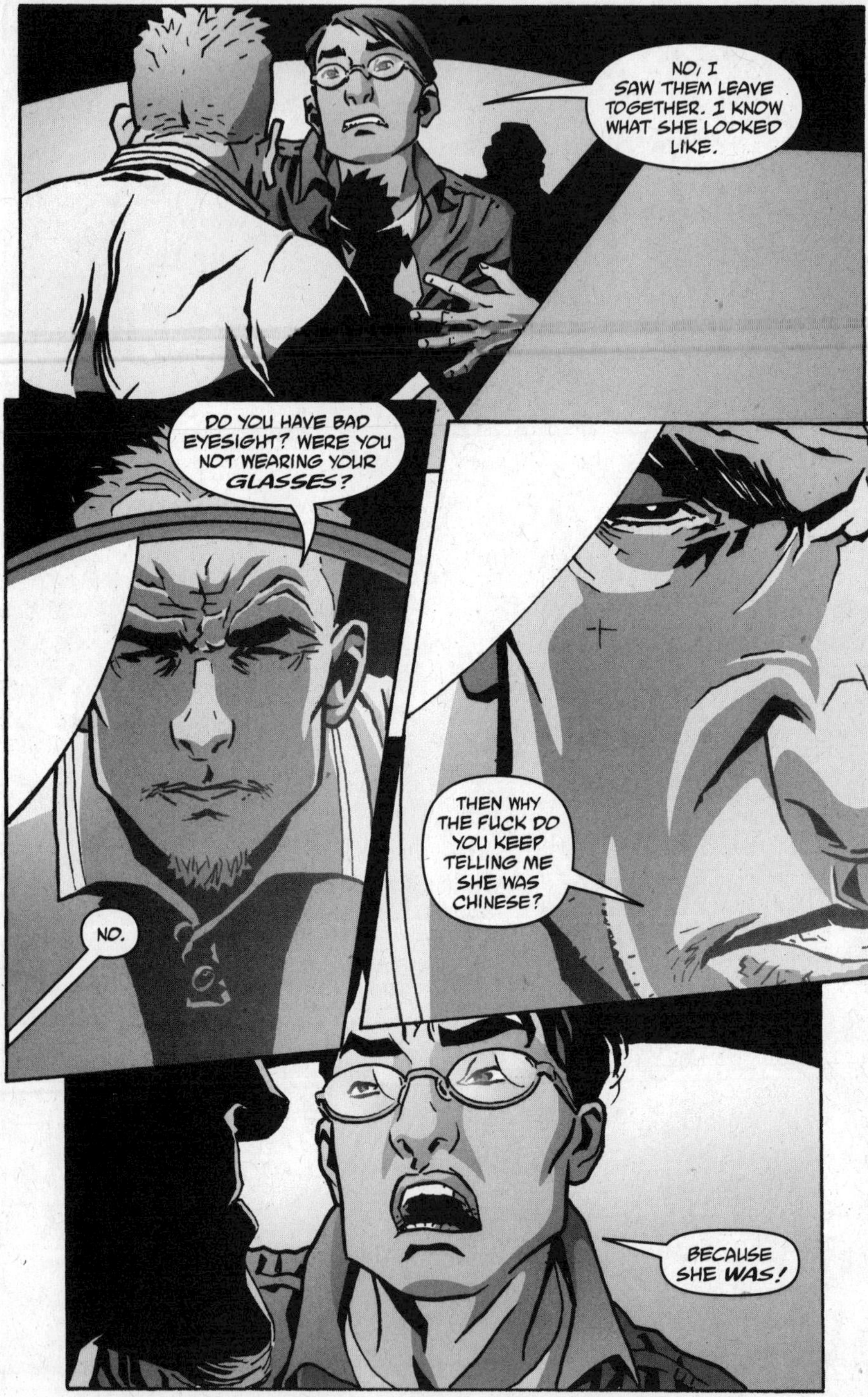
NO, I SAW THEM LEAVE TOGETHER. I KNOW WHAT SHE LOOKED LIKE.
DO YOU HAVE BAD EYESIGHT? WERE YOU NOT WEARING YOUR GLASSES?
NO.
THEN WHY THE FUCK DO YOU KEEP TELLING ME SHE WAS CHINESE?
BECAUSE SHE WAS!

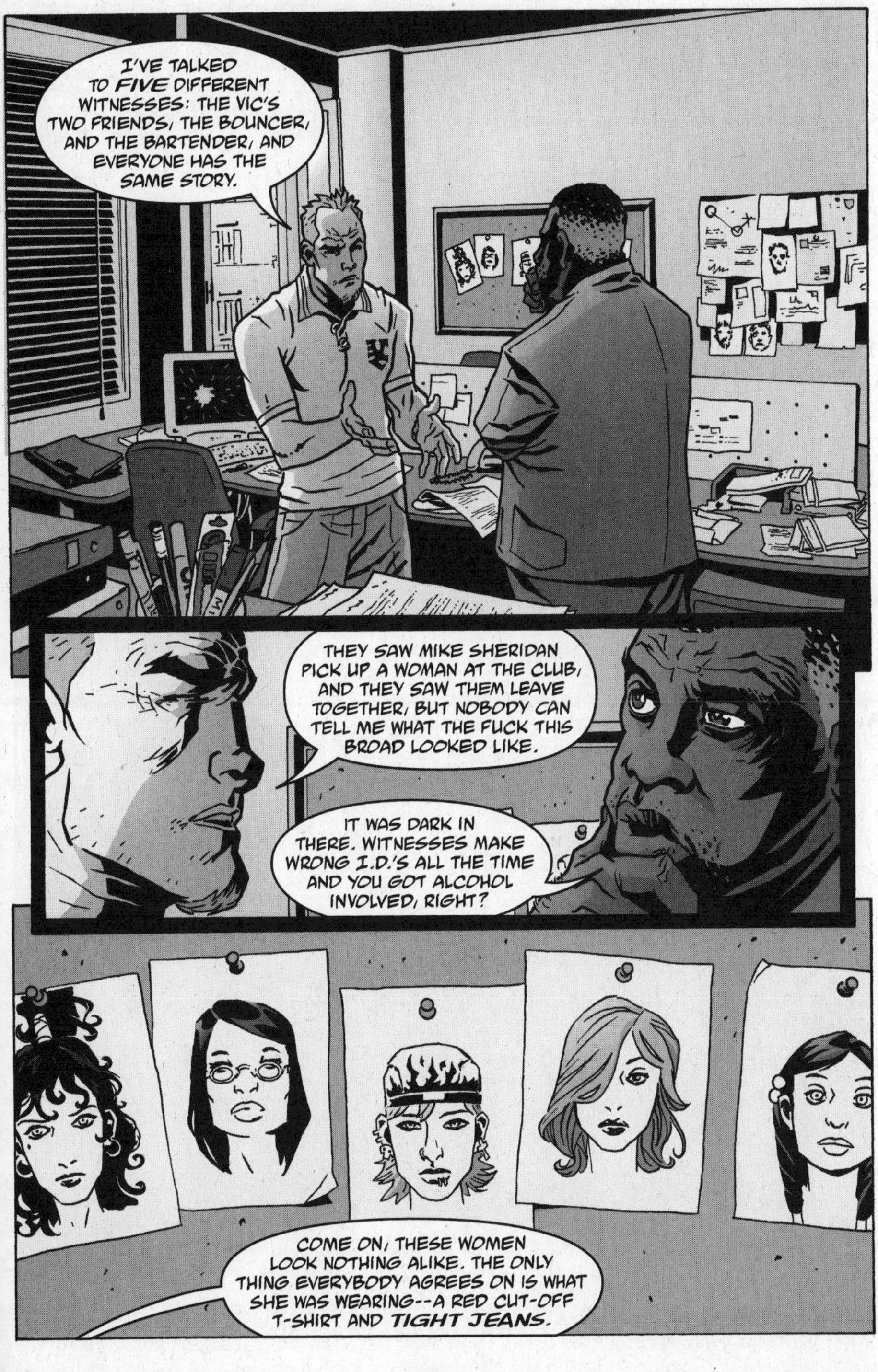
I'VE TALKED TO *FIVE* DIFFERENT WITNESSES: THE VIC'S TWO FRIENDS, THE BOUNCER, AND THE BARTENDER, AND EVERYONE HAS THE SAME STORY.
THEY SAW MIKE SHERIDAN PICK UP A WOMAN AT THE CLUB, AND THEY SAW THEM LEAVE TOGETHER, BUT NOBODY CAN TELL ME WHAT THE FUCK THIS BROAD LOOKED LIKE.
IT WAS DARK IN THERE. WITNESSES MAKE WRONG I.D.'S ALL THE TIME AND YOU GOT ALCOHOL INVOLVED, RIGHT?
COME ON, THESE WOMEN LOOK NOTHING ALIKE. THE ONLY THING EVERYBODY AGREES ON IS WHAT SHE WAS WEARING--A RED CUT-OFF T-SHIRT AND *TIGHT JEANS*.

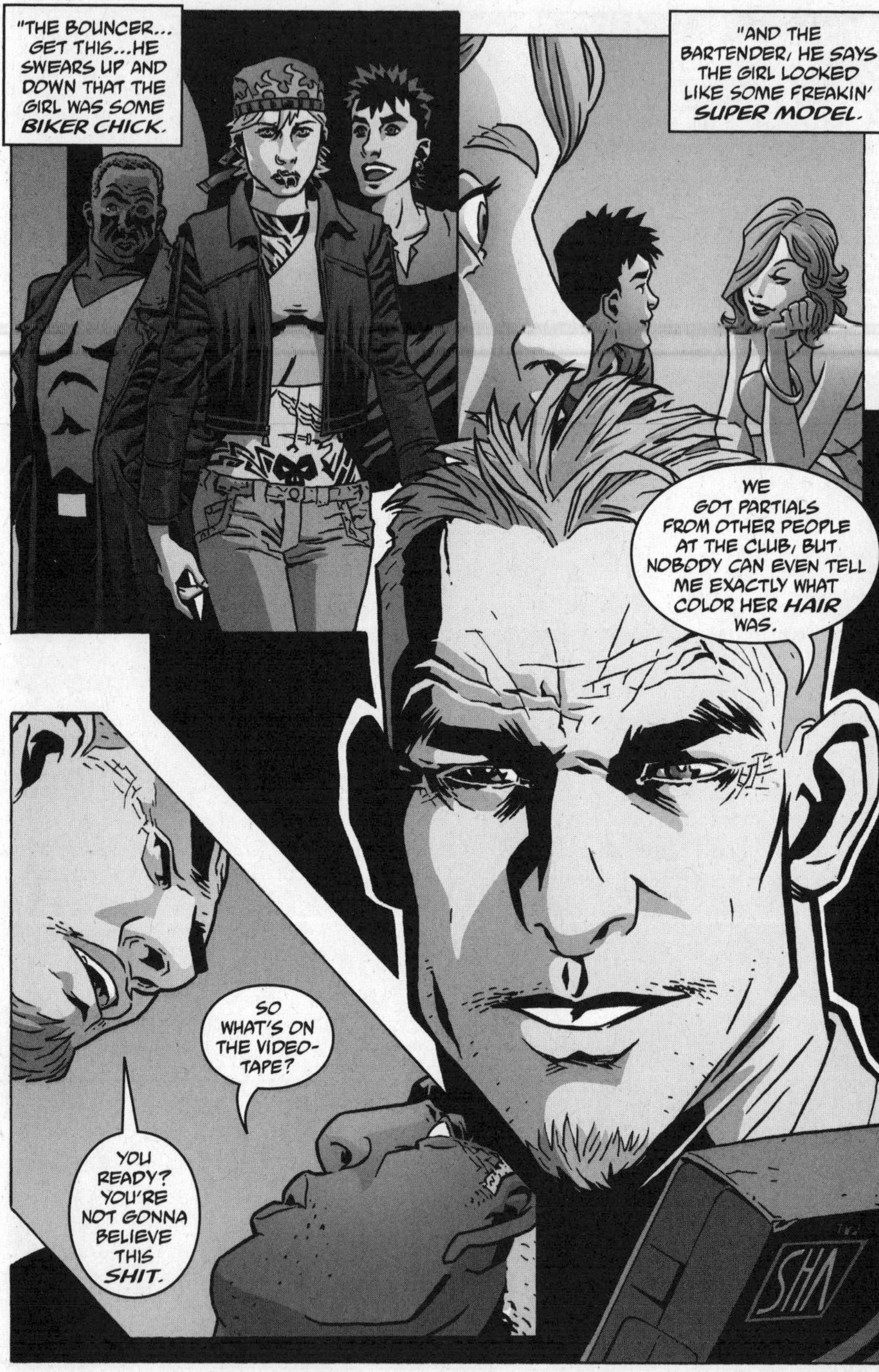
"THE BOUNCER... GET THIS...HE SWEARS UP AND DOWN THAT THE GIRL WAS SOME BIKER CHICK.
"AND THE BARTENDER, HE SAYS THE GIRL LOOKED LIKE SOME FREAKIN' SUPER MODEL.
WE GOT PARTIALS FROM OTHER PEOPLE AT THE CLUB, BUT NOBODY CAN EVEN TELL ME EXACTLY WHAT COLOR HER HAIR WAS.
SO WHAT'S ON THE VIDEO-TAPE?
YOU READY? YOU'RE NOT GONNA BELIEVE THIS SHIT.

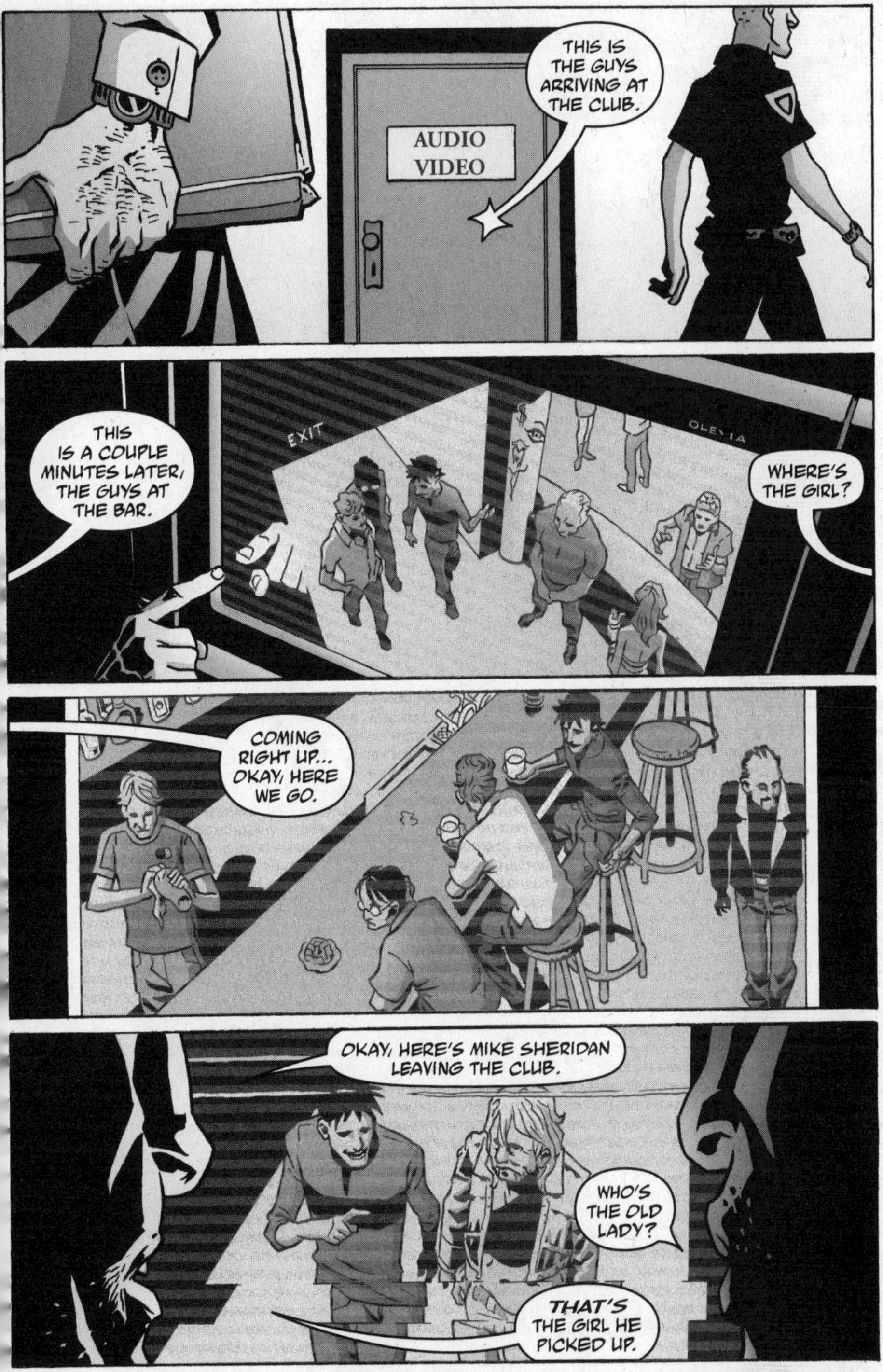
THIS IS THE GUYS ARRIVING AT THE CLUB.
AUDIO VIDEO
THIS IS A COUPLE MINUTES LATER, THE GUYS AT THE BAR.
EXIT
WHERE'S THE GIRL?
COMING RIGHT UP... OKAY, HERE WE GO.
OKAY, HERE'S MIKE SHERIDAN LEAVING THE CLUB.
WHO'S THE OLD LADY?
THAT'S THE GIRL HE PICKED UP.

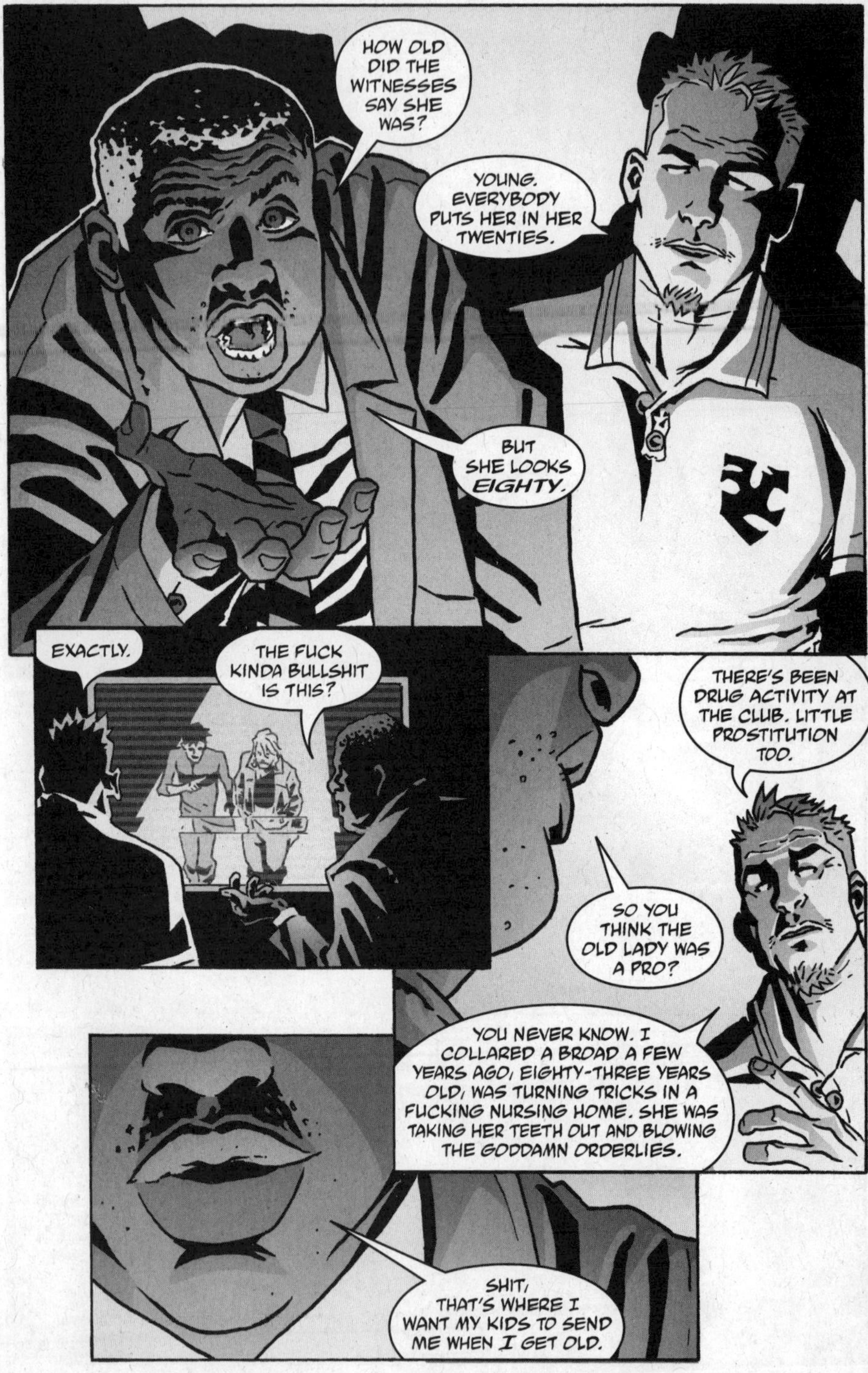
HOW OLD DID THE WITNESSES SAY SHE WAS?
YOUNG. EVERYBODY PUTS HER IN HER TWENTIES.
BUT SHE LOOKS *EIGHTY*.
EXACTLY.
THE FUCK KINDA BULLSHIT IS THIS?
THERE'S BEEN DRUG ACTIVITY AT THE CLUB. LITTLE PROSTITUTION TOO.
SO YOU THINK THE OLD LADY WAS A PRO?
YOU NEVER KNOW. I COLLARED A BROAD A FEW YEARS AGO, EIGHTY-THREE YEARS OLD, WAS TURNING TRICKS IN A FUCKING NURSING HOME. SHE WAS TAKING HER TEETH OUT AND BLOWING THE GODDAMN ORDERLIES.
SHIT, THAT'S WHERE I WANT MY KIDS TO SEND ME WHEN *I* GET OLD.

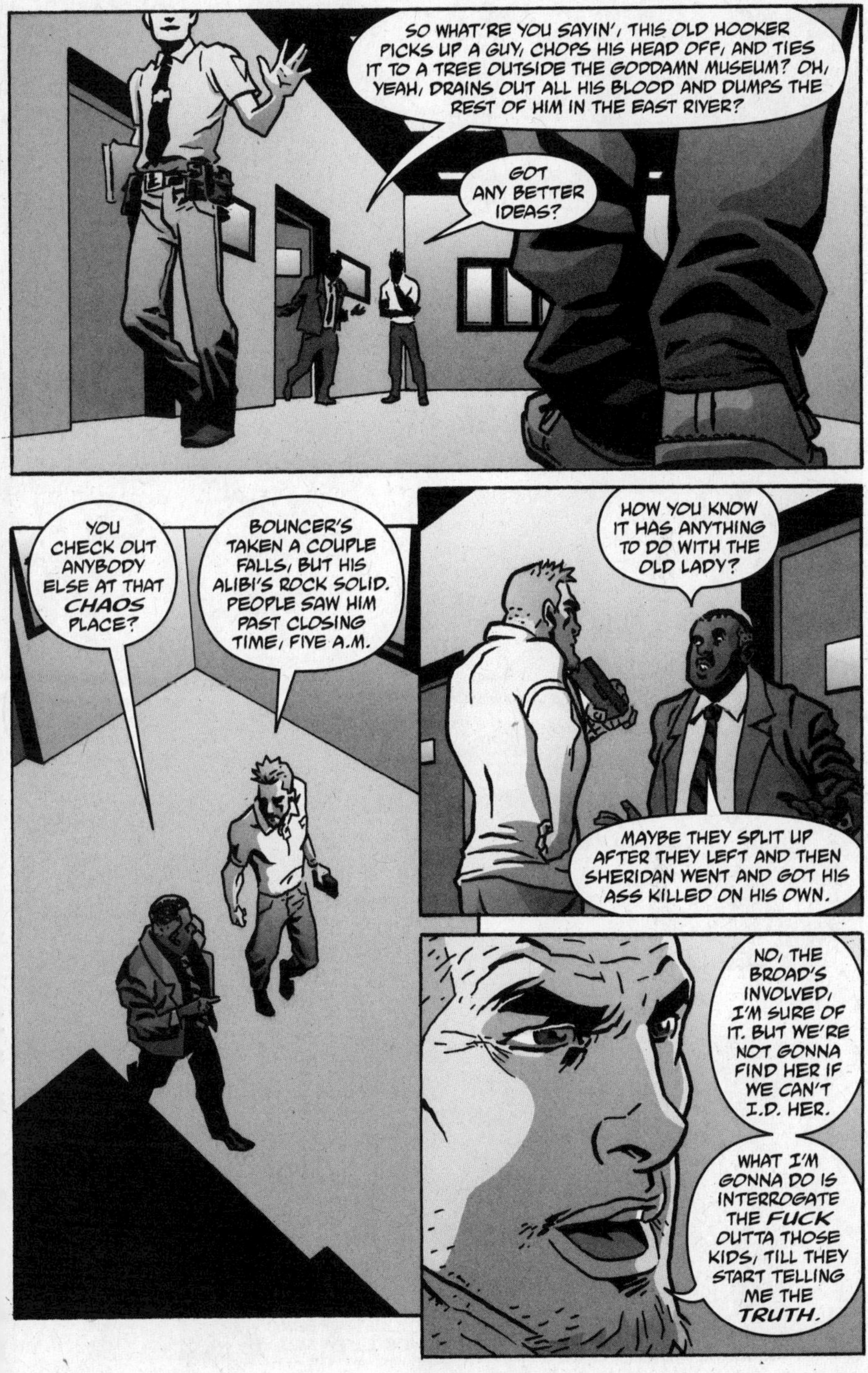
SO WHAT'RE YOU SAYIN', THIS OLD HOOKER PICKS UP A GUY, CHOPS HIS HEAD OFF, AND TIES IT TO A TREE OUTSIDE THE GODDAMN MUSEUM? OH, YEAH, DRAINS OUT ALL HIS BLOOD AND DUMPS THE REST OF HIM IN THE EAST RIVER?
GOT ANY BETTER IDEAS?
YOU CHECK OUT ANYBODY ELSE AT THAT CHAOS PLACE?
BOUNCER'S TAKEN A COUPLE FALLS, BUT HIS ALIBI'S ROCK SOLID. PEOPLE SAW HIM PAST CLOSING TIME, FIVE A.M.
HOW YOU KNOW IT HAS ANYTHING TO DO WITH THE OLD LADY?
MAYBE THEY SPLIT UP AFTER THEY LEFT AND THEN SHERIDAN WENT AND GOT HIS ASS KILLED ON HIS OWN.
NO, THE BROAD'S INVOLVED, I'M SURE OF IT. BUT WE'RE NOT GONNA FIND HER IF WE CAN'T I.D. HER.
WHAT I'M GONNA DO IS INTERROGATE THE FUCK OUTTA THOSE KIDS, TILL THEY START TELLING ME THE TRUTH.

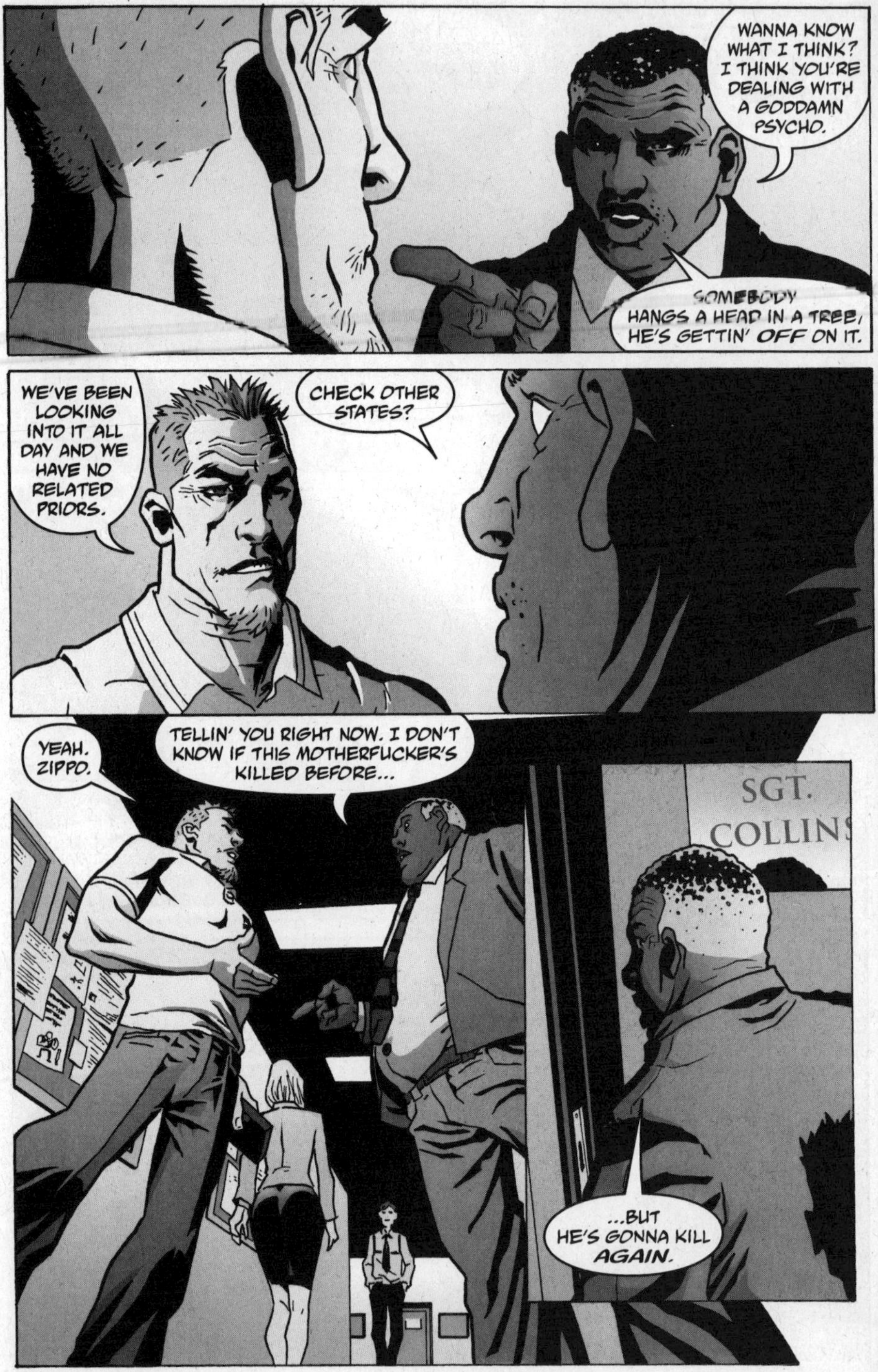
WANNA KNOW WHAT I THINK? I THINK YOU'RE DEALING WITH A GODDAMN PSYCHO.
SOMEBODY HANGS A HEAD IN A TREE, HE'S GETTIN' *OFF* ON IT.
WE'VE BEEN LOOKING INTO IT ALL DAY AND WE HAVE NO RELATED PRIORS.
CHECK OTHER STATES?
YEAH. ZIPPO.
TELLIN' YOU RIGHT NOW. I DON'T KNOW IF THIS MOTHERFUCKER'S KILLED BEFORE...
SGT. COLLINS
...BUT HE'S GONNA KILL *AGAIN*.

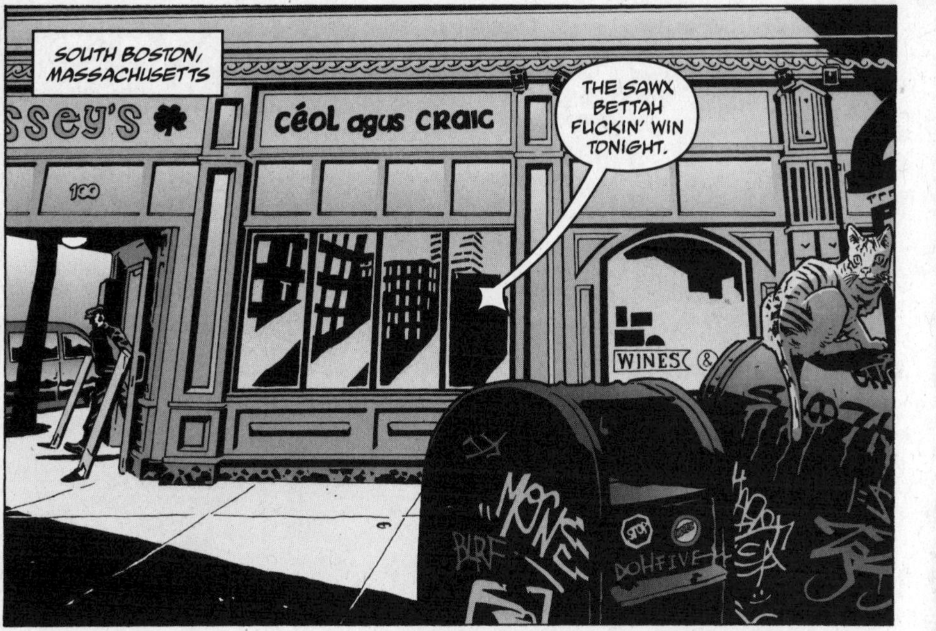
SOUTH BOSTON, MASSACHUSETTS
ssey's
céol agus craic
100
THE SAWX BETTAH FUCKIN' WIN TONIGHT.
WINES &
DOHFIVE

CHAPTER THREE: THE PROTECTOR

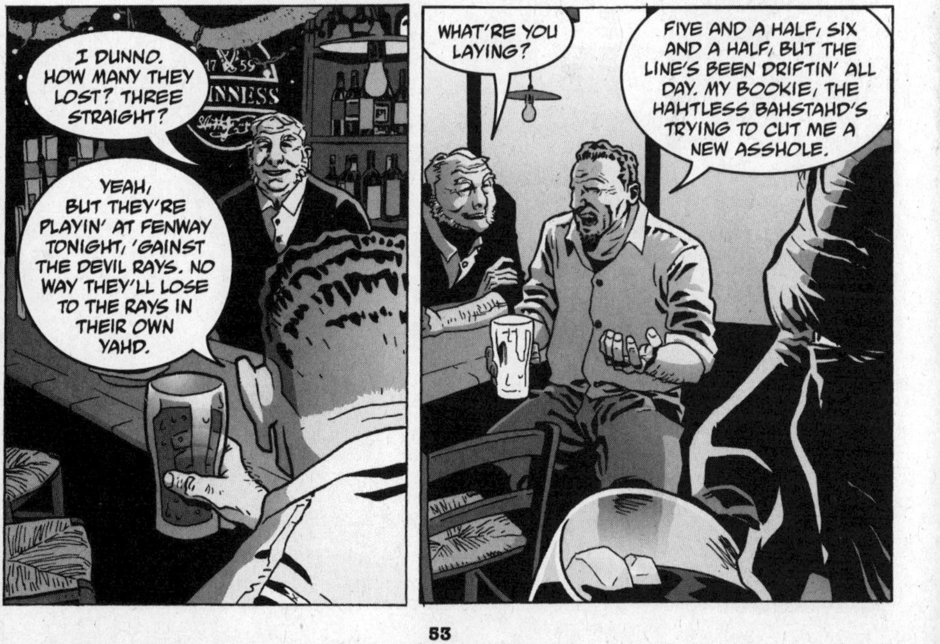
I DUNNO. HOW MANY THEY LOST? THREE STRAIGHT?
YEAH, BUT THEY'RE PLAYIN' AT FENWAY TONIGHT, 'GAINST THE DEVIL RAYS. NO WAY THEY'LL LOSE TO THE RAYS IN THEIR OWN YAHD.
WHAT'RE YOU LAYING?
FIVE AND A HALF, SIX AND A HALF, BUT THE LINE'S BEEN DRIFTIN' ALL DAY. MY BOOKIE, THE HAHTLESS BAHSTAHD'S TRYING TO CUT ME A NEW ASSHOLE.

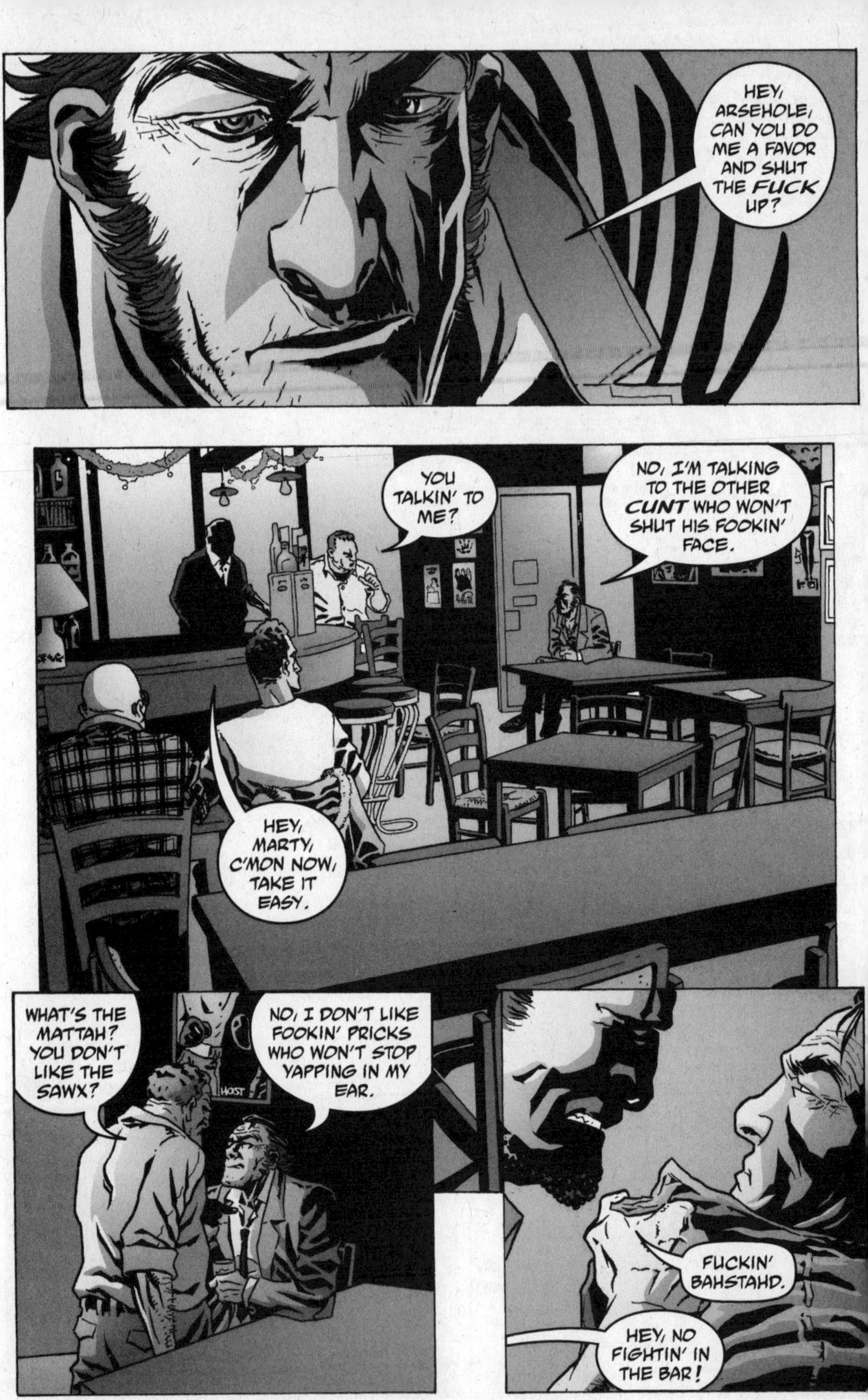
HEY, ARSEHOLE, CAN YOU DO ME A FAVOR AND SHUT THE FUCK UP?
YOU TALKIN' TO ME?
NO, I'M TALKING TO THE OTHER CUNT WHO WON'T SHUT HIS FOOKIN' FACE.
HEY, MARTY, C'MON NOW, TAKE IT EASY.
WHAT'S THE MATTAH? YOU DON'T LIKE THE SAWX?
NO, I DON'T LIKE FOOKIN' PRICKS WHO WON'T STOP YAPPING IN MY EAR.
FUCKIN' BAHSTAHD.
HEY, NO FIGHTIN' IN THE BAR!

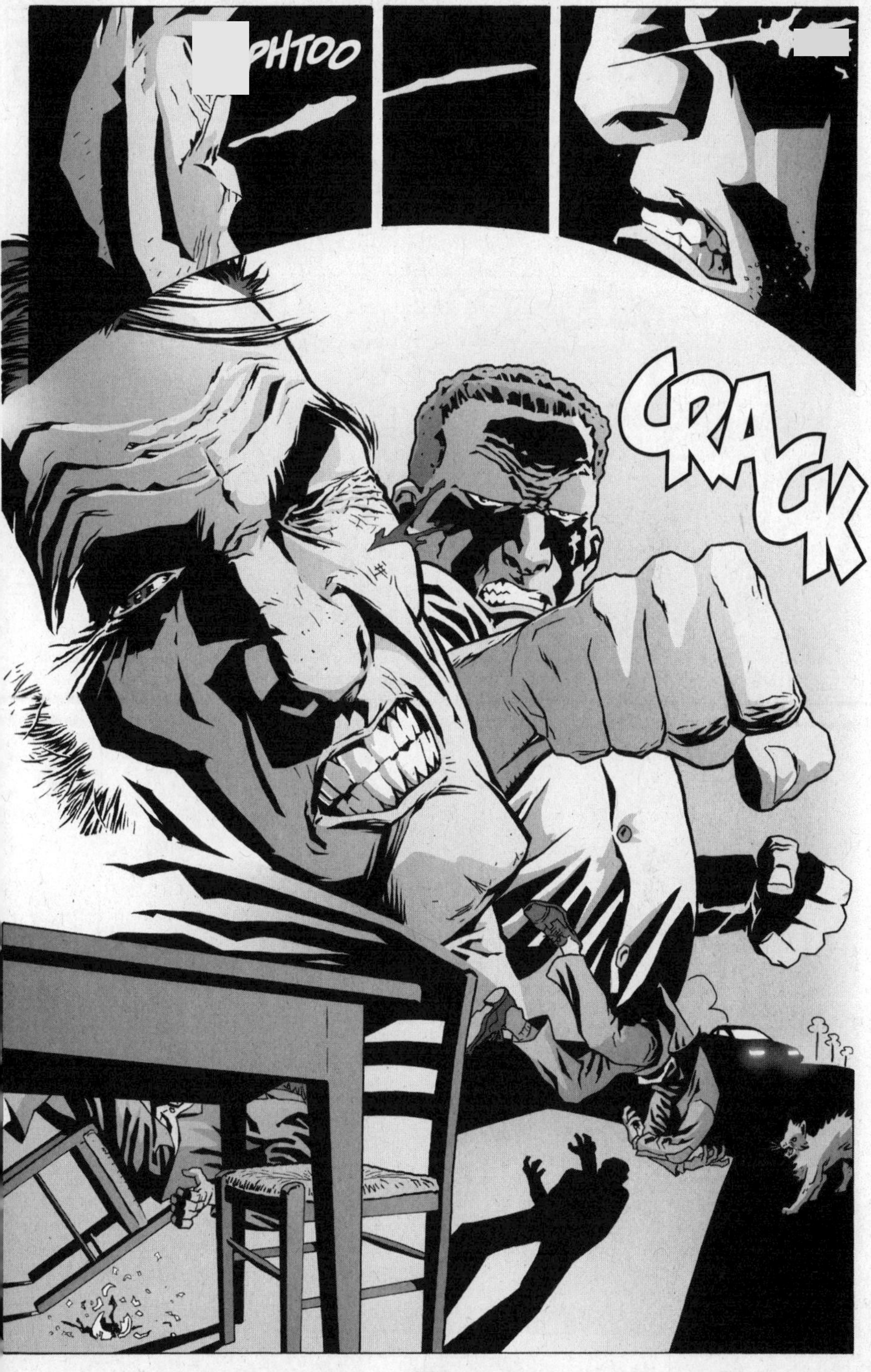
PHTOO
CRACK

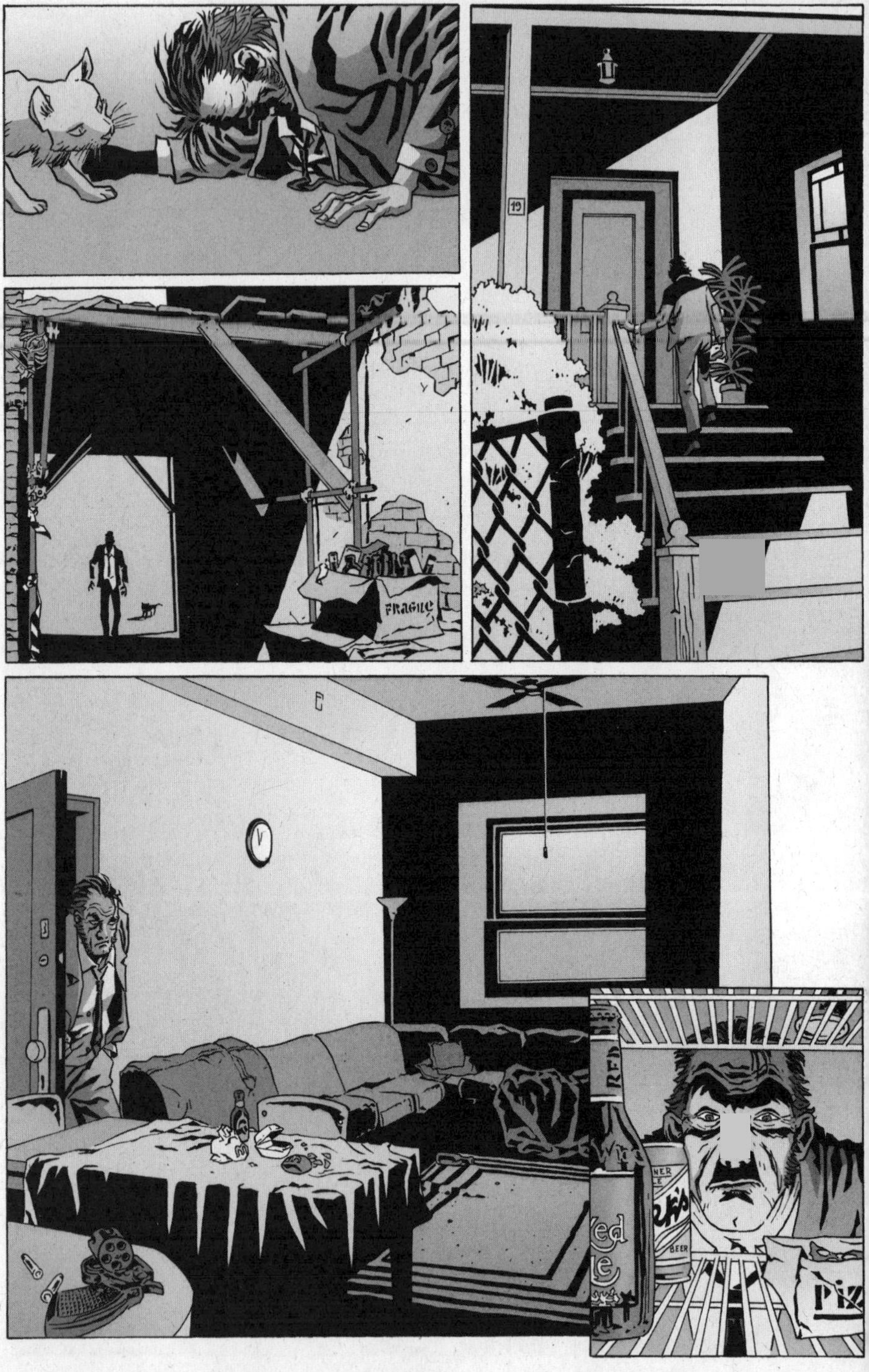
19
FRAGILE
BEER

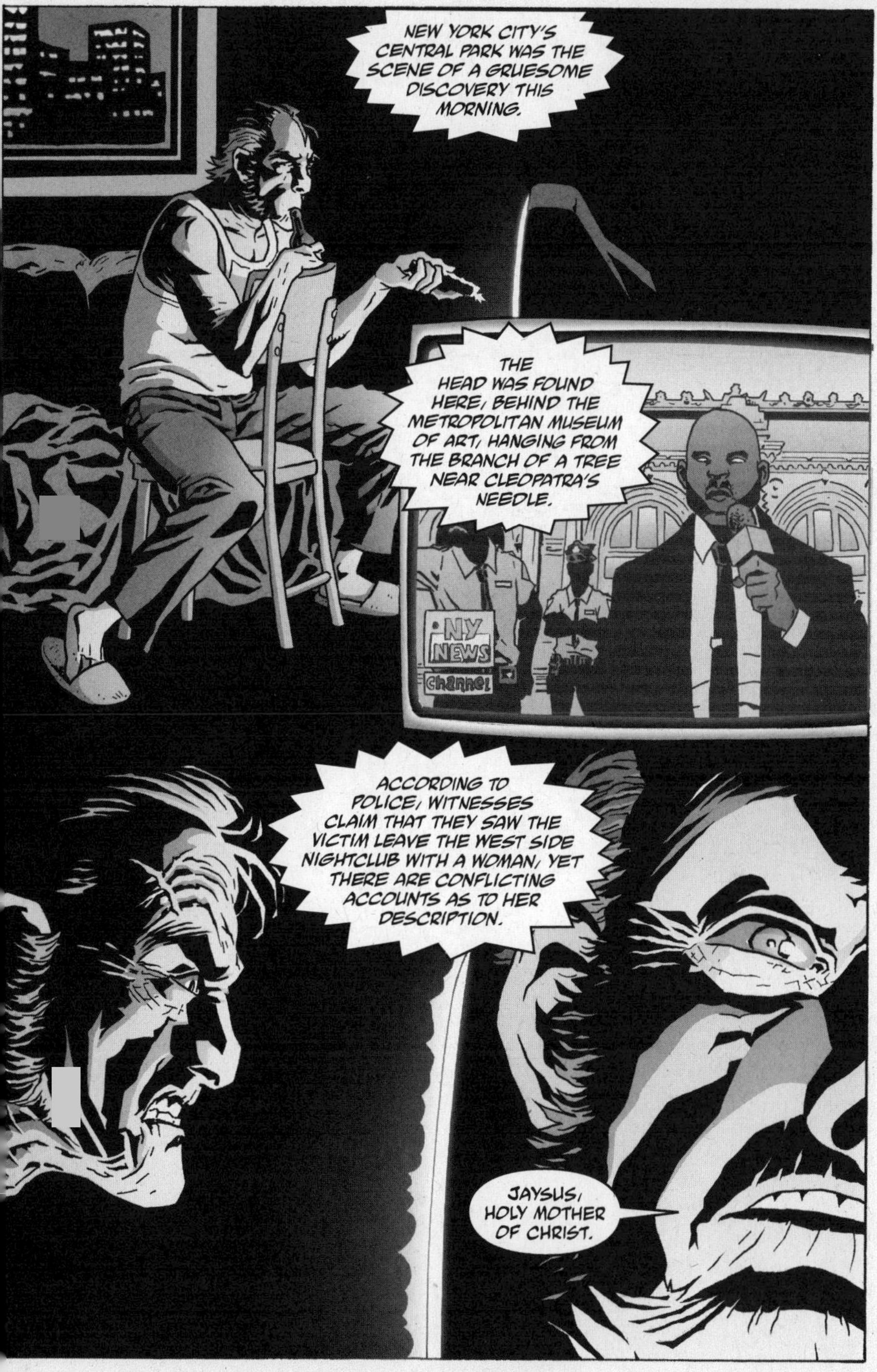
NEW YORK CITY'S CENTRAL PARK WAS THE SCENE OF A GRUESOME DISCOVERY THIS MORNING.
THE HEAD WAS FOUND HERE, BEHIND THE METROPOLITAN MUSEUM OF ART, HANGING FROM THE BRANCH OF A TREE NEAR CLEOPATRA'S NEEDLE.
NY NEWS
Channel
ACCORDING TO POLICE, WITNESSES CLAIM THAT THEY SAW THE VICTIM LEAVE THE WEST SIDE NIGHTCLUB WITH A WOMAN, YET THERE ARE CONFLICTING ACCOUNTS AS TO HER DESCRIPTION.
JAYSUS, HOLY MOTHER OF CHRIST.

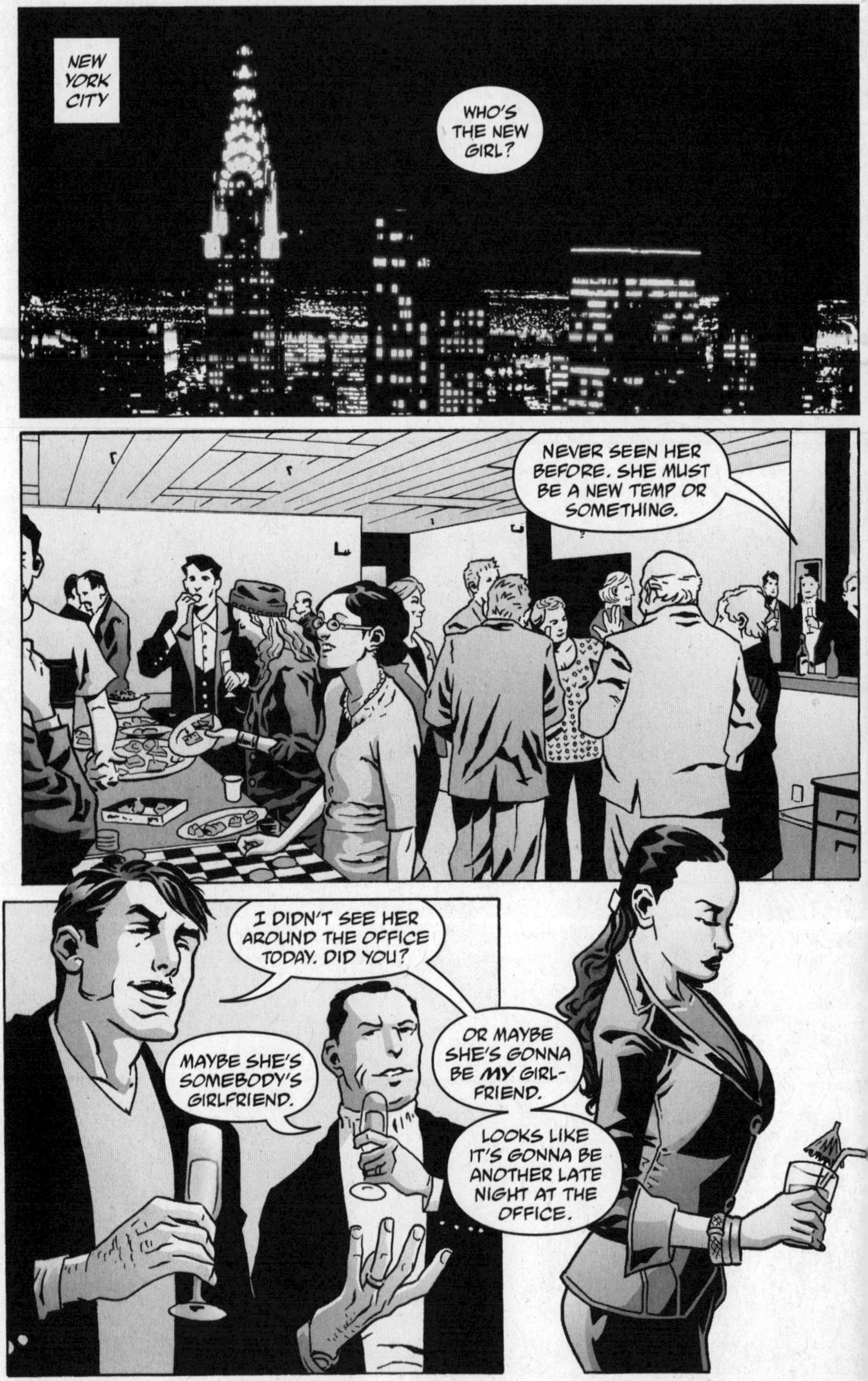
NEW YORK CITY
WHO'S THE NEW GIRL?
NEVER SEEN HER BEFORE. SHE MUST BE A NEW TEMP OR SOMETHING.
I DIDN'T SEE HER AROUND THE OFFICE TODAY. DID YOU?
MAYBE SHE'S SOMEBODY'S GIRLFRIEND.
OR MAYBE SHE'S GONNA BE *MY* GIRL-FRIEND.
LOOKS LIKE IT'S GONNA BE ANOTHER LATE NIGHT AT THE OFFICE.

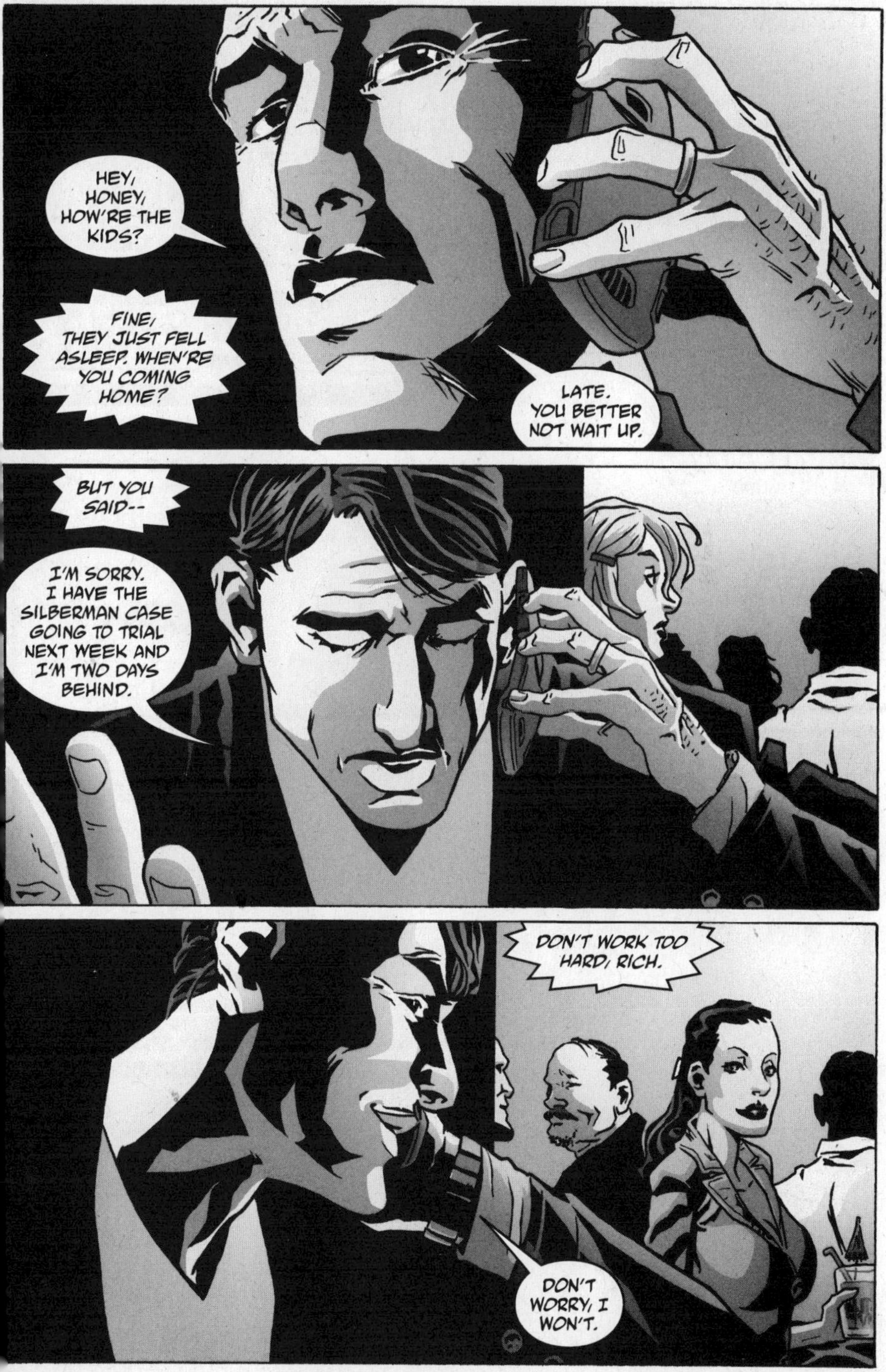
HEY, HONEY, HOW'RE THE KIDS?
FINE, THEY JUST FELL ASLEEP. WHEN'RE YOU COMING HOME?
LATE. YOU BETTER NOT WAIT UP.
BUT YOU SAID--
I'M SORRY. I HAVE THE SILBERMAN CASE GOING TO TRIAL NEXT WEEK AND I'M TWO DAYS BEHIND.
DON'T WORK TOO HARD, RICH.
DON'T WORRY, I WON'T.

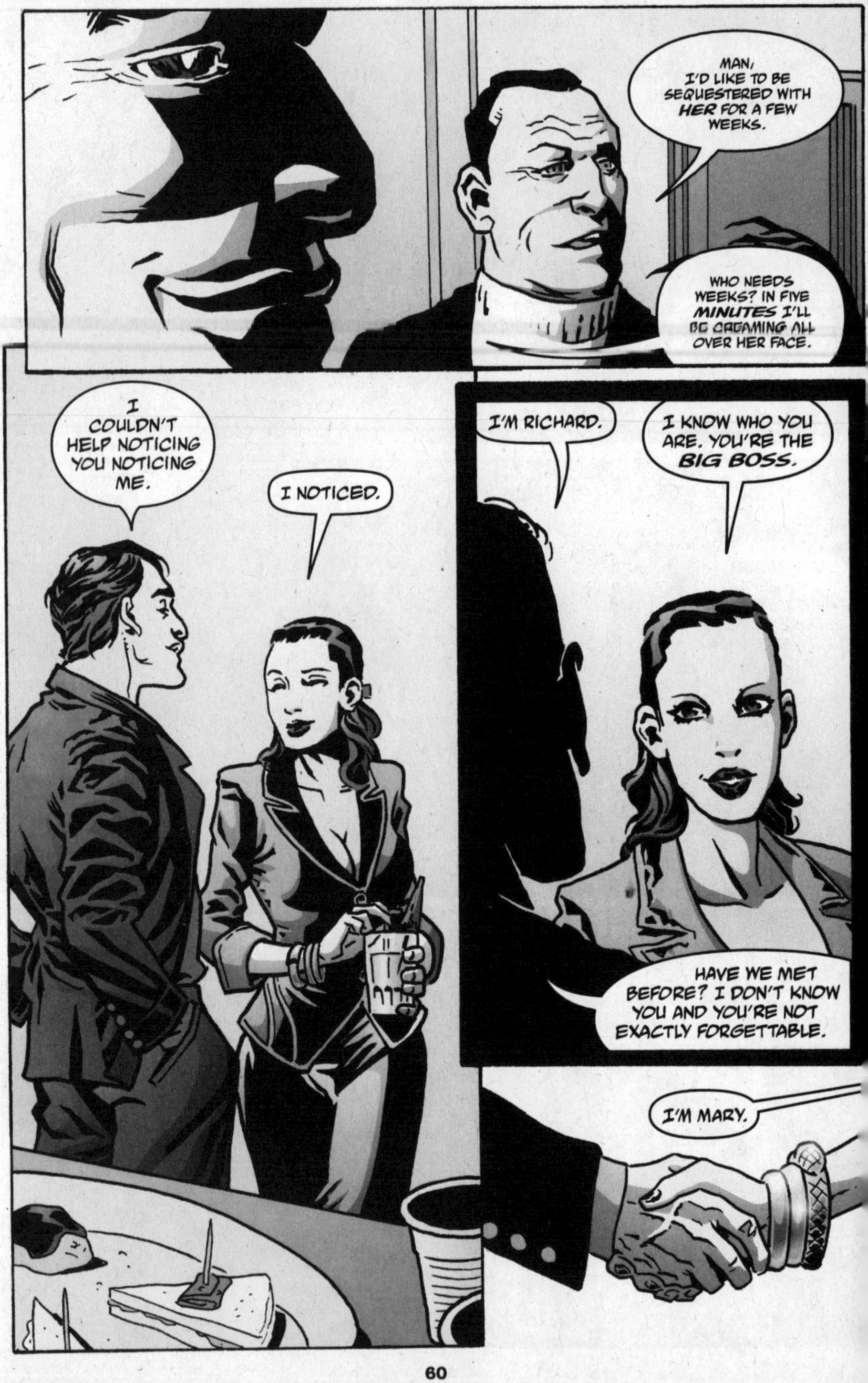
MAN, I'D LIKE TO BE SEQUESTERED WITH HER FOR A FEW WEEKS.
WHO NEEDS WEEKS? IN FIVE MINUTES I'LL BE CREAMING ALL OVER HER FACE.
I COULDN'T HELP NOTICING YOU NOTICING ME.
I NOTICED.
I'M RICHARD.
I KNOW WHO YOU ARE. YOU'RE THE BIG BOSS.
HAVE WE MET BEFORE? I DON'T KNOW YOU AND YOU'RE NOT EXACTLY FORGETTABLE.
I'M MARY.

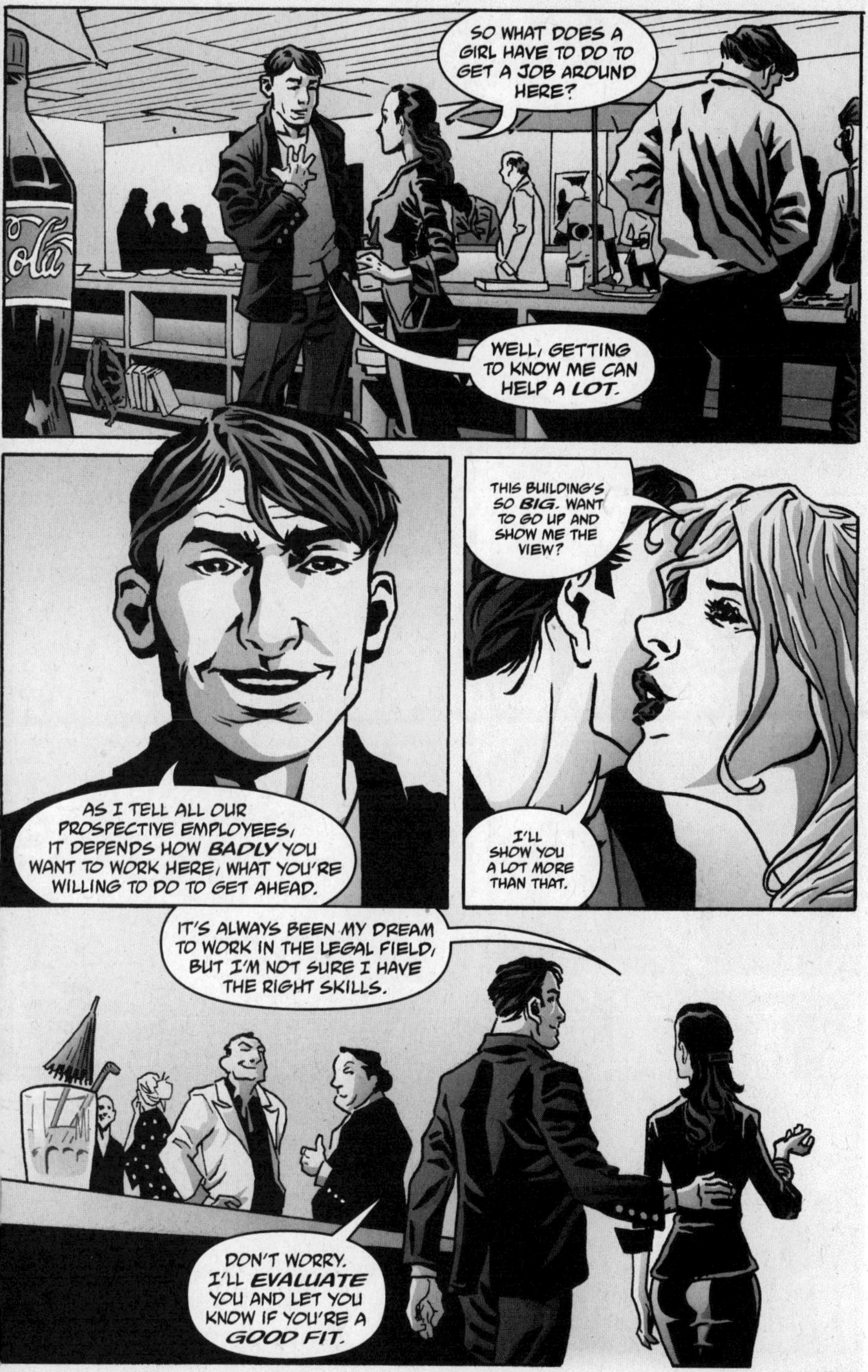

SO WHAT DOES A GIRL HAVE TO DO TO GET A JOB AROUND HERE?
WELL, GETTING TO KNOW ME CAN HELP A LOT.
AS I TELL ALL OUR PROSPECTIVE EMPLOYEES, IT DEPENDS HOW BADLY YOU WANT TO WORK HERE, WHAT YOU'RE WILLING TO DO TO GET AHEAD.
THIS BUILDING'S SO BIG. WANT TO GO UP AND SHOW ME THE VIEW?
I'LL SHOW YOU A LOT MORE THAN THAT.
IT'S ALWAYS BEEN MY DREAM TO WORK IN THE LEGAL FIELD, BUT I'M NOT SURE I HAVE THE RIGHT SKILLS.
DON'T WORRY. I'LL EVALUATE YOU AND LET YOU KNOW IF YOU'RE A GOOD FIT.

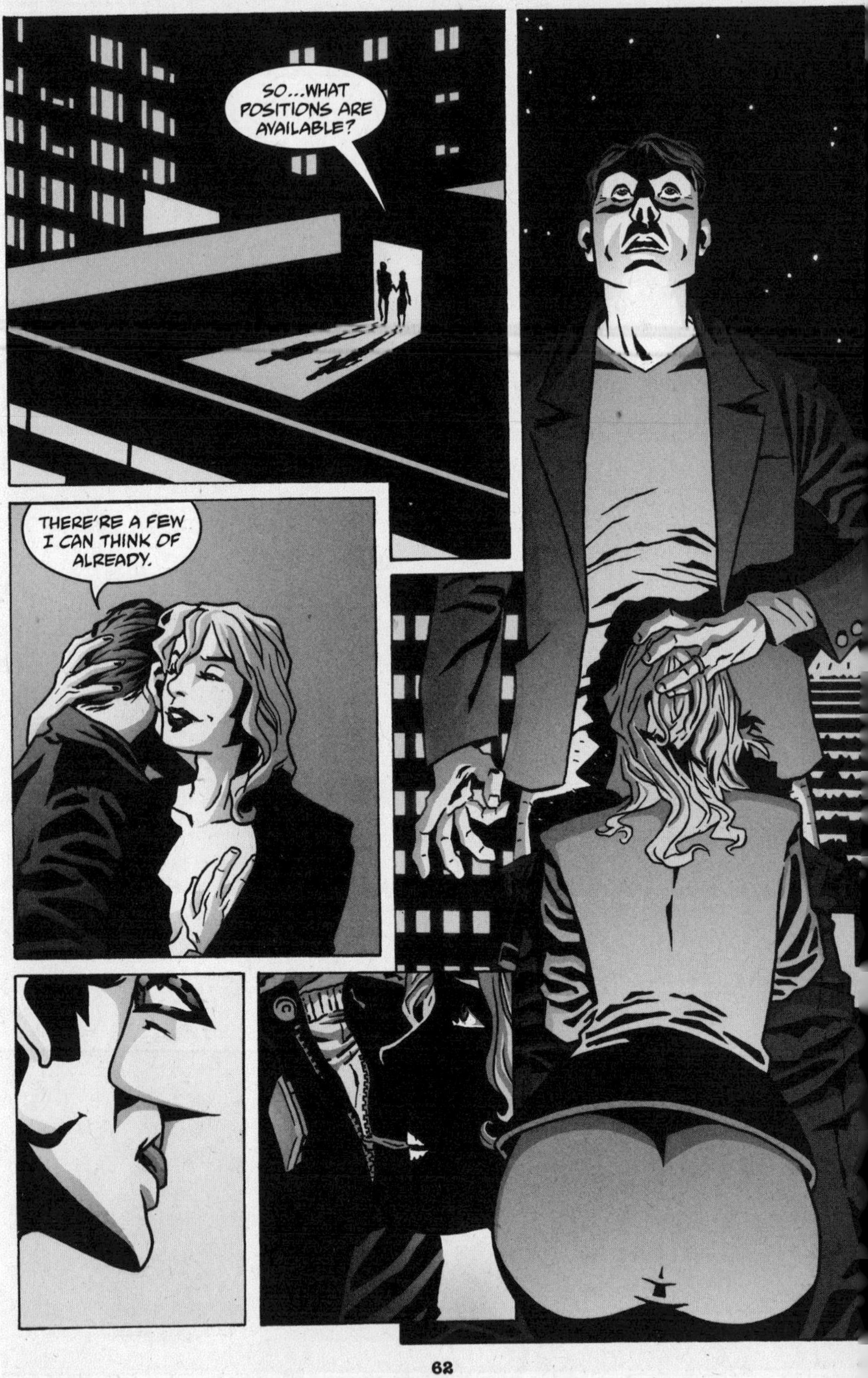
SO...WHAT POSITIONS ARE AVAILABLE?
THERE'RE A FEW I CAN THINK OF ALREADY.

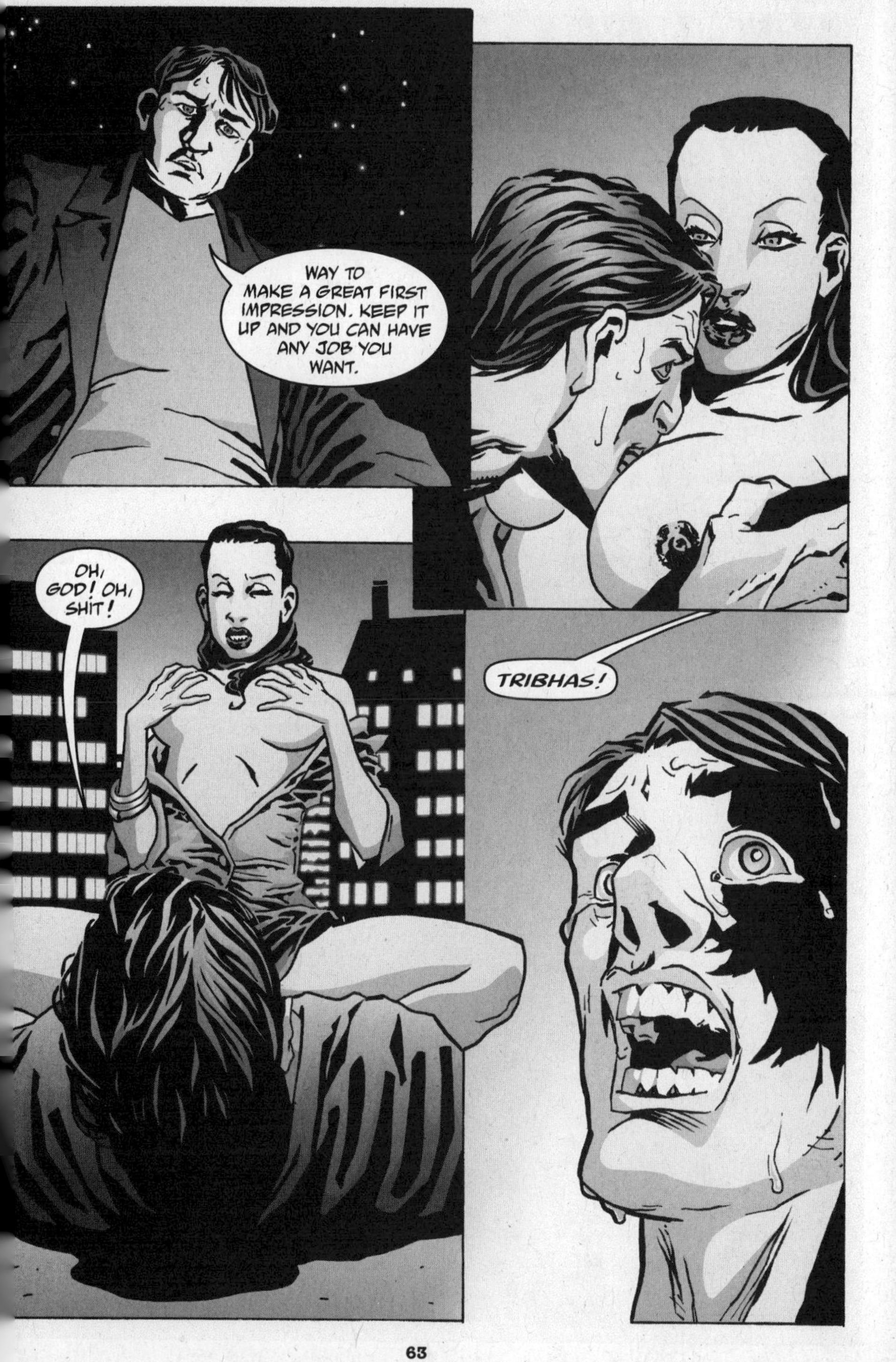
WAY TO MAKE A GREAT FIRST IMPRESSION. KEEP IT UP AND YOU CAN HAVE ANY JOB YOU WANT.
OH, GOD! OH, SHIT!
TRIBHAS!

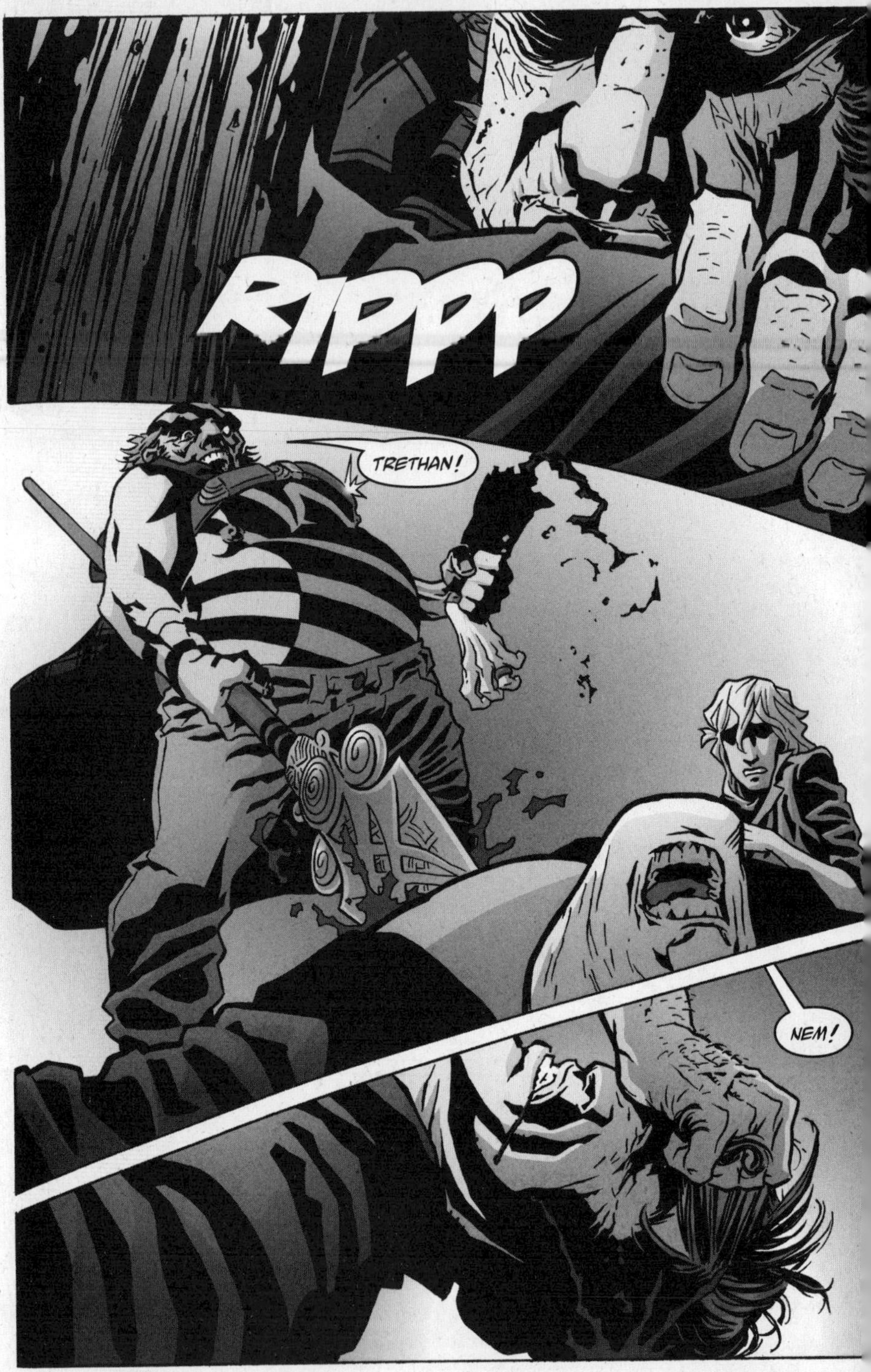
RIPPP
TRETHAN!
NEM!

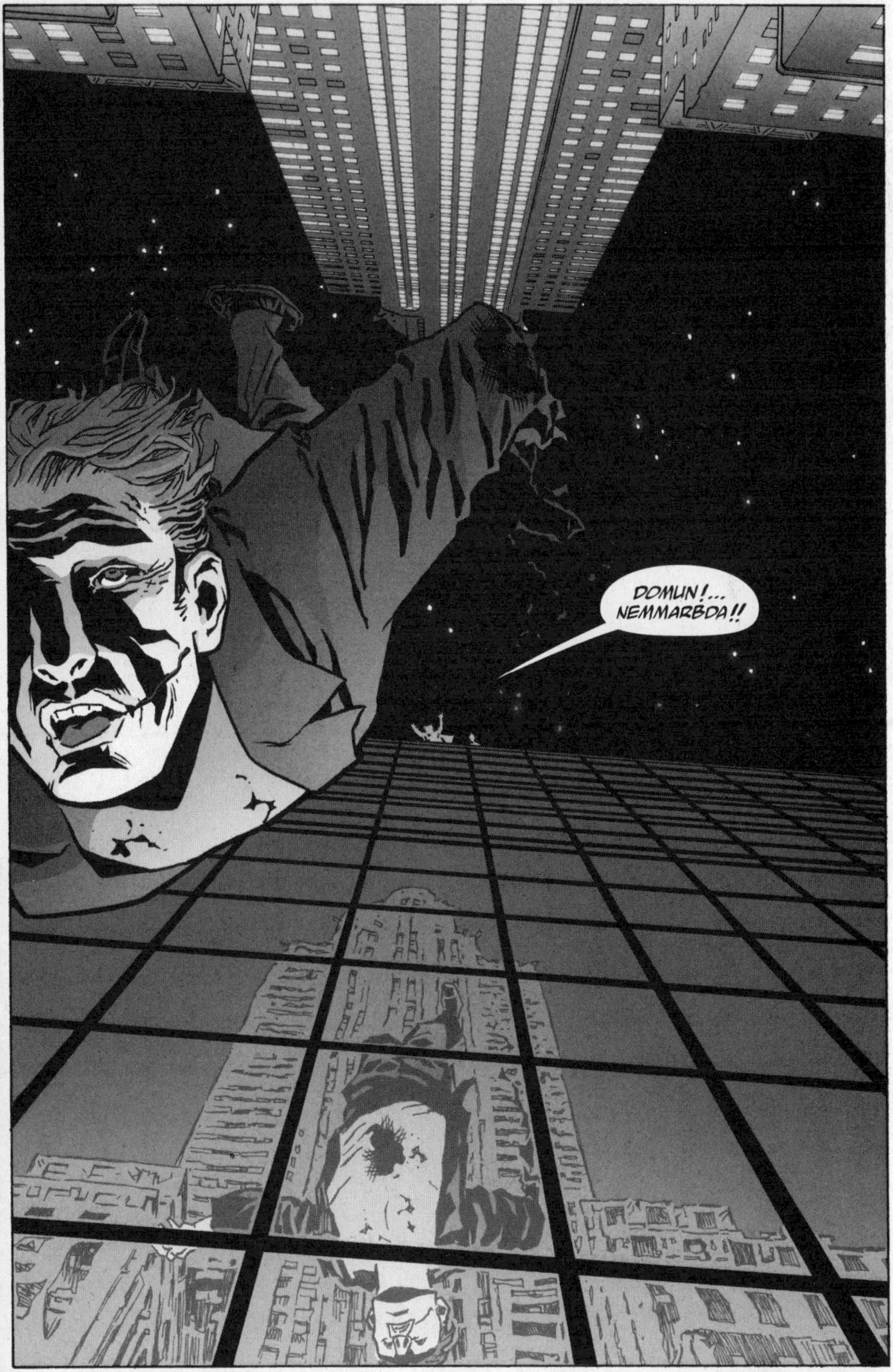
DOMUN!... NEMMARBDA!!

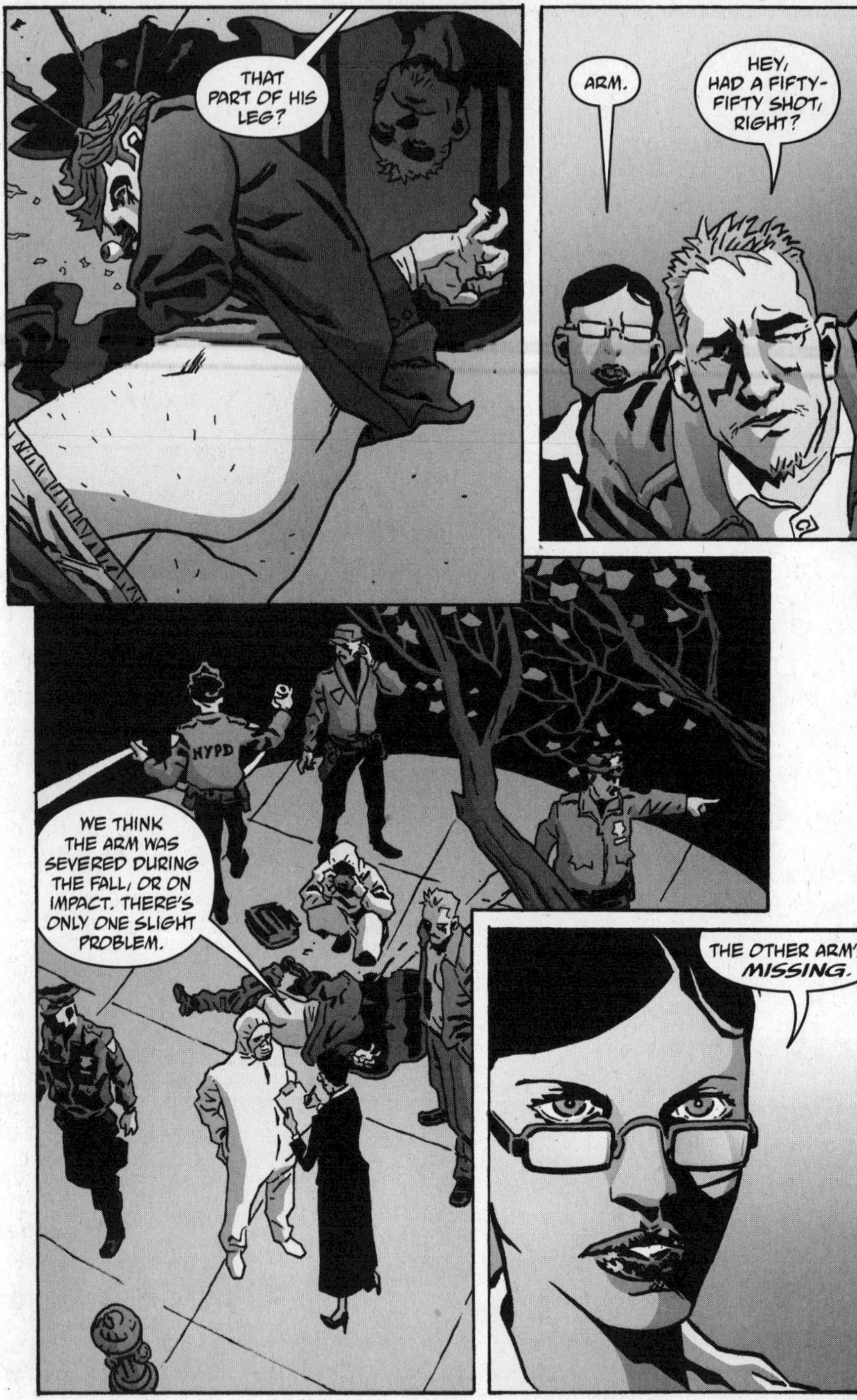
THAT PART OF HIS LEG?
ARM.
HEY, HAD A FIFTY-FIFTY SHOT, RIGHT?
NYPD
WE THINK THE ARM WAS SEVERED DURING THE FALL, OR ON IMPACT. THERE'S ONLY ONE SLIGHT PROBLEM.
THE OTHER ARM'S *MISSING.*

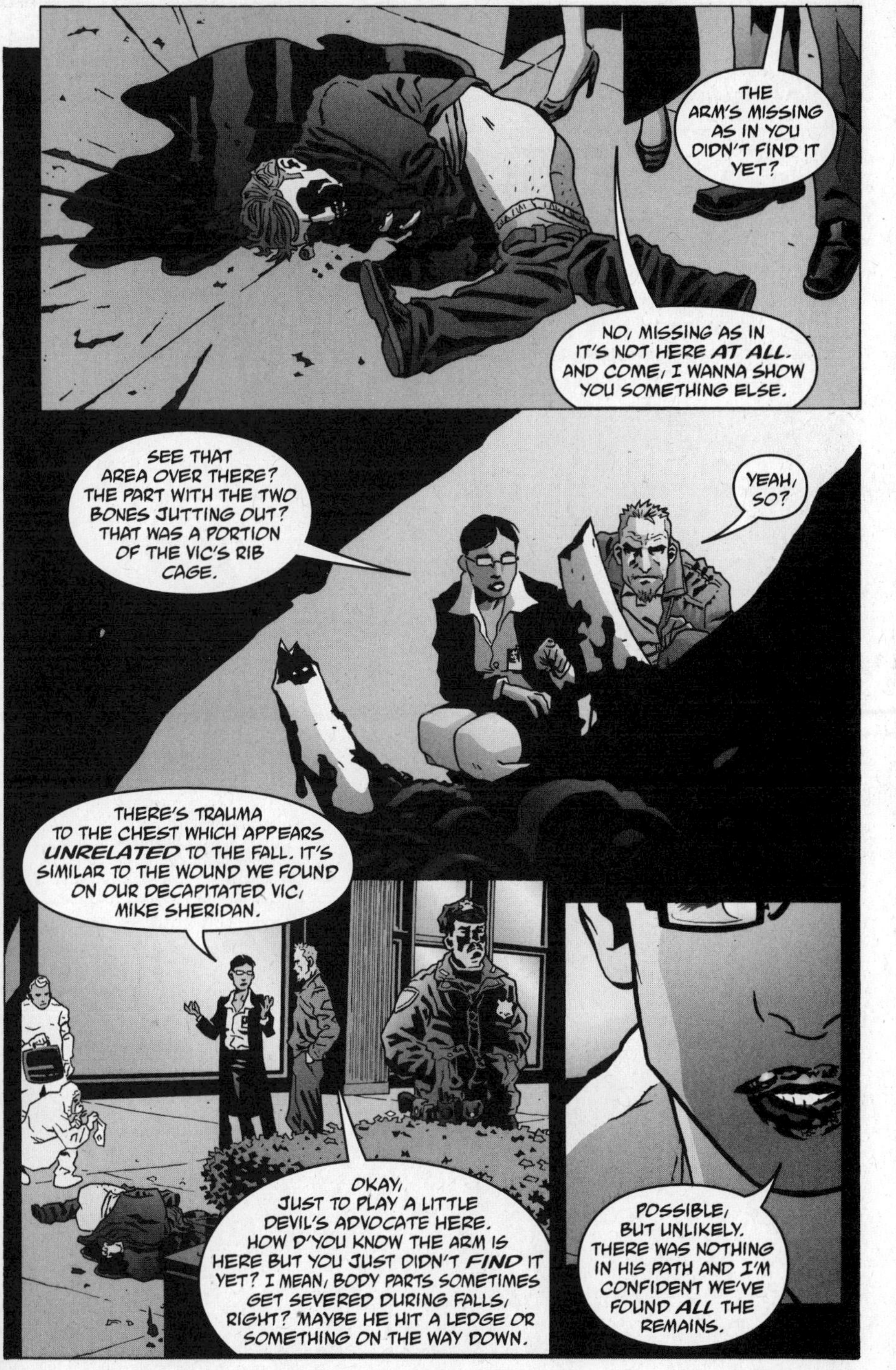
THE ARM'S MISSING AS IN YOU DIDN'T FIND IT YET?
NO, MISSING AS IN IT'S NOT HERE AT ALL. AND COME, I WANNA SHOW YOU SOMETHING ELSE.
SEE THAT AREA OVER THERE? THE PART WITH THE TWO BONES JUTTING OUT? THAT WAS A PORTION OF THE VIC'S RIB CAGE.
YEAH, SO?
THERE'S TRAUMA TO THE CHEST WHICH APPEARS UNRELATED TO THE FALL. IT'S SIMILAR TO THE WOUND WE FOUND ON OUR DECAPITATED VIC, MIKE SHERIDAN.
OKAY, JUST TO PLAY A LITTLE DEVIL'S ADVOCATE HERE. HOW D'YOU KNOW THE ARM IS HERE BUT YOU JUST DIDN'T FIND IT YET? I MEAN, BODY PARTS SOMETIMES GET SEVERED DURING FALLS, RIGHT? MAYBE HE HIT A LEDGE OR SOMETHING ON THE WAY DOWN.
POSSIBLE, BUT UNLIKELY. THERE WAS NOTHING IN HIS PATH AND I'M CONFIDENT WE'VE FOUND ALL THE REMAINS.

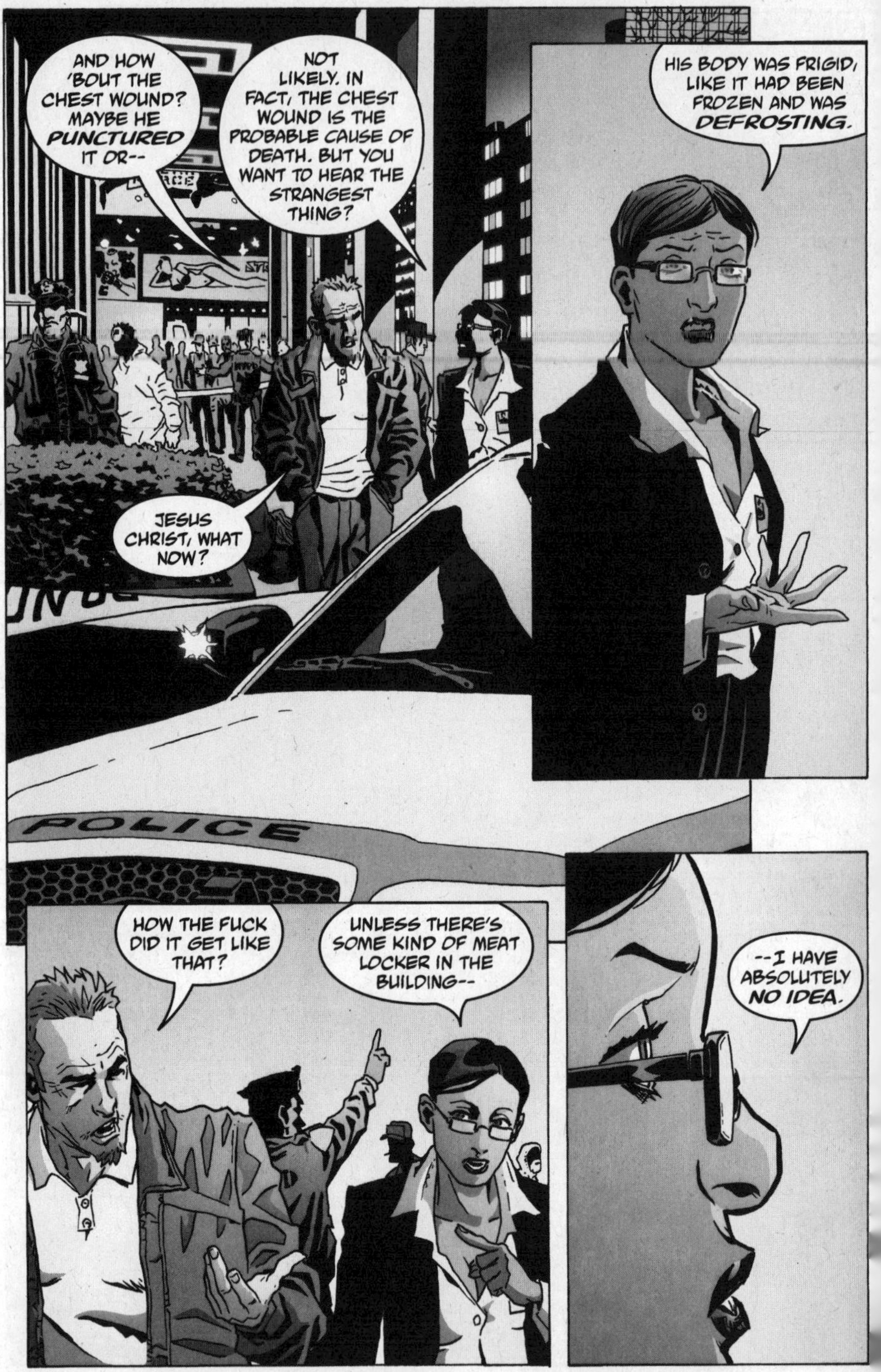
AND HOW 'BOUT THE CHEST WOUND? MAYBE HE PUNCTURED IT OR--
NOT LIKELY. IN FACT, THE CHEST WOUND IS THE PROBABLE CAUSE OF DEATH. BUT YOU WANT TO HEAR THE STRANGEST THING?
JESUS CHRIST, WHAT NOW?
HIS BODY WAS FRIGID, LIKE IT HAD BEEN FROZEN AND WAS DEFROSTING.
POLICE
HOW THE FUCK DID IT GET LIKE THAT?
UNLESS THERE'S SOME KIND OF MEAT LOCKER IN THE BUILDING--
--I HAVE ABSOLUTELY NO IDEA.

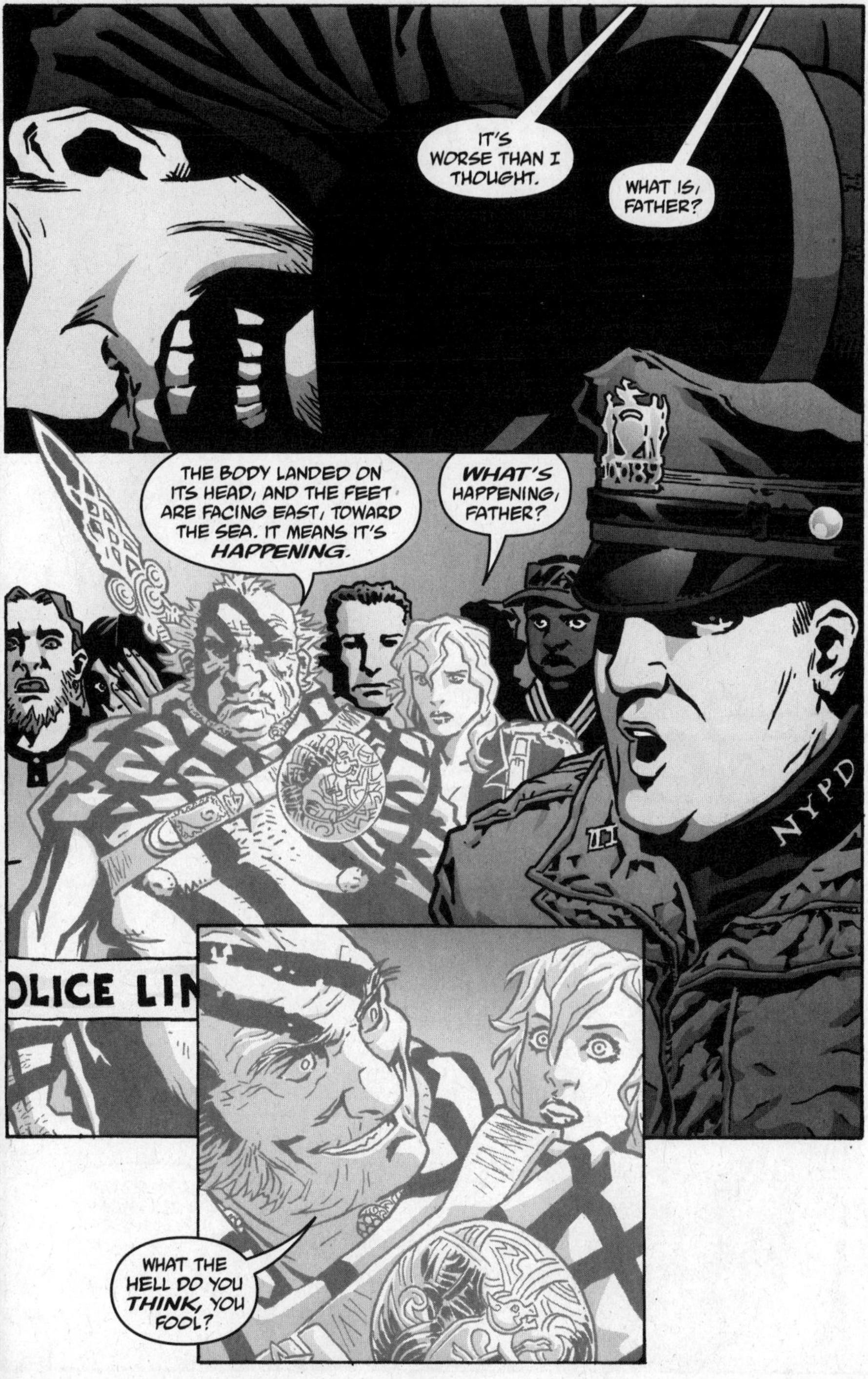
IT'S WORSE THAN I THOUGHT.
WHAT IS, FATHER?
THE BODY LANDED ON ITS HEAD, AND THE FEET ARE FACING EAST, TOWARD THE SEA. IT MEANS IT'S HAPPENING.
WHAT'S HAPPENING, FATHER?
NYPD
OLICE LIN
WHAT THE HELL DO YOU THINK, YOU FOOL?

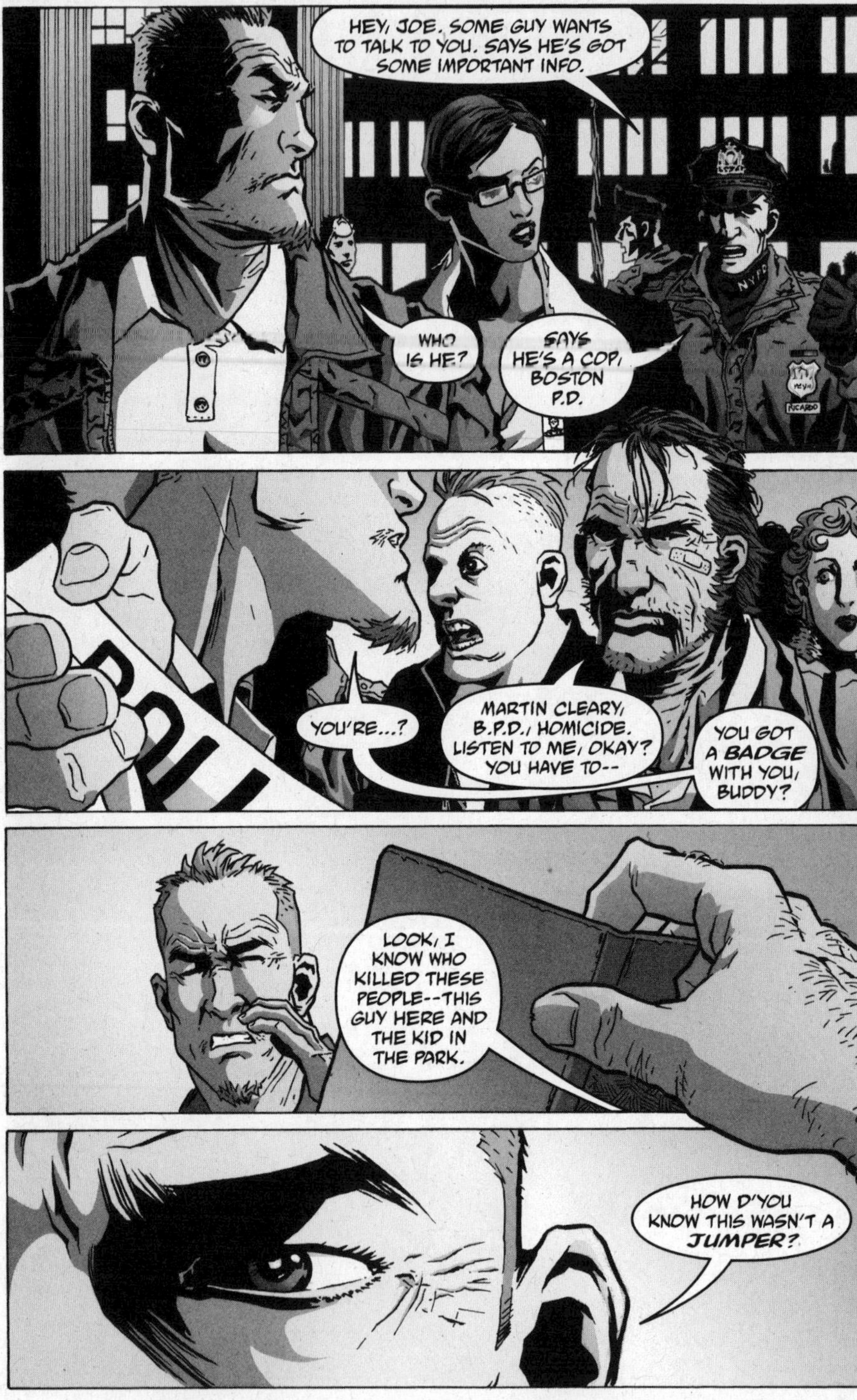
HEY, JOE. SOME GUY WANTS TO TALK TO YOU. SAYS HE'S GOT SOME IMPORTANT INFO.
WHO IS HE?
SAYS HE'S A COP, BOSTON P.D.
YOU'RE...?
MARTIN CLEARY, B.P.D., HOMICIDE. LISTEN TO ME, OKAY? YOU HAVE TO--
YOU GOT A BADGE WITH YOU, BUDDY?
LOOK, I KNOW WHO KILLED THESE PEOPLE--THIS GUY HERE AND THE KID IN THE PARK.
HOW D'YOU KNOW THIS WASN'T A JUMPER?

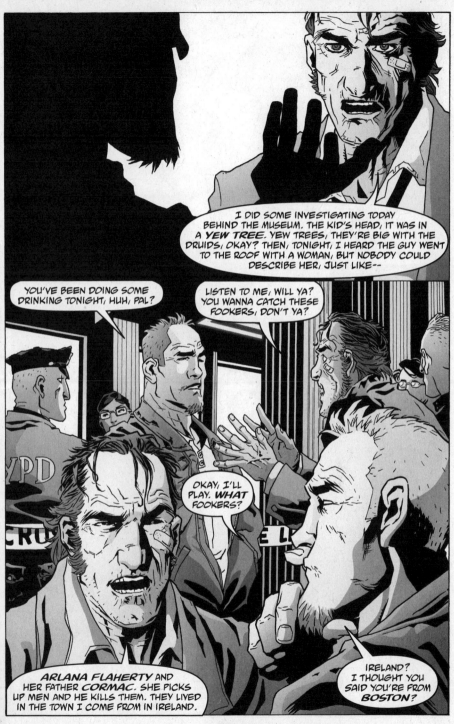

I DID SOME INVESTIGATING TODAY BEHIND THE MUSEUM. THE KID'S HEAD, IT WAS IN A *YEW TREE*. YEW TREES, THEY'RE BIG WITH THE DRUIDS, OKAY? THEN, TONIGHT, I HEARD THE GUY WENT TO THE ROOF WITH A WOMAN, BUT NOBODY COULD DESCRIBE HER, JUST LIKE--

YOU'VE BEEN DOING SOME DRINKING TONIGHT, HUH, PAL?

LISTEN TO ME, WILL YA? YOU WANNA CATCH THESE FOOKERS, DON'T YA?

OKAY, I'LL PLAY. *WHAT* FOOKERS?

ARLANA FLAHERTY AND HER FATHER CORMAC. SHE PICKS UP MEN AND HE KILLS THEM. THEY LIVED IN THE TOWN I COME FROM IN IRELAND.

IRELAND? I THOUGHT YOU SAID YOU'RE FROM BOSTON?

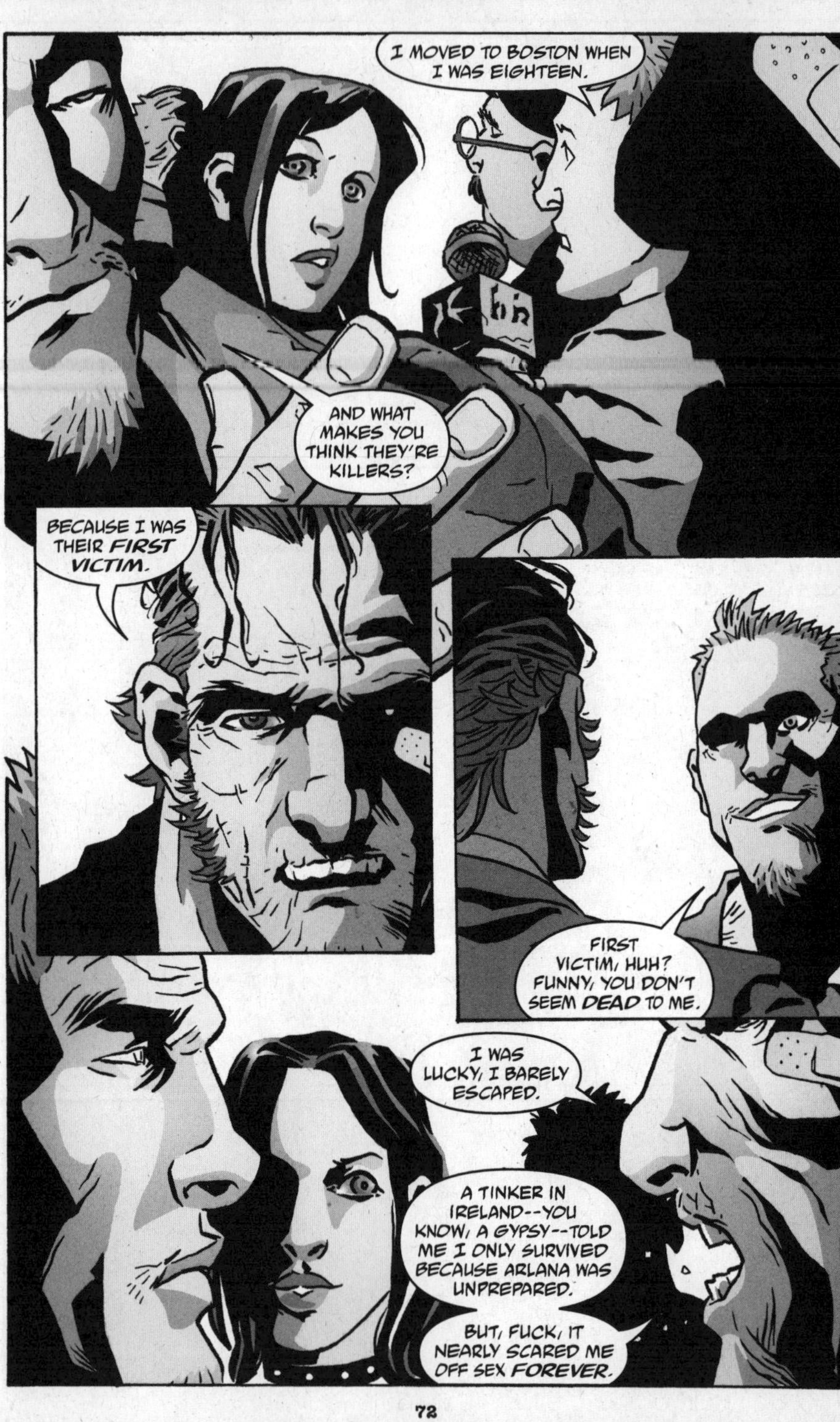
I MOVED TO BOSTON WHEN I WAS EIGHTEEN.
AND WHAT MAKES YOU THINK THEY'RE KILLERS?
BECAUSE I WAS THEIR *FIRST VICTIM*.
FIRST VICTIM, HUH? FUNNY, YOU DON'T SEEM *DEAD* TO ME.
I WAS LUCKY, I BARELY ESCAPED.
A TINKER IN IRELAND--YOU KNOW, A *GYPSY*--TOLD ME I ONLY SURVIVED BECAUSE ARLANA WAS UNPREPARED.
BUT, FUCK, IT NEARLY SCARED ME OFF SEX *FOREVER*.

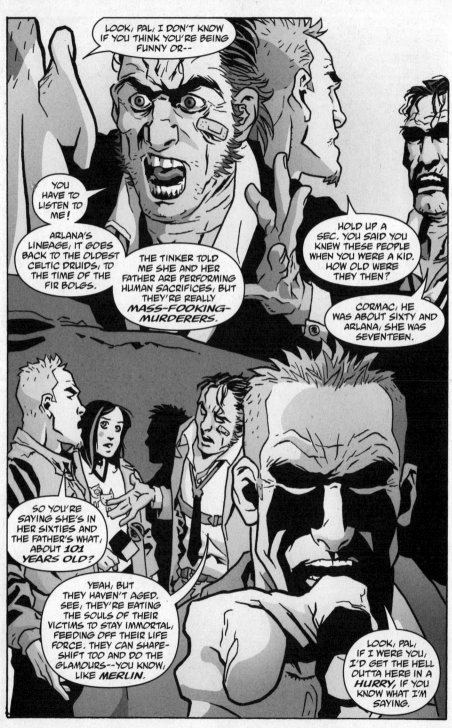

LOOK, PAL, I DON'T KNOW IF YOU THINK YOU'RE BEING FUNNY OR--

YOU HAVE TO LISTEN TO ME!

ARLANA'S LINEAGE, IT GOES BACK TO THE OLDEST CELTIC DRUIDS, TO THE TIME OF THE FIR BOLGS.

THE TINKER TOLD ME SHE AND HER FATHER ARE PERFORMING HUMAN SACRIFICES, BUT THEY'RE REALLY MASS-FOOKING-MURDERERS.

HOLD UP A SEC. YOU SAID YOU KNEW THESE PEOPLE WHEN YOU WERE A KID. HOW OLD WERE THEY THEN?

CORMAC, HE WAS ABOUT SIXTY AND ARLANA, SHE WAS SEVENTEEN.

SO YOU'RE SAYING SHE'S IN HER SIXTIES AND THE FATHER'S WHAT, ABOUT 101 YEARS OLD?

YEAH, BUT THEY HAVEN'T AGED. SEE, THEY'RE EATING THE SOULS OF THEIR VICTIMS TO STAY IMMORTAL, FEEDING OFF THEIR LIFE FORCE. THEY CAN SHAPE-SHIFT TOO AND DO THE GLAMOURS--YOU KNOW, LIKE MERLIN.

LOOK, PAL, IF I WERE YOU, I'D GET THE HELL OUTTA HERE IN A HURRY, IF YOU KNOW WHAT I'M SAYING.

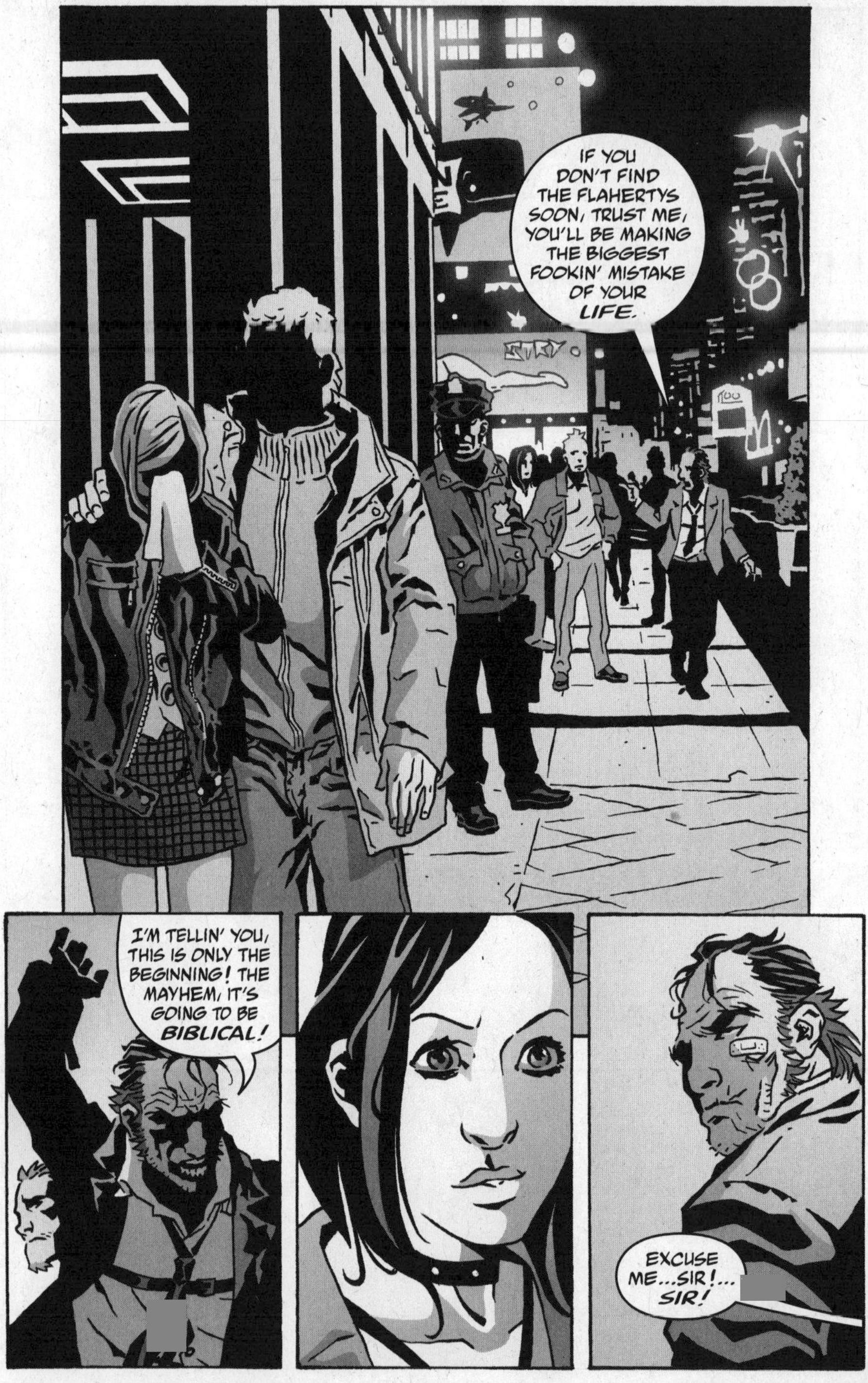
IF YOU DON'T FIND THE FLAHERTYS SOON, TRUST ME, YOU'LL BE MAKING THE BIGGEST FOOKIN' MISTAKE OF YOUR LIFE.
I'M TELLIN' YOU, THIS IS ONLY THE BEGINNING! THE MAYHEM, IT'S GOING TO BE BIBLICAL!
EXCUSE ME...SIR!... SIR!

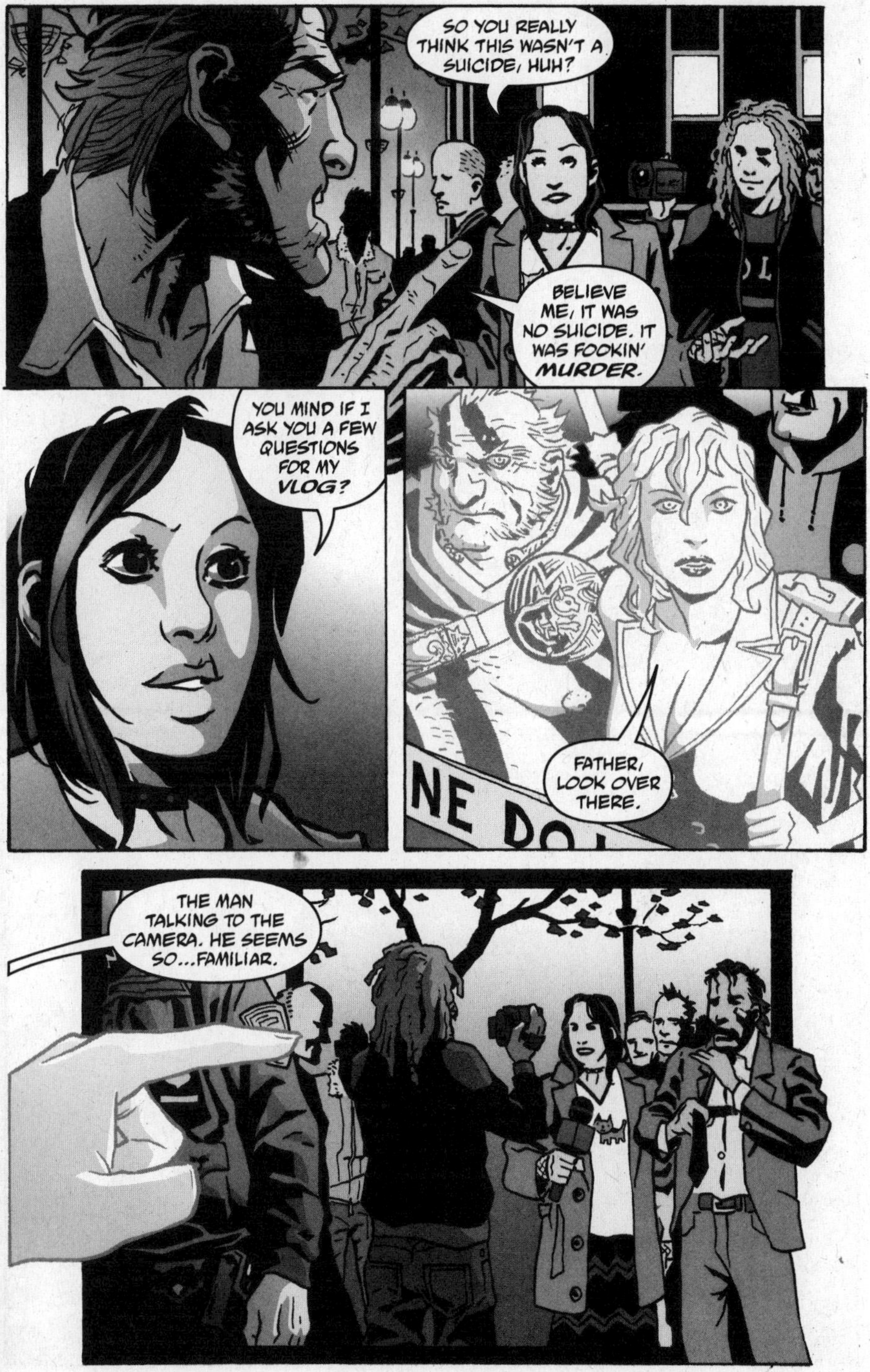
SO YOU REALLY THINK THIS WASN'T A SUICIDE, HUH?
BELIEVE ME, IT WAS NO SUICIDE. IT WAS FOOKIN' MURDER.
YOU MIND IF I ASK YOU A FEW QUESTIONS FOR MY VLOG?
FATHER, LOOK OVER THERE.
NE DO
THE MAN TALKING TO THE CAMERA. HE SEEMS SO...FAMILIAR.

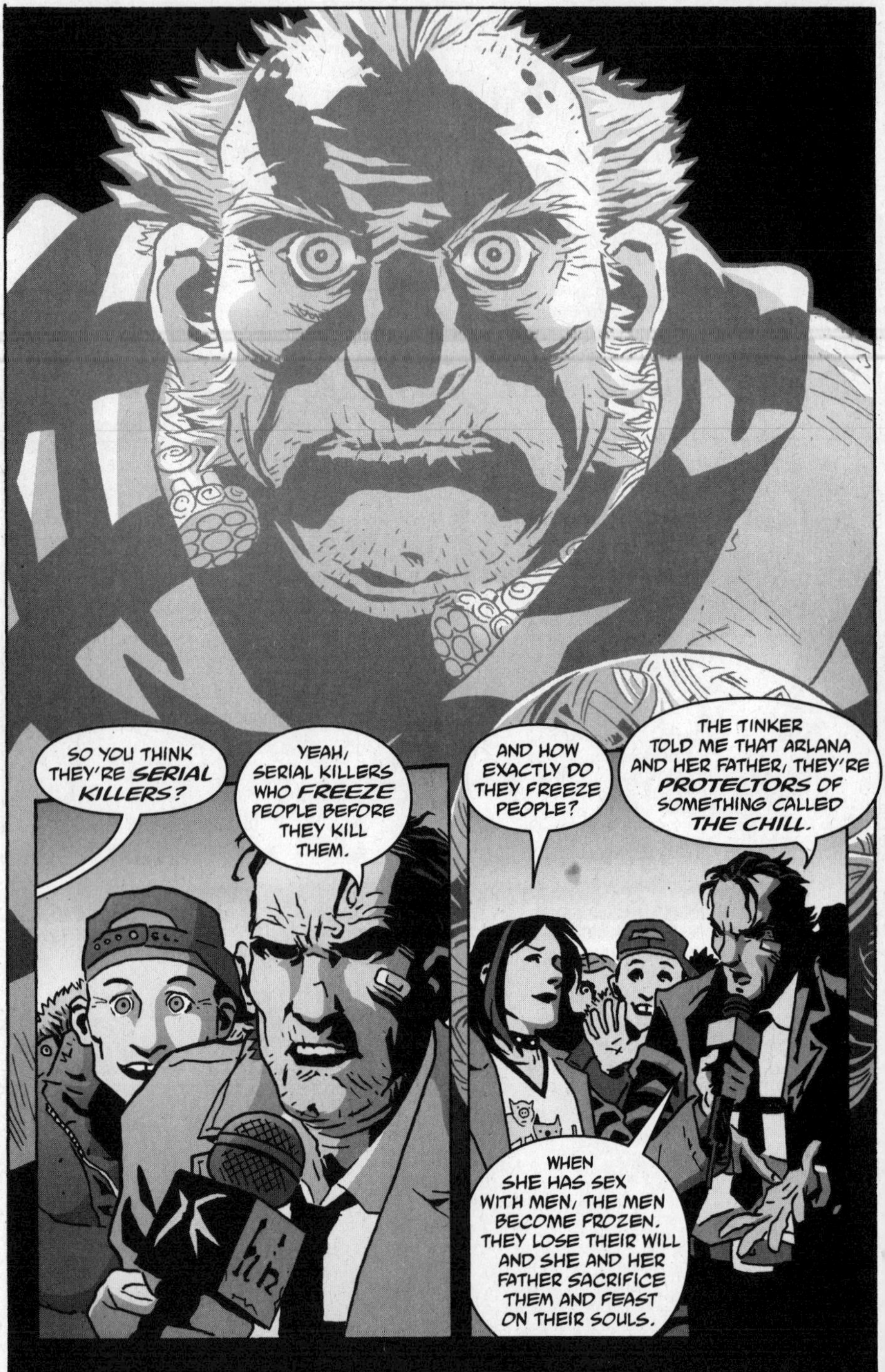
SO YOU THINK THEY'RE SERIAL KILLERS?
YEAH, SERIAL KILLERS WHO FREEZE PEOPLE BEFORE THEY KILL THEM.
AND HOW EXACTLY DO THEY FREEZE PEOPLE?
THE TINKER TOLD ME THAT ARLANA AND HER FATHER, THEY'RE PROTECTORS OF SOMETHING CALLED THE CHILL.
WHEN SHE HAS SEX WITH MEN, THE MEN BECOME FROZEN. THEY LOSE THEIR WILL AND SHE AND HER FATHER SACRIFICE THEM AND FEAST ON THEIR SOULS.

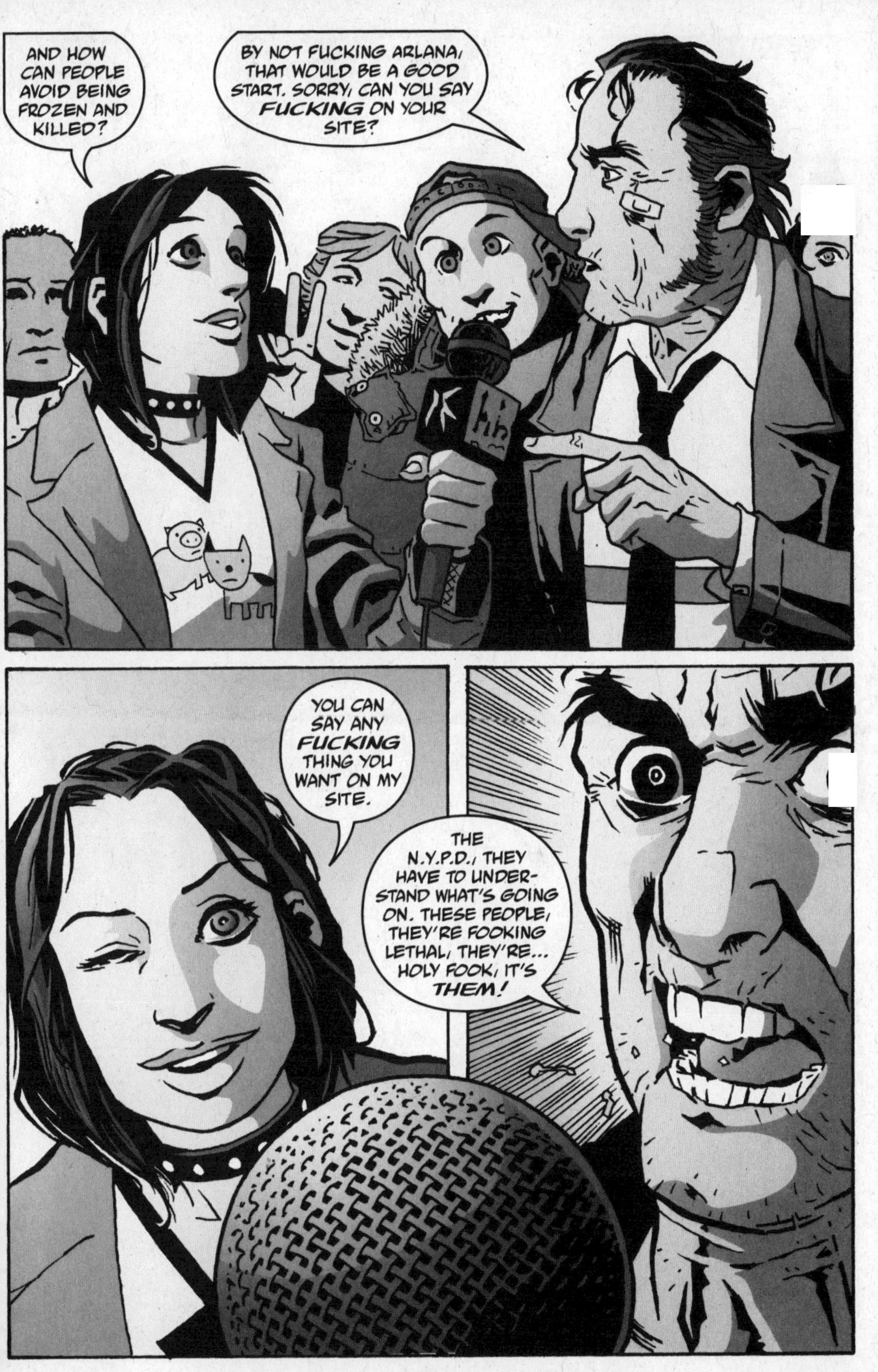
AND HOW CAN PEOPLE AVOID BEING FROZEN AND KILLED?
BY NOT FUCKING ARLANA, THAT WOULD BE A GOOD START. SORRY, CAN YOU SAY FUCKING ON YOUR SITE?
YOU CAN SAY ANY FUCKING THING YOU WANT ON MY SITE.
THE N.Y.P.D., THEY HAVE TO UNDER-STAND WHAT'S GOING ON. THESE PEOPLE, THEY'RE FOOKING LETHAL, THEY'RE... HOLY FOOK, IT'S THEM!

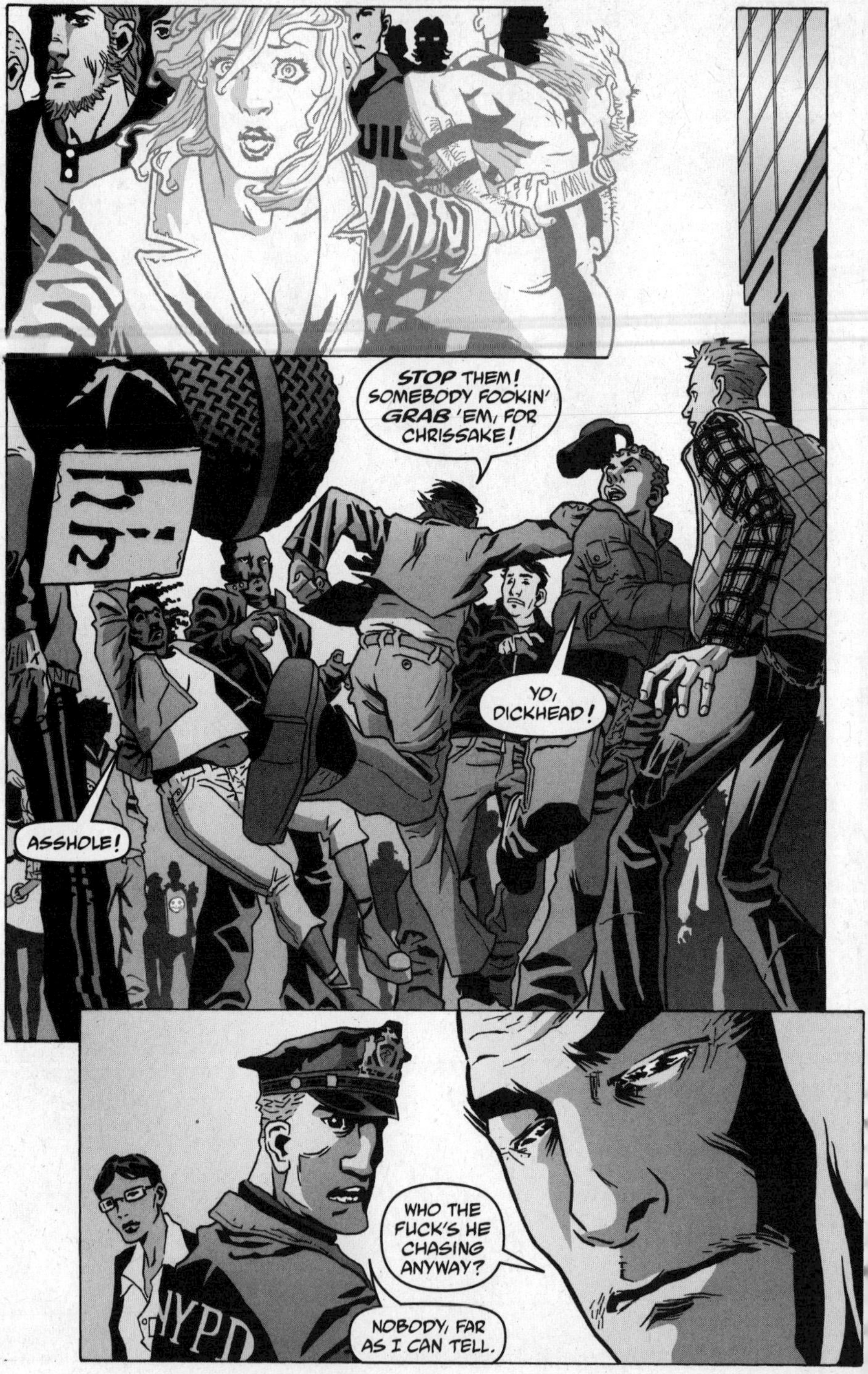
STOP THEM! SOMEBODY FOOKIN' GRAB 'EM, FOR CHRISSAKE!
YO, DICKHEAD!
ASSHOLE!
NYPD
WHO THE FUCK'S HE CHASING ANYWAY?
NOBODY, FAR AS I CAN TELL.

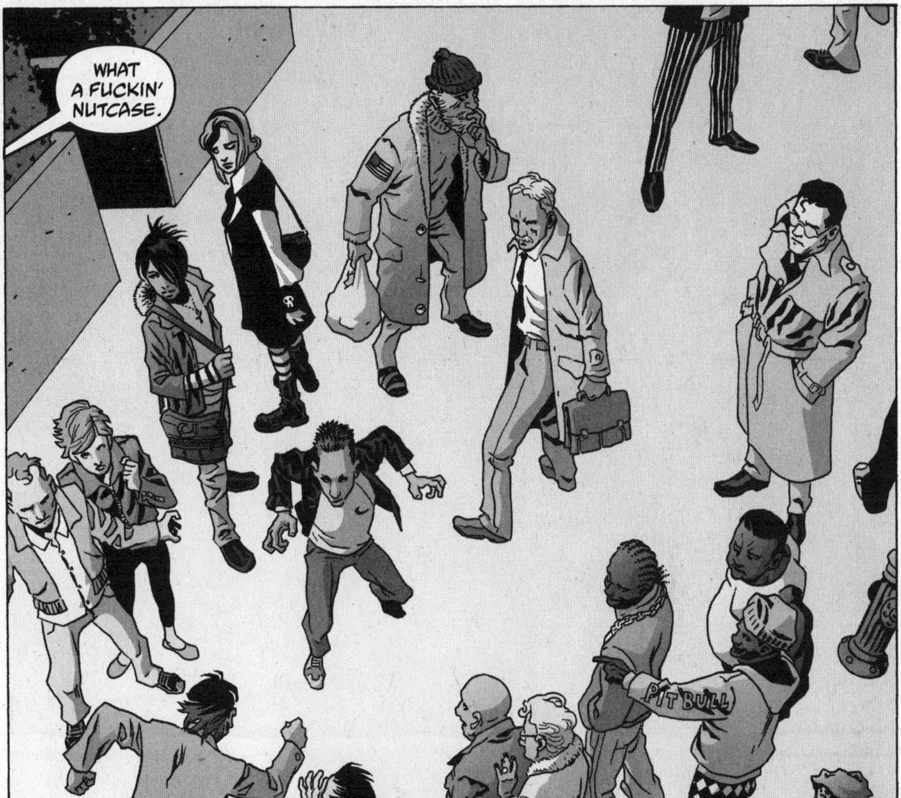
WHAT A FUCKIN' NUTCASE.
PIT BULL

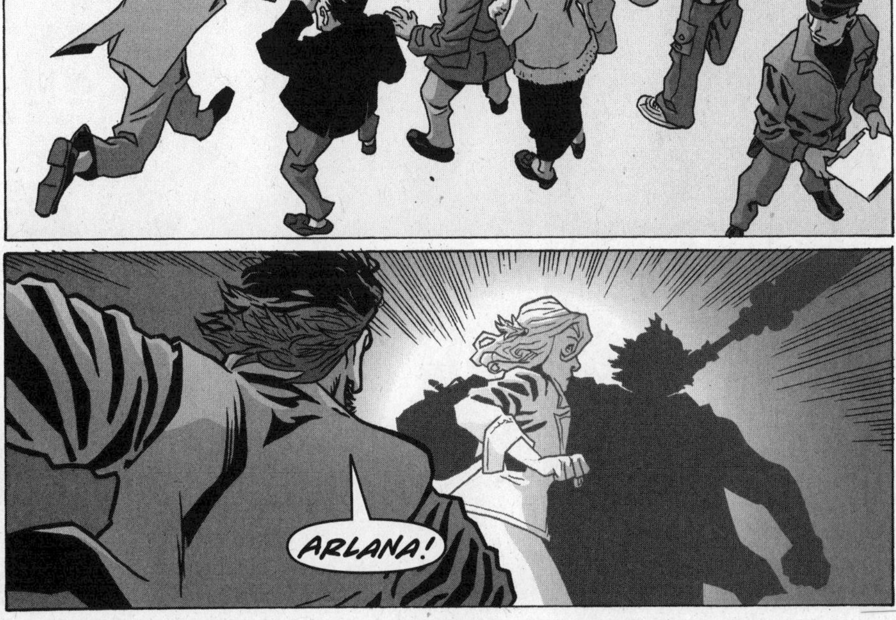
ARLANA!

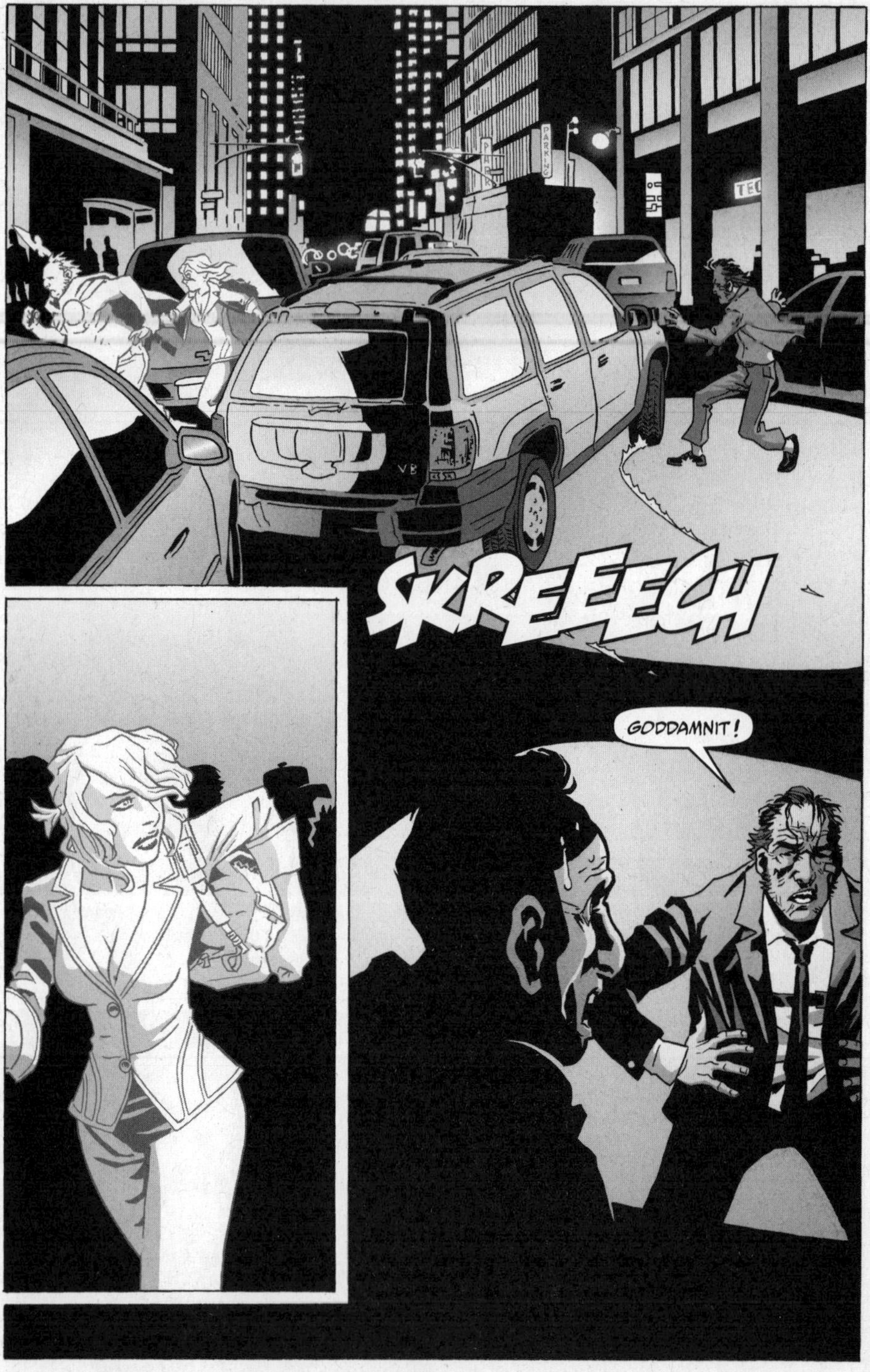
PARKING
SKREEECH
GODDAMNIT!

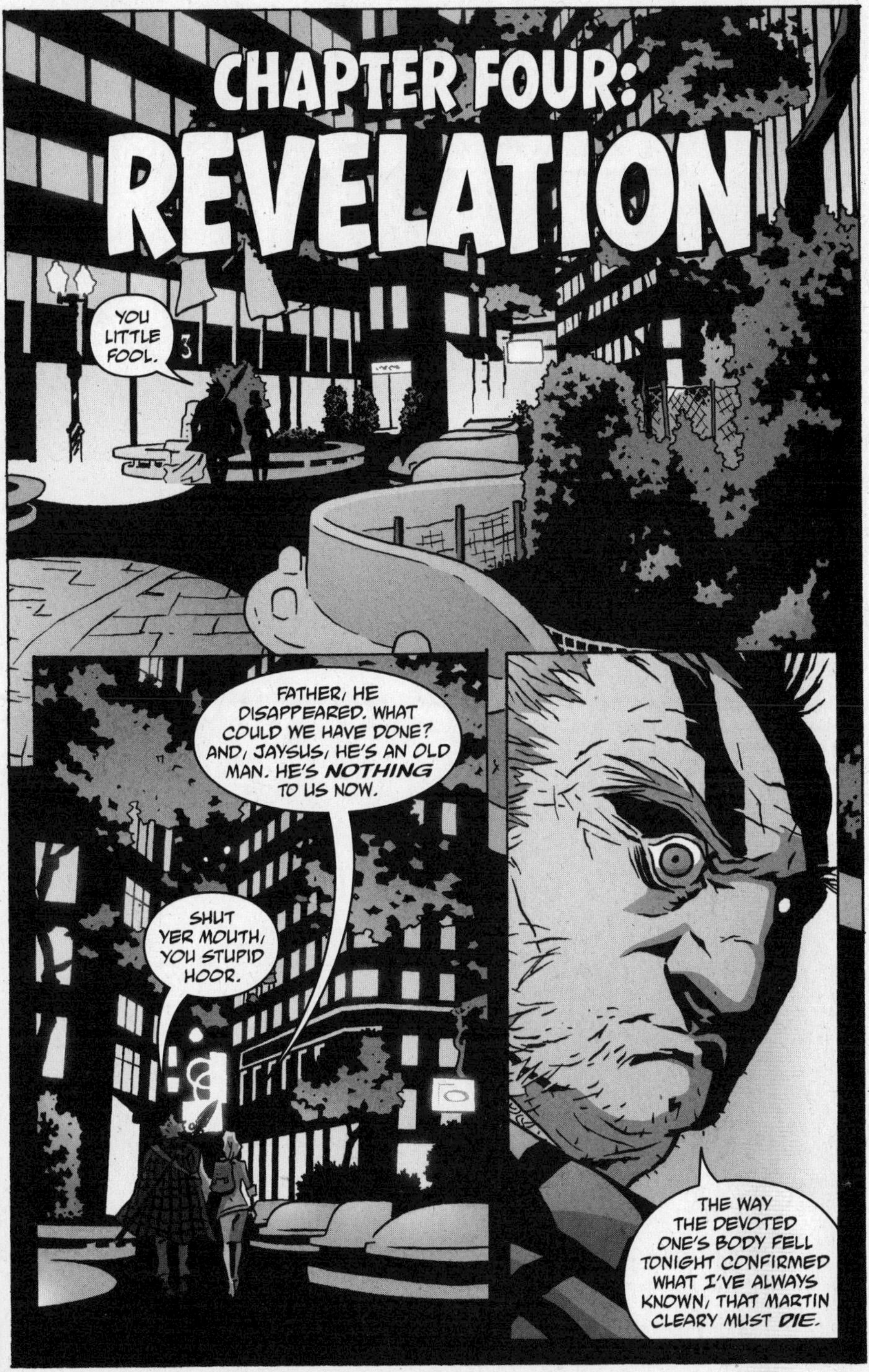
CHAPTER FOUR:
REVELATION
YOU LITTLE FOOL.
FATHER, HE DISAPPEARED. WHAT COULD WE HAVE DONE? AND, JAYSUS, HE'S AN OLD MAN. HE'S NOTHING TO US NOW.
SHUT YER MOUTH, YOU STUPID HOOR.
THE WAY THE DEVOTED ONE'S BODY FELL TONIGHT CONFIRMED WHAT I'VE ALWAYS KNOWN, THAT MARTIN CLEARY MUST DIE.

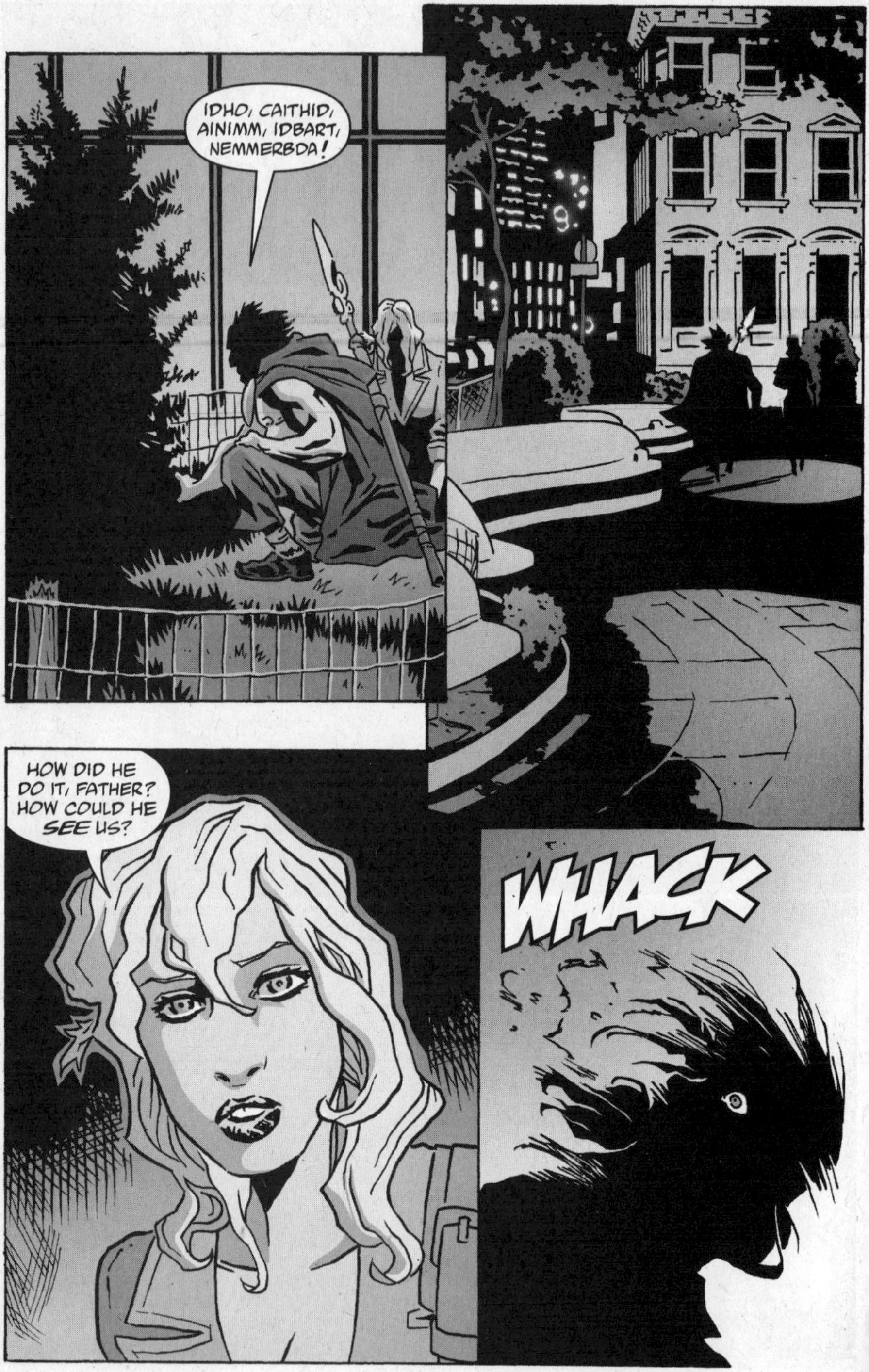
IDHO, CAITHID, AINIMM, IDBART, NEMMERBDA!
HOW DID HE DO IT, FATHER? HOW COULD HE SEE US?
WHACK

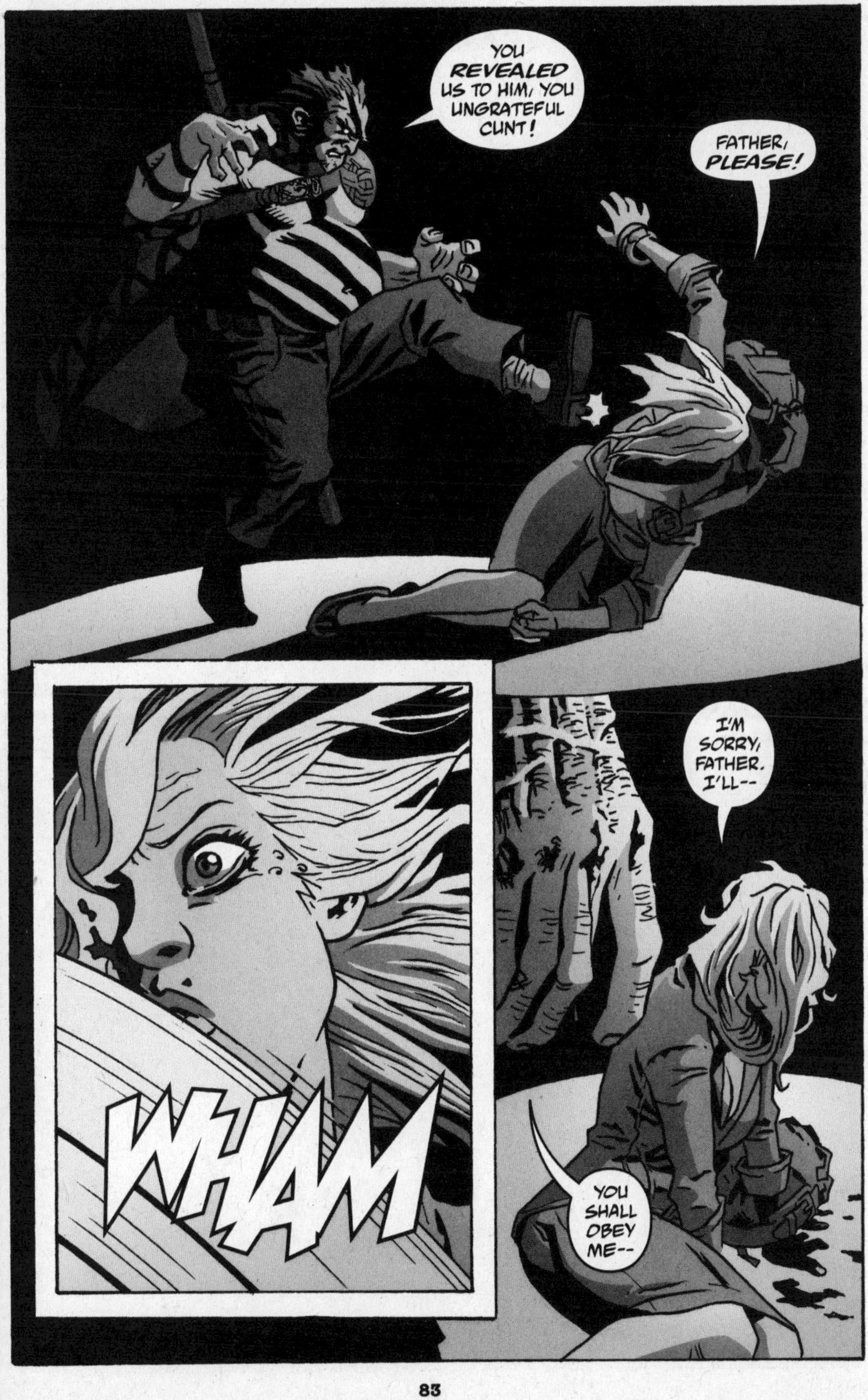
YOU REVEALED US TO HIM, YOU UNGRATEFUL CUNT!
FATHER, PLEASE!
I'M SORRY, FATHER. I'LL--
WHAM
YOU SHALL OBEY ME--

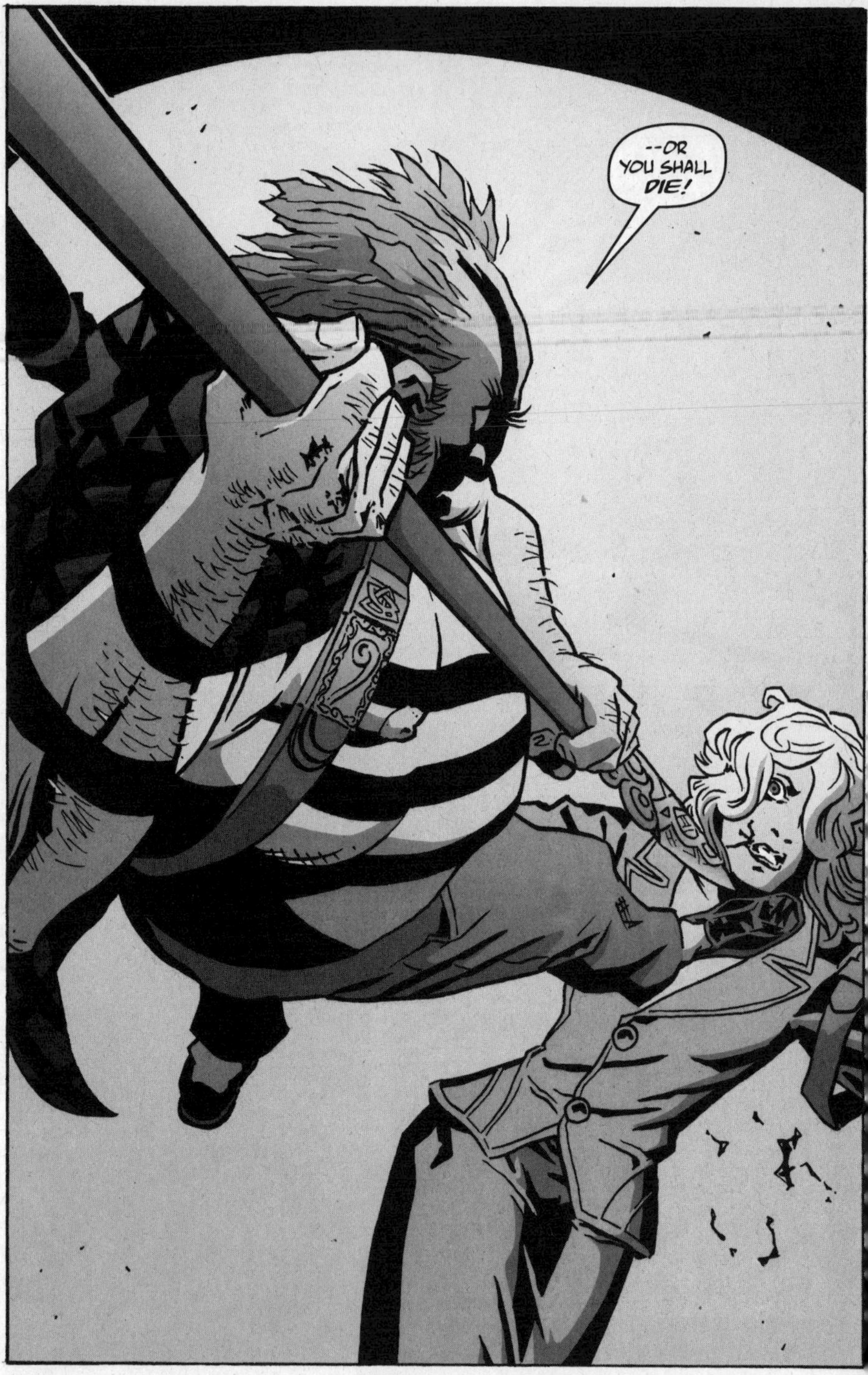
--OR YOU SHALL DIE!

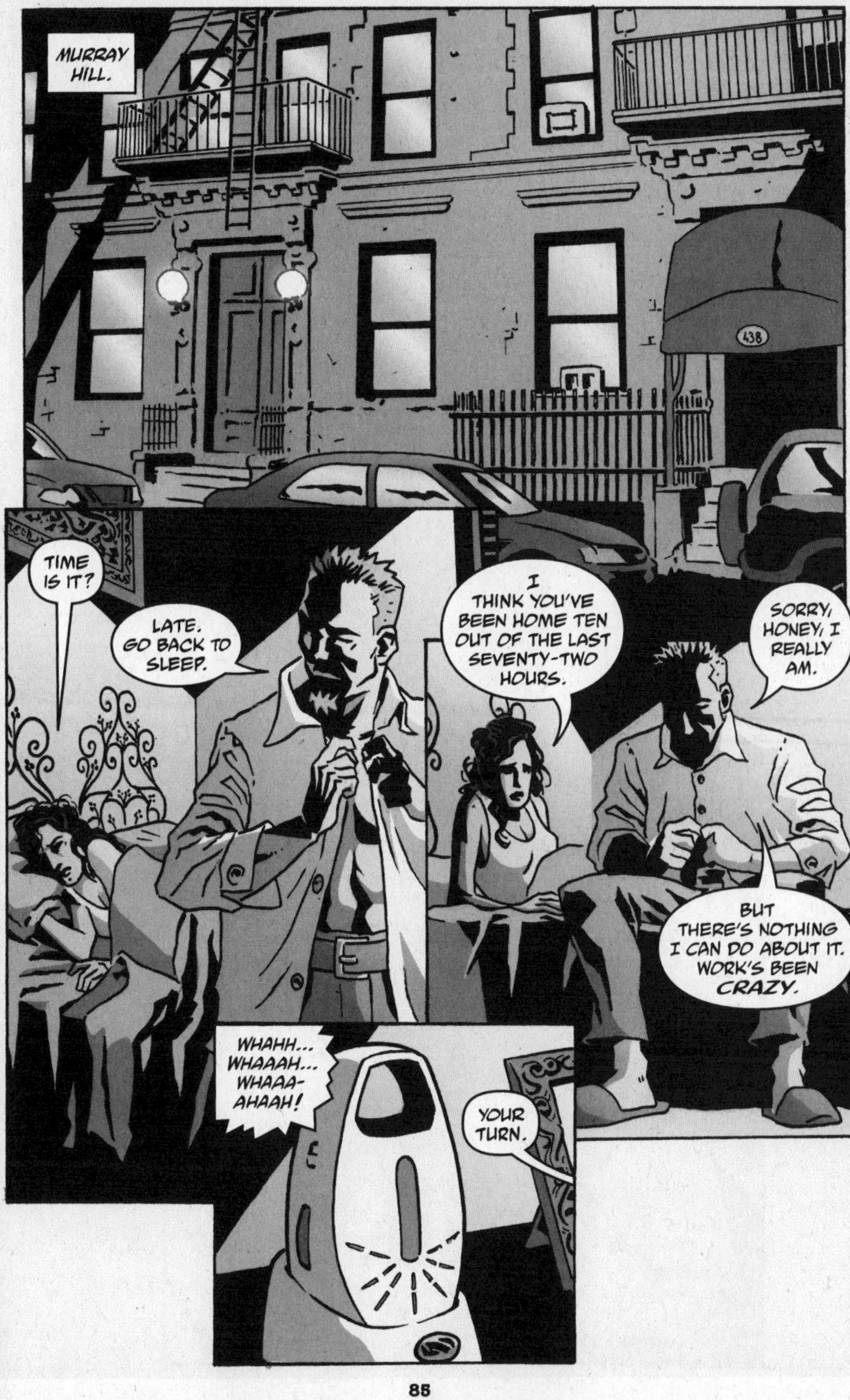
MURRAY HILL.
TIME IS IT?
LATE. GO BACK TO SLEEP.
I THINK YOU'VE BEEN HOME TEN OUT OF THE LAST SEVENTY-TWO HOURS.
SORRY, HONEY, I REALLY AM.
BUT THERE'S NOTHING I CAN DO ABOUT IT. WORK'S BEEN CRAZY.
WHAHH... WHAAAH... WHAAA-AHAAH!
YOUR TURN.
438

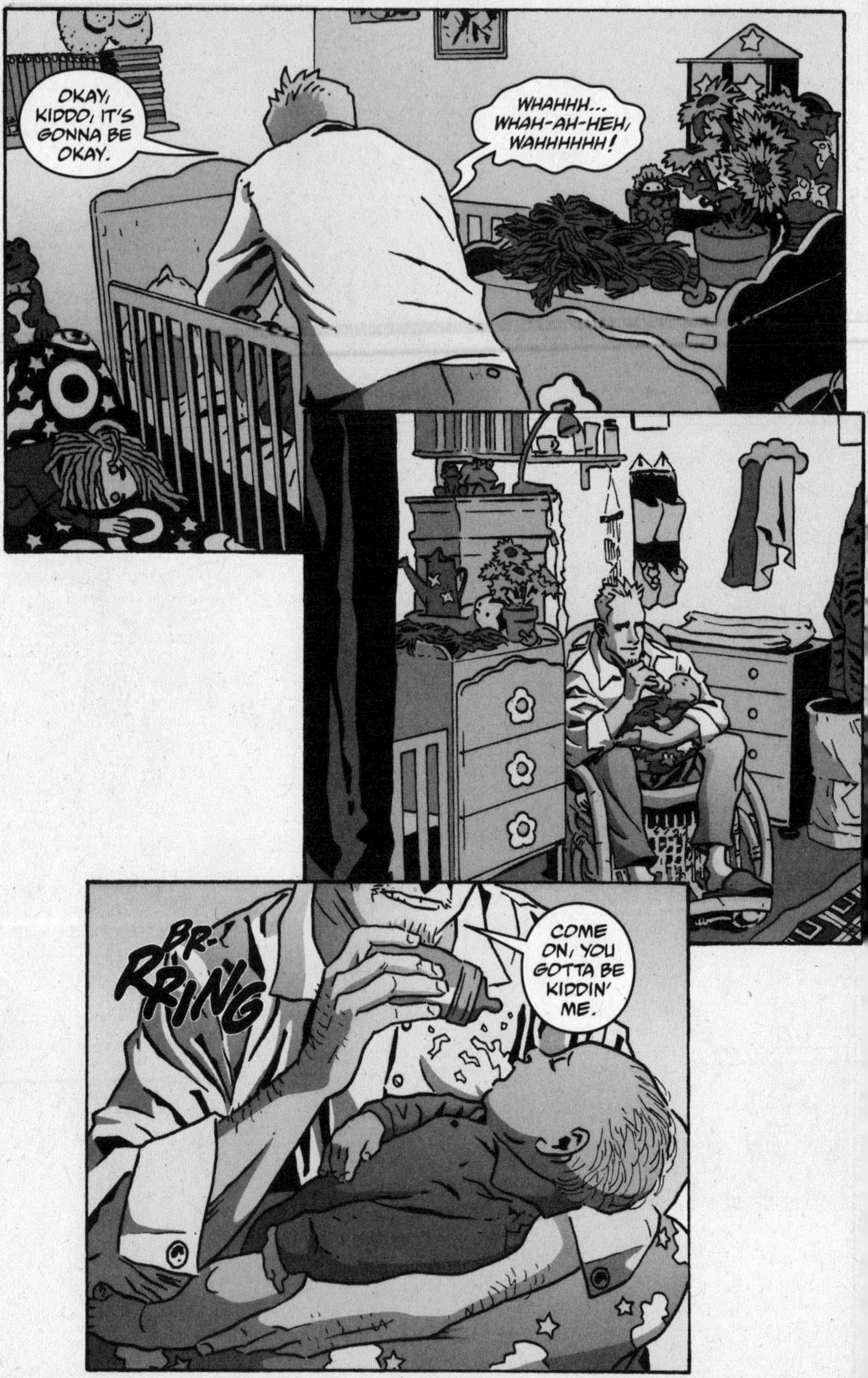
OKAY, KIDDO, IT'S GONNA BE OKAY.
WHAHHH... WHAH-AH-HEH, WAHHHHHH!
BR-RRING
COME ON, YOU GOTTA BE KIDDIN' ME.

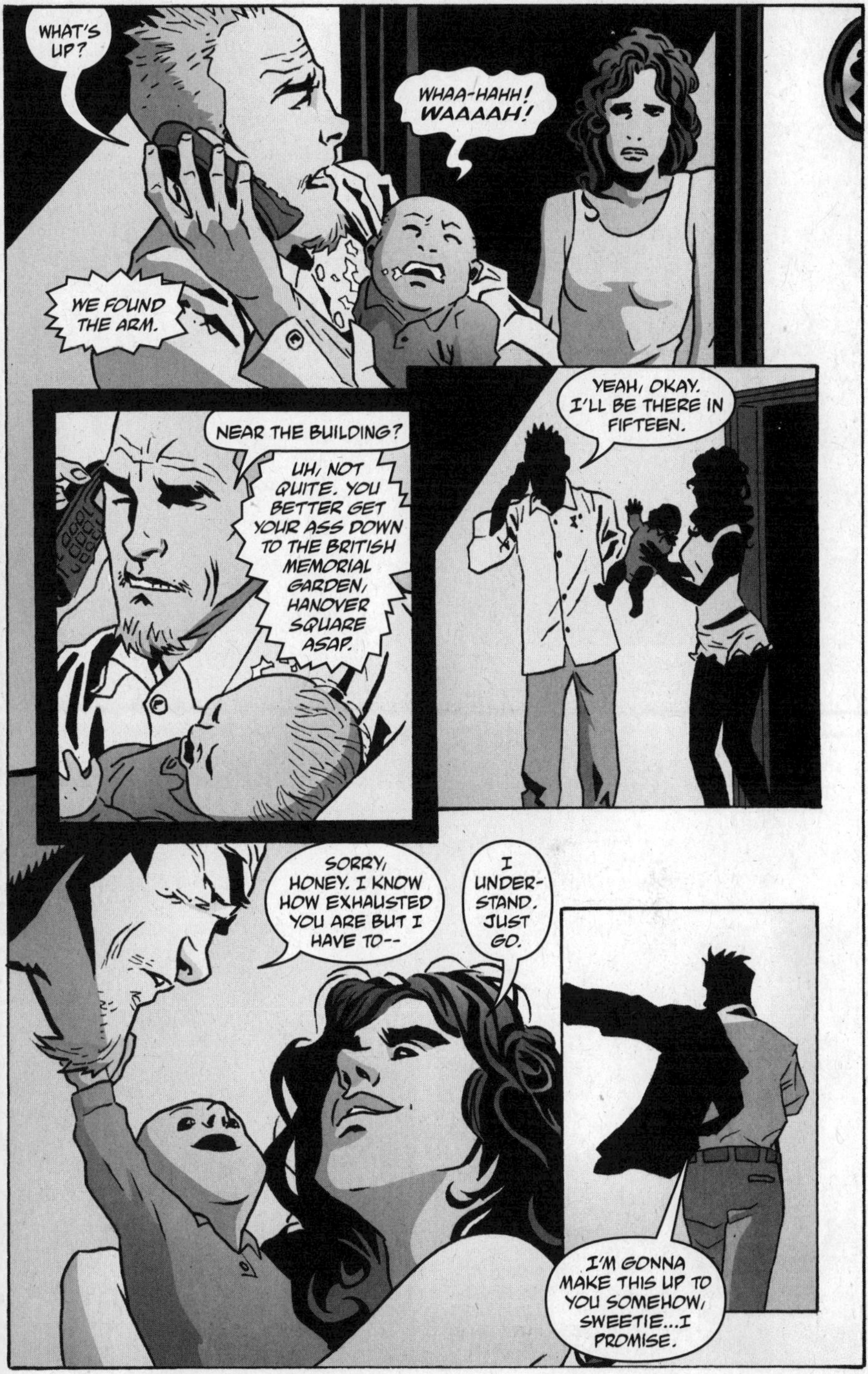
WHAT'S UP?
WHAA-HAHH! WAAAAH!
WE FOUND THE ARM.
NEAR THE BUILDING?
UH, NOT QUITE. YOU BETTER GET YOUR ASS DOWN TO THE BRITISH MEMORIAL GARDEN, HANOVER SQUARE ASAP.
YEAH, OKAY. I'LL BE THERE IN FIFTEEN.
SORRY, HONEY. I KNOW HOW EXHAUSTED YOU ARE BUT I HAVE TO--
I UNDER-STAND. JUST GO.
I'M GONNA MAKE THIS UP TO YOU SOMEHOW, SWEETIE...I PROMISE.

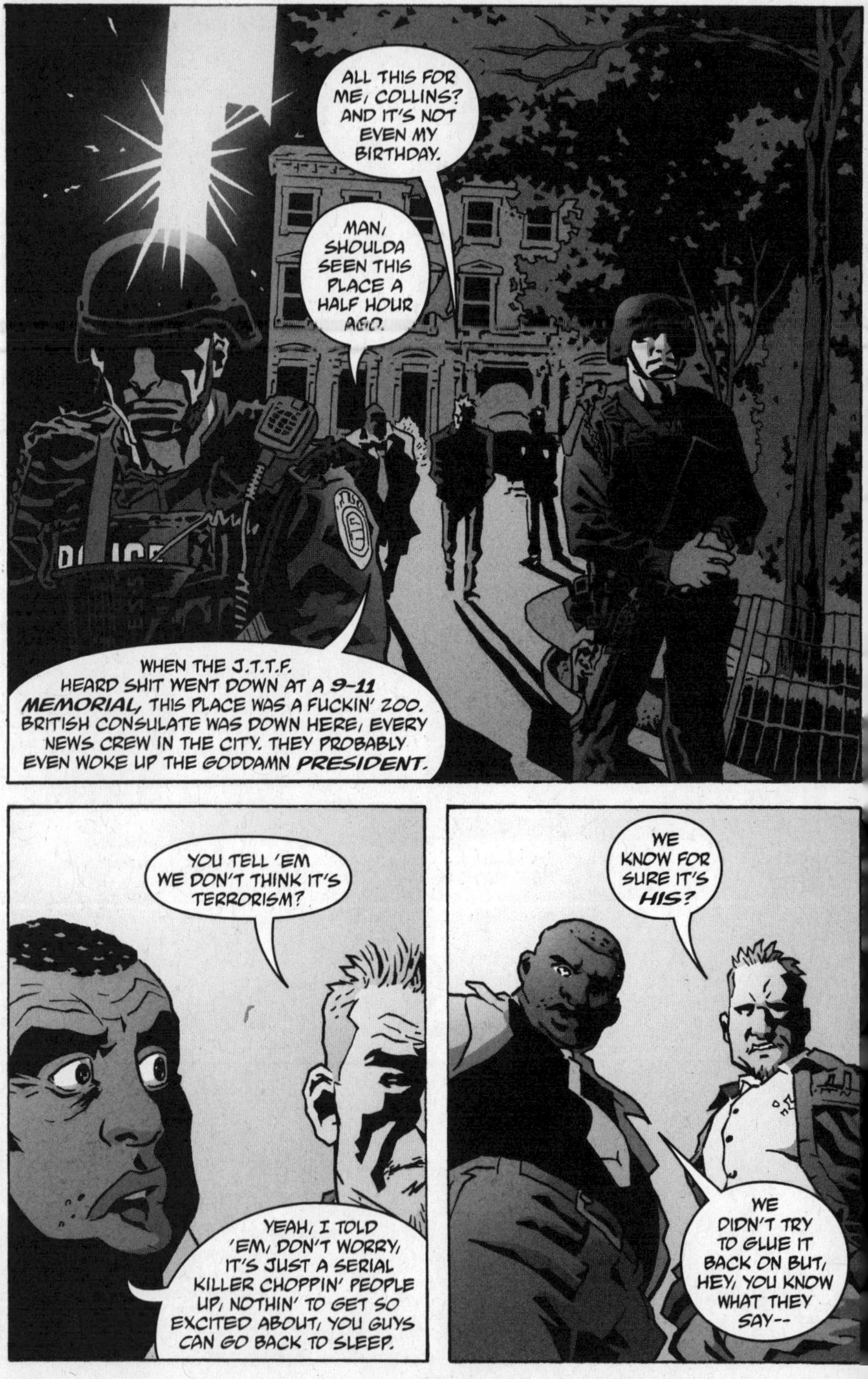
ALL THIS FOR ME, COLLINS? AND IT'S NOT EVEN MY BIRTHDAY.
MAN, SHOULDA SEEN THIS PLACE A HALF HOUR AGO.
WHEN THE J.T.T.F. HEARD SHIT WENT DOWN AT A 9-11 MEMORIAL, THIS PLACE WAS A FUCKIN' ZOO. BRITISH CONSULATE WAS DOWN HERE, EVERY NEWS CREW IN THE CITY. THEY PROBABLY EVEN WOKE UP THE GODDAMN PRESIDENT.
YOU TELL 'EM WE DON'T THINK IT'S TERRORISM?
YEAH, I TOLD 'EM, DON'T WORRY, IT'S JUST A SERIAL KILLER CHOPPIN' PEOPLE UP, NOTHIN' TO GET SO EXCITED ABOUT, YOU GUYS CAN GO BACK TO SLEEP.
WE KNOW FOR SURE IT'S HIS?
WE DIDN'T TRY TO GLUE IT BACK ON BUT, HEY, YOU KNOW WHAT THEY SAY--

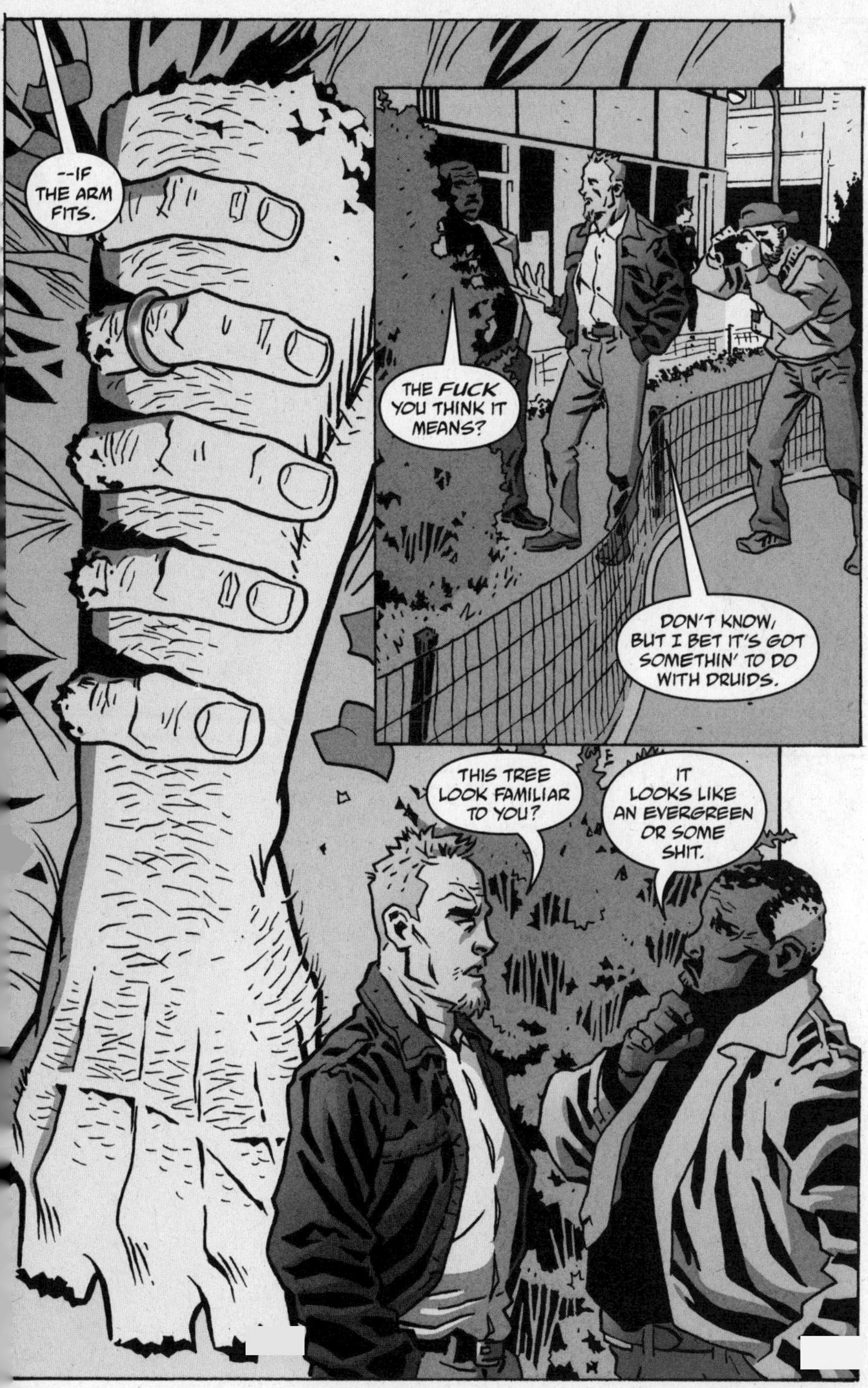
--IF THE ARM FITS.
THE FUCK YOU THINK IT MEANS?
DON'T KNOW, BUT I BET IT'S GOT SOMETHIN' TO DO WITH DRUIDS.
THIS TREE LOOK FAMILIAR TO YOU?
IT LOOKS LIKE AN EVERGREEN OR SOME SHIT.

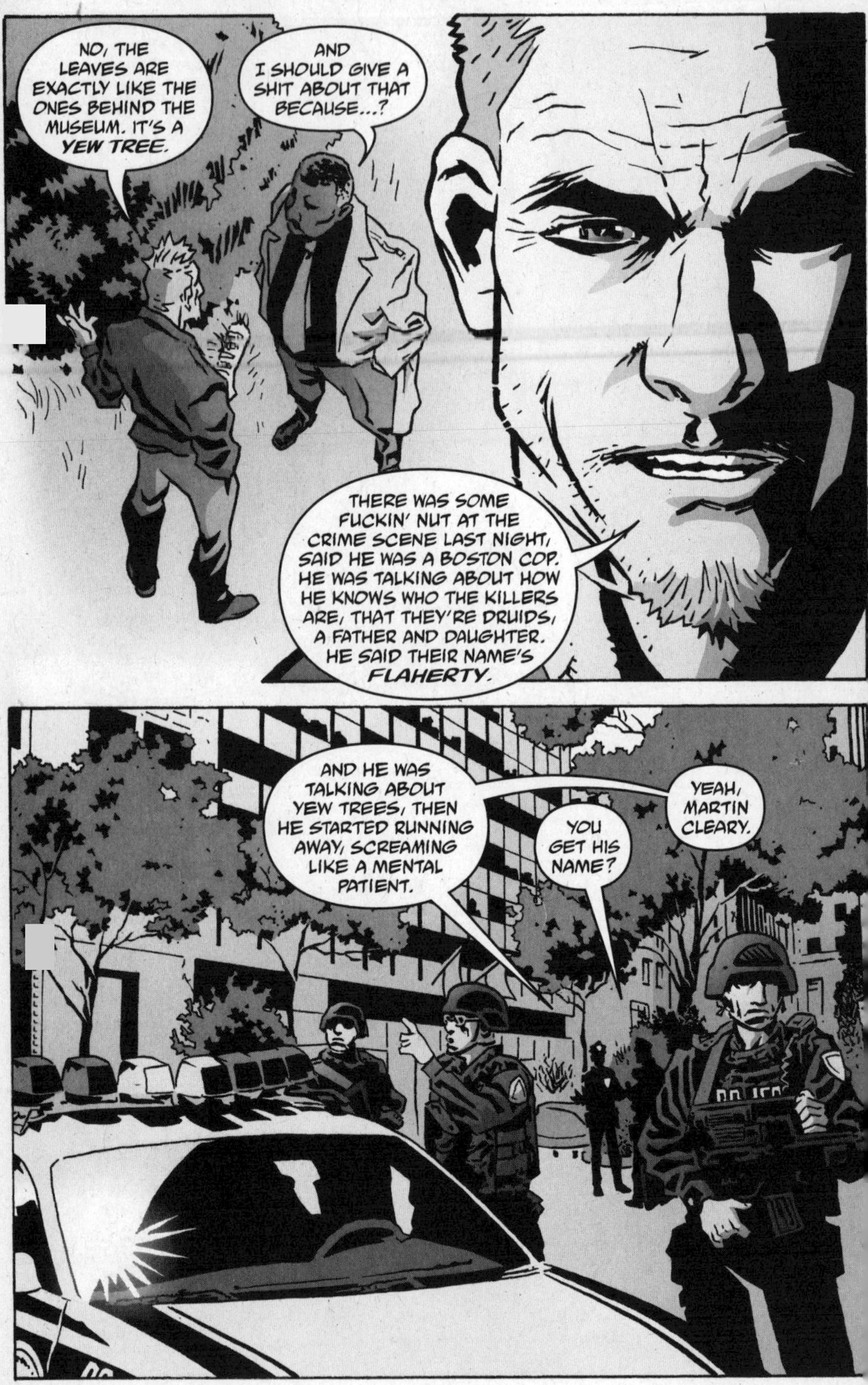
NO, THE LEAVES ARE EXACTLY LIKE THE ONES BEHIND THE MUSEUM. IT'S A YEW TREE.
AND I SHOULD GIVE A SHIT ABOUT THAT BECAUSE...?
THERE WAS SOME FUCKIN' NUT AT THE CRIME SCENE LAST NIGHT, SAID HE WAS A BOSTON COP. HE WAS TALKING ABOUT HOW HE KNOWS WHO THE KILLERS ARE, THAT THEY'RE DRUIDS, A FATHER AND DAUGHTER. HE SAID THEIR NAME'S FLAHERTY.
AND HE WAS TALKING ABOUT YEW TREES, THEN HE STARTED RUNNING AWAY, SCREAMING LIKE A MENTAL PATIENT.
YOU GET HIS NAME?
YEAH, MARTIN CLEARY.

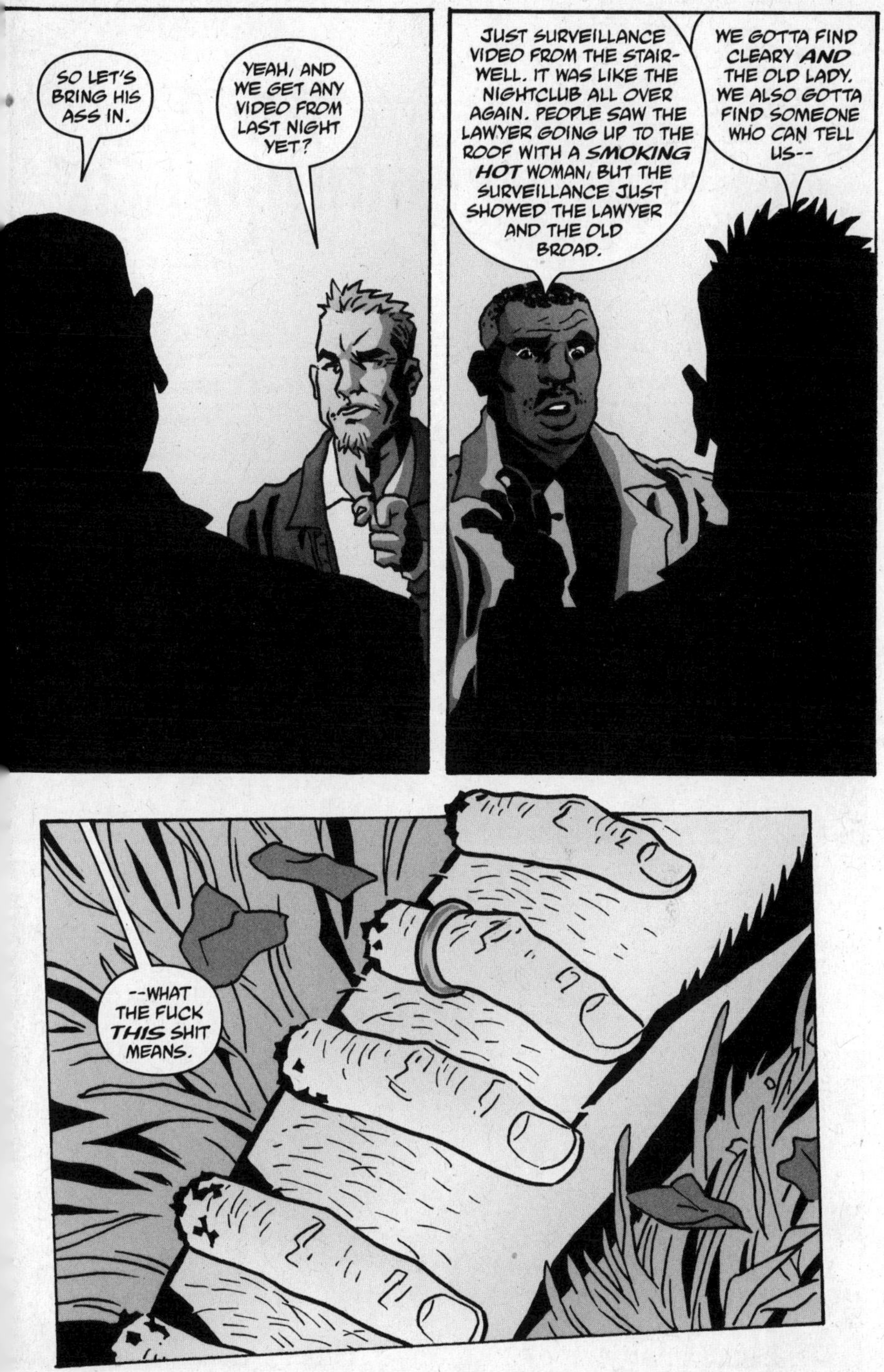
SO LET'S BRING HIS ASS IN.
YEAH, AND WE GET ANY VIDEO FROM LAST NIGHT YET?
JUST SURVEILLANCE VIDEO FROM THE STAIR-WELL. IT WAS LIKE THE NIGHTCLUB ALL OVER AGAIN. PEOPLE SAW THE LAWYER GOING UP TO THE ROOF WITH A SMOKING HOT WOMAN, BUT THE SURVEILLANCE JUST SHOWED THE LAWYER AND THE OLD BROAD.
WE GOTTA FIND CLEARY AND THE OLD LADY. WE ALSO GOTTA FIND SOMEONE WHO CAN TELL US--
--WHAT THE FUCK THIS SHIT MEANS.

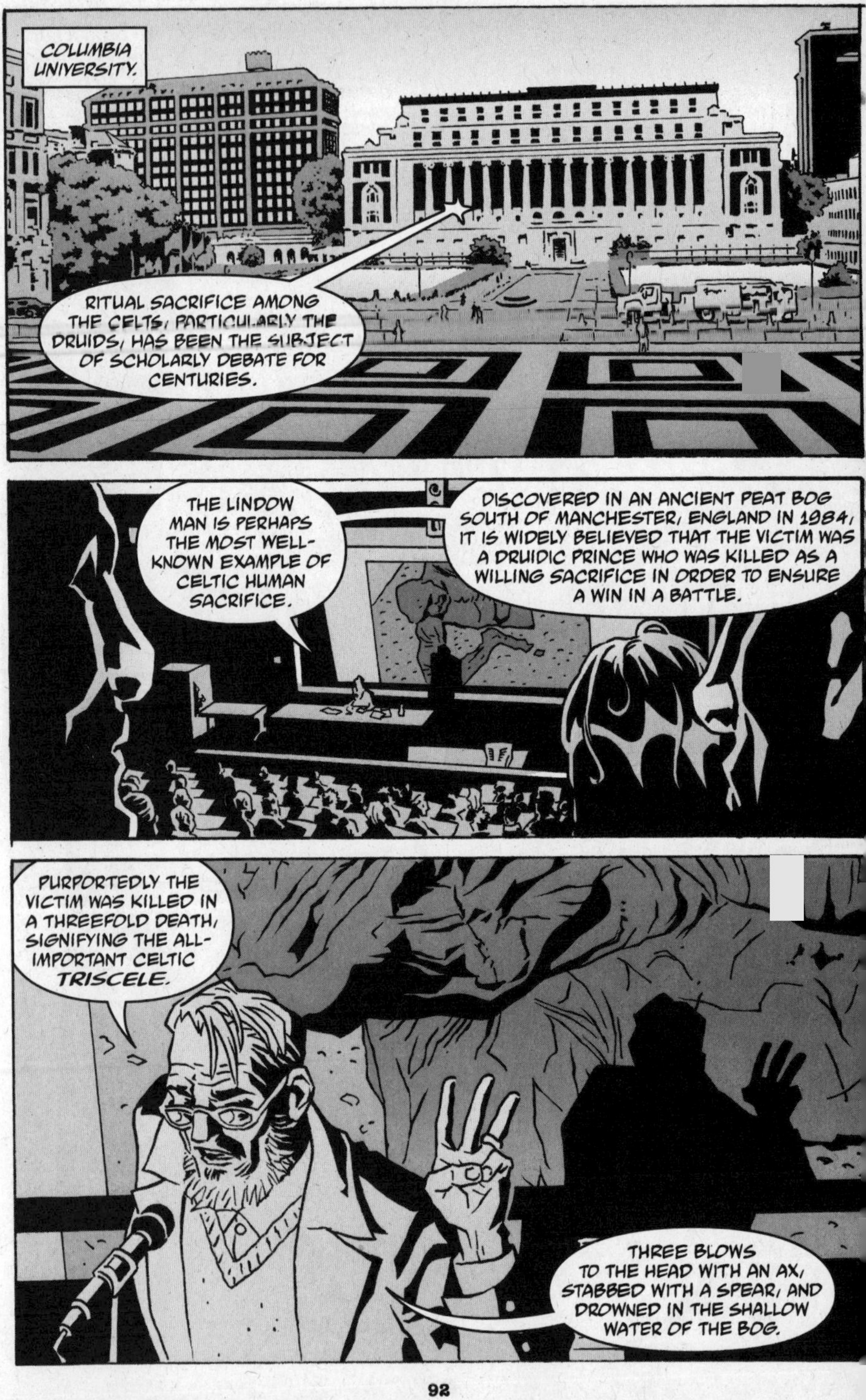
COLUMBIA UNIVERSITY.
RITUAL SACRIFICE AMONG THE CELTS, PARTICULARLY THE DRUIDS, HAS BEEN THE SUBJECT OF SCHOLARLY DEBATE FOR CENTURIES.
THE LINDOW MAN IS PERHAPS THE MOST WELL-KNOWN EXAMPLE OF CELTIC HUMAN SACRIFICE.
DISCOVERED IN AN ANCIENT PEAT BOG SOUTH OF MANCHESTER, ENGLAND IN 1984, IT IS WIDELY BELIEVED THAT THE VICTIM WAS A DRUIDIC PRINCE WHO WAS KILLED AS A WILLING SACRIFICE IN ORDER TO ENSURE A WIN IN A BATTLE.
PURPORTEDLY THE VICTIM WAS KILLED IN A THREEFOLD DEATH, SIGNIFYING THE ALL-IMPORTANT CELTIC *TRISCELE.*
THREE BLOWS TO THE HEAD WITH AN AX, STABBED WITH A SPEAR, AND DROWNED IN THE SHALLOW WATER OF THE BOG.

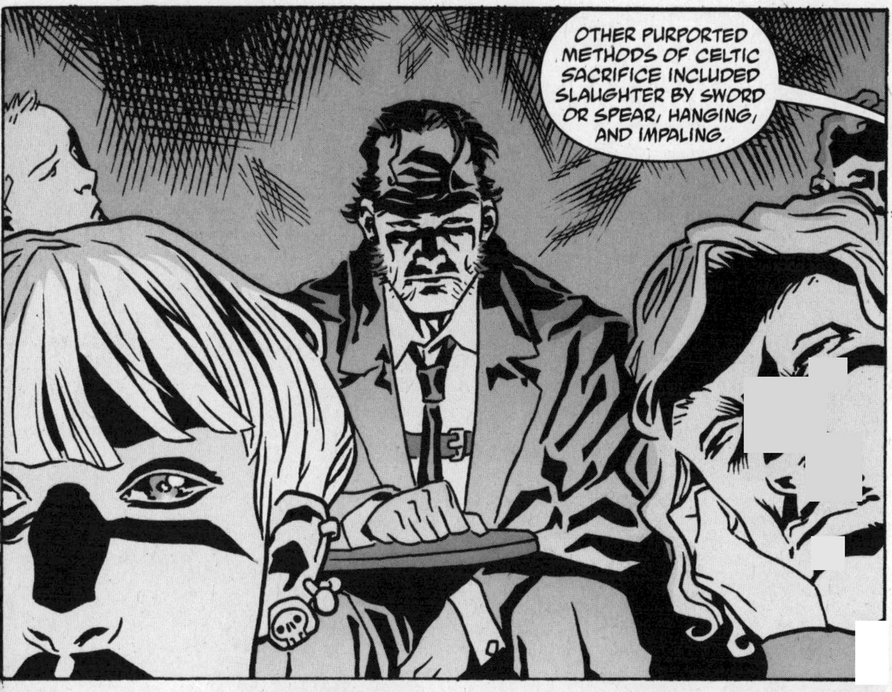
OTHER PURPORTED METHODS OF CELTIC SACRIFICE INCLUDED SLAUGHTER BY SWORD OR SPEAR, HANGING, AND IMPALING.

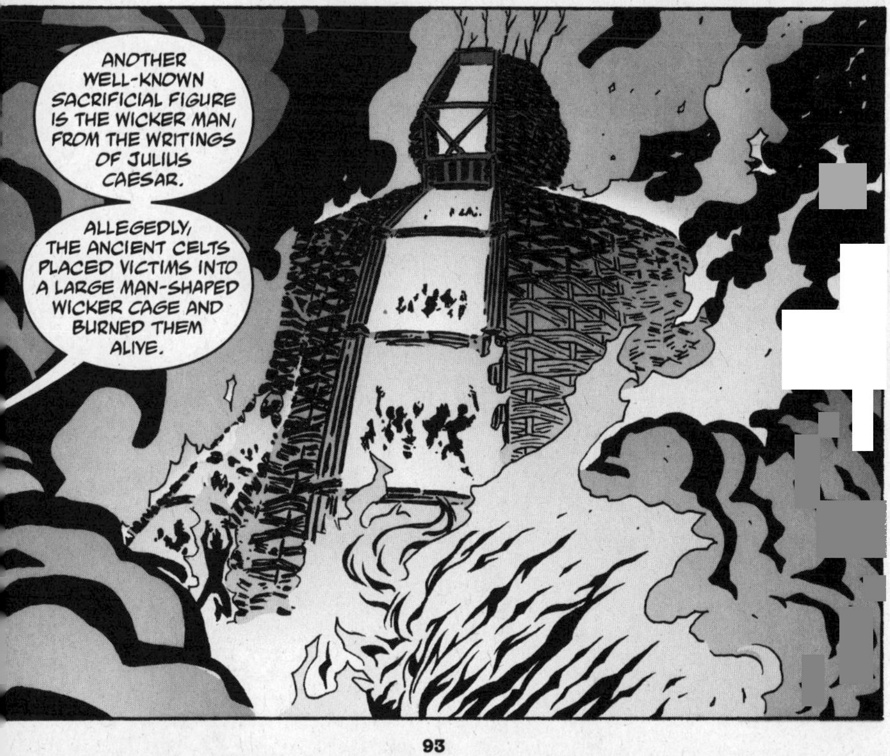
ANOTHER WELL-KNOWN SACRIFICIAL FIGURE IS THE WICKER MAN, FROM THE WRITINGS OF JULIUS CAESAR.
ALLEGEDLY, THE ANCIENT CELTS PLACED VICTIMS INTO A LARGE MAN-SHAPED WICKER CAGE AND BURNED THEM ALIVE.

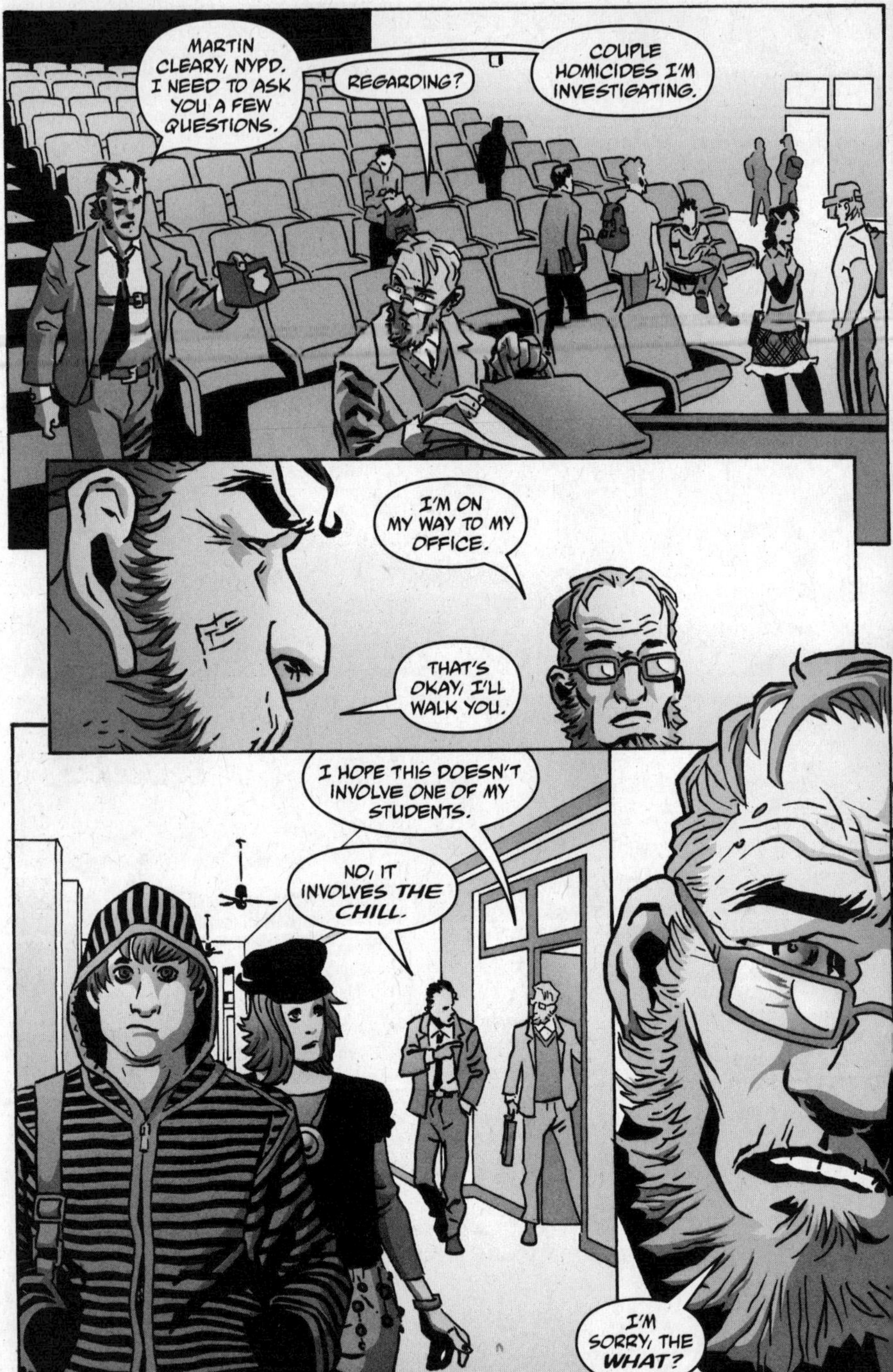
MARTIN CLEARY, NYPD. I NEED TO ASK YOU A FEW QUESTIONS.
REGARDING?
COUPLE HOMICIDES I'M INVESTIGATING.
I'M ON MY WAY TO MY OFFICE.
THAT'S OKAY, I'LL WALK YOU.
I HOPE THIS DOESN'T INVOLVE ONE OF MY STUDENTS.
NO, IT INVOLVES *THE CHILL*.
I'M SORRY, THE *WHAT*?

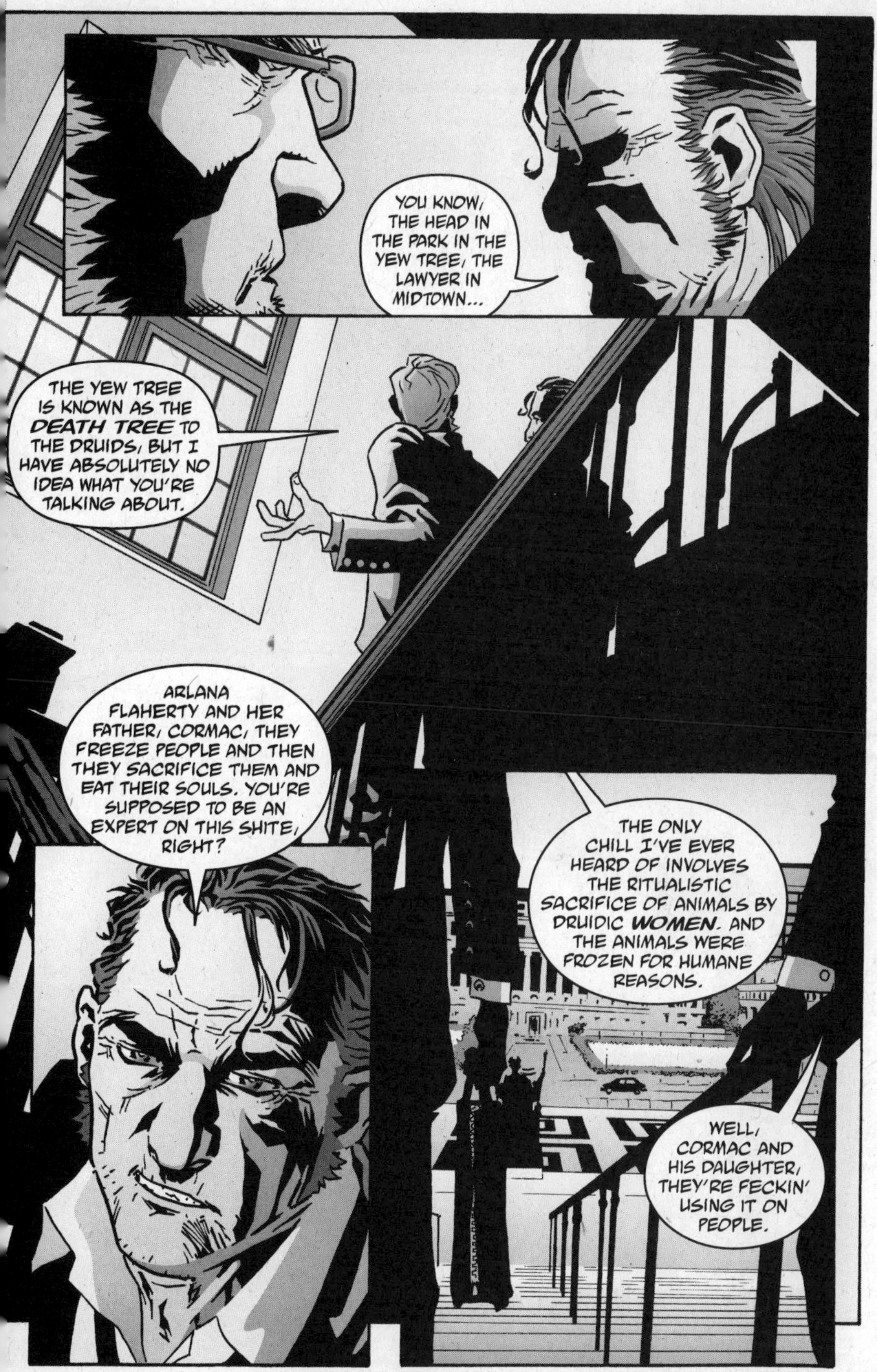
YOU KNOW, THE HEAD IN THE PARK IN THE YEW TREE, THE LAWYER IN MIDTOWN...
THE YEW TREE IS KNOWN AS THE DEATH TREE TO THE DRUIDS, BUT I HAVE ABSOLUTELY NO IDEA WHAT YOU'RE TALKING ABOUT.
ARLANA FLAHERTY AND HER FATHER, CORMAC, THEY FREEZE PEOPLE AND THEN THEY SACRIFICE THEM AND EAT THEIR SOULS. YOU'RE SUPPOSED TO BE AN EXPERT ON THIS SHITE, RIGHT?
THE ONLY CHILL I'VE EVER HEARD OF INVOLVES THE RITUALISTIC SACRIFICE OF ANIMALS BY DRUIDIC WOMEN. AND THE ANIMALS WERE FROZEN FOR HUMANE REASONS.
WELL, CORMAC AND HIS DAUGHTER, THEY'RE FECKIN' USING IT ON PEOPLE.

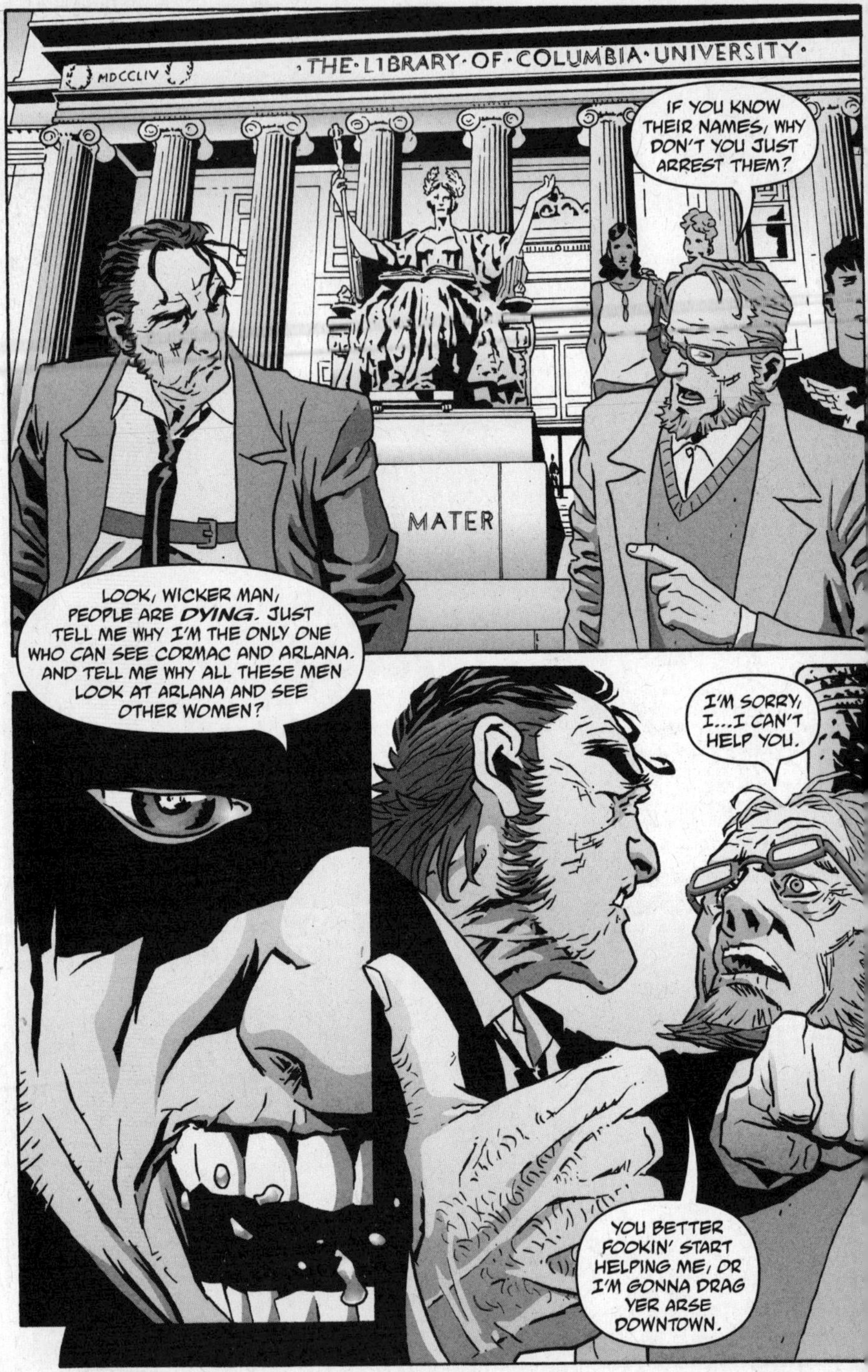
·THE·LIBRARY·OF·COLUMBIA·UNIVERSITY·
MDCCLIV
IF YOU KNOW THEIR NAMES, WHY DON'T YOU JUST ARREST THEM?
MATER
LOOK, WICKER MAN, PEOPLE ARE DYING. JUST TELL ME WHY I'M THE ONLY ONE WHO CAN SEE CORMAC AND ARLANA. AND TELL ME WHY ALL THESE MEN LOOK AT ARLANA AND SEE OTHER WOMEN?
I'M SORRY, I...I CAN'T HELP YOU.
YOU BETTER FOOKIN' START HELPING ME, OR I'M GONNA DRAG YER ARSE DOWNTOWN.

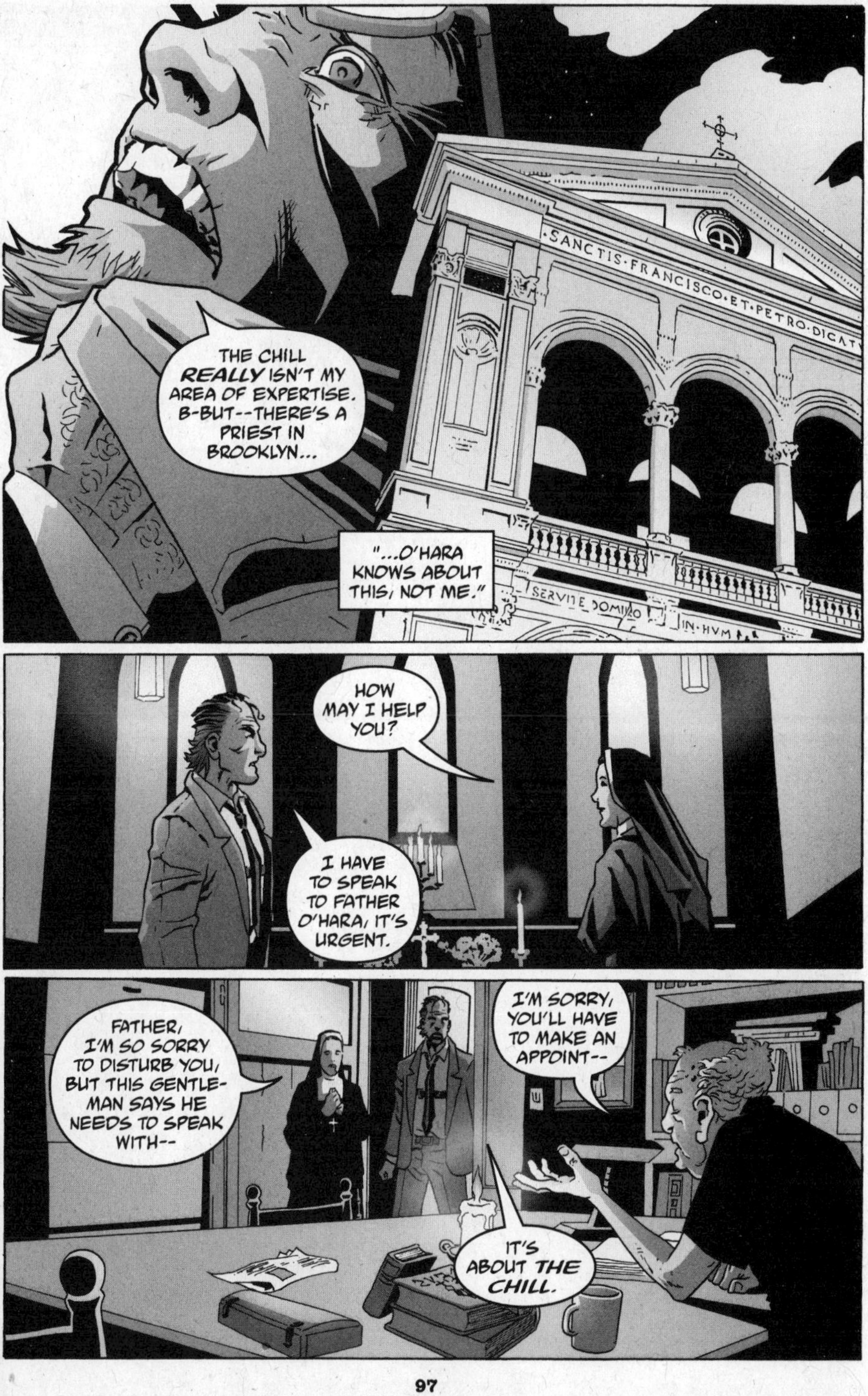
THE CHILL REALLY ISN'T MY AREA OF EXPERTISE. B-BUT--THERE'S A PRIEST IN BROOKLYN...
SANCTIS·FRANCISCO·ET·PETRO·DICAT
"...O'HARA KNOWS ABOUT THIS, NOT ME."
HOW MAY I HELP YOU?
I HAVE TO SPEAK TO FATHER O'HARA, IT'S URGENT.
FATHER, I'M SO SORRY TO DISTURB YOU, BUT THIS GENTLE-MAN SAYS HE NEEDS TO SPEAK WITH--
I'M SORRY, YOU'LL HAVE TO MAKE AN APPOINT--
IT'S ABOUT THE CHILL.

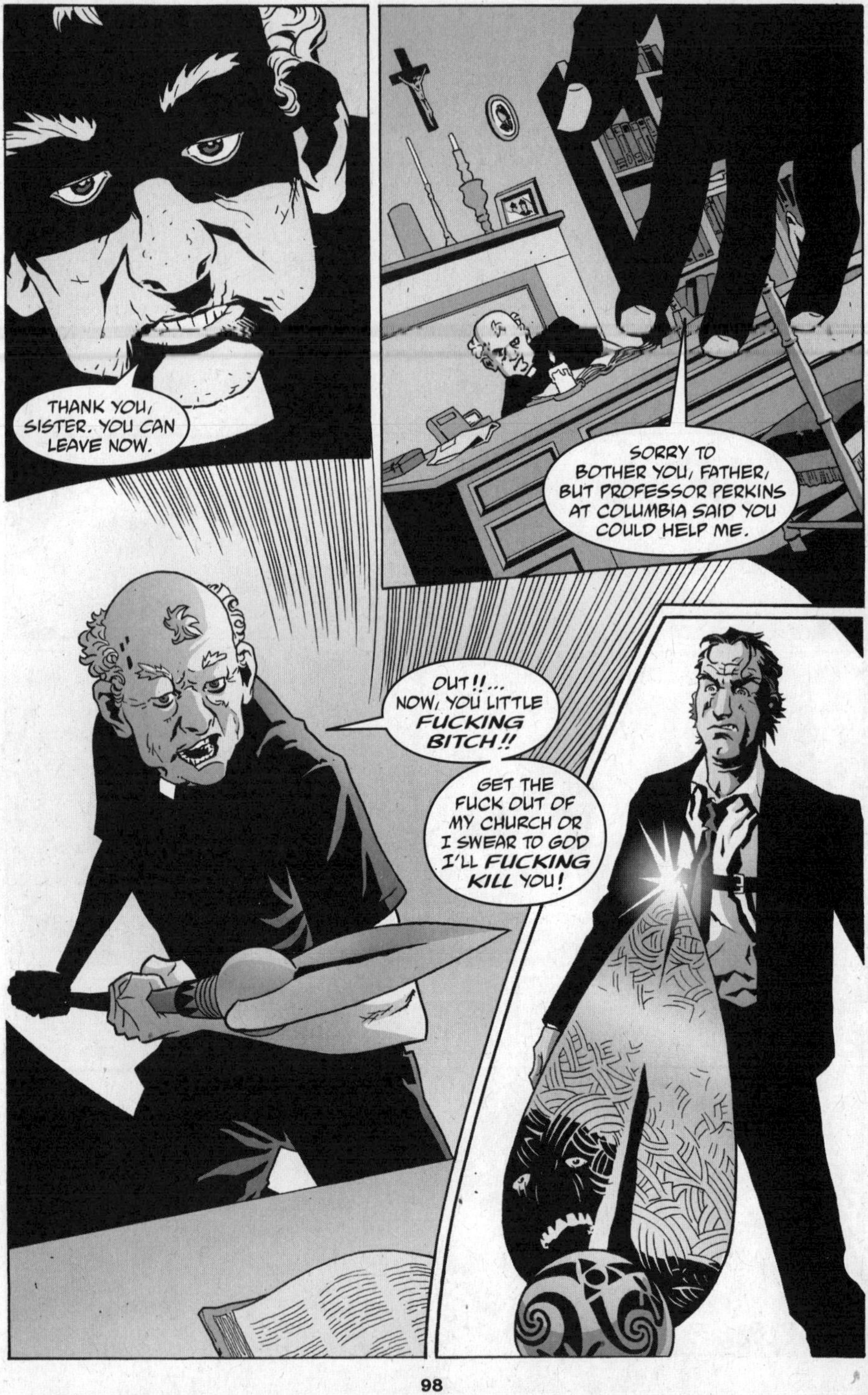
THANK YOU, SISTER. YOU CAN LEAVE NOW.
SORRY TO BOTHER YOU, FATHER, BUT PROFESSOR PERKINS AT COLUMBIA SAID YOU COULD HELP ME.
OUT!!... NOW, YOU LITTLE FUCKING BITCH!!
GET THE FUCK OUT OF MY CHURCH OR I SWEAR TO GOD I'LL FUCKING KILL YOU!

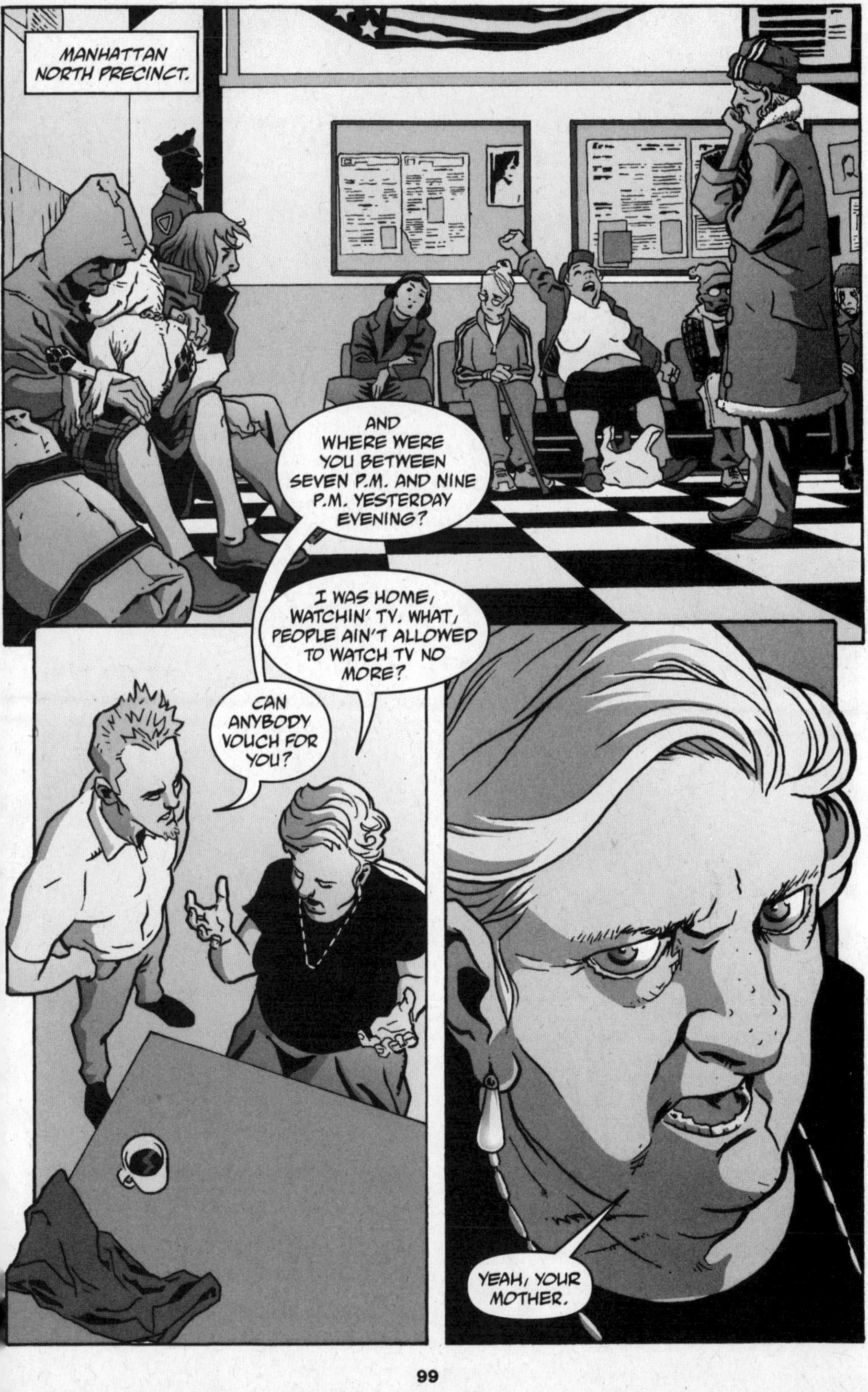
MANHATTAN NORTH PRECINCT.
AND WHERE WERE YOU BETWEEN SEVEN P.M. AND NINE P.M. YESTERDAY EVENING?
I WAS HOME, WATCHIN' TV. WHAT, PEOPLE AIN'T ALLOWED TO WATCH TV NO MORE?
CAN ANYBODY VOUCH FOR YOU?
YEAH, YOUR MOTHER.

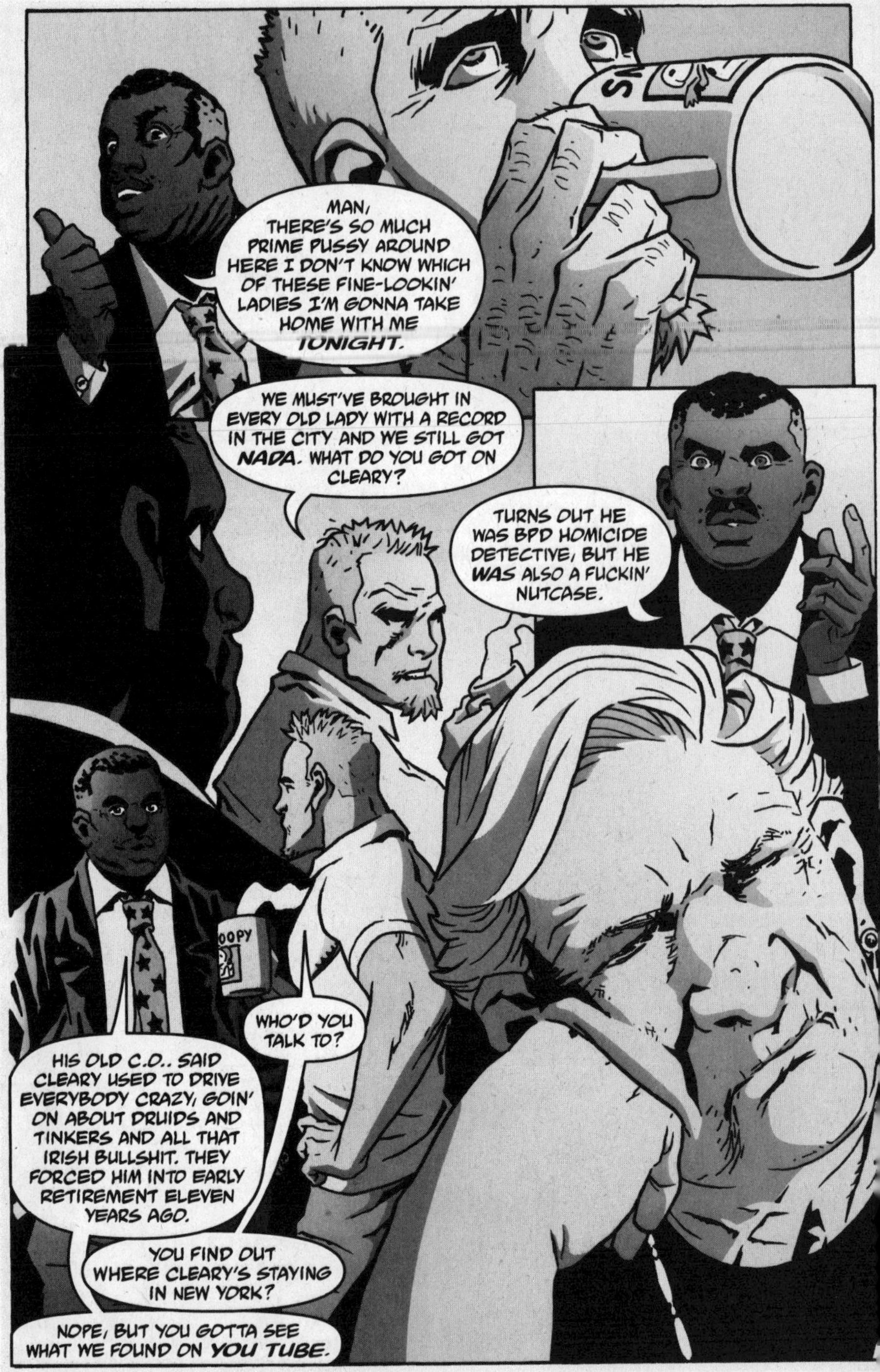
MAN, THERE'S SO MUCH PRIME PUSSY AROUND HERE I DON'T KNOW WHICH OF THESE FINE-LOOKIN' LADIES I'M GONNA TAKE HOME WITH ME *TONIGHT*.
WE MUST'VE BROUGHT IN EVERY OLD LADY WITH A RECORD IN THE CITY AND WE STILL GOT *NADA*. WHAT DO YOU GOT ON CLEARY?
TURNS OUT HE WAS BPD HOMICIDE DETECTIVE, BUT HE *WAS* ALSO A FUCKIN' NUTCASE.
WHO'D YOU TALK TO?
HIS OLD C.O.. SAID CLEARY USED TO DRIVE EVERYBODY CRAZY, GOIN' ON ABOUT DRUIDS AND TINKERS AND ALL THAT IRISH BULLSHIT. THEY FORCED HIM INTO EARLY RETIREMENT ELEVEN YEARS AGO.
YOU FIND OUT WHERE CLEARY'S STAYING IN NEW YORK?
NOPE, BUT YOU GOTTA SEE WHAT WE FOUND ON *YOU TUBE*.

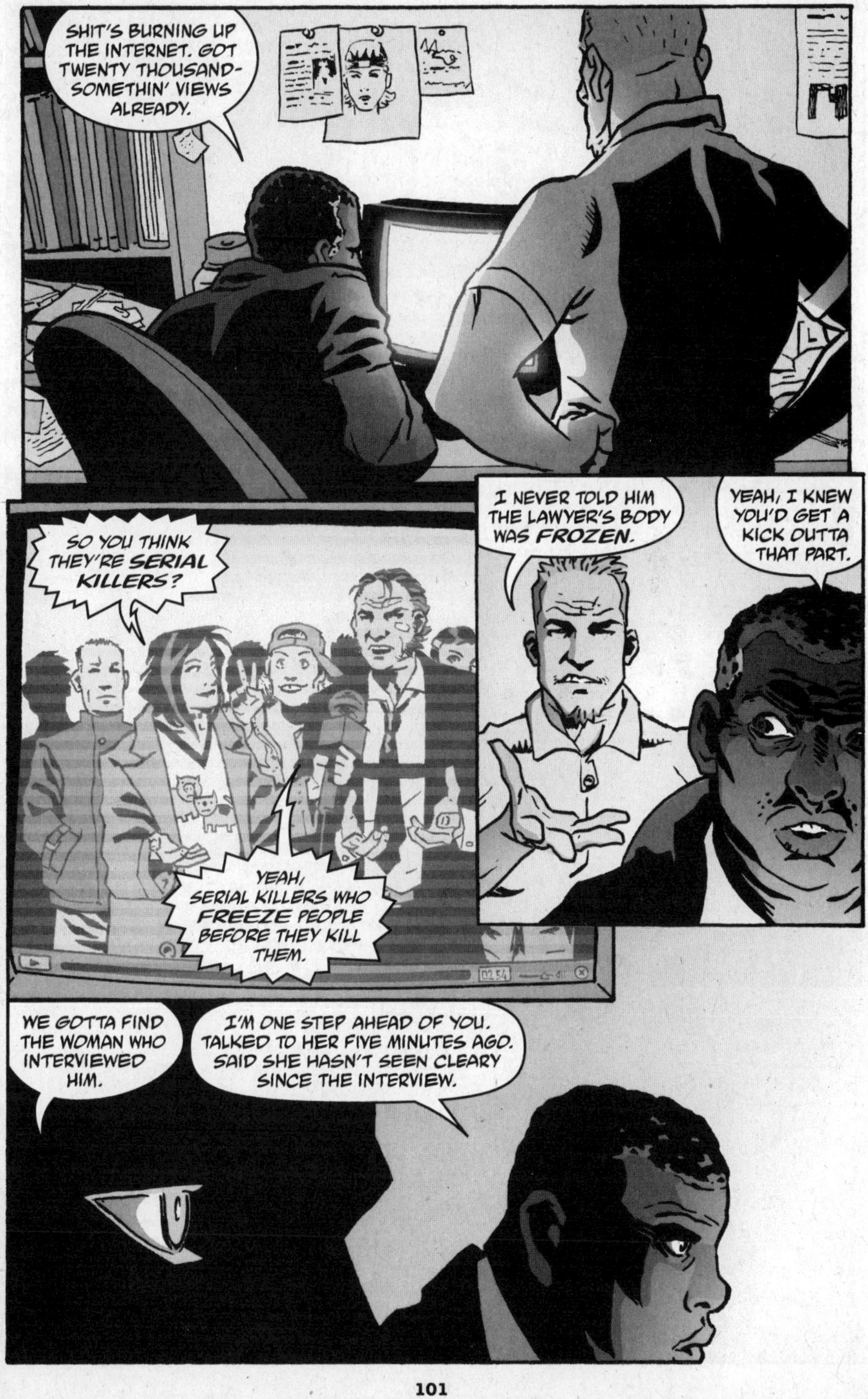
SHIT'S BURNING UP THE INTERNET. GOT TWENTY THOUSAND-SOMETHIN' VIEWS ALREADY.
SO YOU THINK THEY'RE SERIAL KILLERS?
YEAH, SERIAL KILLERS WHO FREEZE PEOPLE BEFORE THEY KILL THEM.
02.54
I NEVER TOLD HIM THE LAWYER'S BODY WAS FROZEN.
YEAH, I KNEW YOU'D GET A KICK OUTTA THAT PART.
WE GOTTA FIND THE WOMAN WHO INTERVIEWED HIM.
I'M ONE STEP AHEAD OF YOU. TALKED TO HER FIVE MINUTES AGO. SAID SHE HASN'T SEEN CLEARY SINCE THE INTERVIEW.

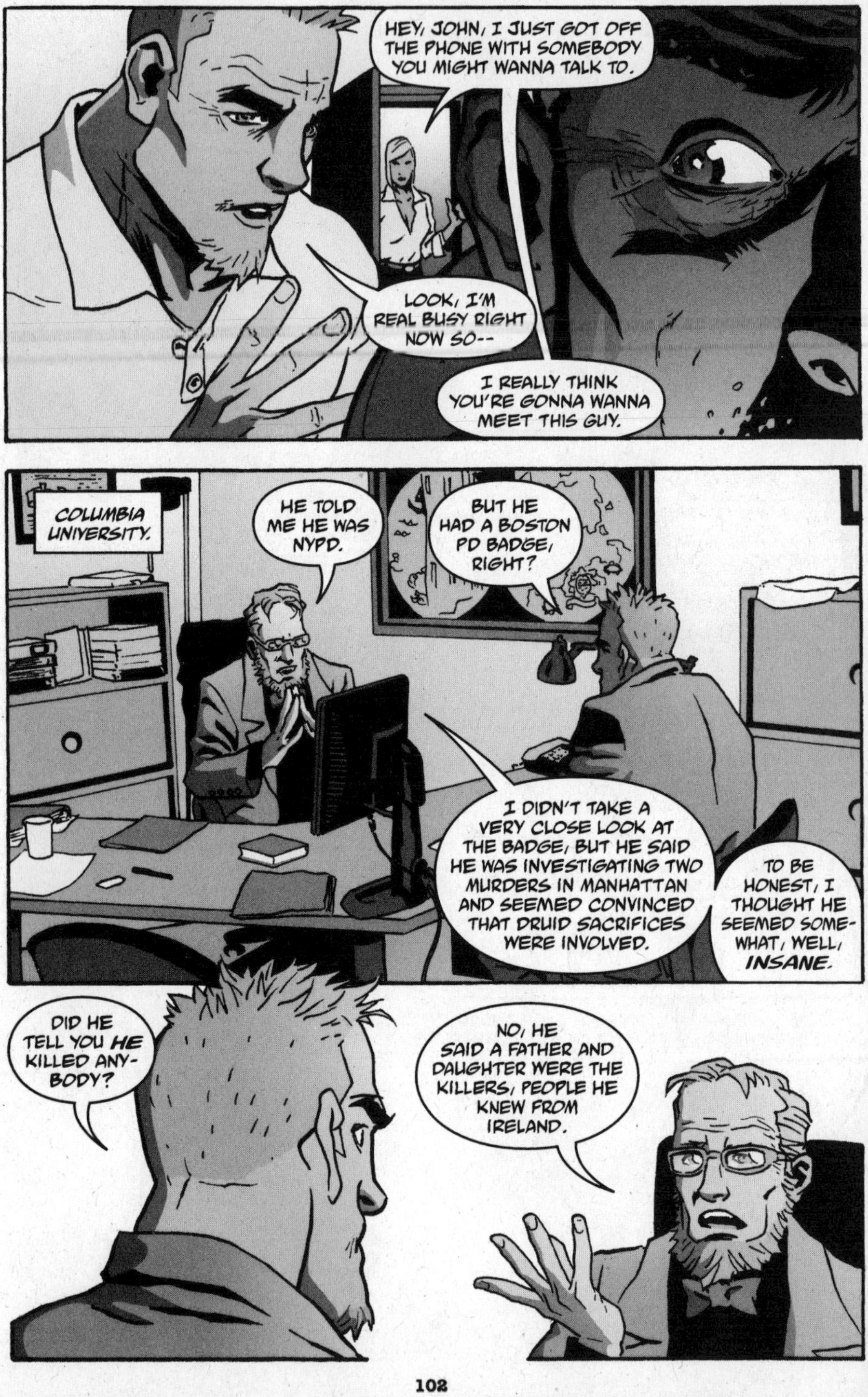
HEY, JOHN, I JUST GOT OFF THE PHONE WITH SOMEBODY YOU MIGHT WANNA TALK TO.
LOOK, I'M REAL BUSY RIGHT NOW SO--
I REALLY THINK YOU'RE GONNA WANNA MEET THIS GUY.
COLUMBIA UNIVERSITY.
HE TOLD ME HE WAS NYPD.
BUT HE HAD A BOSTON PD BADGE, RIGHT?
I DIDN'T TAKE A VERY CLOSE LOOK AT THE BADGE, BUT HE SAID HE WAS INVESTIGATING TWO MURDERS IN MANHATTAN AND SEEMED CONVINCED THAT DRUID SACRIFICES WERE INVOLVED.
TO BE HONEST, I THOUGHT HE SEEMED SOME-WHAT, WELL, *INSANE*.
DID HE TELL YOU *HE* KILLED ANY-BODY?
NO, HE SAID A FATHER AND DAUGHTER WERE THE KILLERS, PEOPLE HE KNEW FROM IRELAND.

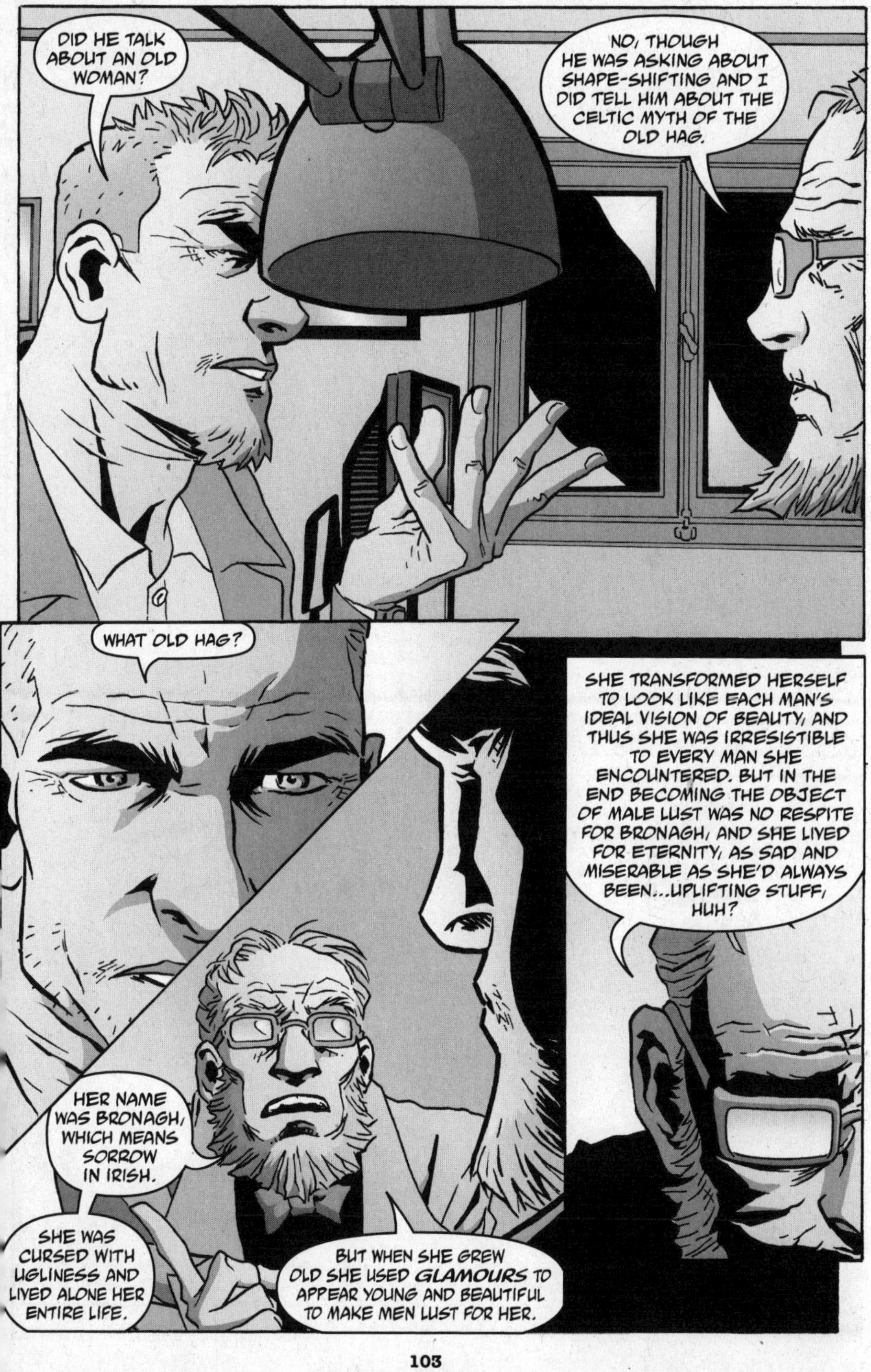
DID HE TALK ABOUT AN OLD WOMAN?
NO, THOUGH HE WAS ASKING ABOUT SHAPE-SHIFTING AND I DID TELL HIM ABOUT THE CELTIC MYTH OF THE OLD HAG.
WHAT OLD HAG?
HER NAME WAS BRONAGH, WHICH MEANS SORROW IN IRISH.
SHE WAS CURSED WITH UGLINESS AND LIVED ALONE HER ENTIRE LIFE.
BUT WHEN SHE GREW OLD SHE USED *GLAMOURS* TO APPEAR YOUNG AND BEAUTIFUL TO MAKE MEN LUST FOR HER.
SHE TRANSFORMED HERSELF TO LOOK LIKE EACH MAN'S IDEAL VISION OF BEAUTY, AND THUS SHE WAS IRRESISTIBLE TO EVERY MAN SHE ENCOUNTERED. BUT IN THE END BECOMING THE OBJECT OF MALE LUST WAS NO RESPITE FOR BRONAGH, AND SHE LIVED FOR ETERNITY, AS SAD AND MISERABLE AS SHE'D ALWAYS BEEN...UPLIFTING STUFF, HUH?

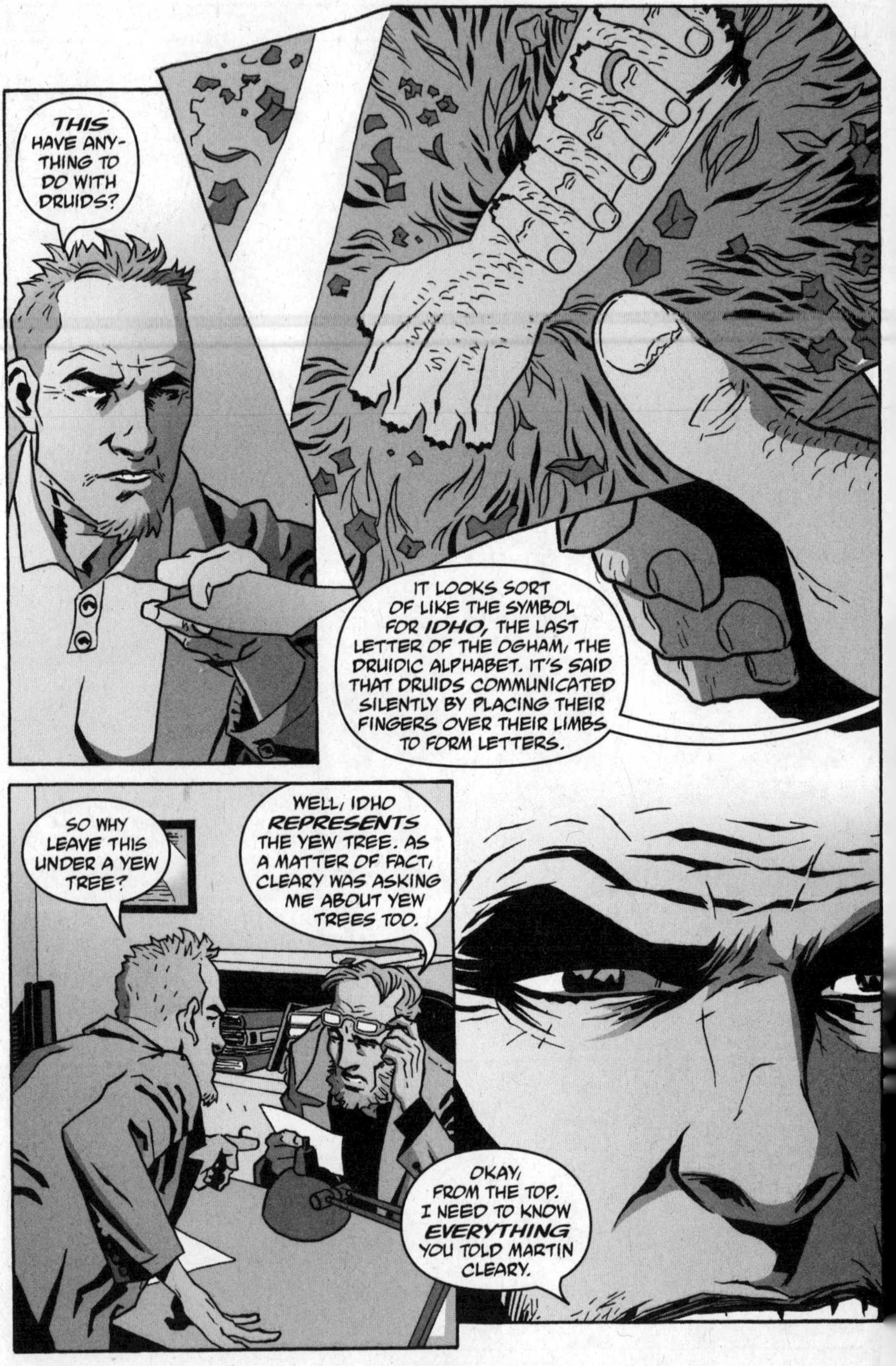
THIS HAVE ANY-THING TO DO WITH DRUIDS?
IT LOOKS SORT OF LIKE THE SYMBOL FOR IDHO, THE LAST LETTER OF THE OGHAM, THE DRUIDIC ALPHABET. IT'S SAID THAT DRUIDS COMMUNICATED SILENTLY BY PLACING THEIR FINGERS OVER THEIR LIMBS TO FORM LETTERS.
SO WHY LEAVE THIS UNDER A YEW TREE?
WELL, IDHO REPRESENTS THE YEW TREE. AS A MATTER OF FACT, CLEARY WAS ASKING ME ABOUT YEW TREES TOO.
OKAY, FROM THE TOP. I NEED TO KNOW EVERYTHING YOU TOLD MARTIN CLEARY.

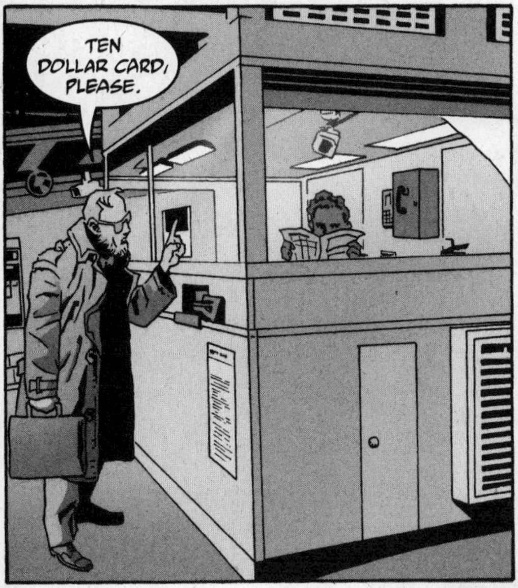
TEN DOLLAR CARD, PLEASE.

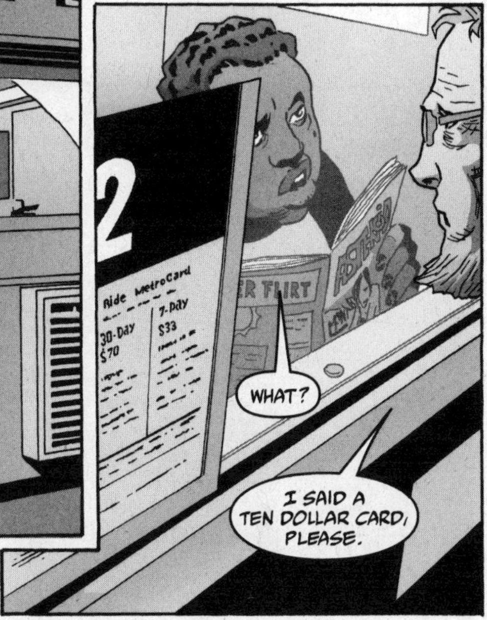
2
Ride MetroCard
30-Day $70
7-Day $33
WHAT?
I SAID A TEN DOLLAR CARD, PLEASE.

CHAPTER FIVE: GLAMOURS

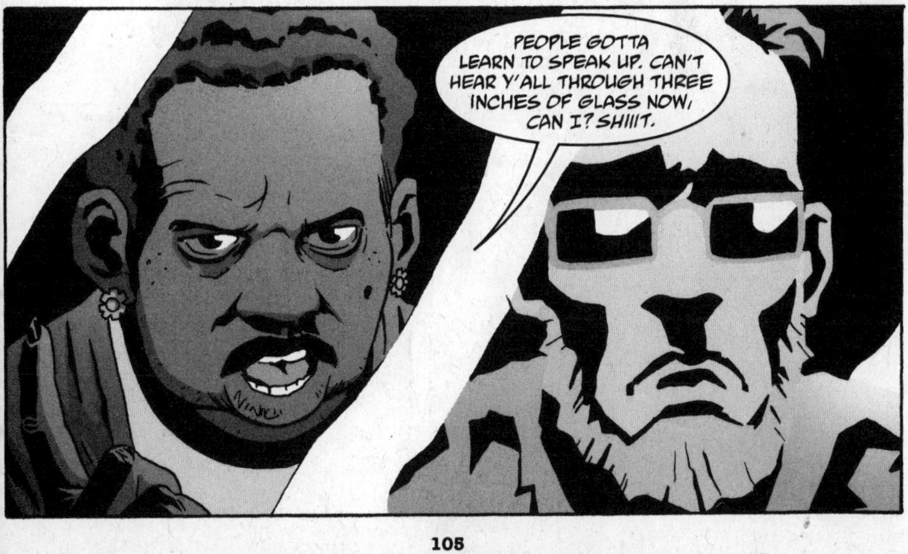
PEOPLE GOTTA LEARN TO SPEAK UP. CAN'T HEAR Y'ALL THROUGH THREE INCHES OF GLASS NOW, CAN I? SHIIIT.

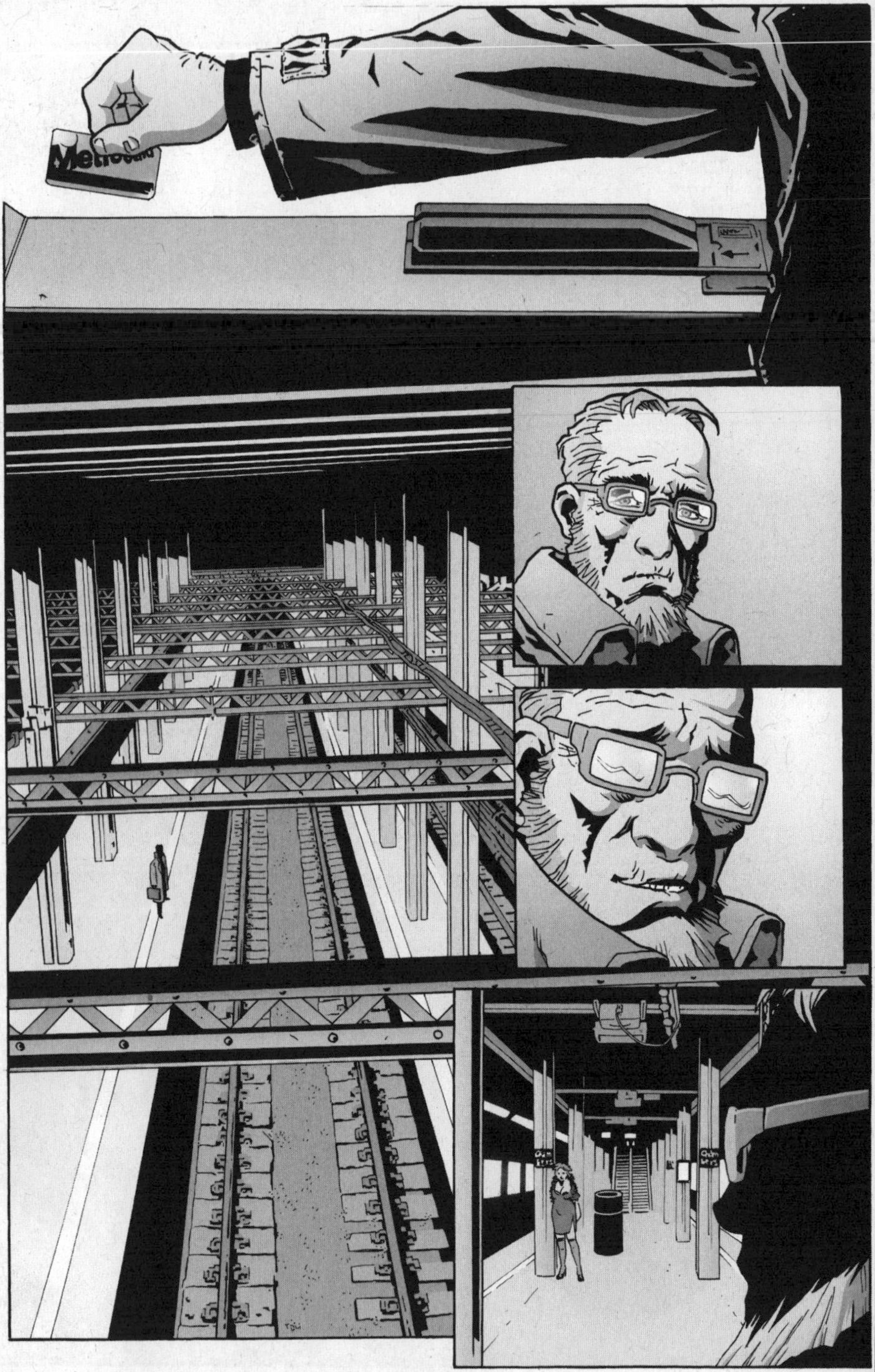

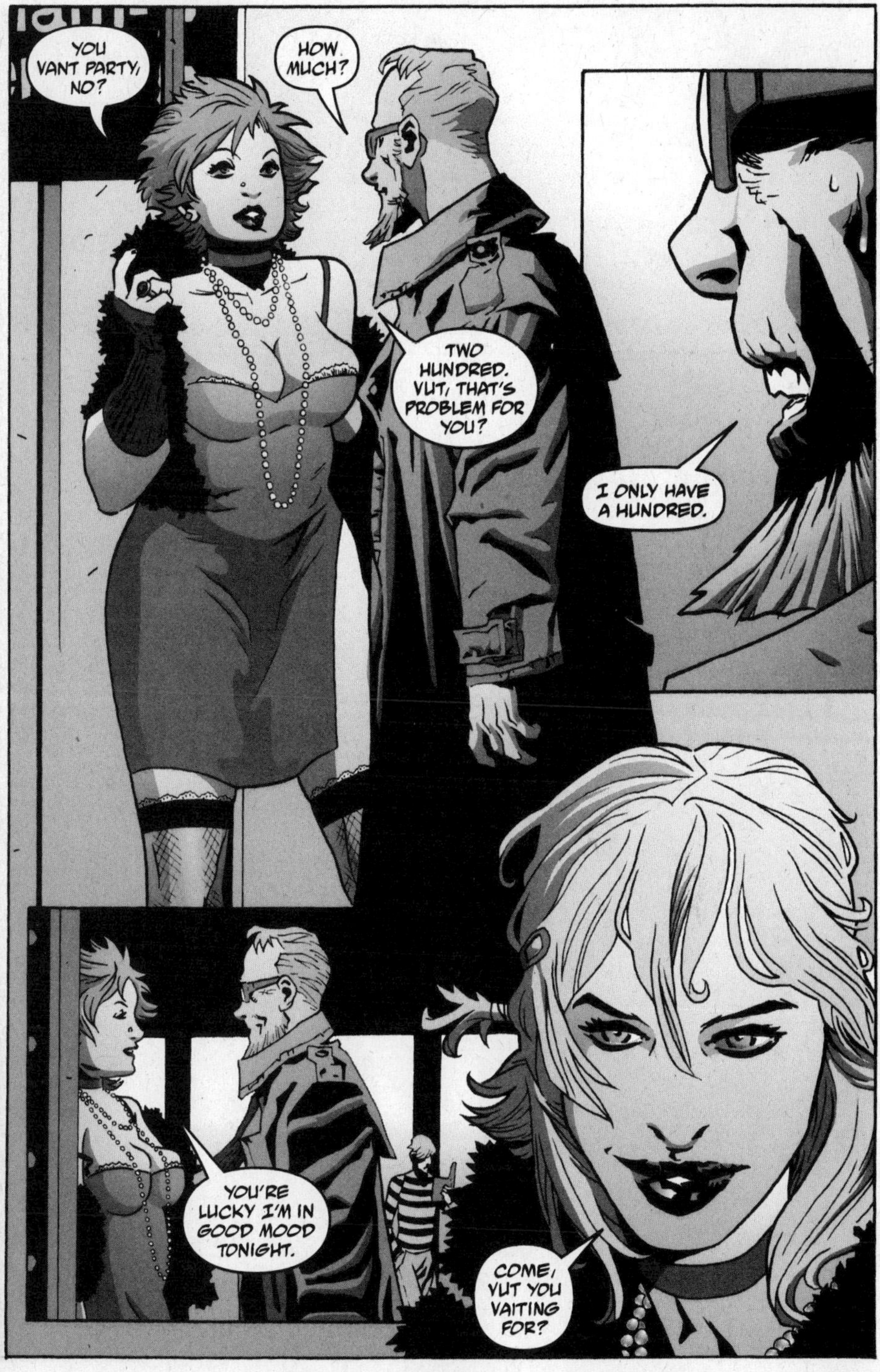
YOU VANT PARTY, NO?
HOW MUCH?
TWO HUNDRED. VUT, THAT'S PROBLEM FOR YOU?
I ONLY HAVE A HUNDRED.
YOU'RE LUCKY I'M IN GOOD MOOD TONIGHT.
COME, VUT YOU VAITING FOR?

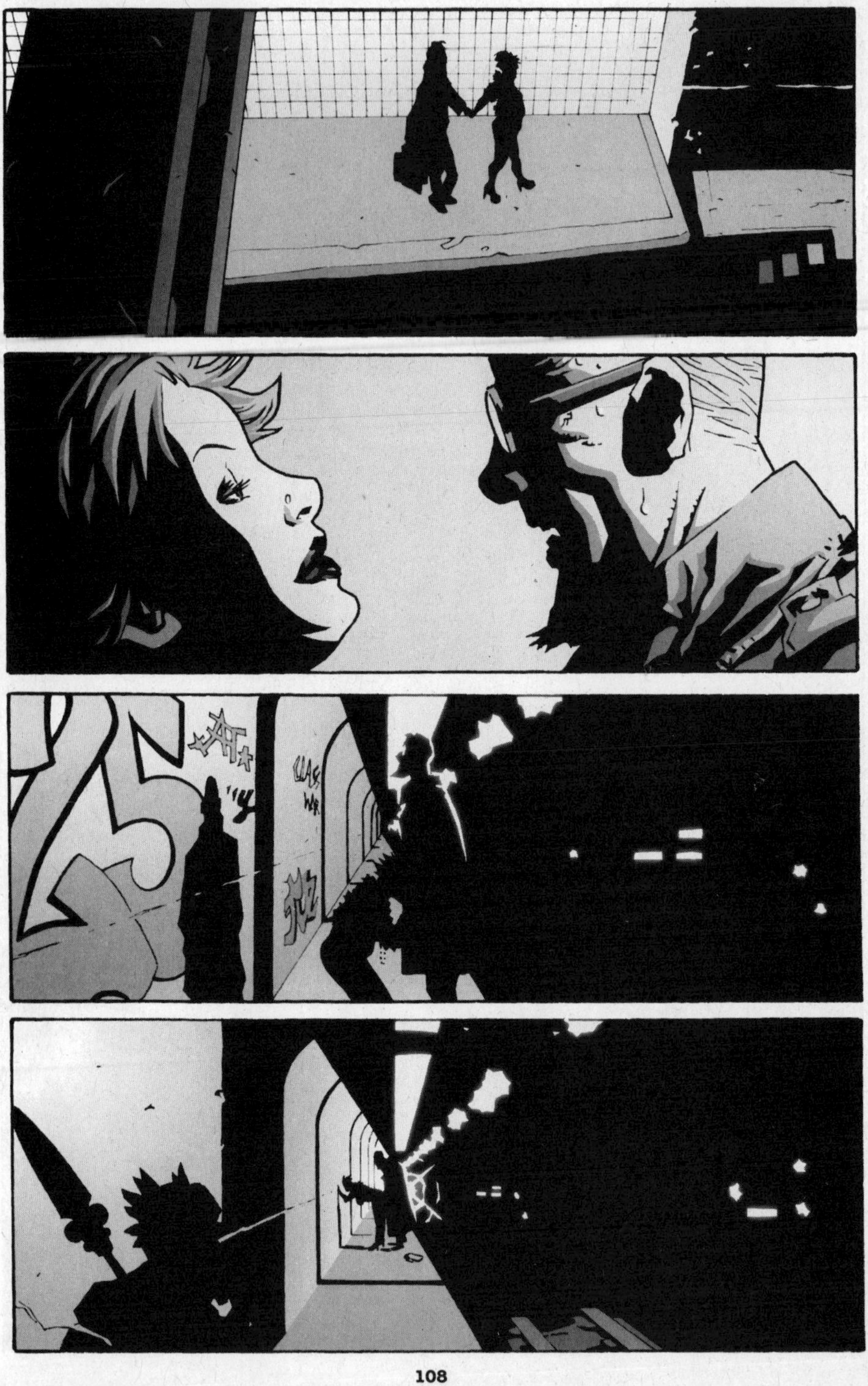

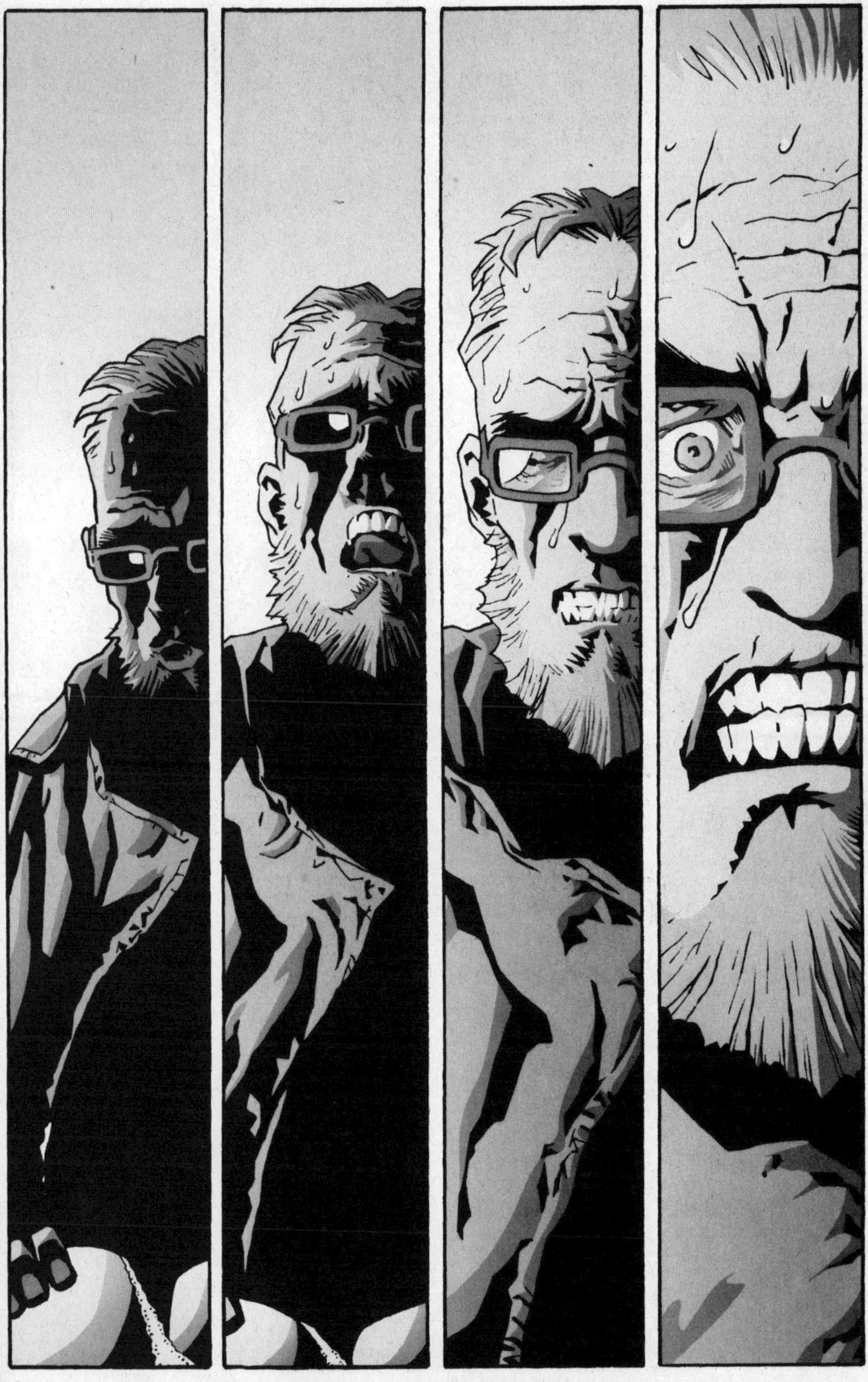

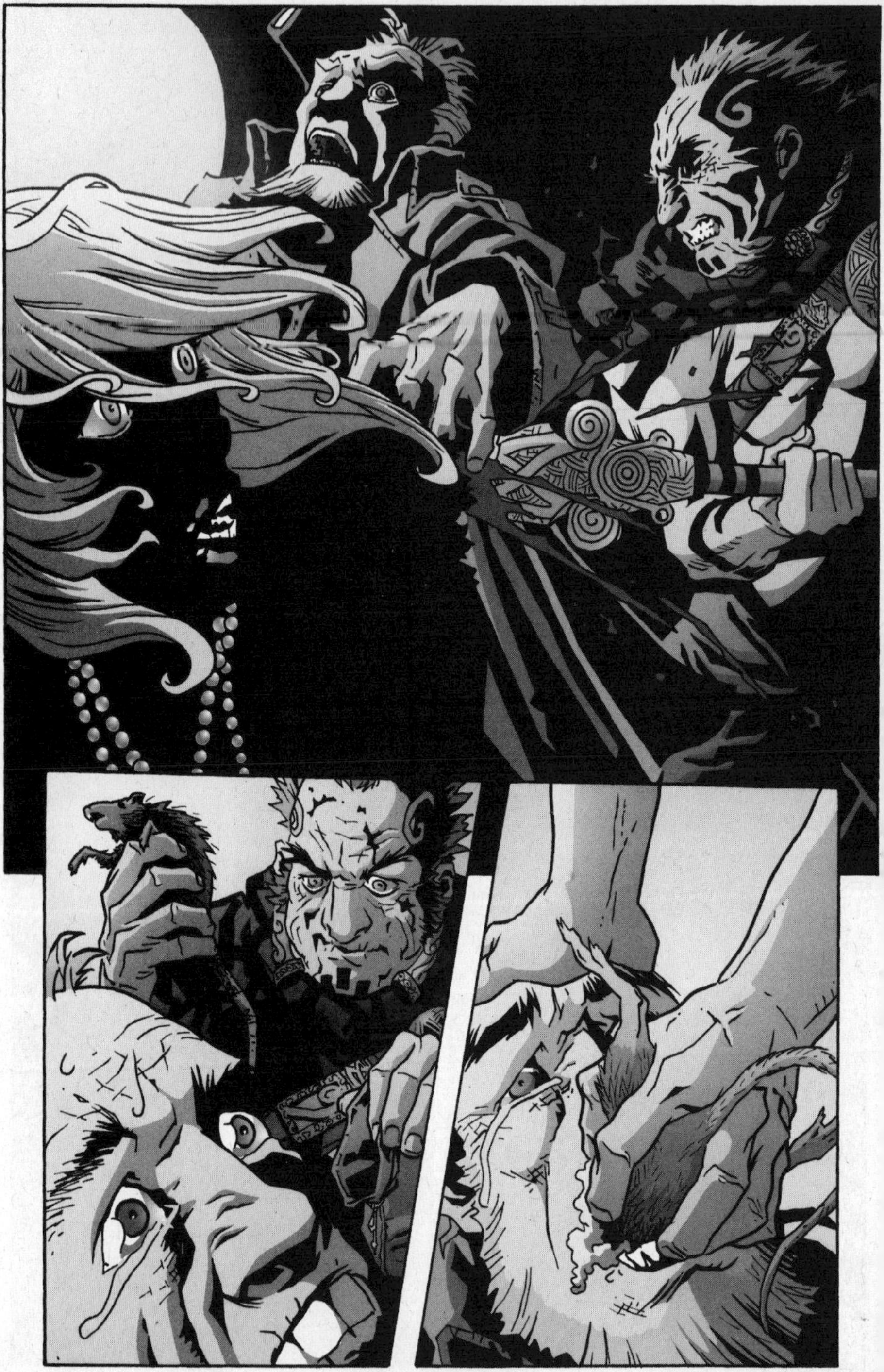

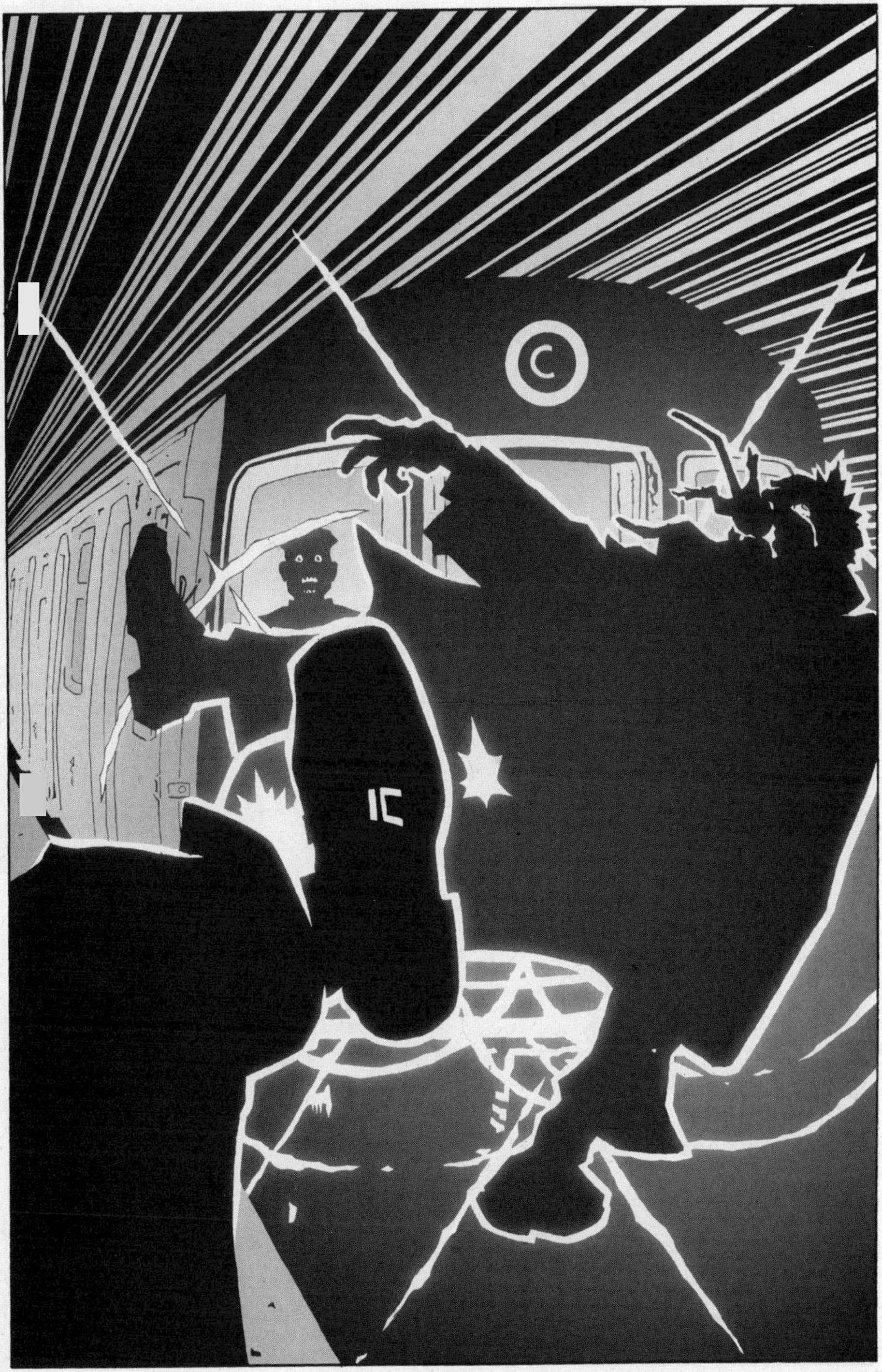
C

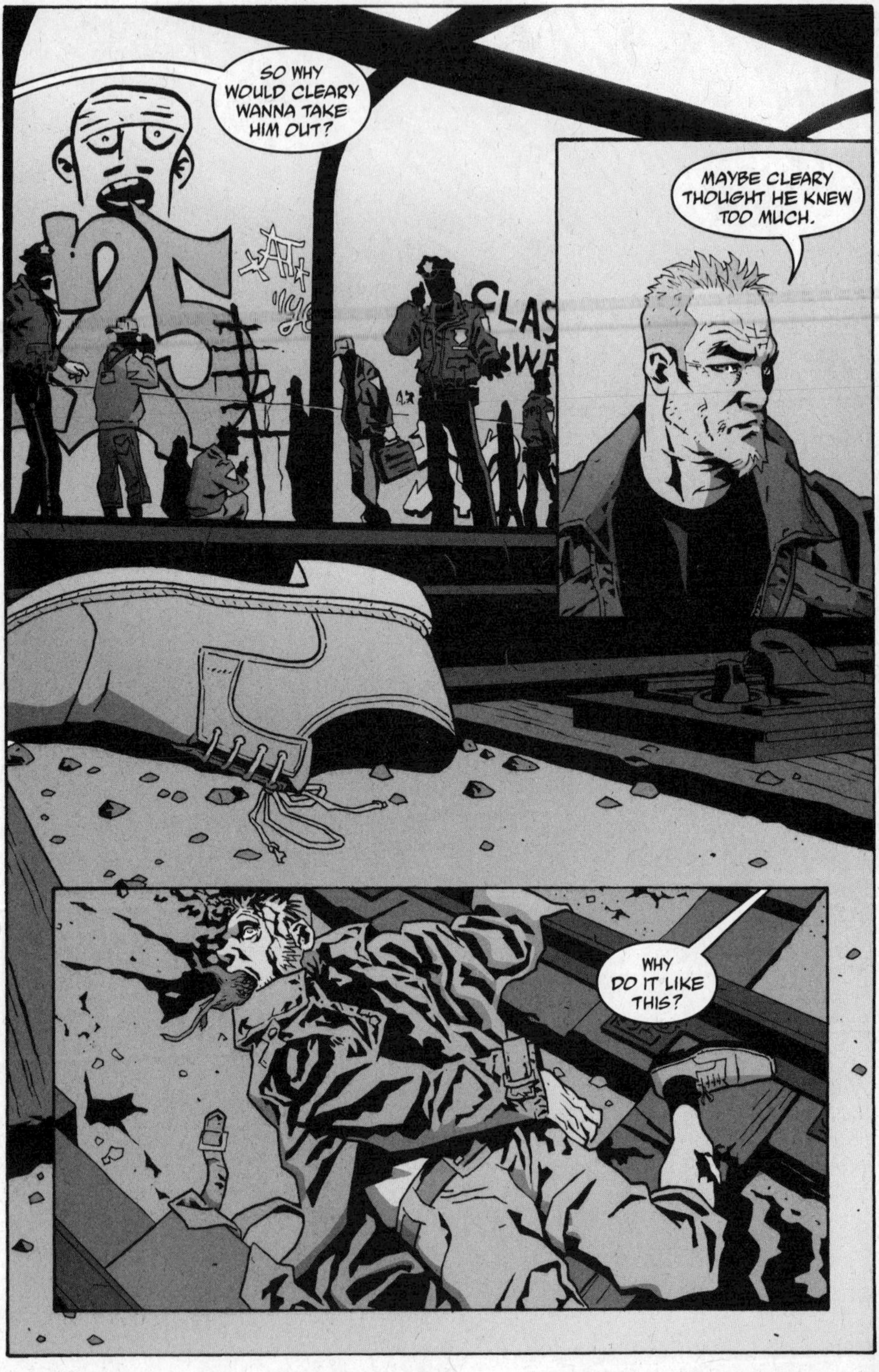
SO WHY WOULD CLEARY WANNA TAKE HIM OUT?
MAYBE CLEARY THOUGHT HE KNEW TOO MUCH.
WHY DO IT LIKE THIS?

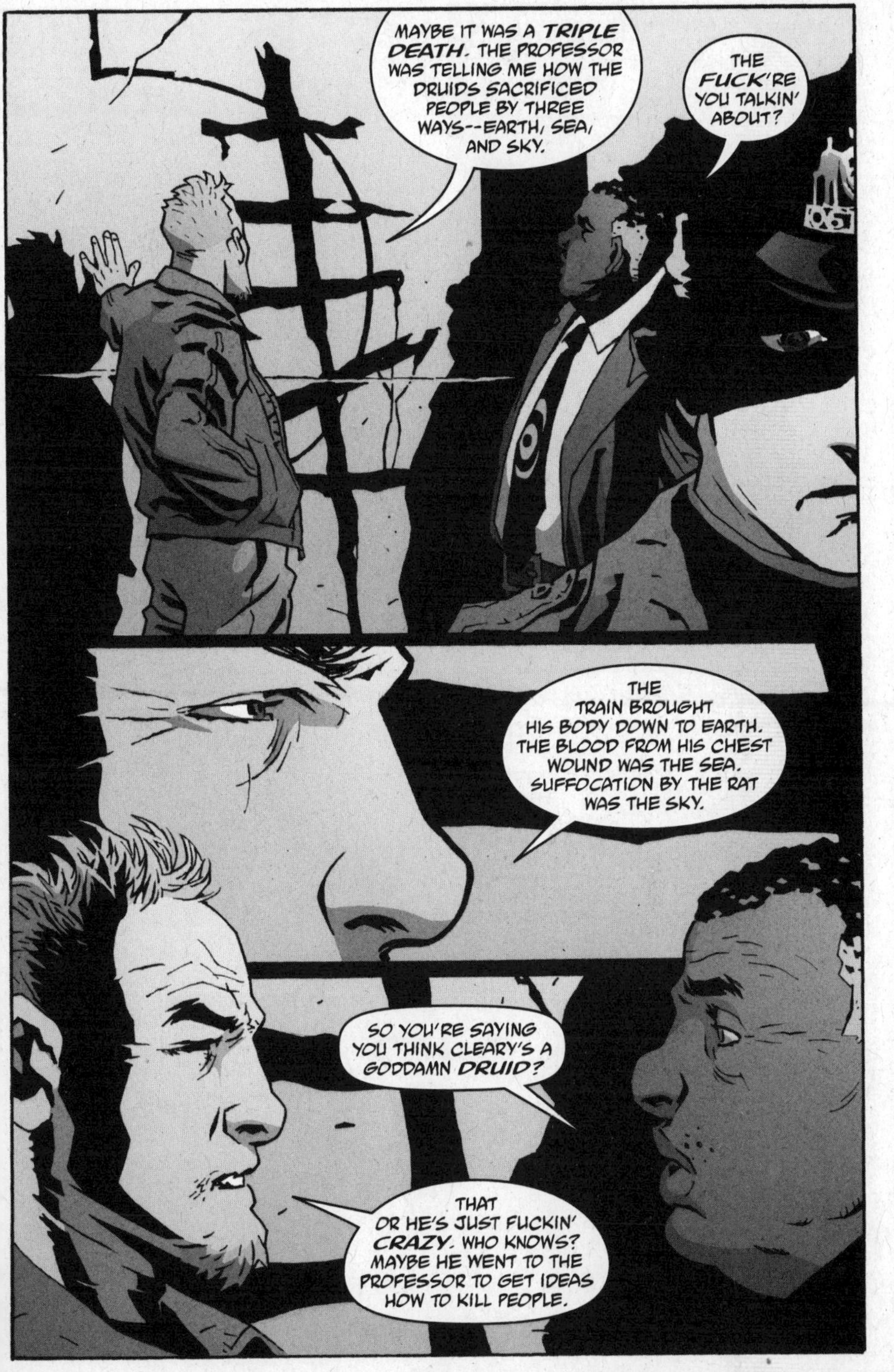
MAYBE IT WAS A TRIPLE DEATH. THE PROFESSOR WAS TELLING ME HOW THE DRUIDS SACRIFICED PEOPLE BY THREE WAYS--EARTH, SEA, AND SKY.
THE FUCK'RE YOU TALKIN' ABOUT?
THE TRAIN BROUGHT HIS BODY DOWN TO EARTH. THE BLOOD FROM HIS CHEST WOUND WAS THE SEA. SUFFOCATION BY THE RAT WAS THE SKY.
SO YOU'RE SAYING YOU THINK CLEARY'S A GODDAMN DRUID?
THAT OR HE'S JUST FUCKIN' CRAZY. WHO KNOWS? MAYBE HE WENT TO THE PROFESSOR TO GET IDEAS HOW TO KILL PEOPLE.

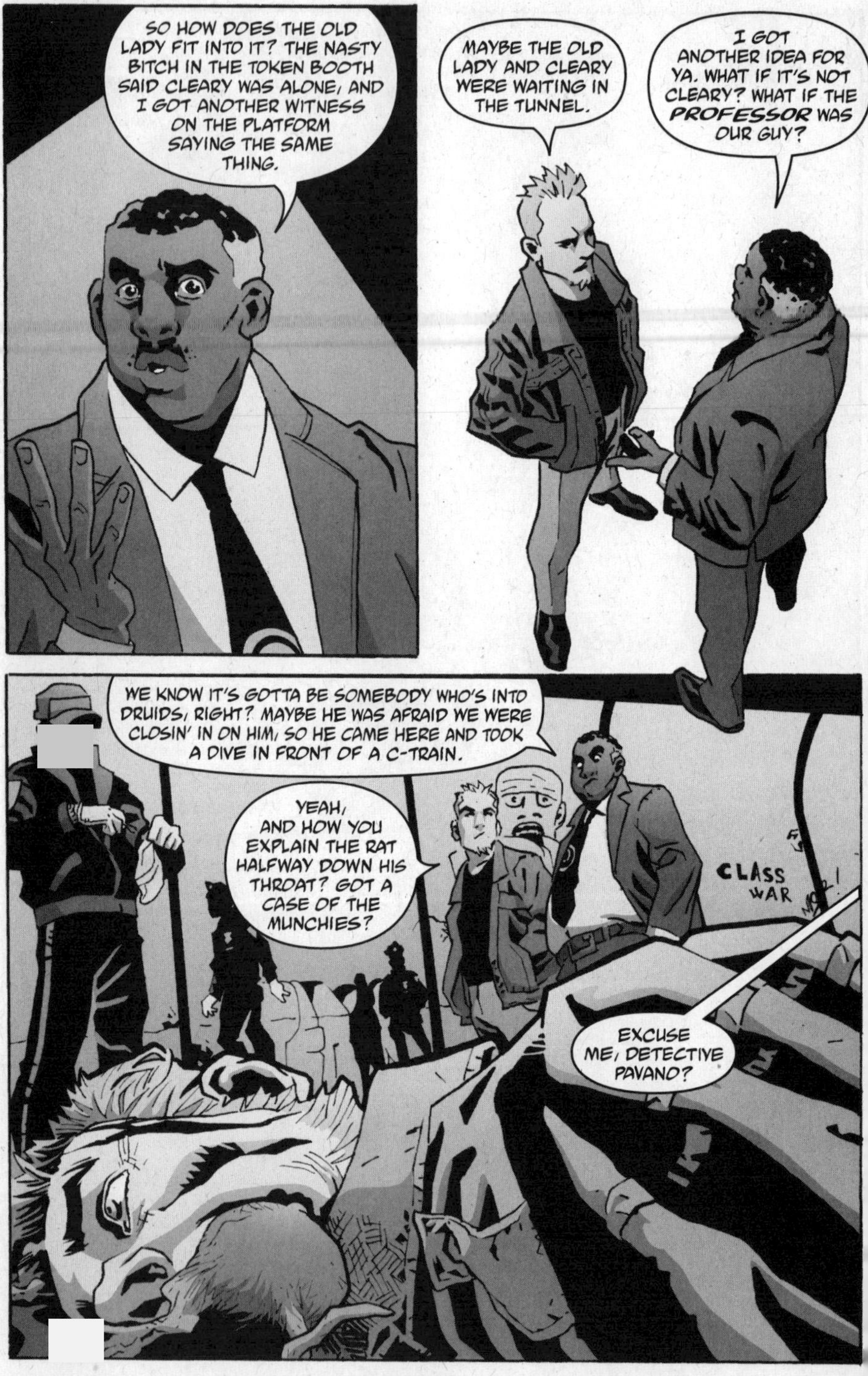

SO HOW DOES THE OLD LADY FIT INTO IT? THE NASTY BITCH IN THE TOKEN BOOTH SAID CLEARY WAS ALONE, AND I GOT ANOTHER WITNESS ON THE PLATFORM SAYING THE SAME THING.
MAYBE THE OLD LADY AND CLEARY WERE WAITING IN THE TUNNEL.
I GOT ANOTHER IDEA FOR YA. WHAT IF IT'S NOT CLEARY? WHAT IF THE PROFESSOR WAS OUR GUY?
WE KNOW IT'S GOTTA BE SOMEBODY WHO'S INTO DRUIDS, RIGHT? MAYBE HE WAS AFRAID WE WERE CLOSIN' IN ON HIM, SO HE CAME HERE AND TOOK A DIVE IN FRONT OF A C-TRAIN.
YEAH, AND HOW YOU EXPLAIN THE RAT HALFWAY DOWN HIS THROAT? GOT A CASE OF THE MUNCHIES?
CLASS WAR
EXCUSE ME, DETECTIVE PAVANO?

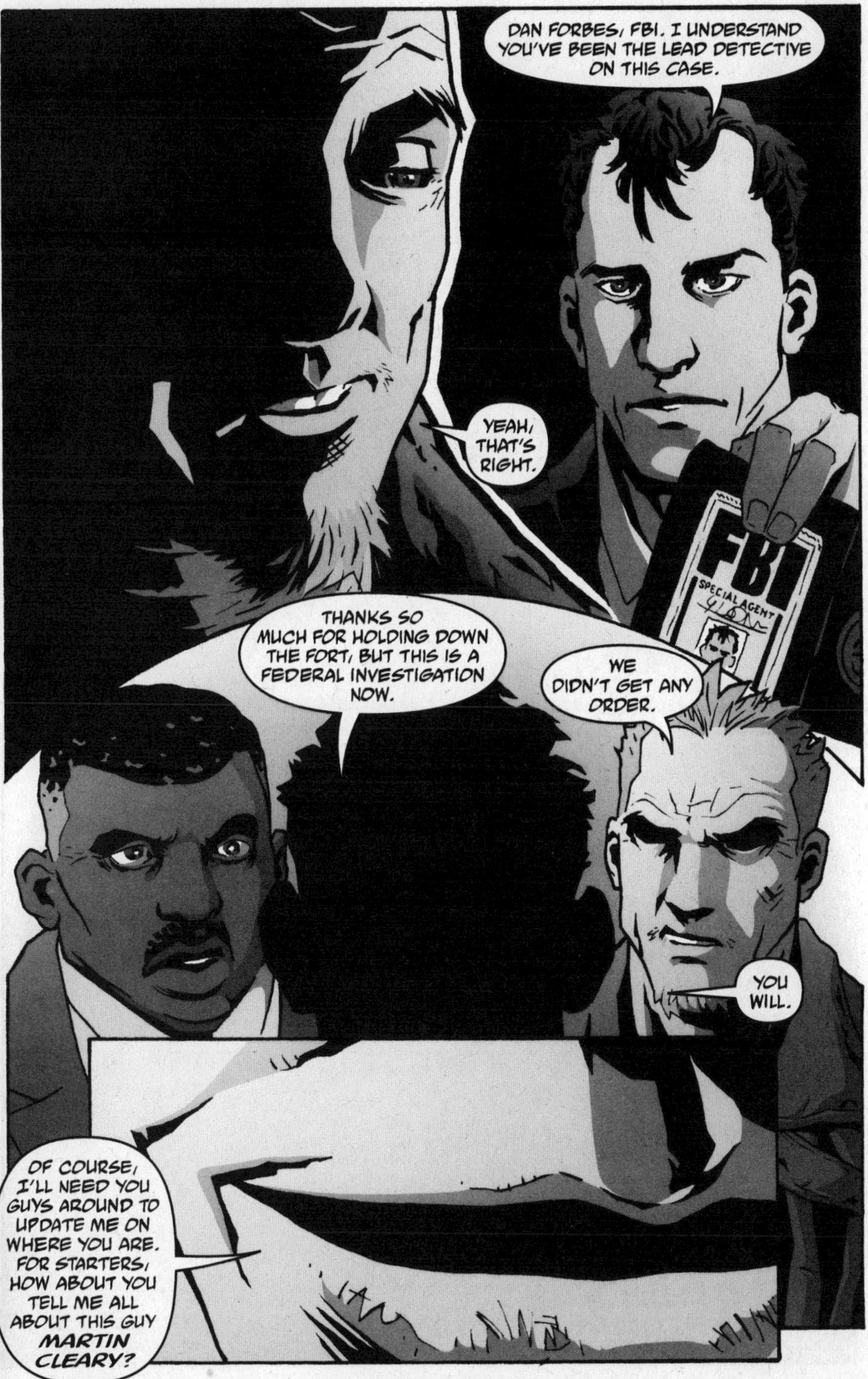
DAN FORBES, FBI. I UNDERSTAND YOU'VE BEEN THE LEAD DETECTIVE ON THIS CASE.
YEAH, THAT'S RIGHT.
FBI
SPECIAL AGENT
THANKS SO MUCH FOR HOLDING DOWN THE FORT, BUT THIS IS A FEDERAL INVESTIGATION NOW.
WE DIDN'T GET ANY ORDER.
YOU WILL.
OF COURSE, I'LL NEED YOU GUYS AROUND TO UPDATE ME ON WHERE YOU ARE. FOR STARTERS, HOW ABOUT YOU TELL ME ALL ABOUT THIS GUY *MARTIN CLEARY*?

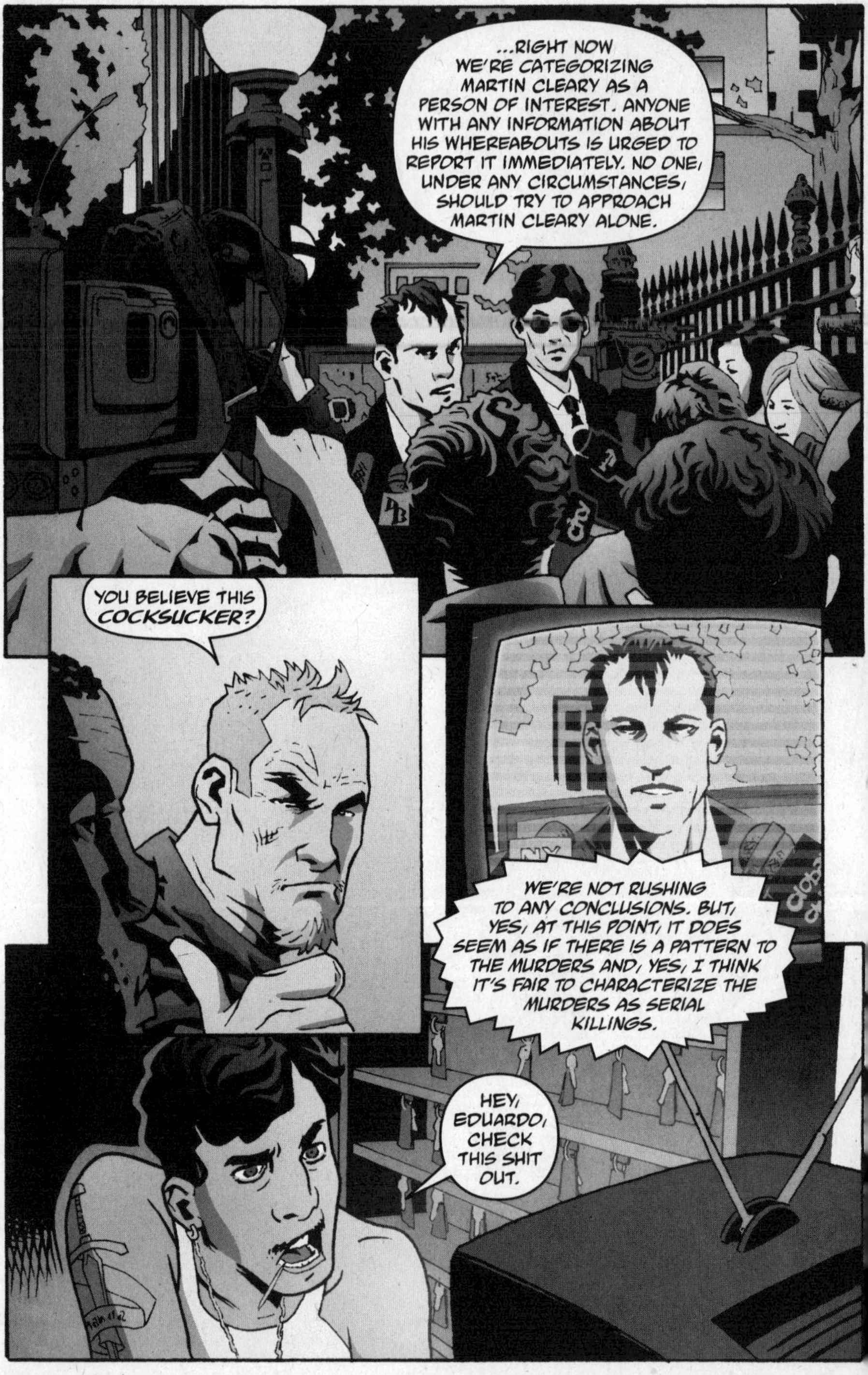
...RIGHT NOW WE'RE CATEGORIZING MARTIN CLEARY AS A PERSON OF INTEREST. ANYONE WITH ANY INFORMATION ABOUT HIS WHEREABOUTS IS URGED TO REPORT IT IMMEDIATELY. NO ONE, UNDER ANY CIRCUMSTANCES, SHOULD TRY TO APPROACH MARTIN CLEARY ALONE.
YOU BELIEVE THIS *COCKSUCKER?*
WE'RE NOT RUSHING TO ANY CONCLUSIONS. BUT, YES, AT THIS POINT, IT DOES SEEM AS IF THERE IS A PATTERN TO THE MURDERS AND, YES, I THINK IT'S FAIR TO CHARACTERIZE THE MURDERS AS SERIAL KILLINGS.
HEY, EDUARDO, CHECK THIS SHIT OUT.

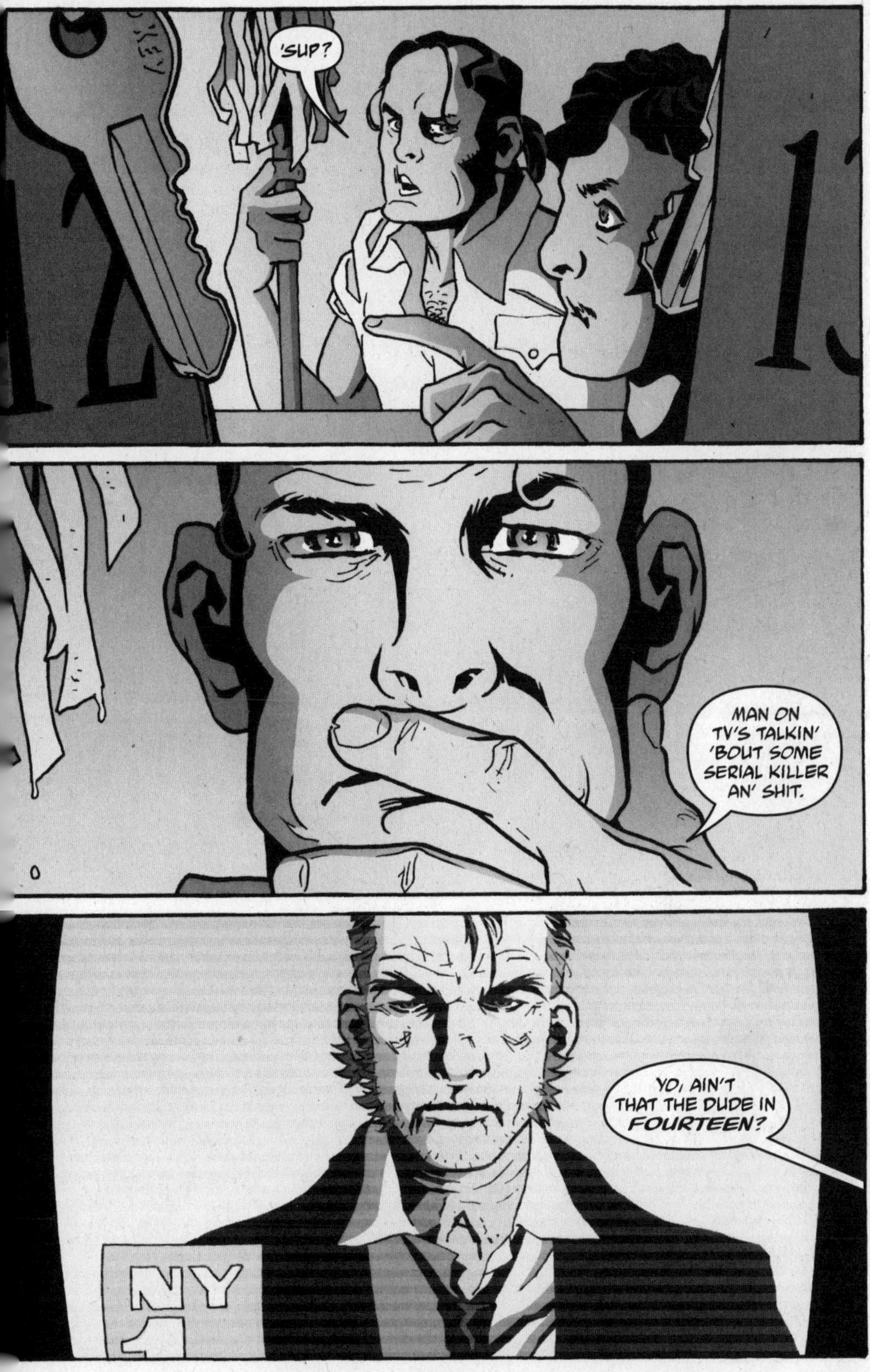
'SUP?
MAN ON TV'S TALKIN' 'BOUT SOME SERIAL KILLER AN' SHIT.
YO, AIN'T THAT THE DUDE IN FOURTEEN?
NY 1

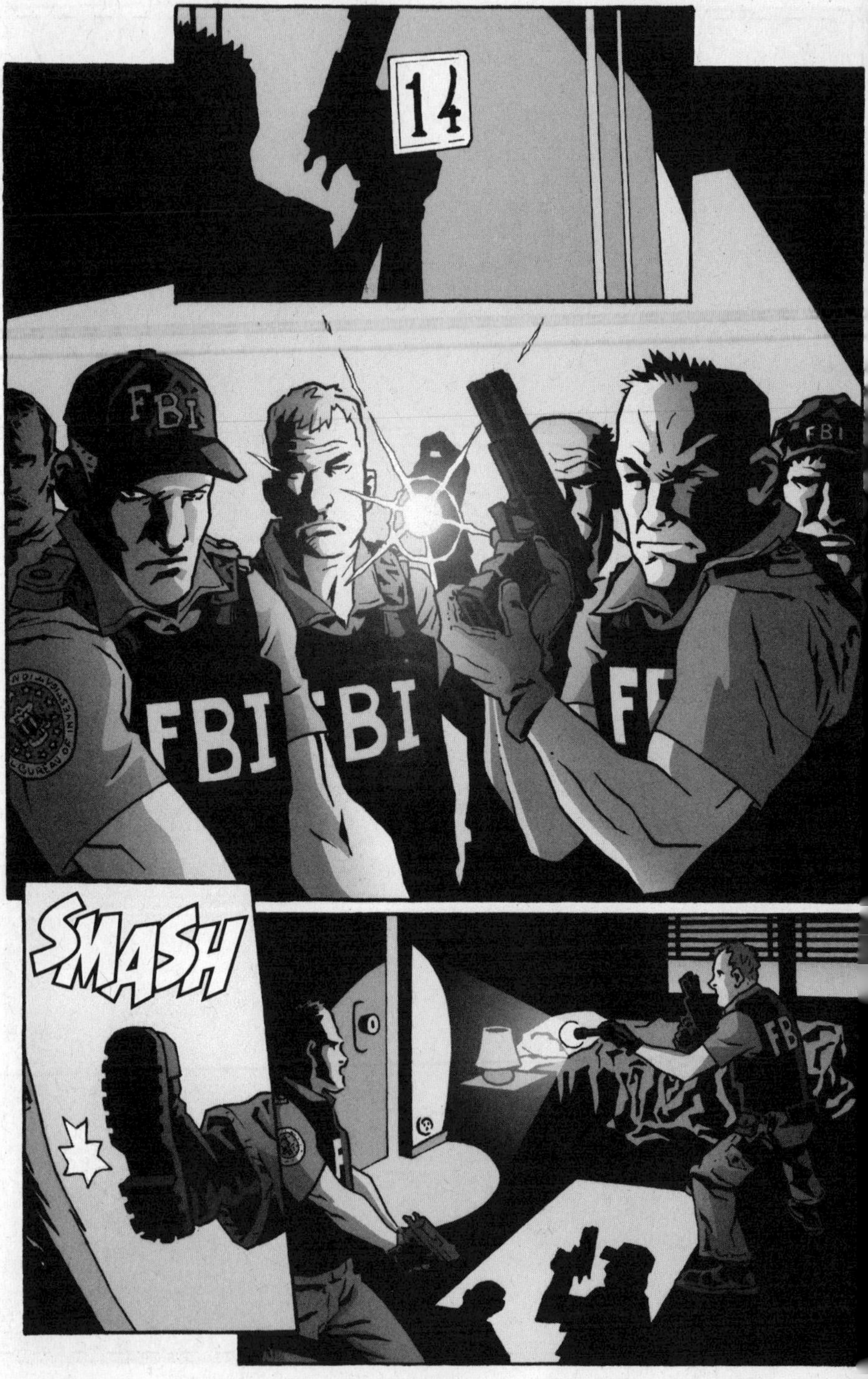
14
FBI
FBI
FBI
FBI
SMASH

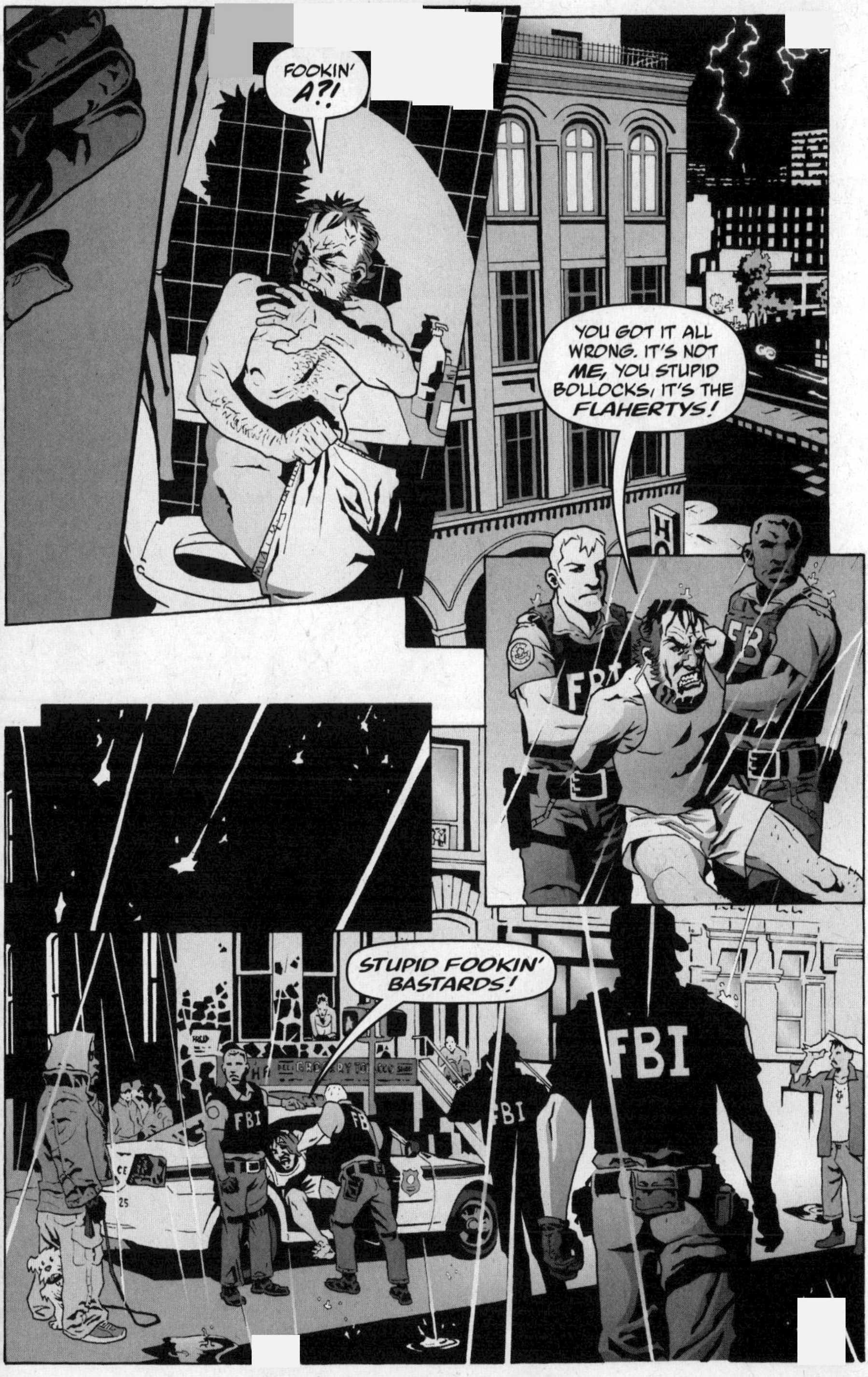
FOOKIN' A?!
YOU GOT IT ALL WRONG. IT'S NOT ME, YOU STUPID BOLLOCKS, IT'S THE FLAHERTYS!
FBI
STUPID FOOKIN' BASTARDS!
FBI
FBI
FBI

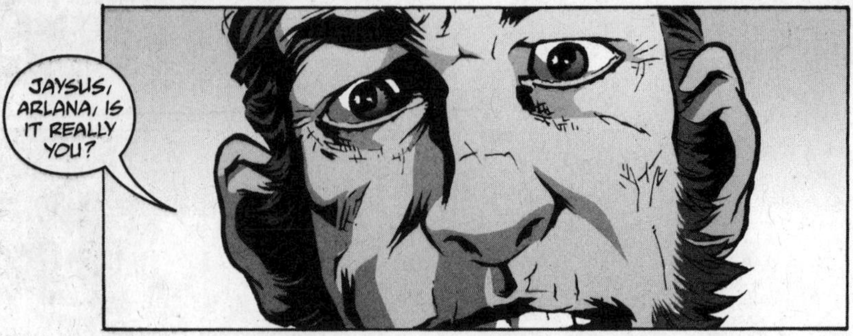
JAYSUS, ARLANA, IS IT REALLY YOU?

CHAPTER SIX: THE VISIT

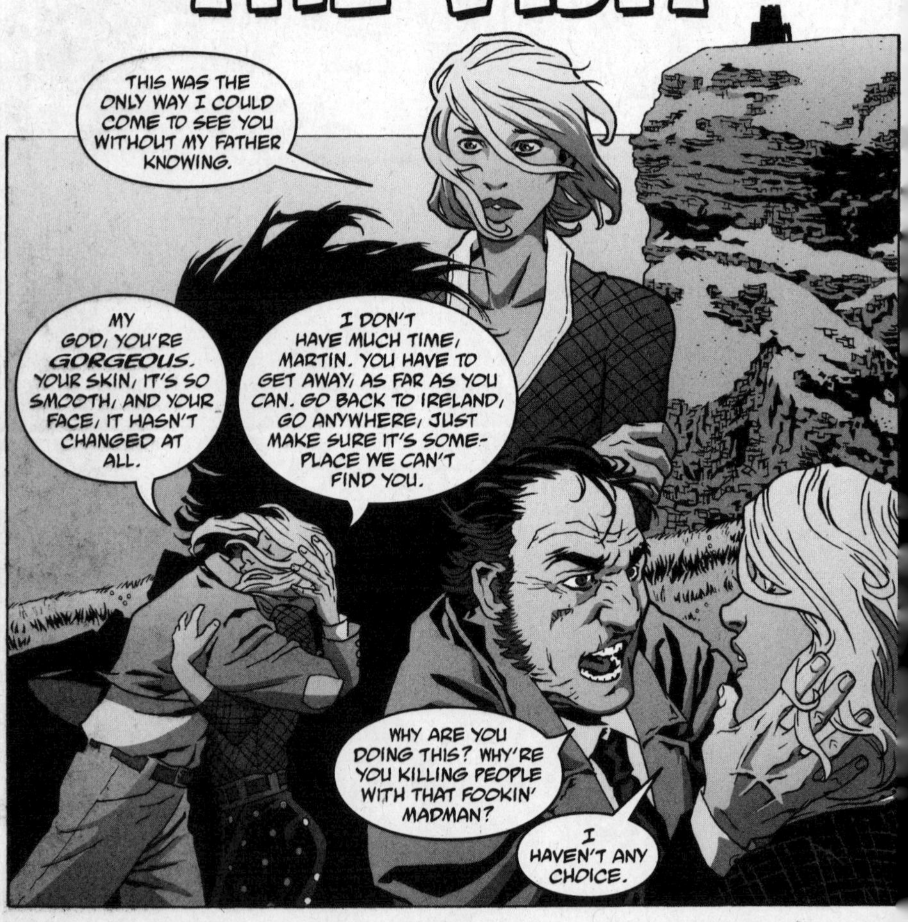
THIS WAS THE ONLY WAY I COULD COME TO SEE YOU WITHOUT MY FATHER KNOWING.
MY GOD, YOU'RE *GORGEOUS*. YOUR SKIN, IT'S SO SMOOTH, AND YOUR FACE, IT HASN'T CHANGED AT ALL.
I DON'T HAVE MUCH TIME, MARTIN. YOU HAVE TO GET AWAY, AS FAR AS YOU CAN. GO BACK TO IRELAND, GO ANYWHERE, JUST MAKE SURE IT'S SOME-PLACE WE CAN'T FIND YOU.
WHY ARE YOU DOING THIS? WHY'RE YOU KILLING PEOPLE WITH THAT FOOKIN' MADMAN?
I HAVEN'T ANY CHOICE.

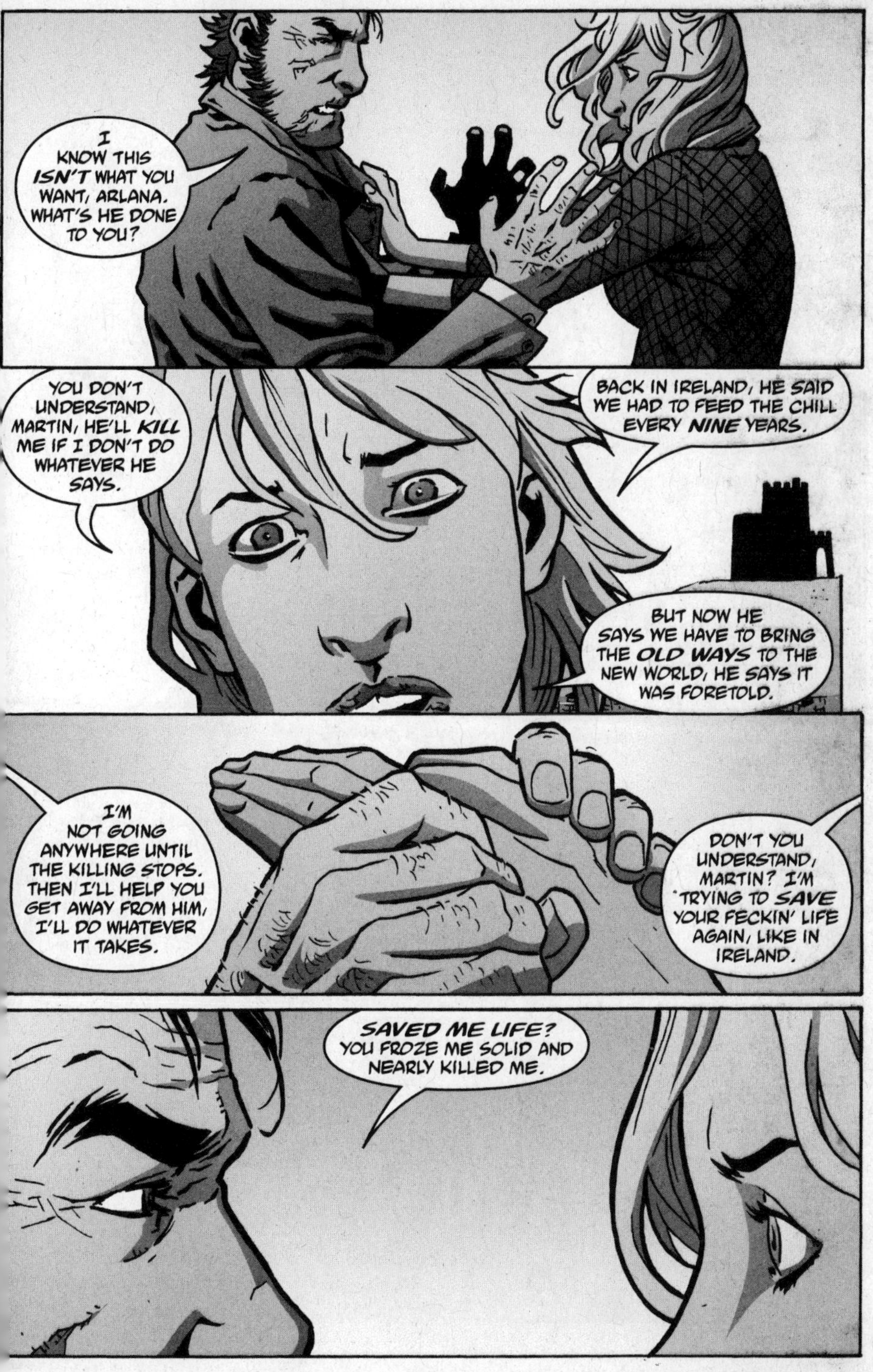
I KNOW THIS ISN'T WHAT YOU WANT, ARLANA. WHAT'S HE DONE TO YOU?
YOU DON'T UNDERSTAND, MARTIN, HE'LL KILL ME IF I DON'T DO WHATEVER HE SAYS.
BACK IN IRELAND, HE SAID WE HAD TO FEED THE CHILL EVERY NINE YEARS.
BUT NOW HE SAYS WE HAVE TO BRING THE OLD WAYS TO THE NEW WORLD, HE SAYS IT WAS FORETOLD.
I'M NOT GOING ANYWHERE UNTIL THE KILLING STOPS. THEN I'LL HELP YOU GET AWAY FROM HIM, I'LL DO WHATEVER IT TAKES.
DON'T YOU UNDERSTAND, MARTIN? I'M TRYING TO SAVE YOUR FECKIN' LIFE AGAIN, LIKE IN IRELAND.
SAVED ME LIFE? YOU FROZE ME SOLID AND NEARLY KILLED ME.

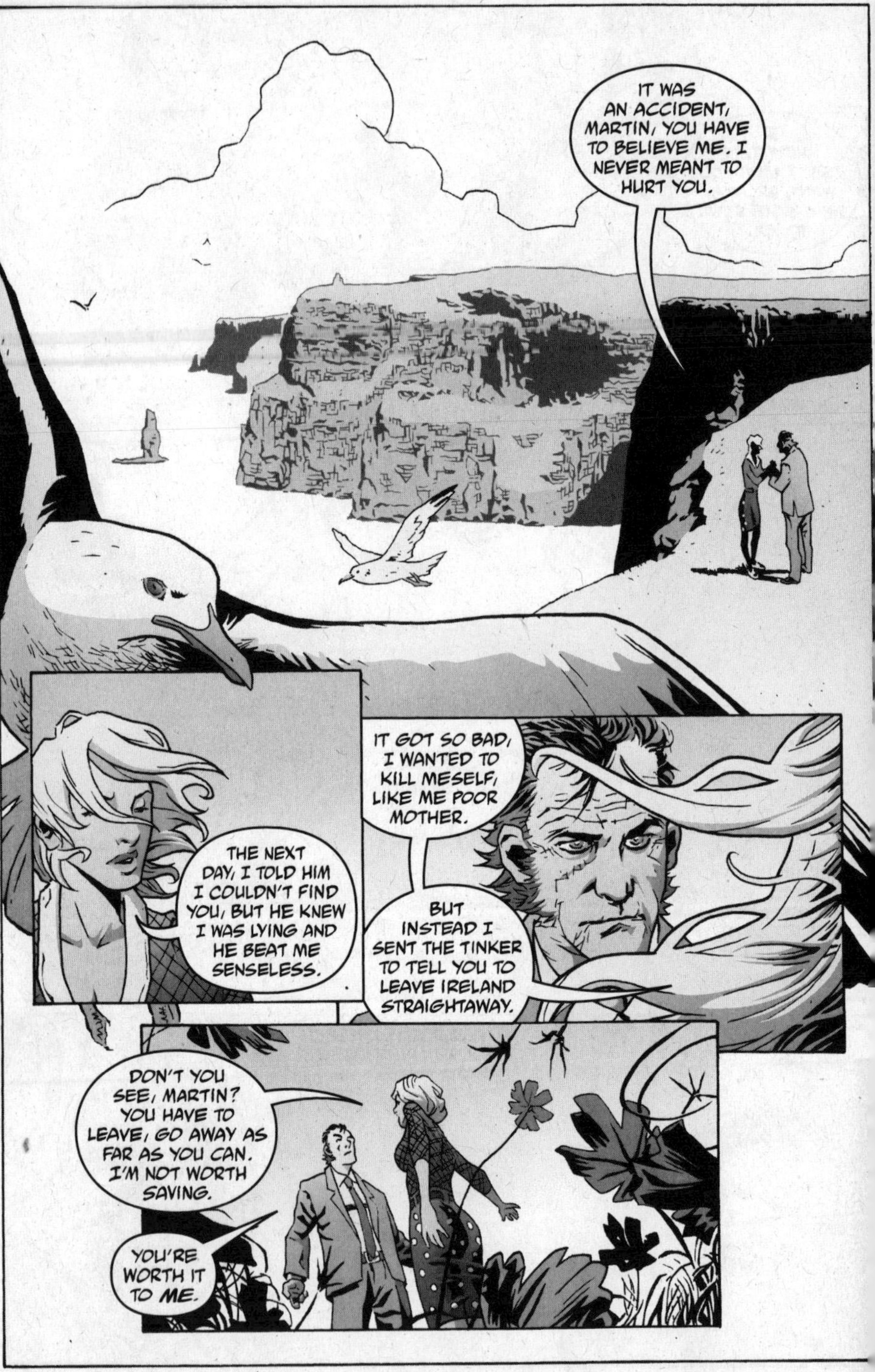
IT WAS AN ACCIDENT, MARTIN, YOU HAVE TO BELIEVE ME. I NEVER MEANT TO HURT YOU.
THE NEXT DAY, I TOLD HIM I COULDN'T FIND YOU, BUT HE KNEW I WAS LYING AND HE BEAT ME SENSELESS.
IT GOT SO BAD, I WANTED TO KILL MESELF, LIKE ME POOR MOTHER.
BUT INSTEAD I SENT THE TINKER TO TELL YOU TO LEAVE IRELAND STRAIGHTAWAY.
DON'T YOU SEE, MARTIN? YOU HAVE TO LEAVE, GO AWAY AS FAR AS YOU CAN. I'M NOT WORTH SAVING.
YOU'RE WORTH IT TO *ME*.

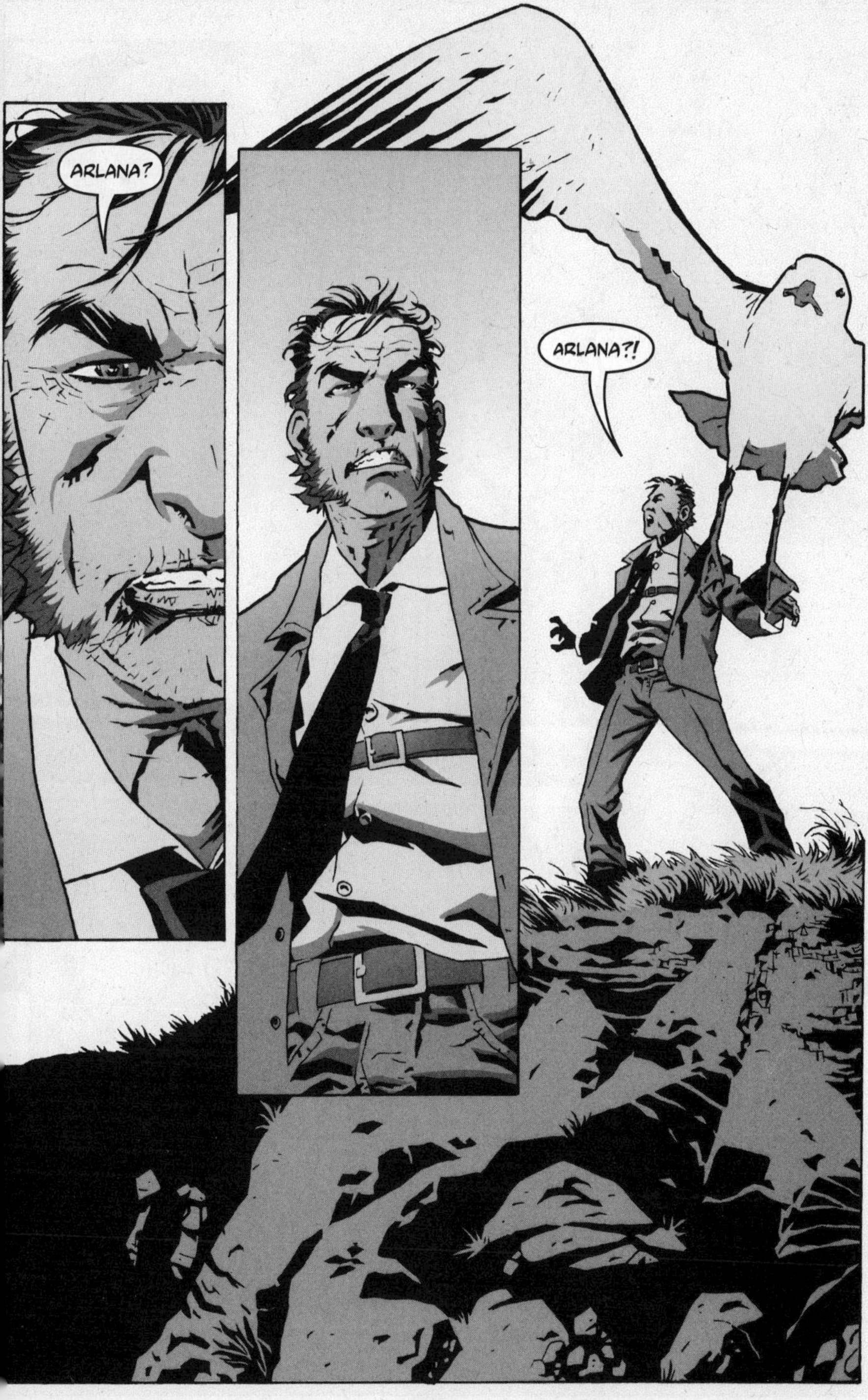
ARLANA?
ARLANA?!

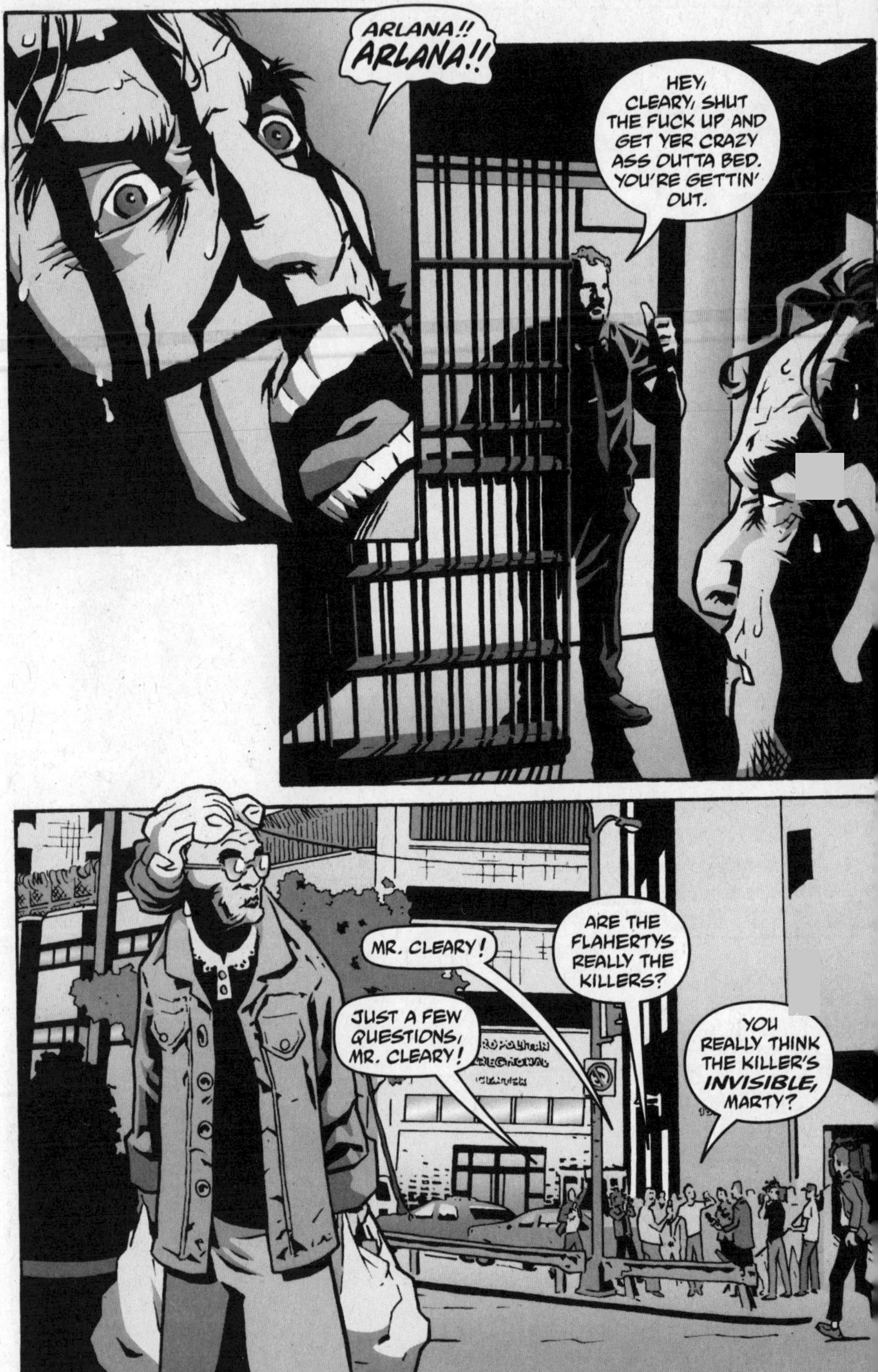
ARLANA!! ARLANA!!
HEY, CLEARY, SHUT THE FUCK UP AND GET YER CRAZY ASS OUTTA BED. YOU'RE GETTIN' OUT.
MR. CLEARY!
JUST A FEW QUESTIONS, MR. CLEARY!
ARE THE FLAHERTYS REALLY THE KILLERS?
YOU REALLY THINK THE KILLER'S *INVISIBLE,* MARTY?

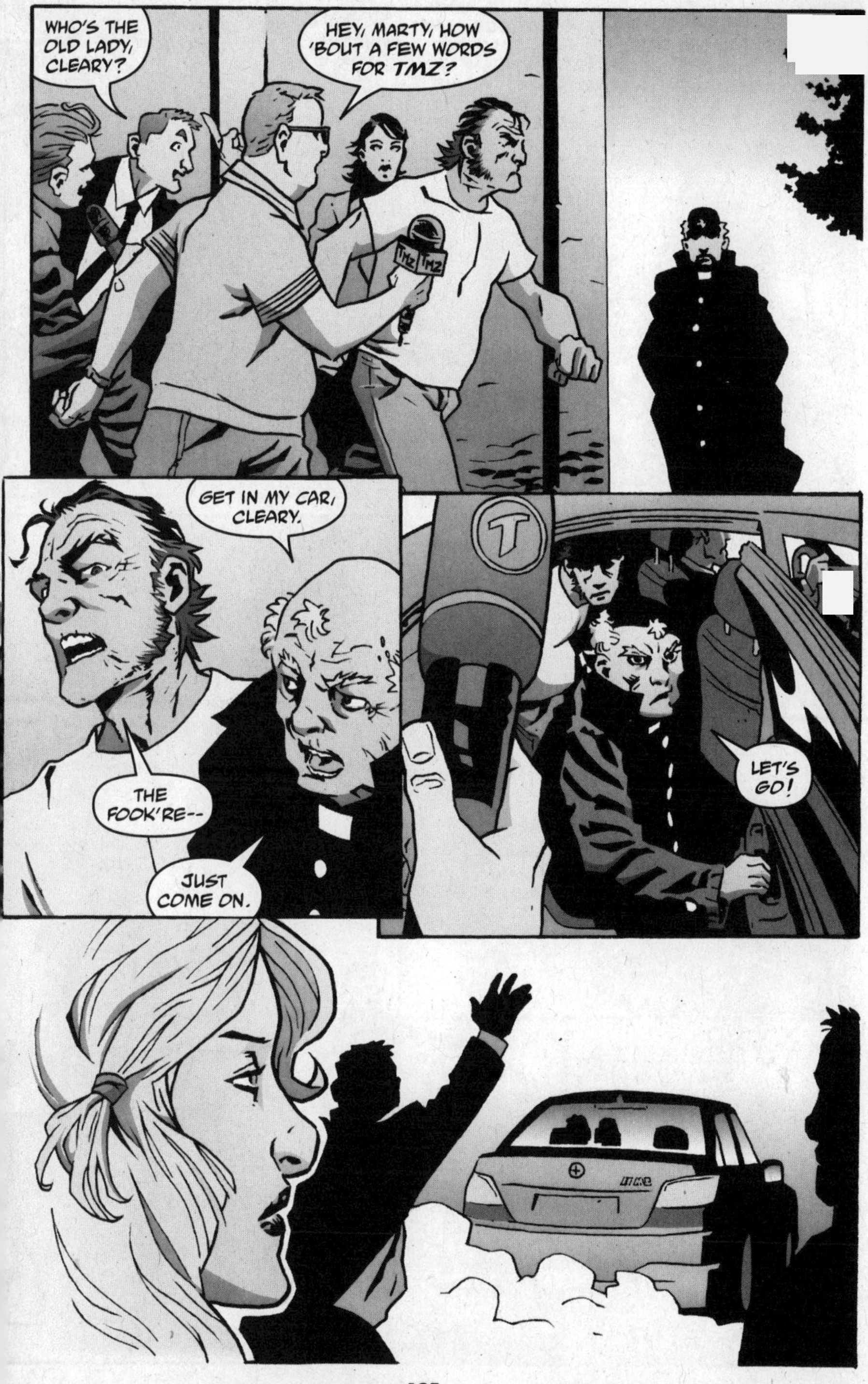
WHO'S THE OLD LADY, CLEARY?
HEY, MARTY, HOW 'BOUT A FEW WORDS FOR TMZ?
TMZ
GET IN MY CAR, CLEARY.
THE FOOK'RE--
JUST COME ON.
LET'S GO!

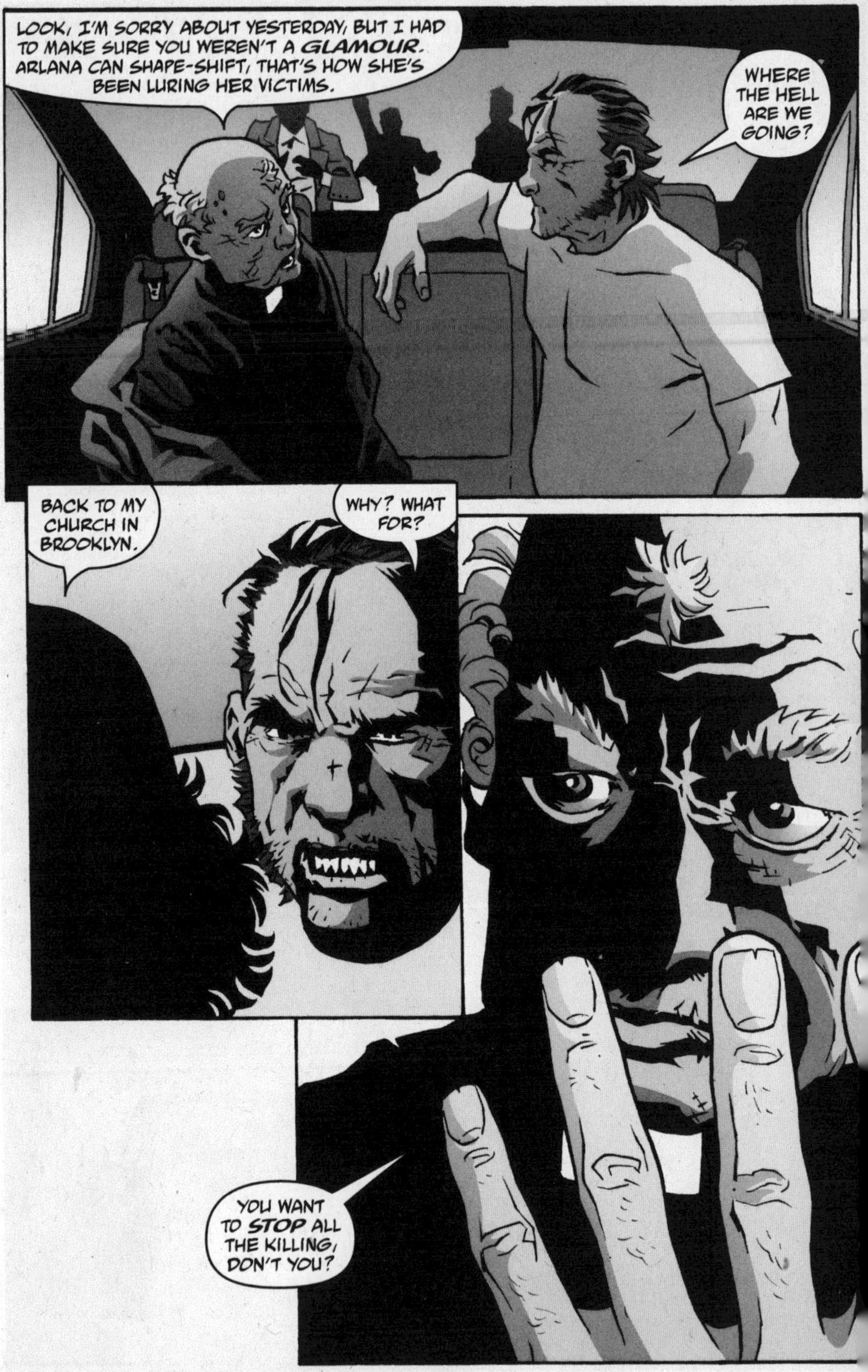
LOOK, I'M SORRY ABOUT YESTERDAY, BUT I HAD TO MAKE SURE YOU WEREN'T A GLAMOUR. ARLANA CAN SHAPE-SHIFT, THAT'S HOW SHE'S BEEN LURING HER VICTIMS.
WHERE THE HELL ARE WE GOING?
BACK TO MY CHURCH IN BROOKLYN.
WHY? WHAT FOR?
YOU WANT TO STOP ALL THE KILLING, DON'T YOU?

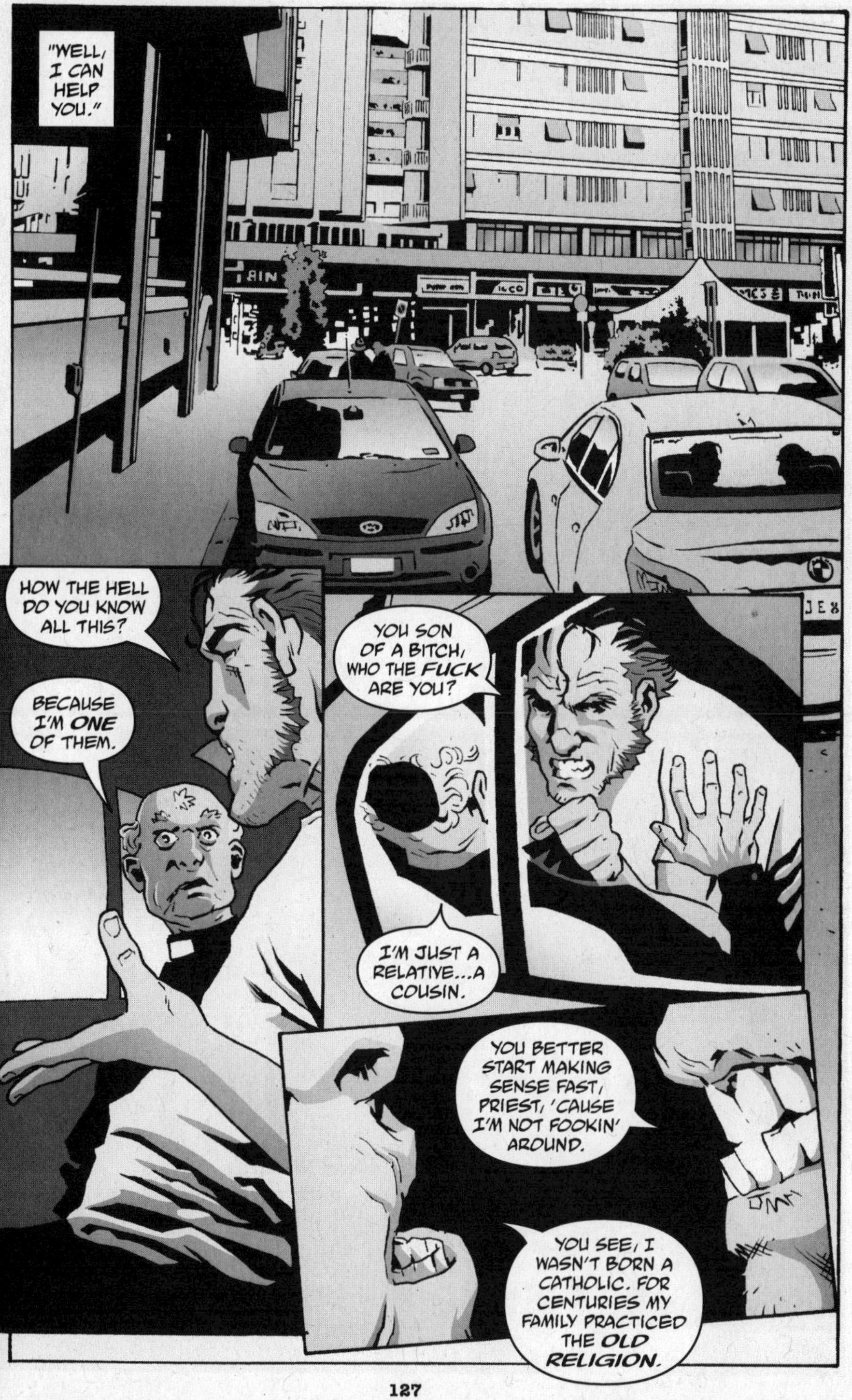
"WELL, I CAN HELP YOU."
HOW THE HELL DO YOU KNOW ALL THIS?
BECAUSE I'M *ONE* OF THEM.
YOU SON OF A BITCH, WHO THE *FUCK* ARE YOU?
I'M JUST A RELATIVE...A COUSIN.
YOU BETTER START MAKING SENSE FAST, PRIEST, 'CAUSE I'M NOT FOOKIN' AROUND.
YOU SEE, I WASN'T BORN A CATHOLIC. FOR CENTURIES MY FAMILY PRACTICED THE *OLD RELIGION*.

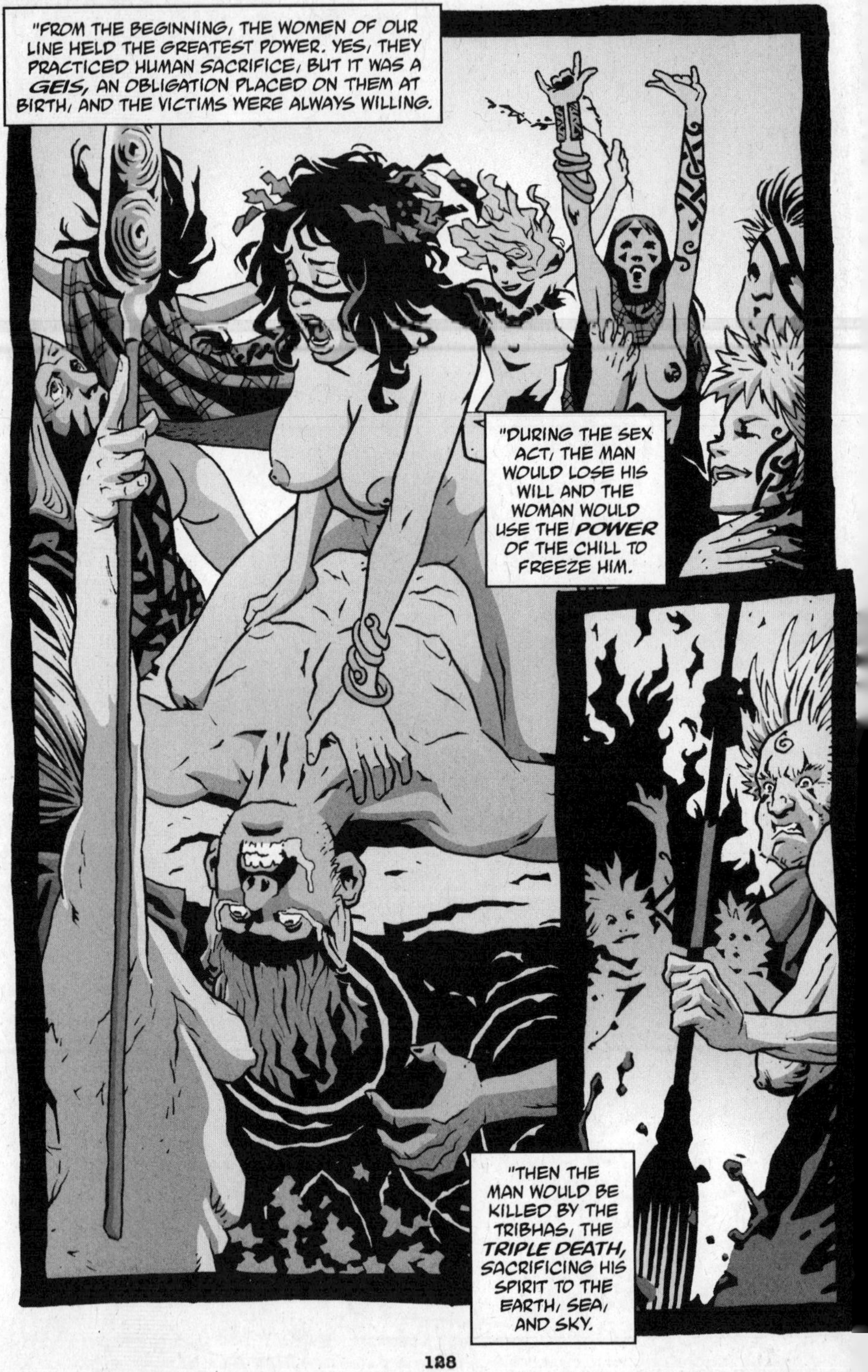
"FROM THE BEGINNING, THE WOMEN OF OUR LINE HELD THE GREATEST POWER. YES, THEY PRACTICED HUMAN SACRIFICE, BUT IT WAS A *GEIS*, AN OBLIGATION PLACED ON THEM AT BIRTH, AND THE VICTIMS WERE ALWAYS WILLING.
"DURING THE SEX ACT, THE MAN WOULD LOSE HIS WILL AND THE WOMAN WOULD USE THE *POWER* OF THE CHILL TO FREEZE HIM.
"THEN THE MAN WOULD BE KILLED BY THE TRIBHAS, THE *TRIPLE DEATH*, SACRIFICING HIS SPIRIT TO THE EARTH, SEA, AND SKY.

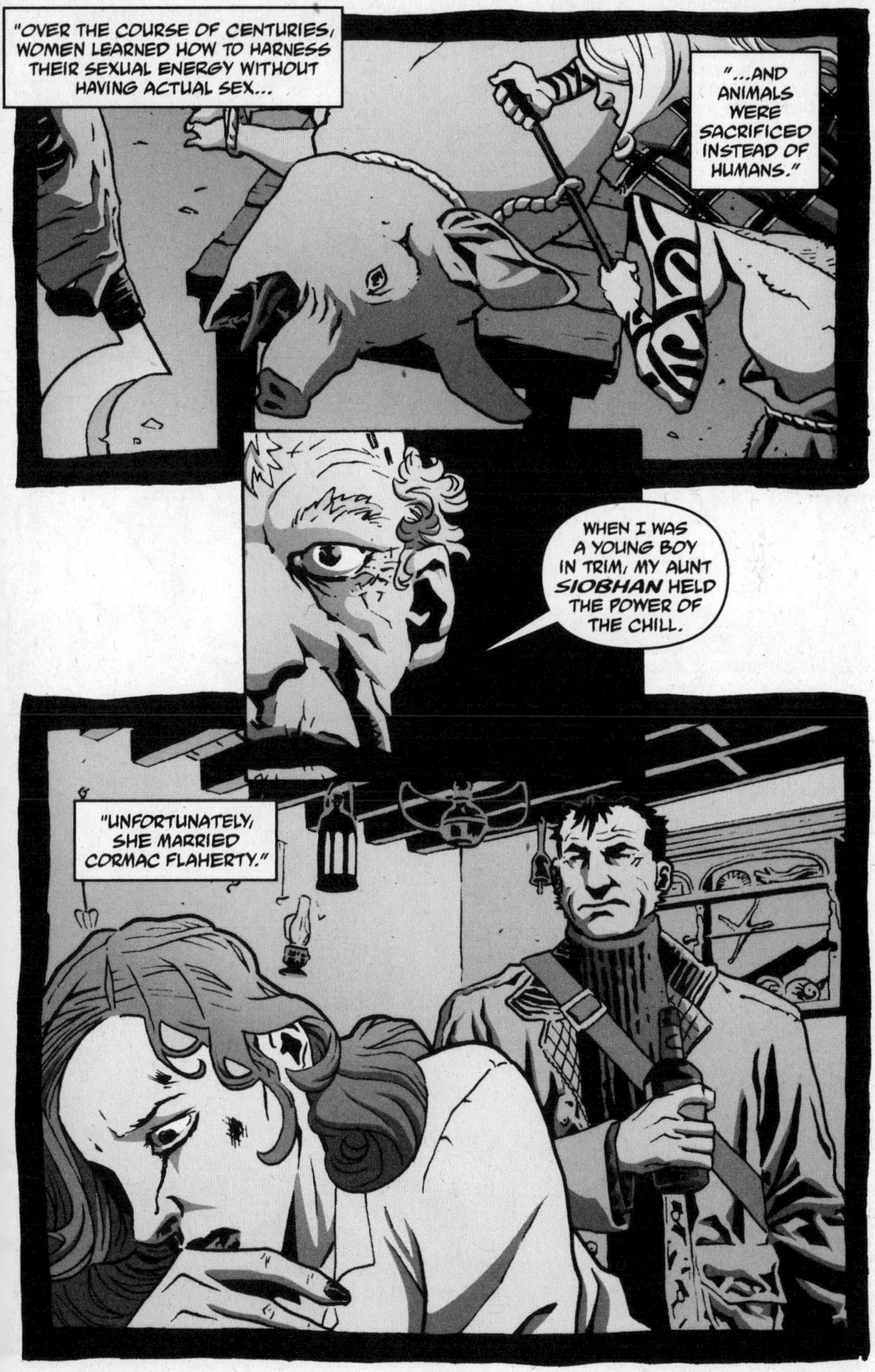
"OVER THE COURSE OF CENTURIES, WOMEN LEARNED HOW TO HARNESS THEIR SEXUAL ENERGY WITHOUT HAVING ACTUAL SEX...
"...AND ANIMALS WERE SACRIFICED INSTEAD OF HUMANS."
WHEN I WAS A YOUNG BOY IN TRIM, MY AUNT *SIOBHAN* HELD THE POWER OF THE CHILL.
"UNFORTUNATELY, SHE MARRIED CORMAC FLAHERTY."

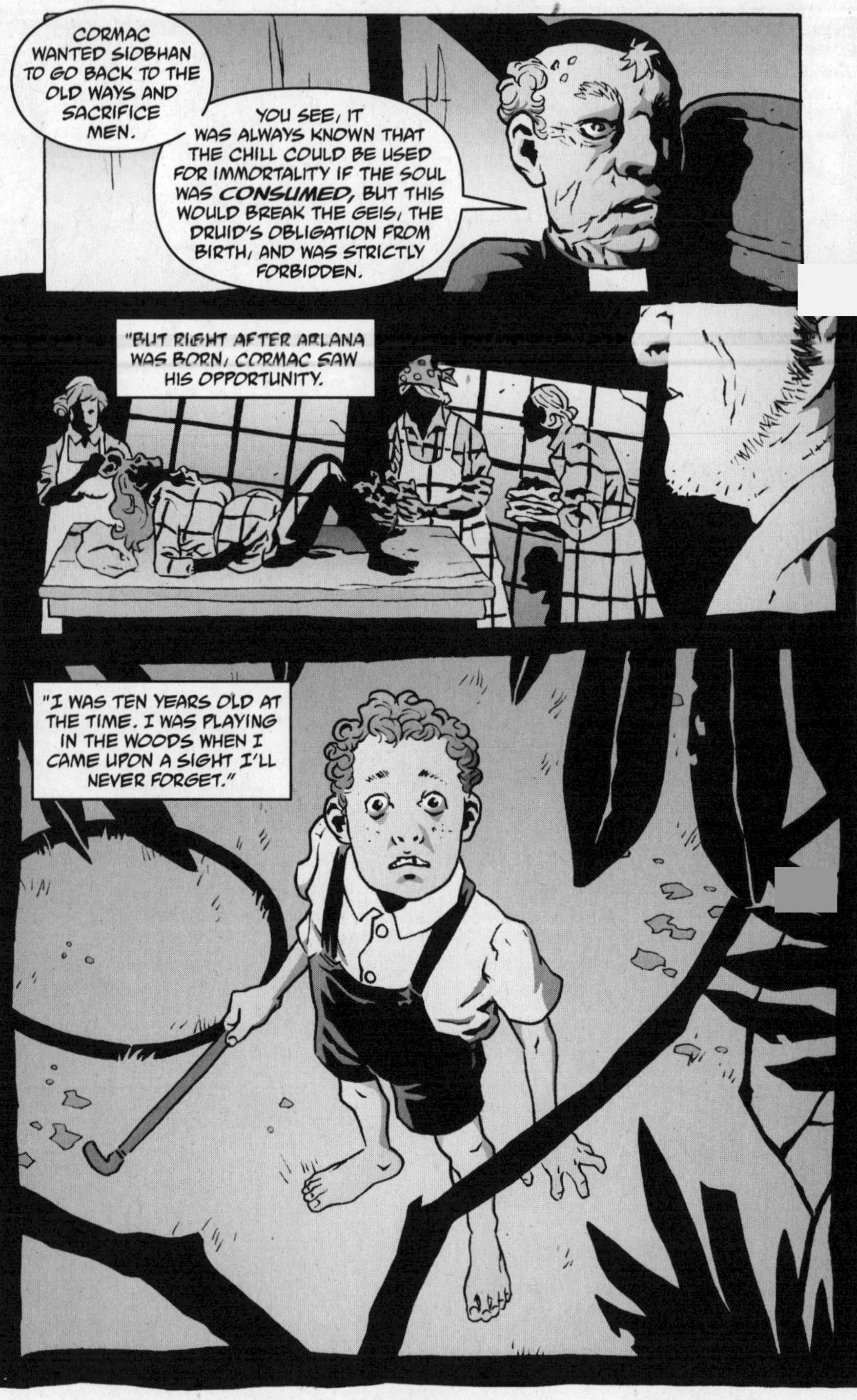
CORMAC WANTED SIOBHAN TO GO BACK TO THE OLD WAYS AND SACRIFICE MEN.
YOU SEE, IT WAS ALWAYS KNOWN THAT THE CHILL COULD BE USED FOR IMMORTALITY IF THE SOUL WAS CONSUMED, BUT THIS WOULD BREAK THE GEIS, THE DRUID'S OBLIGATION FROM BIRTH, AND WAS STRICTLY FORBIDDEN.
"BUT RIGHT AFTER ARLANA WAS BORN, CORMAC SAW HIS OPPORTUNITY.
"I WAS TEN YEARS OLD AT THE TIME. I WAS PLAYING IN THE WOODS WHEN I CAME UPON A SIGHT I'LL NEVER FORGET."

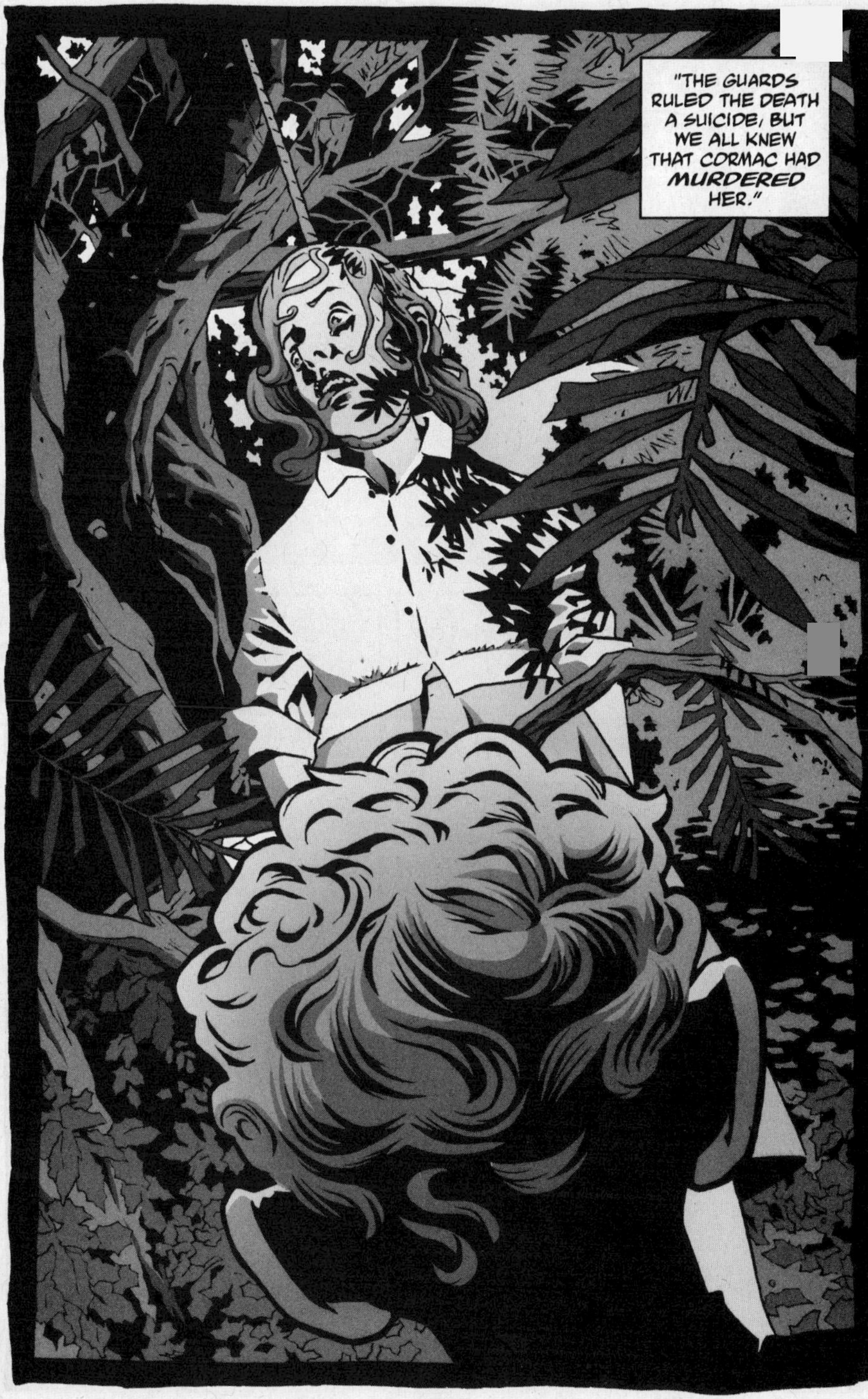
"THE GUARDS RULED THE DEATH A SUICIDE, BUT WE ALL KNEW THAT CORMAC HAD MURDERED HER."

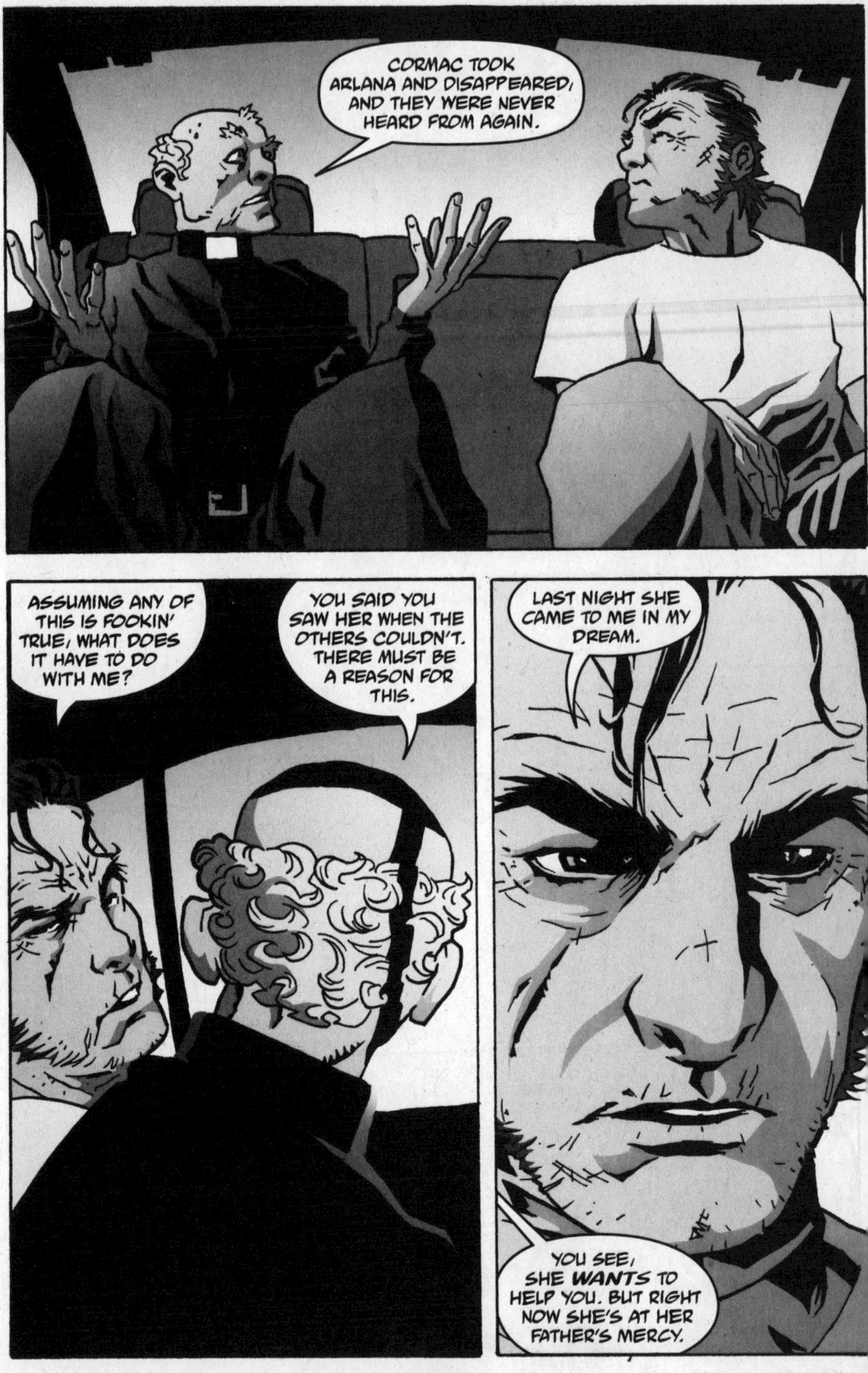
CORMAC TOOK ARLANA AND DISAPPEARED, AND THEY WERE NEVER HEARD FROM AGAIN.
ASSUMING ANY OF THIS IS FOOKIN' TRUE, WHAT DOES IT HAVE TO DO WITH ME?
YOU SAID YOU SAW HER WHEN THE OTHERS COULDN'T. THERE MUST BE A REASON FOR THIS.
LAST NIGHT SHE CAME TO ME IN MY DREAM.
YOU SEE, SHE *WANTS* TO HELP YOU. BUT RIGHT NOW SHE'S AT HER FATHER'S MERCY.

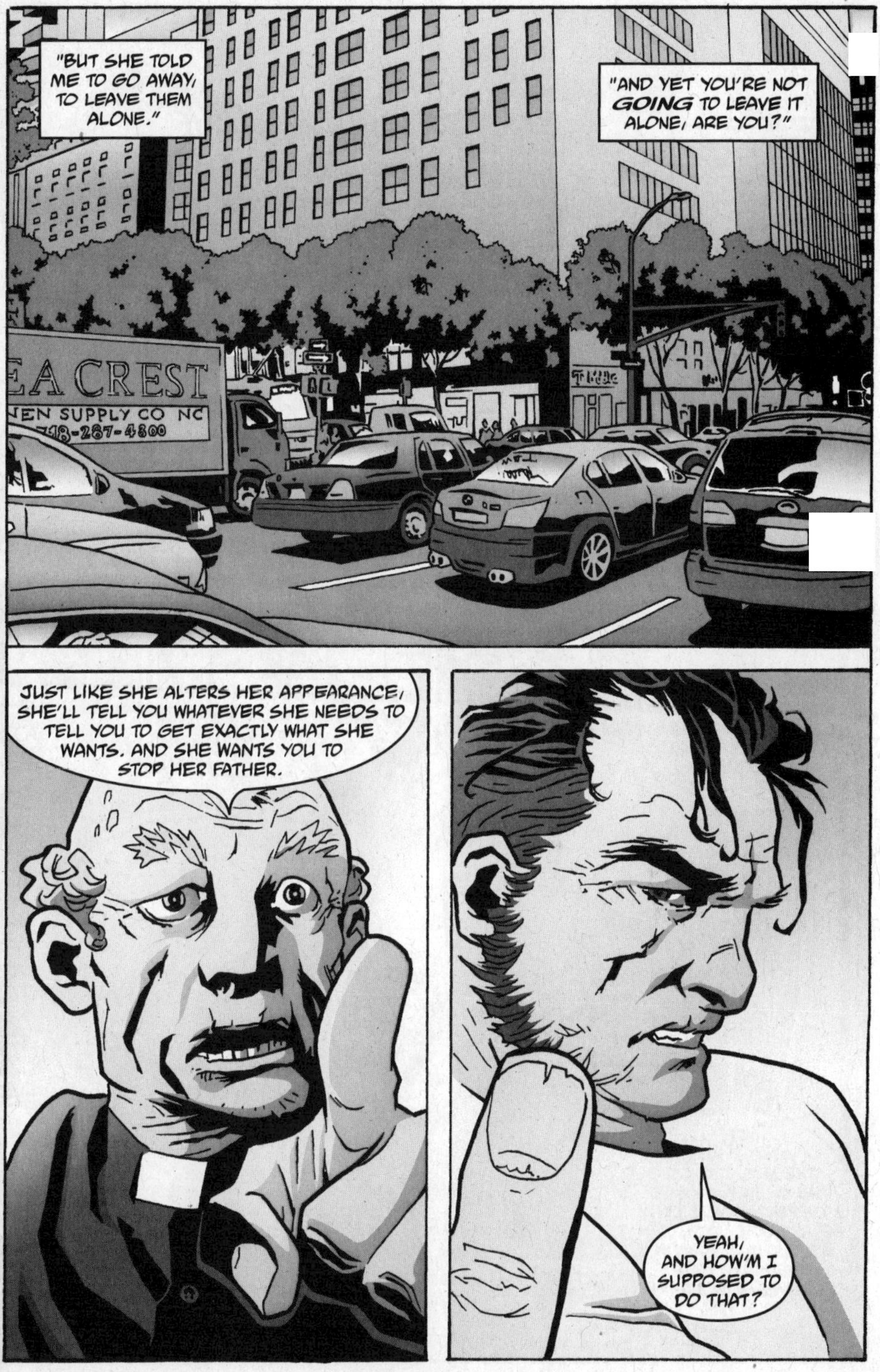
"BUT SHE TOLD ME TO GO AWAY, TO LEAVE THEM ALONE."
"AND YET YOU'RE NOT GOING TO LEAVE IT ALONE, ARE YOU?"
EA CREST
NEN SUPPLY CO NC
718-287-4300
JUST LIKE SHE ALTERS HER APPEARANCE, SHE'LL TELL YOU WHATEVER SHE NEEDS TO TELL YOU TO GET EXACTLY WHAT SHE WANTS. AND SHE WANTS YOU TO STOP HER FATHER.
YEAH, AND HOW'M I SUPPOSED TO DO THAT?

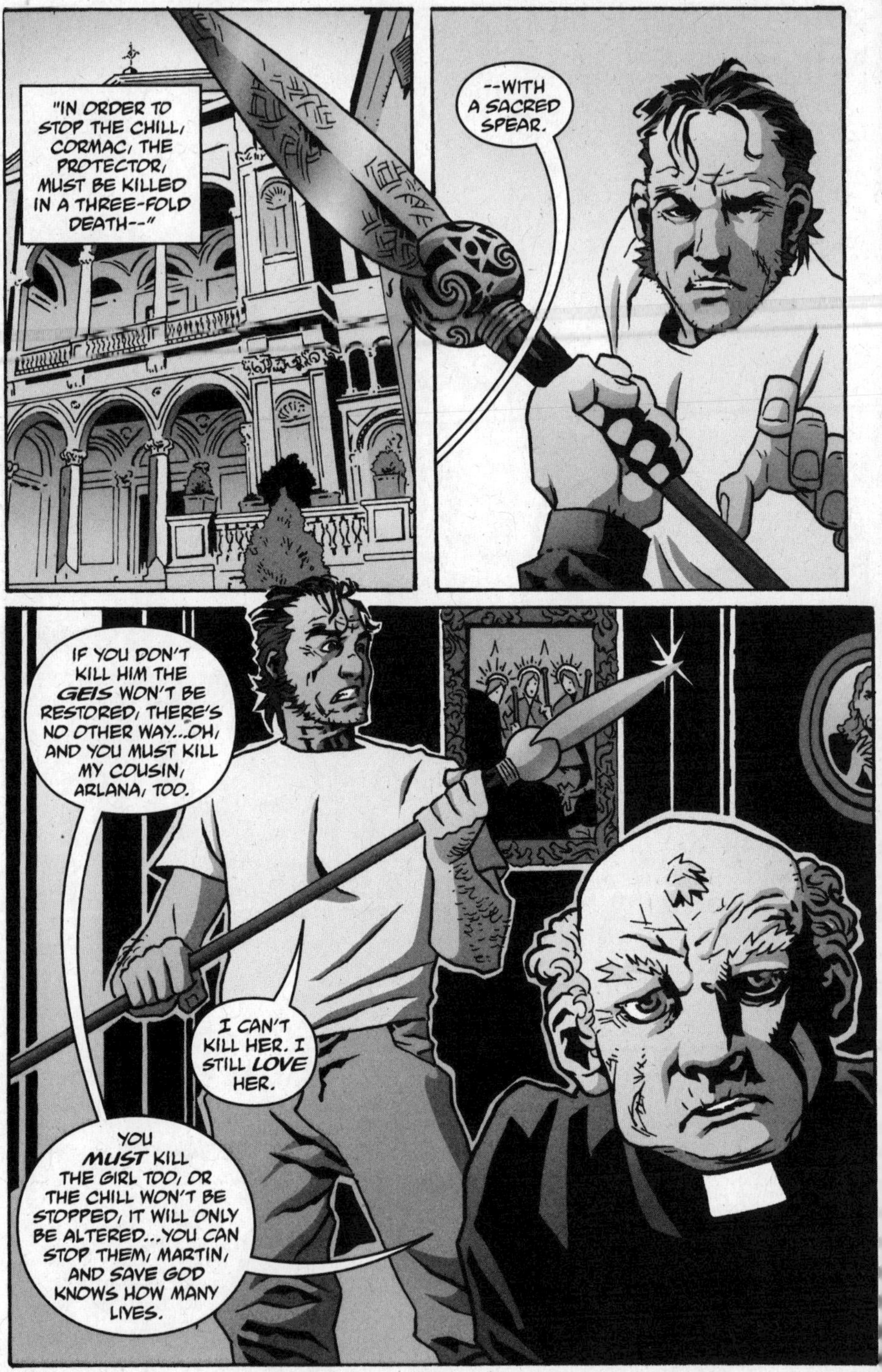
"IN ORDER TO STOP THE CHILL, CORMAC, THE PROTECTOR, MUST BE KILLED IN A THREE-FOLD DEATH--"
--WITH A SACRED SPEAR.
IF YOU DON'T KILL HIM THE *GEIS* WON'T BE RESTORED, THERE'S NO OTHER WAY...OH, AND YOU MUST KILL MY COUSIN, ARLANA, TOO.
I CAN'T KILL HER. I STILL *LOVE* HER.
YOU *MUST* KILL THE GIRL TOO, OR THE CHILL WON'T BE STOPPED, IT WILL ONLY BE ALTERED...YOU CAN STOP THEM, MARTIN, AND SAVE GOD KNOWS HOW MANY LIVES.

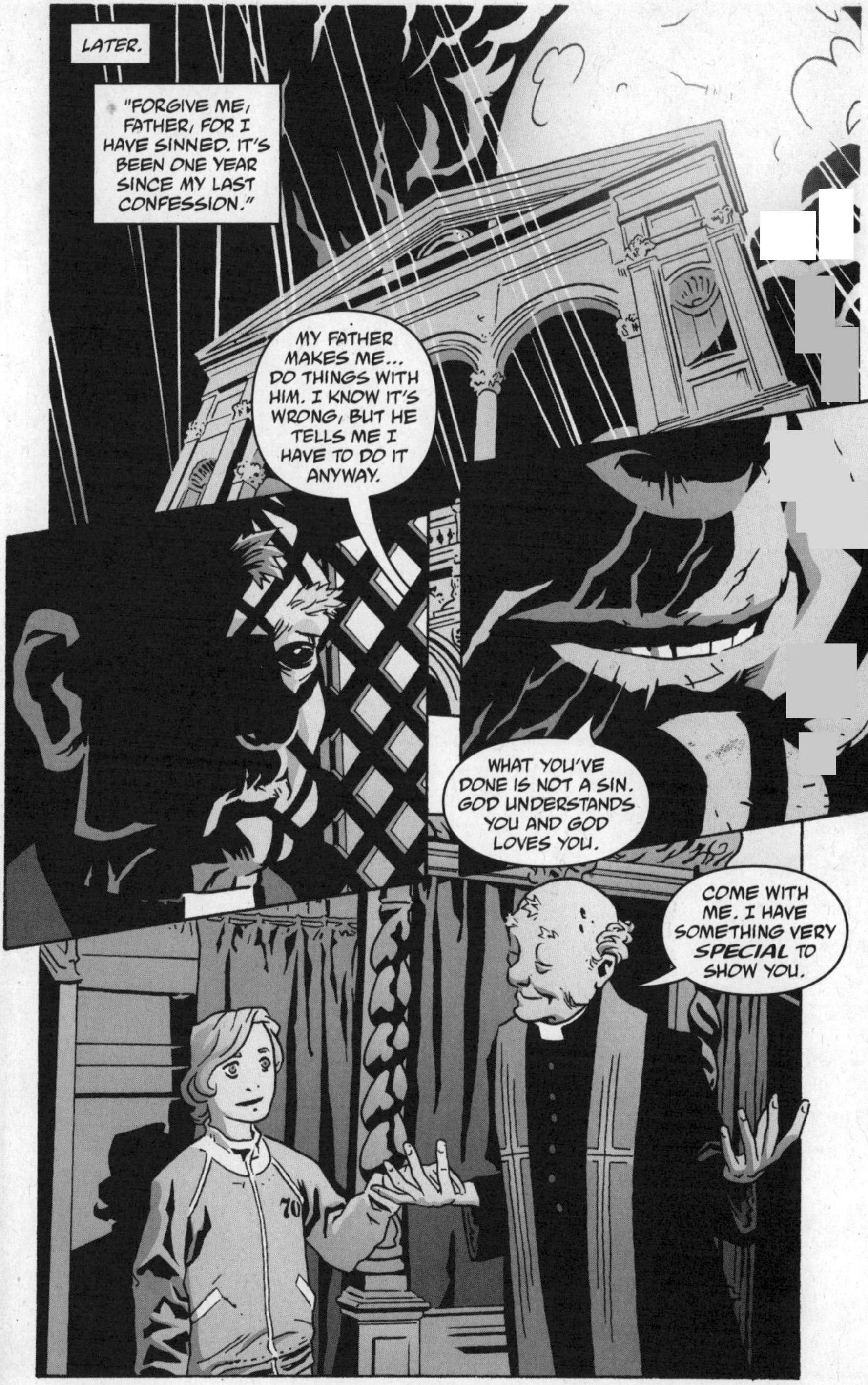
LATER.
"FORGIVE ME, FATHER, FOR I HAVE SINNED. IT'S BEEN ONE YEAR SINCE MY LAST CONFESSION."
MY FATHER MAKES ME... DO THINGS WITH HIM. I KNOW IT'S WRONG, BUT HE TELLS ME I HAVE TO DO IT ANYWAY.
WHAT YOU'VE DONE IS NOT A SIN. GOD UNDERSTANDS YOU AND GOD LOVES YOU.
COME WITH ME. I HAVE SOMETHING VERY SPECIAL TO SHOW YOU.

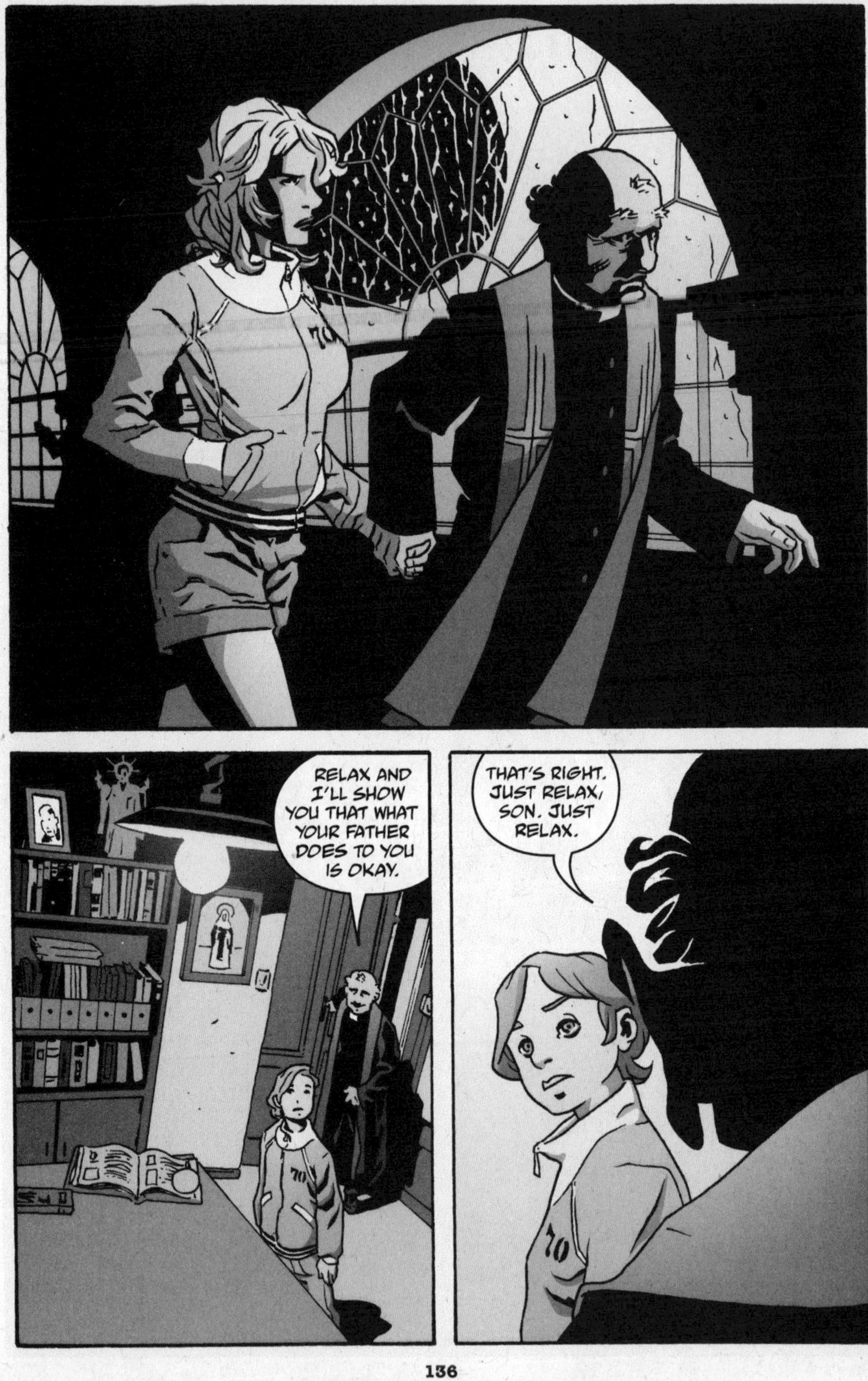
RELAX AND I'LL SHOW YOU THAT WHAT YOUR FATHER DOES TO YOU IS OKAY.
THAT'S RIGHT. JUST RELAX, SON. JUST RELAX.

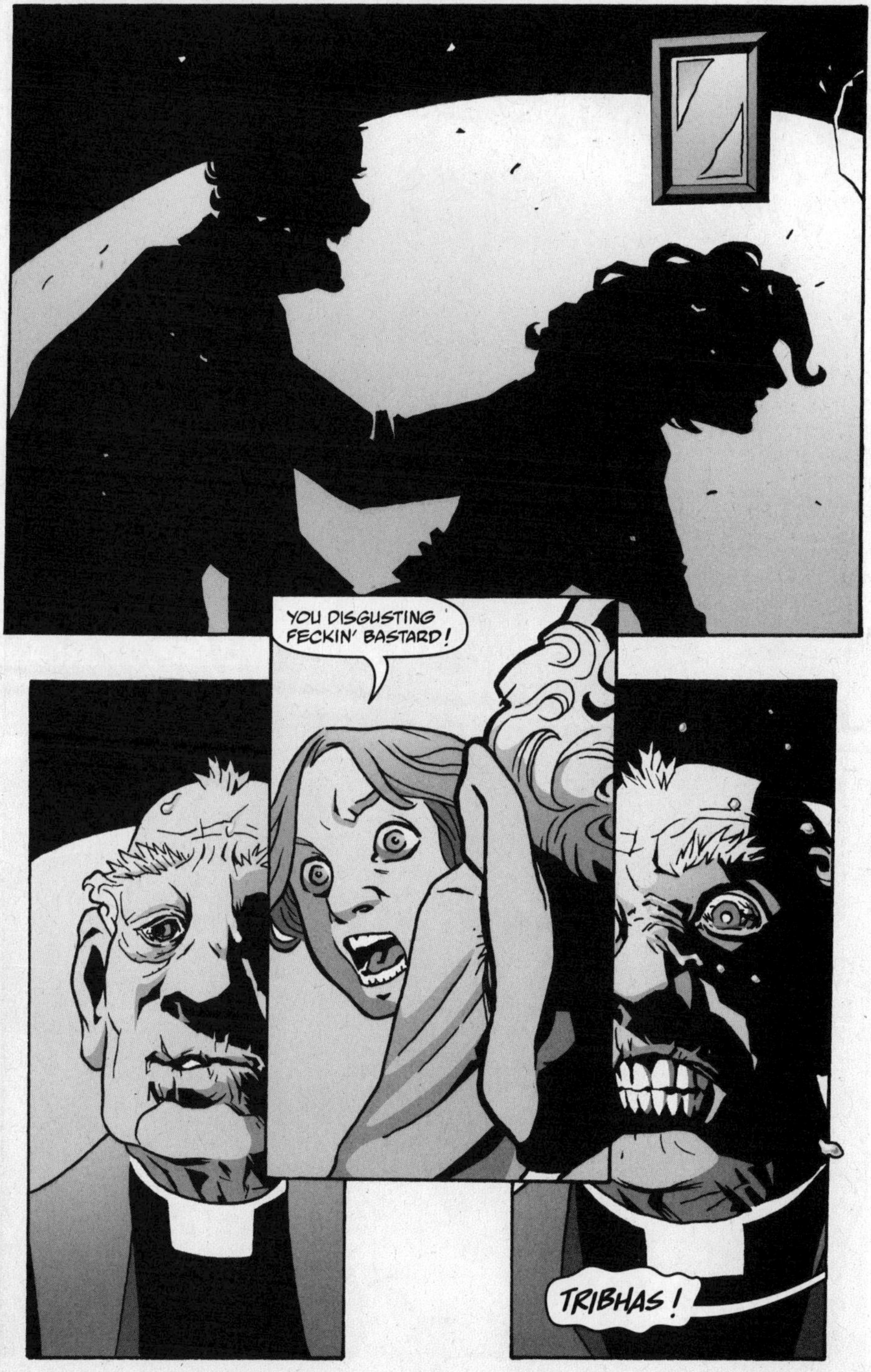
YOU DISGUSTING FECKIN' BASTARD!
TRIBHAS!

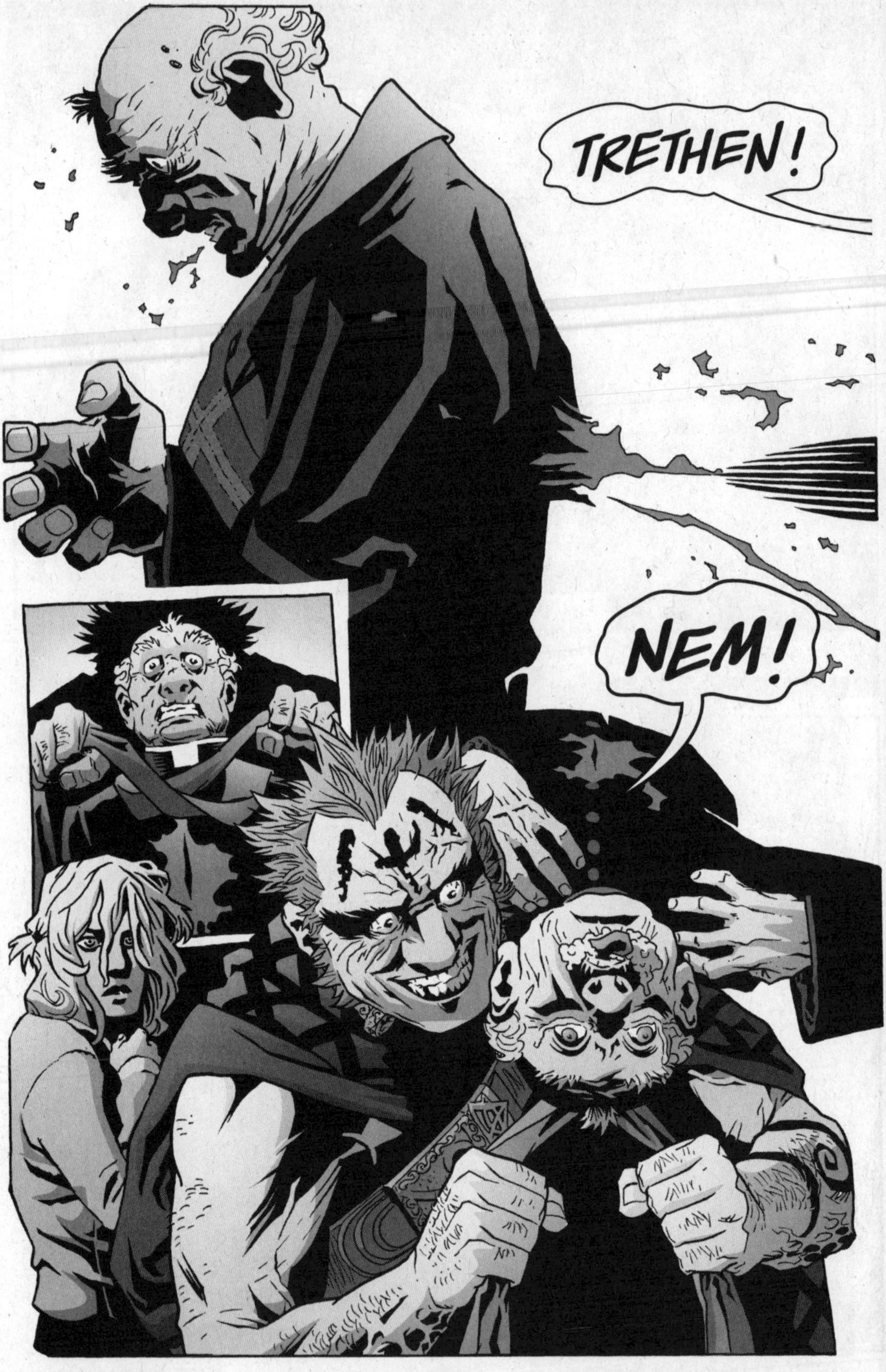
TRETHEN!
NEM!

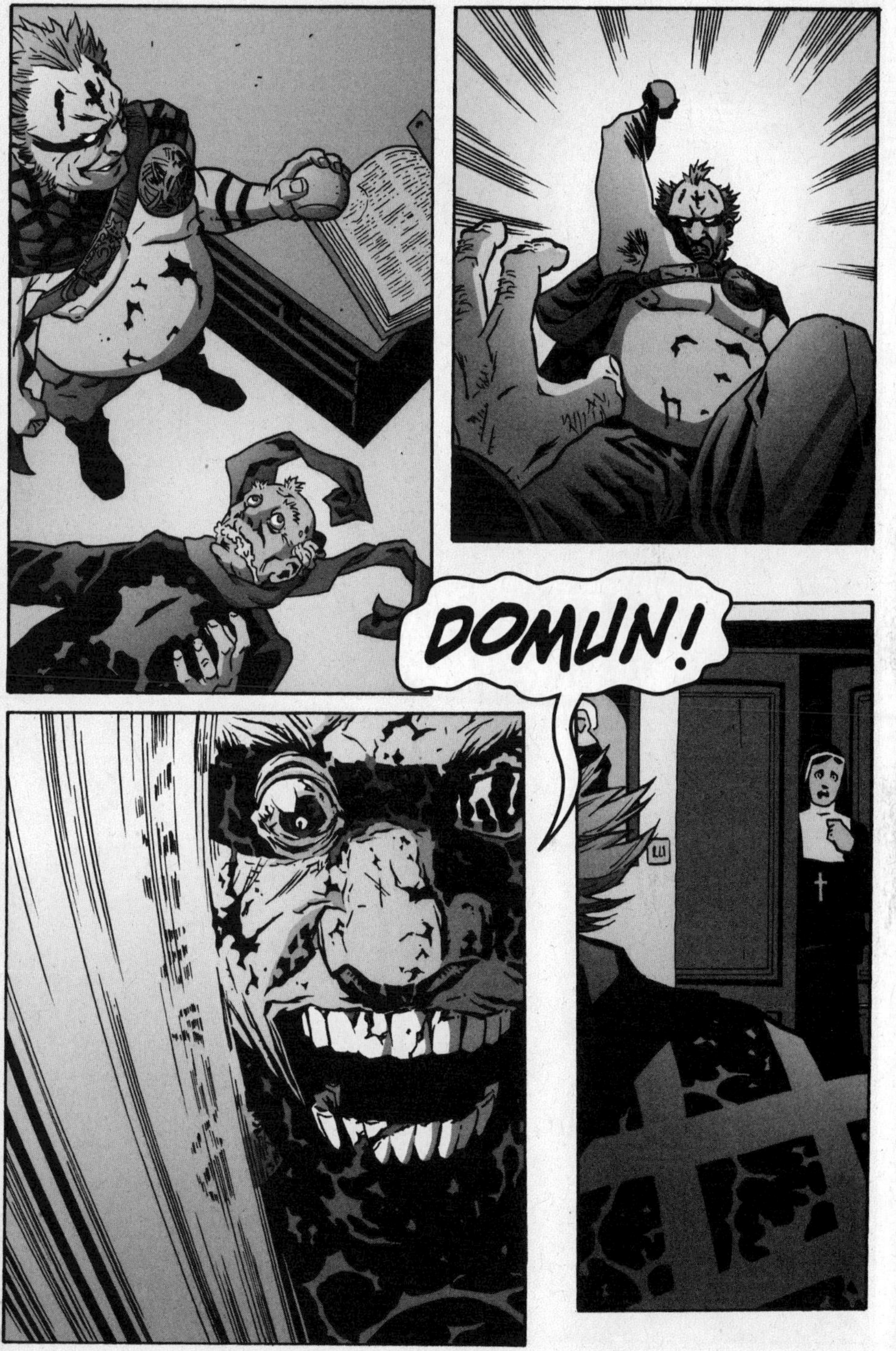
DOMUN!

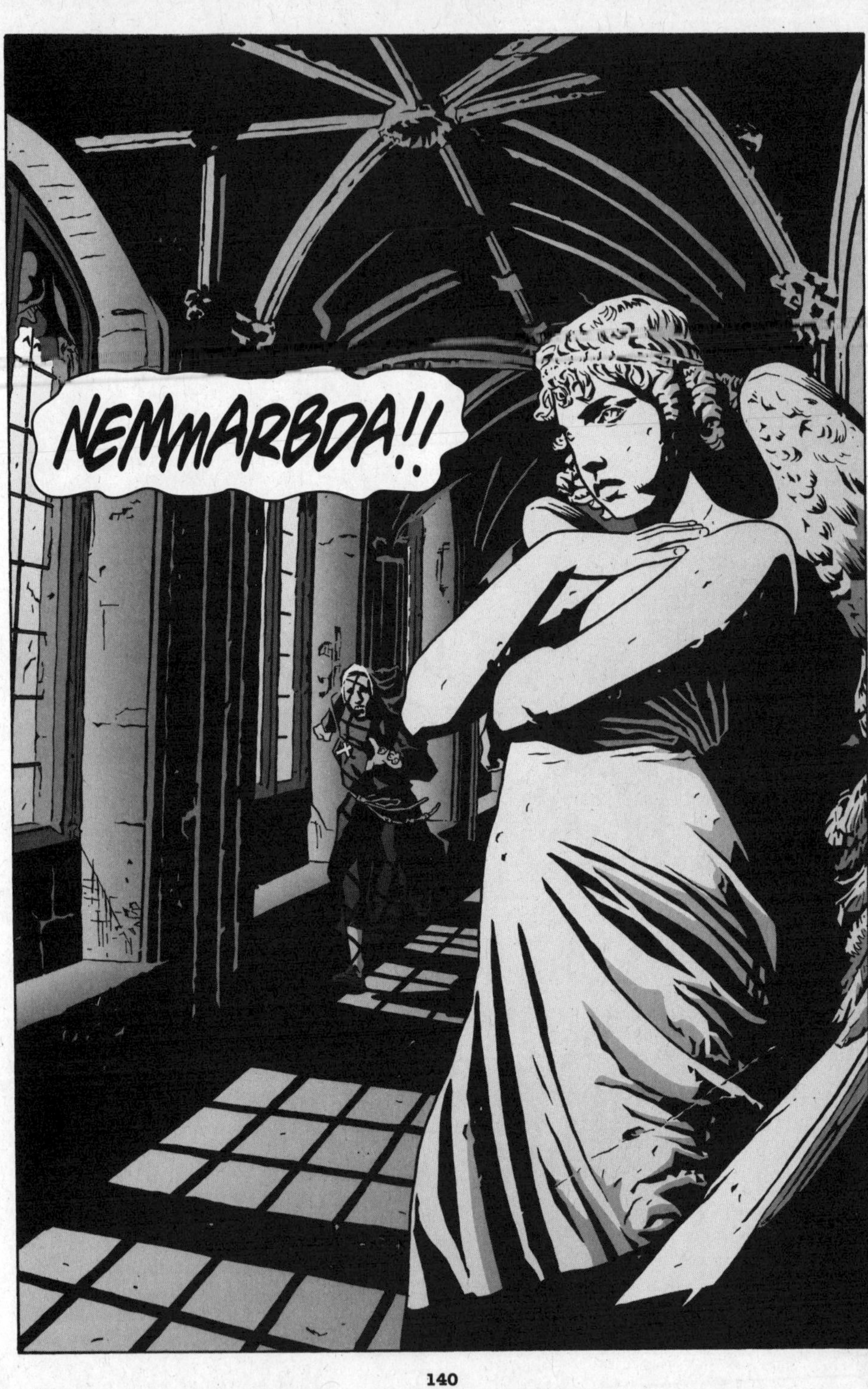
NEMMARBDA!!

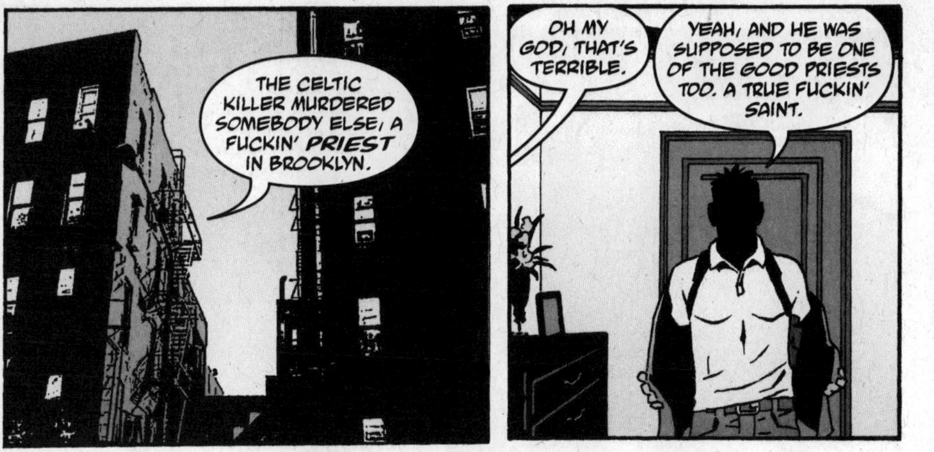
THE CELTIC KILLER MURDERED SOMEBODY ELSE, A FUCKIN' *PRIEST* IN BROOKLYN.
OH MY GOD, THAT'S TERRIBLE.
YEAH, AND HE WAS SUPPOSED TO BE ONE OF THE GOOD PRIESTS TOO. A TRUE FUCKIN' SAINT.

CHAPTER SEVEN:
DEFIANCE

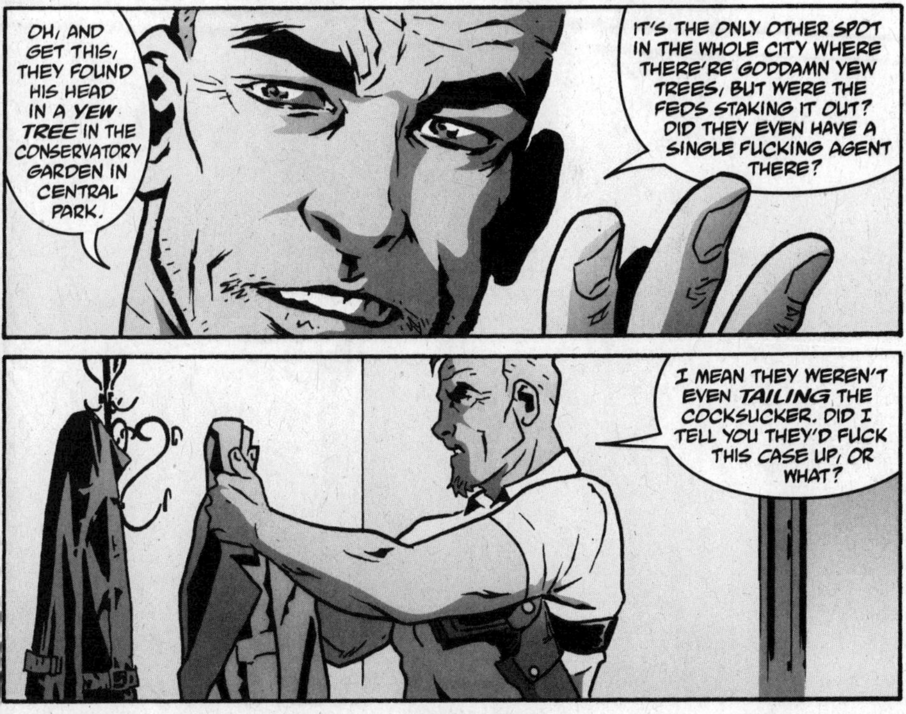
OH, AND GET THIS, THEY FOUND HIS HEAD IN A *YEW TREE* IN THE CONSERVATORY GARDEN IN CENTRAL PARK.
IT'S THE ONLY OTHER SPOT IN THE WHOLE CITY WHERE THERE'RE GODDAMN YEW TREES, BUT WERE THE FEDS STAKING IT OUT? DID THEY EVEN HAVE A SINGLE FUCKING AGENT THERE?
I MEAN THEY WEREN'T EVEN *TAILING* THE COCKSUCKER. DID I TELL YOU THEY'D FUCK THIS CASE UP, OR WHAT?

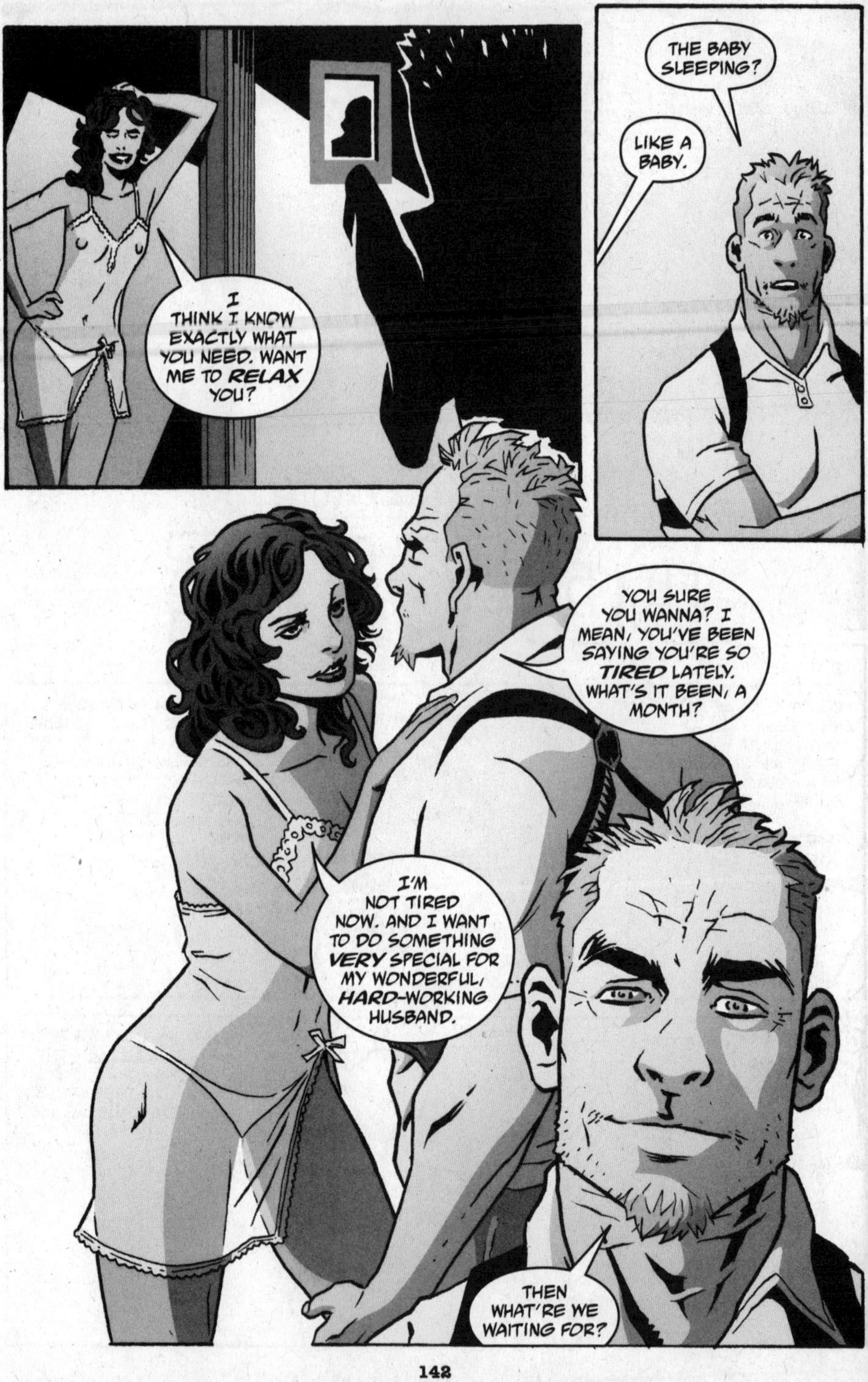
I THINK I KNOW EXACTLY WHAT YOU NEED. WANT ME TO RELAX YOU?
THE BABY SLEEPING?
LIKE A BABY.
YOU SURE YOU WANNA? I MEAN, YOU'VE BEEN SAYING YOU'RE SO TIRED LATELY. WHAT'S IT BEEN, A MONTH?
I'M NOT TIRED NOW. AND I WANT TO DO SOMETHING VERY SPECIAL FOR MY WONDERFUL, HARD-WORKING HUSBAND.
THEN WHAT'RE WE WAITING FOR?

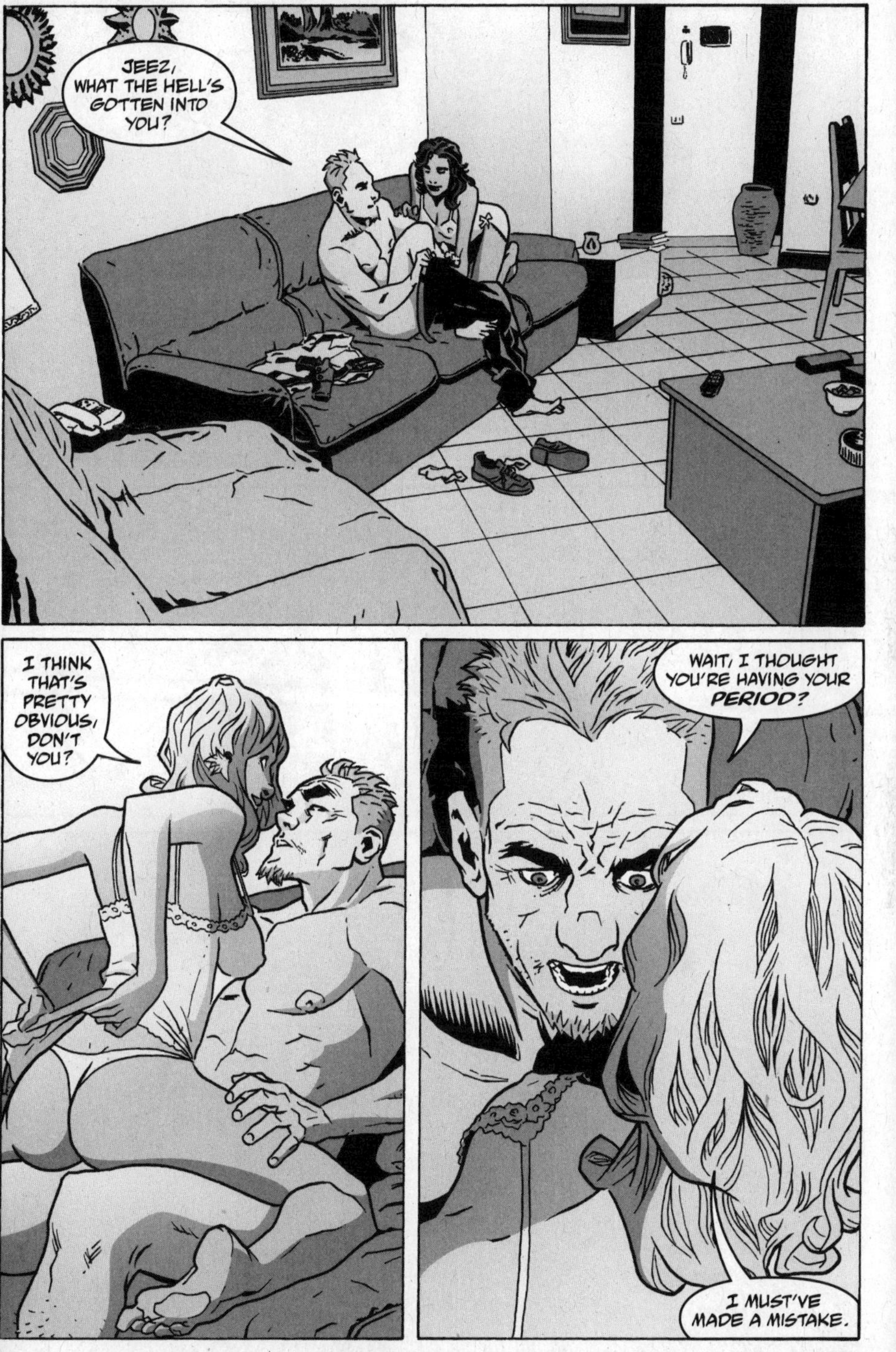
JEEZ, WHAT THE HELL'S GOTTEN INTO YOU?
I THINK THAT'S PRETTY OBVIOUS, DON'T YOU?
WAIT, I THOUGHT YOU'RE HAVING YOUR *PERIOD?*
I MUST'VE MADE A MISTAKE.

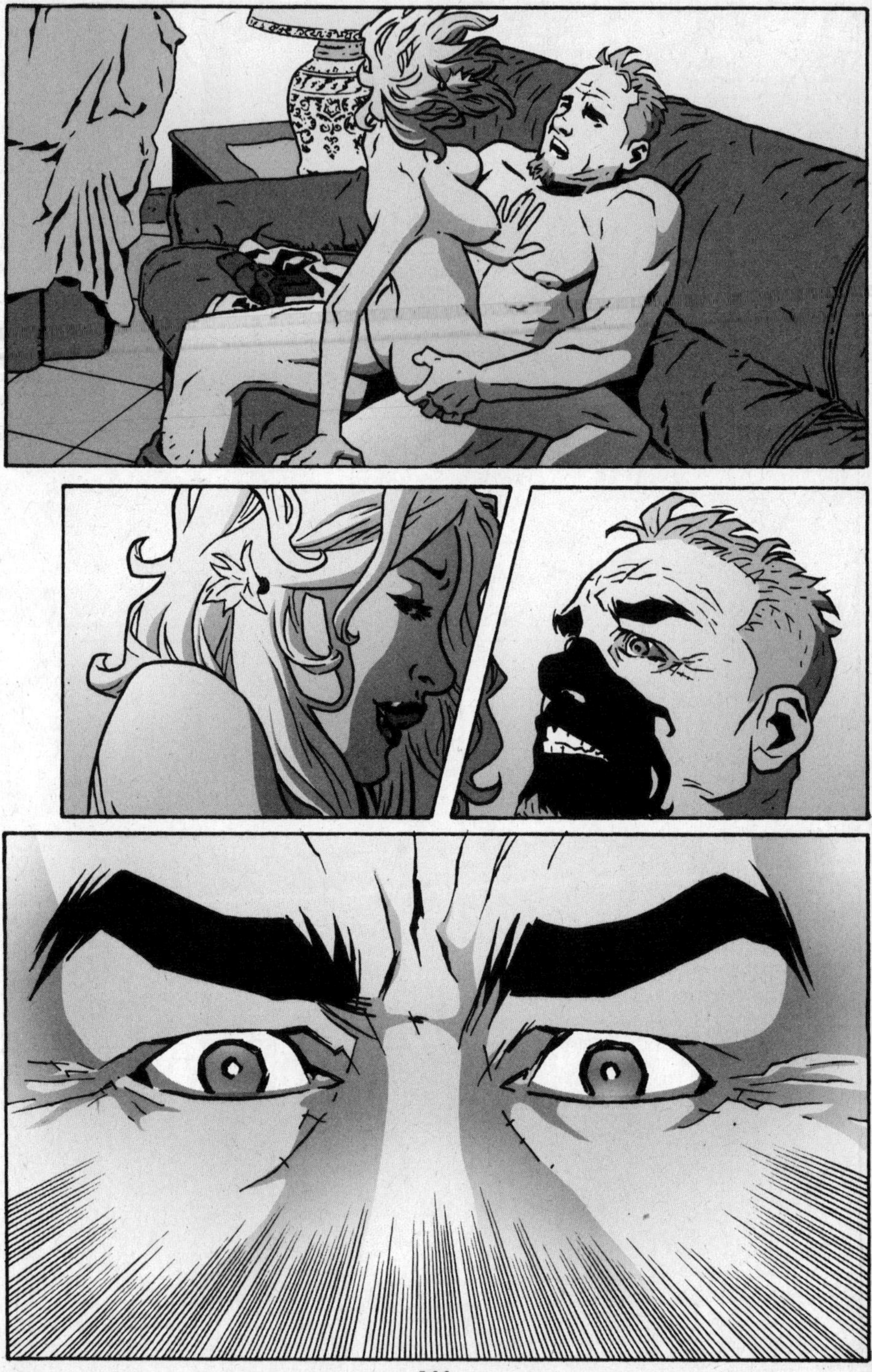

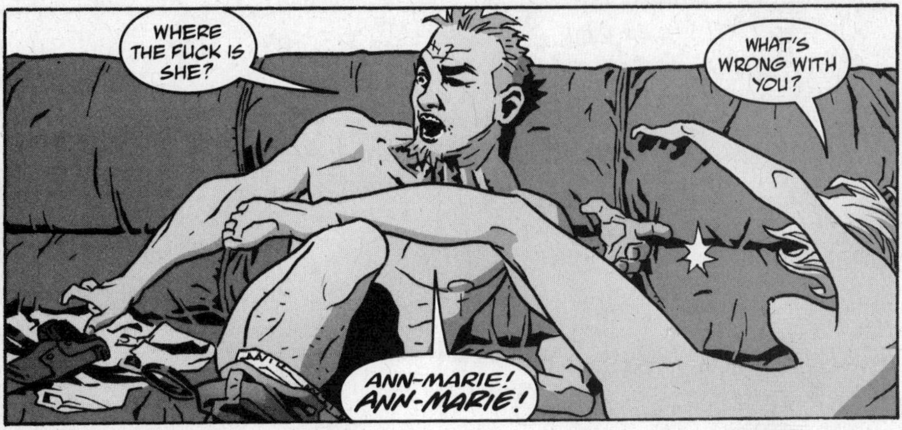
WHERE THE FUCK IS SHE?
WHAT'S WRONG WITH YOU?
ANN-MARIE! ANN-MARIE!

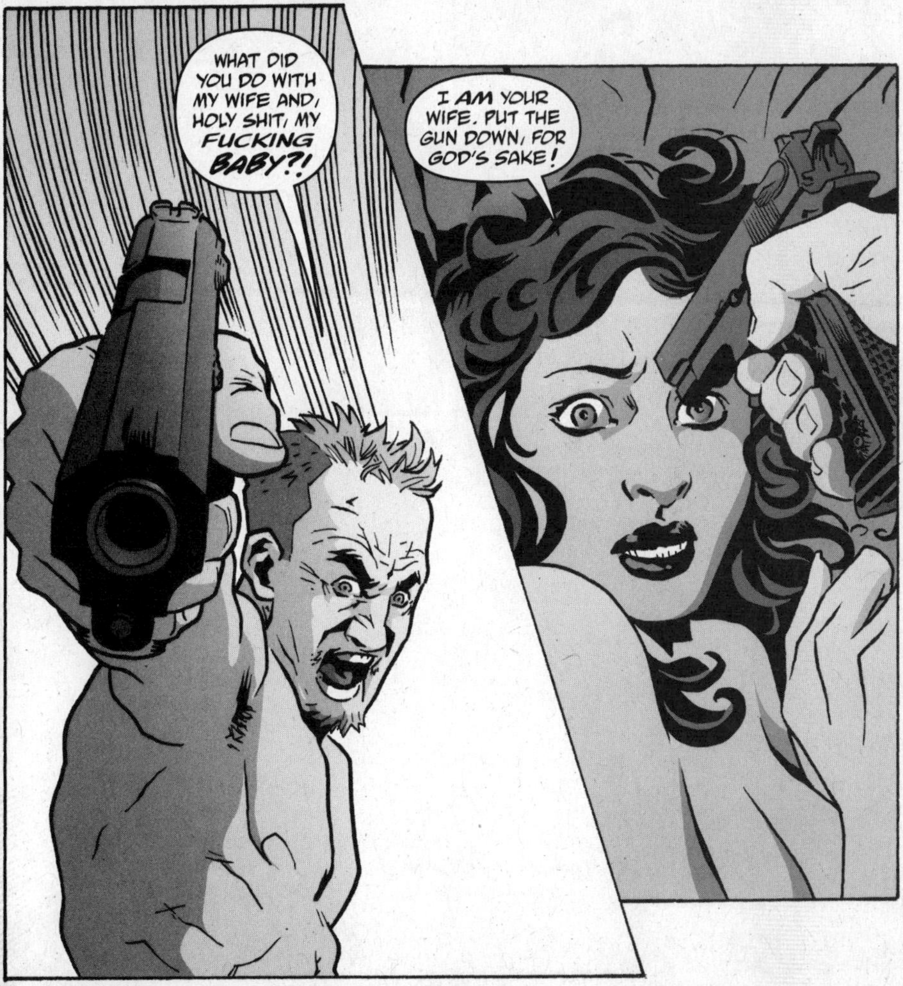
WHAT DID YOU DO WITH MY WIFE AND, HOLY SHIT, MY FUCKING BABY?!
I AM YOUR WIFE. PUT THE GUN DOWN, FOR GOD'S SAKE!

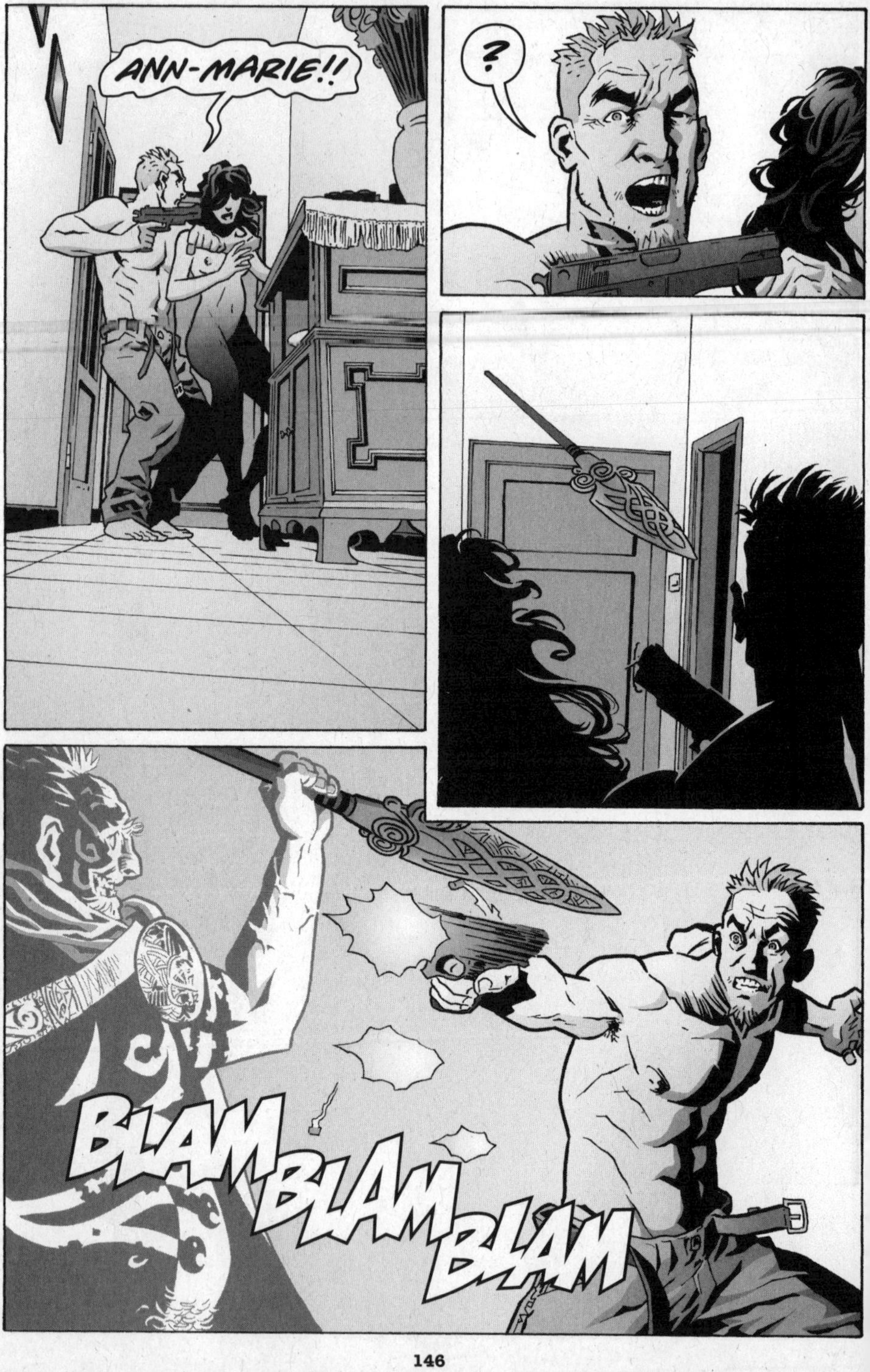
ANN-MARIE!!
?
BLAM BLAM BLAM

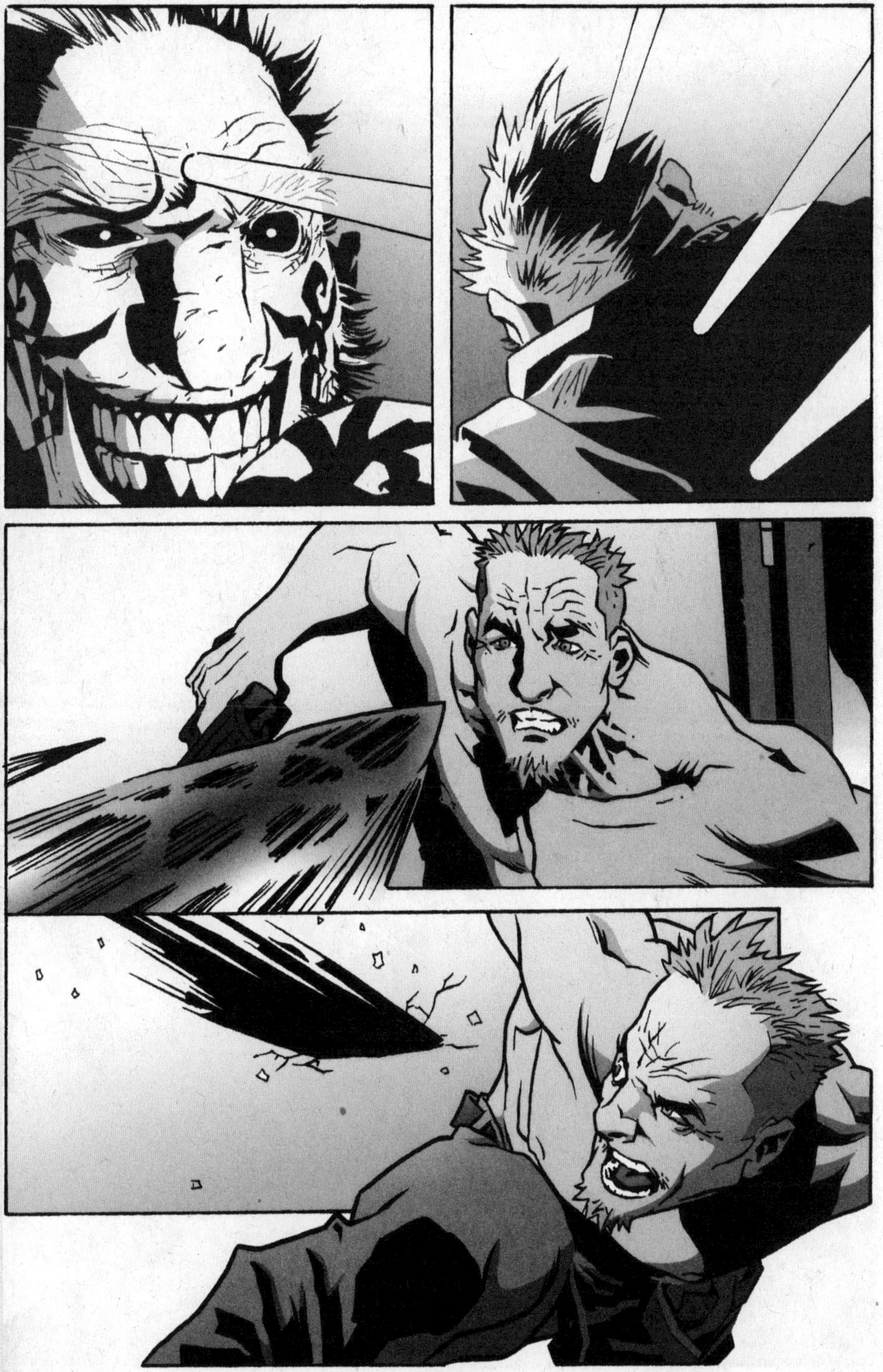

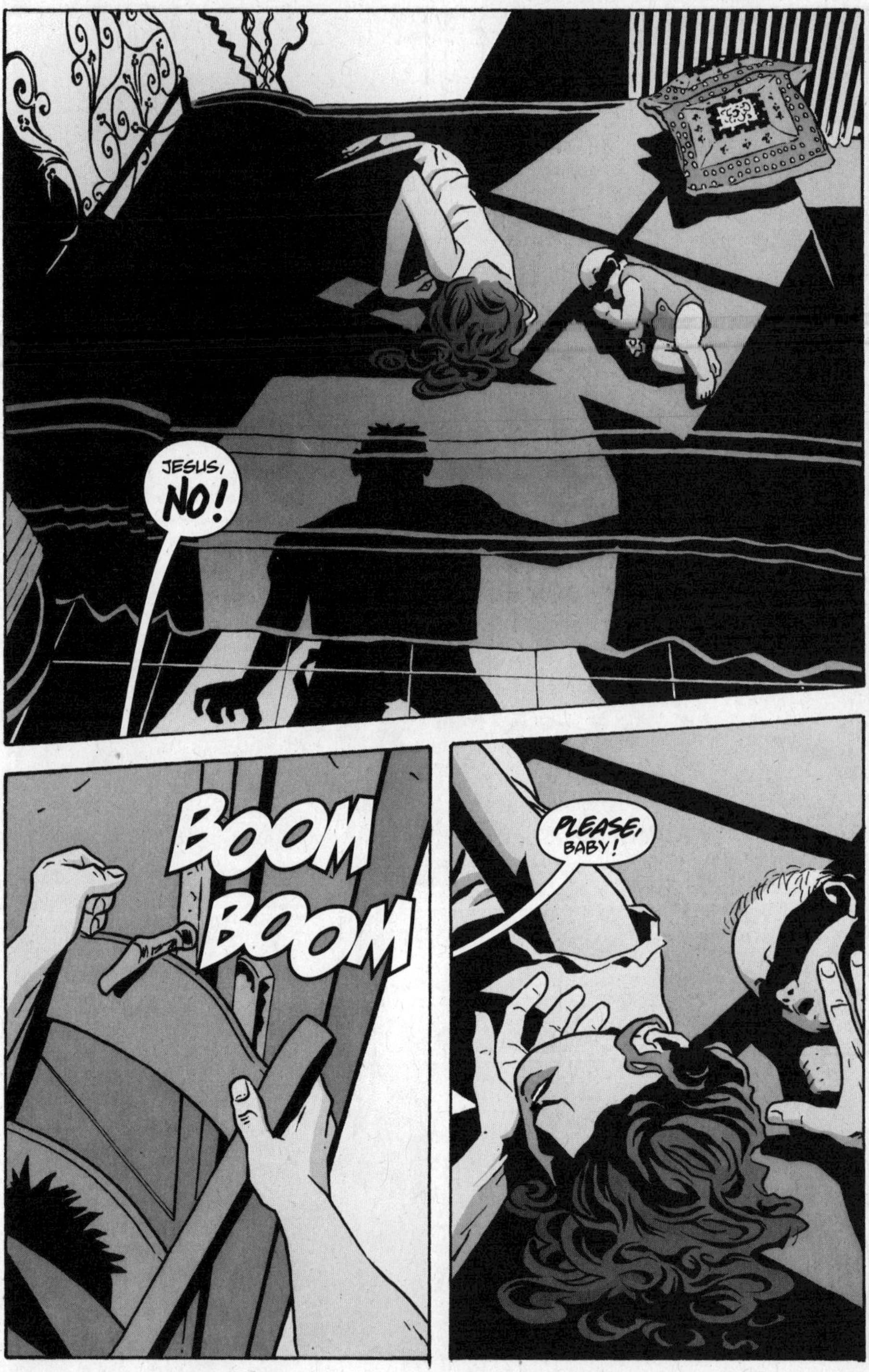
JESUS, NO!
BOOM BOOM
PLEASE, BABY!

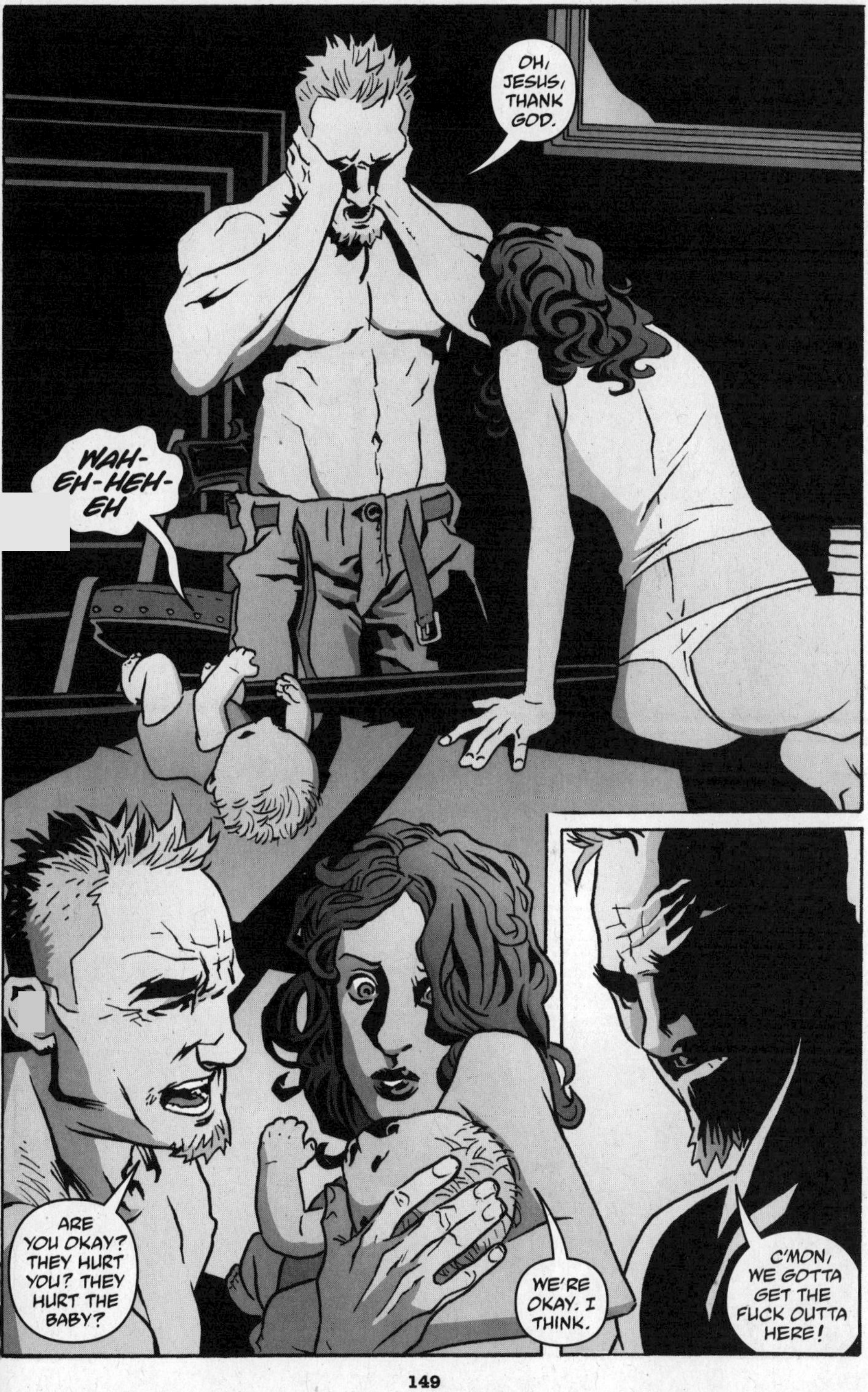
OH, JESUS, THANK GOD.
WAH-EH-HEH-EH
ARE YOU OKAY? THEY HURT YOU? THEY HURT THE BABY?
WE'RE OKAY. I THINK.
C'MON, WE GOTTA GET THE FUCK OUTTA HERE!

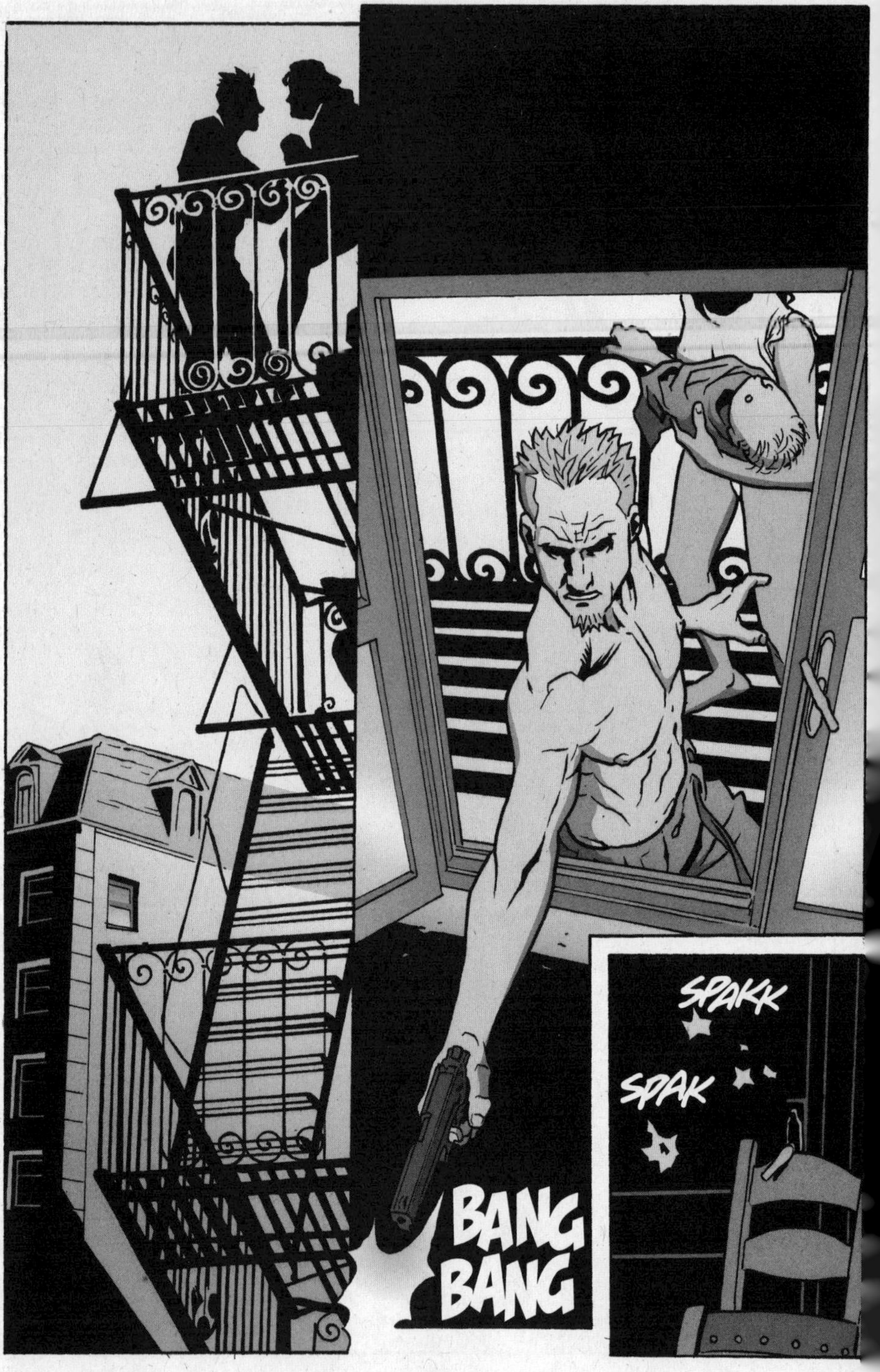
BANG
BANG
SPAKK
SPAK

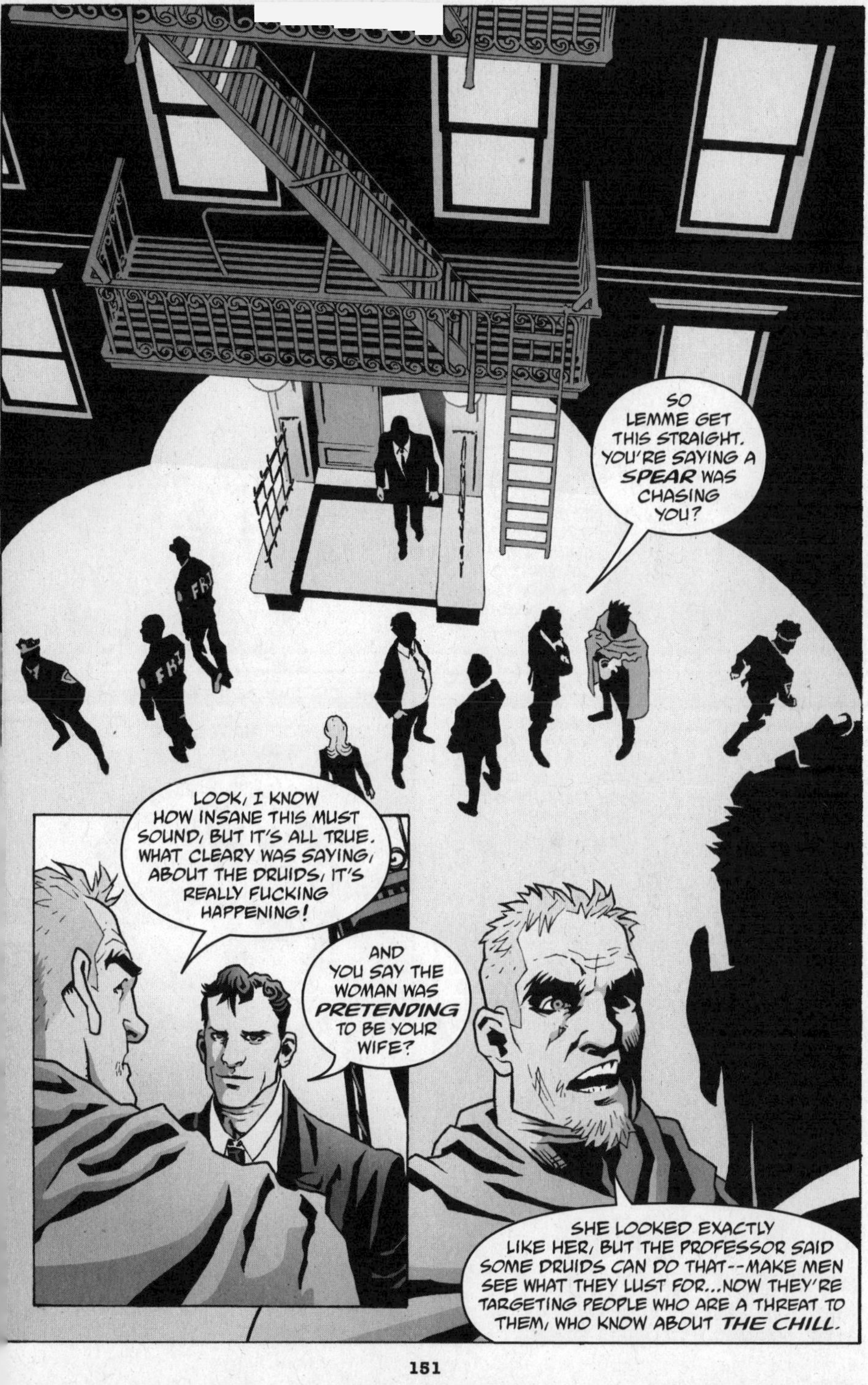

SO LEMME GET THIS STRAIGHT. YOU'RE SAYING A SPEAR WAS CHASING YOU?
LOOK, I KNOW HOW INSANE THIS MUST SOUND, BUT IT'S ALL TRUE. WHAT CLEARY WAS SAYING, ABOUT THE DRUIDS, IT'S REALLY FUCKING HAPPENING!
AND YOU SAY THE WOMAN WAS PRETENDING TO BE YOUR WIFE?
SHE LOOKED EXACTLY LIKE HER, BUT THE PROFESSOR SAID SOME DRUIDS CAN DO THAT--MAKE MEN SEE WHAT THEY LUST FOR...NOW THEY'RE TARGETING PEOPLE WHO ARE A THREAT TO THEM, WHO KNOW ABOUT THE CHILL.

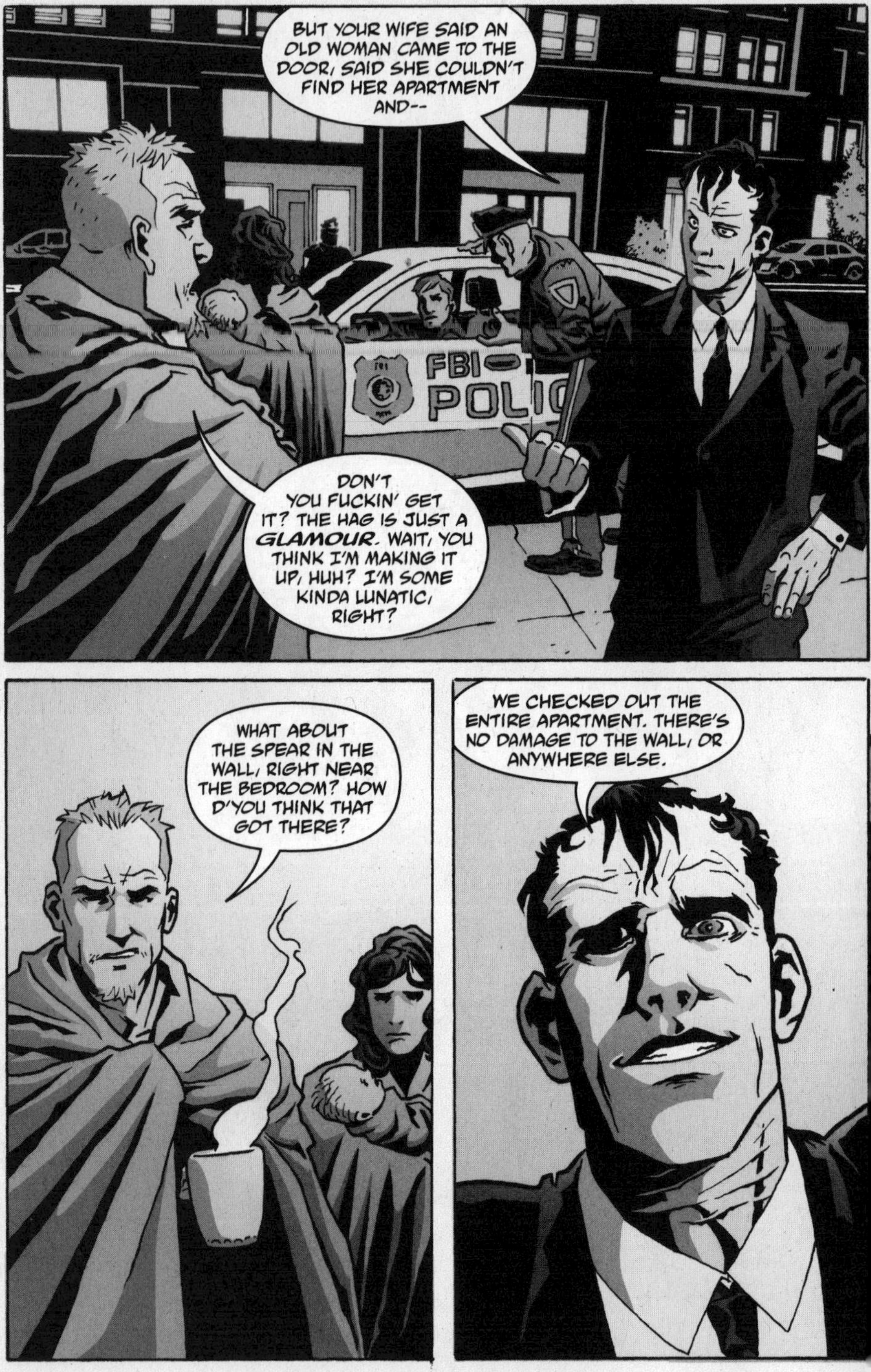
BUT YOUR WIFE SAID AN OLD WOMAN CAME TO THE DOOR, SAID SHE COULDN'T FIND HER APARTMENT AND--
FBI POLIC
DON'T YOU FUCKIN' GET IT? THE HAG IS JUST A GLAMOUR. WAIT, YOU THINK I'M MAKING IT UP, HUH? I'M SOME KINDA LUNATIC, RIGHT?
WHAT ABOUT THE SPEAR IN THE WALL, RIGHT NEAR THE BEDROOM? HOW D'YOU THINK THAT GOT THERE?
WE CHECKED OUT THE ENTIRE APARTMENT. THERE'S NO DAMAGE TO THE WALL, OR ANYWHERE ELSE.

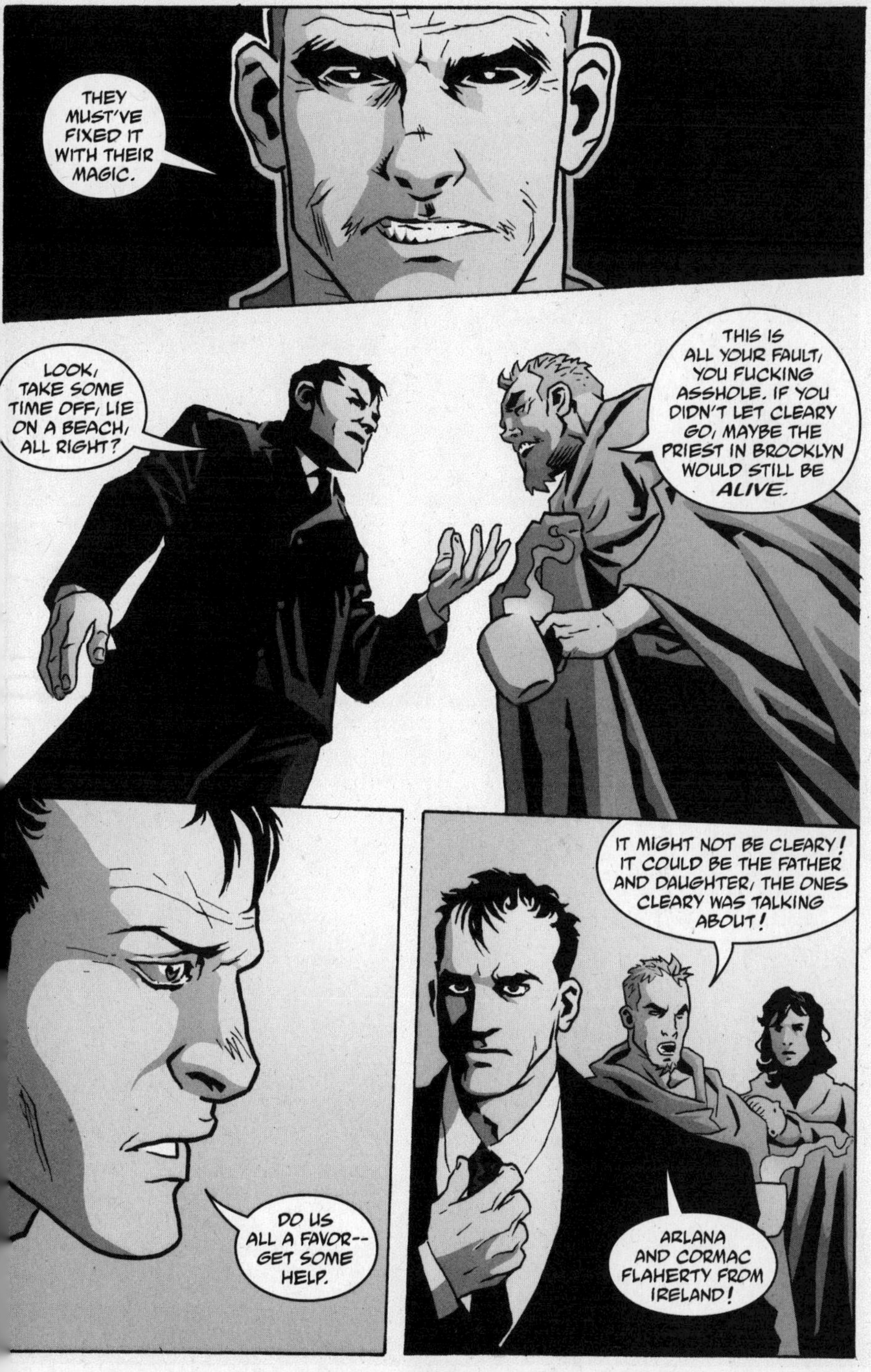
THEY MUST'VE FIXED IT WITH THEIR MAGIC.
LOOK, TAKE SOME TIME OFF, LIE ON A BEACH, ALL RIGHT?
THIS IS ALL YOUR FAULT, YOU FUCKING ASSHOLE. IF YOU DIDN'T LET CLEARY GO, MAYBE THE PRIEST IN BROOKLYN WOULD STILL BE ALIVE.
DO US ALL A FAVOR--GET SOME HELP.
IT MIGHT NOT BE CLEARY! IT COULD BE THE FATHER AND DAUGHTER, THE ONES CLEARY WAS TALKING ABOUT!
ARLANA AND CORMAC FLAHERTY FROM IRELAND!

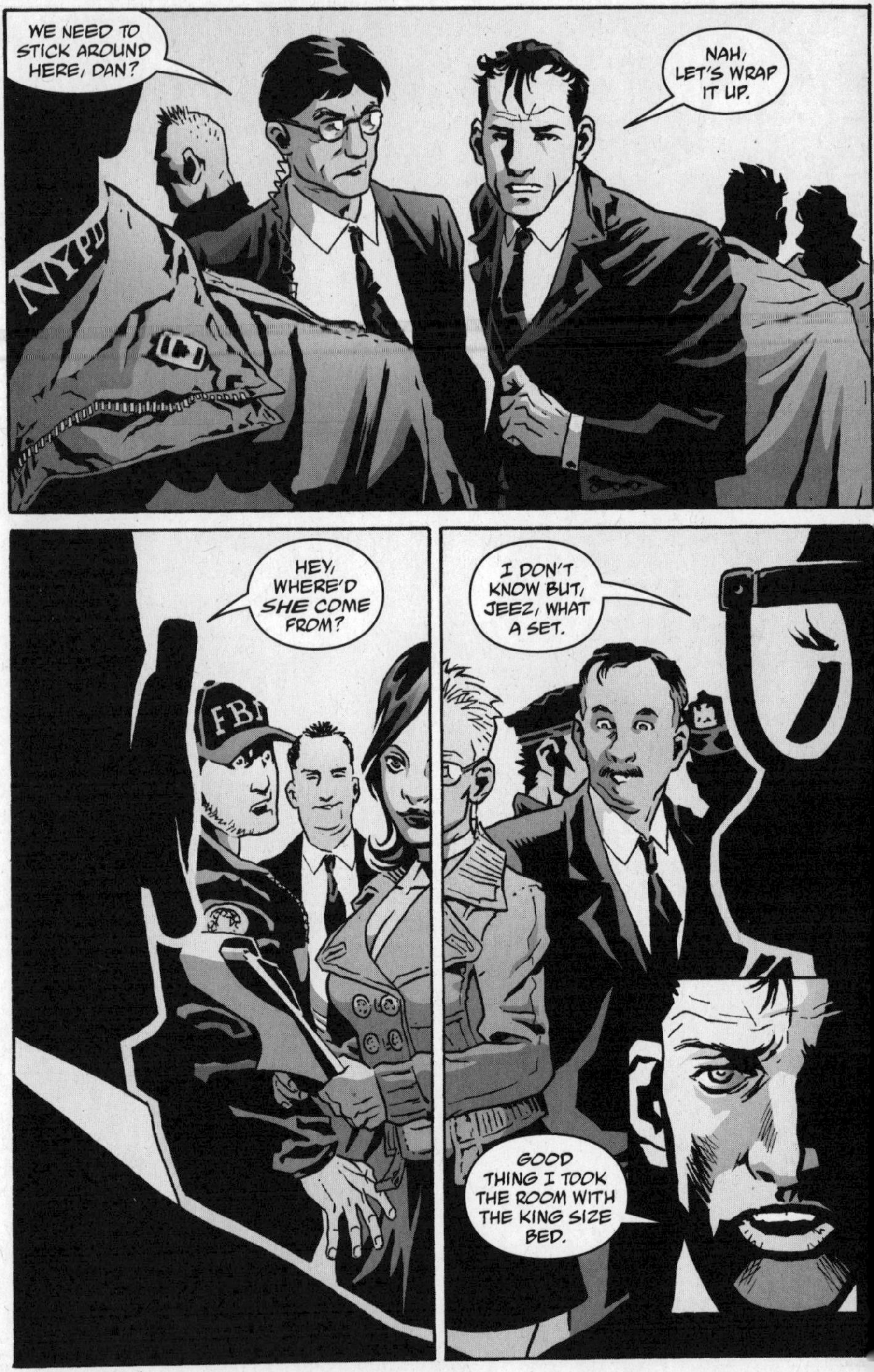
WE NEED TO STICK AROUND HERE, DAN?
NAH, LET'S WRAP IT UP.
NYPD
HEY, WHERE'D *SHE* COME FROM?
FBI
I DON'T KNOW BUT, JEEZ, WHAT A SET.
GOOD THING I TOOK THE ROOM WITH THE KING SIZE BED.

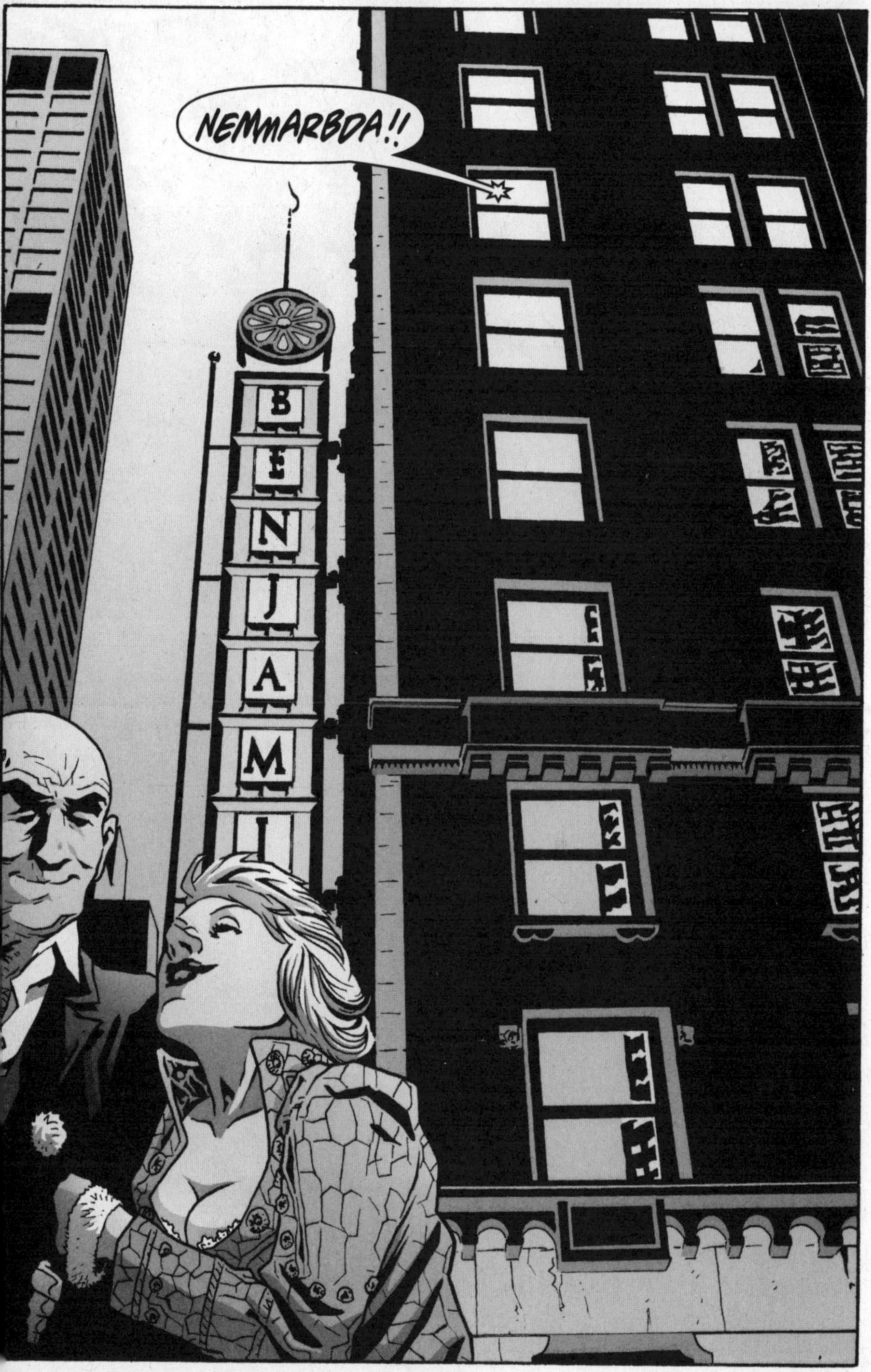
NEMMARBDA!!
B
E
N
J
A
M
I

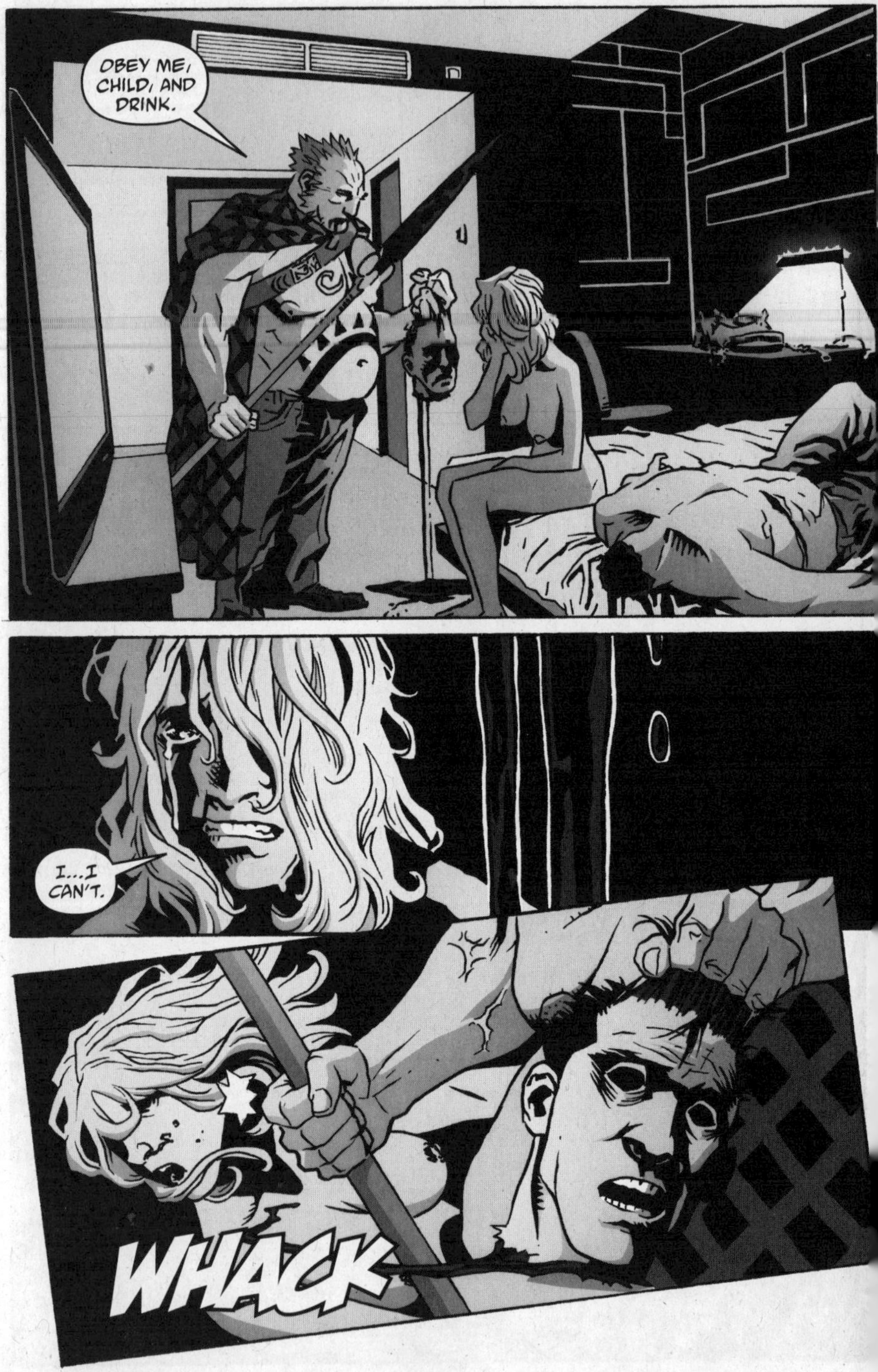
OBEY ME, CHILD, AND DRINK.
I...I CAN'T.
WHACK

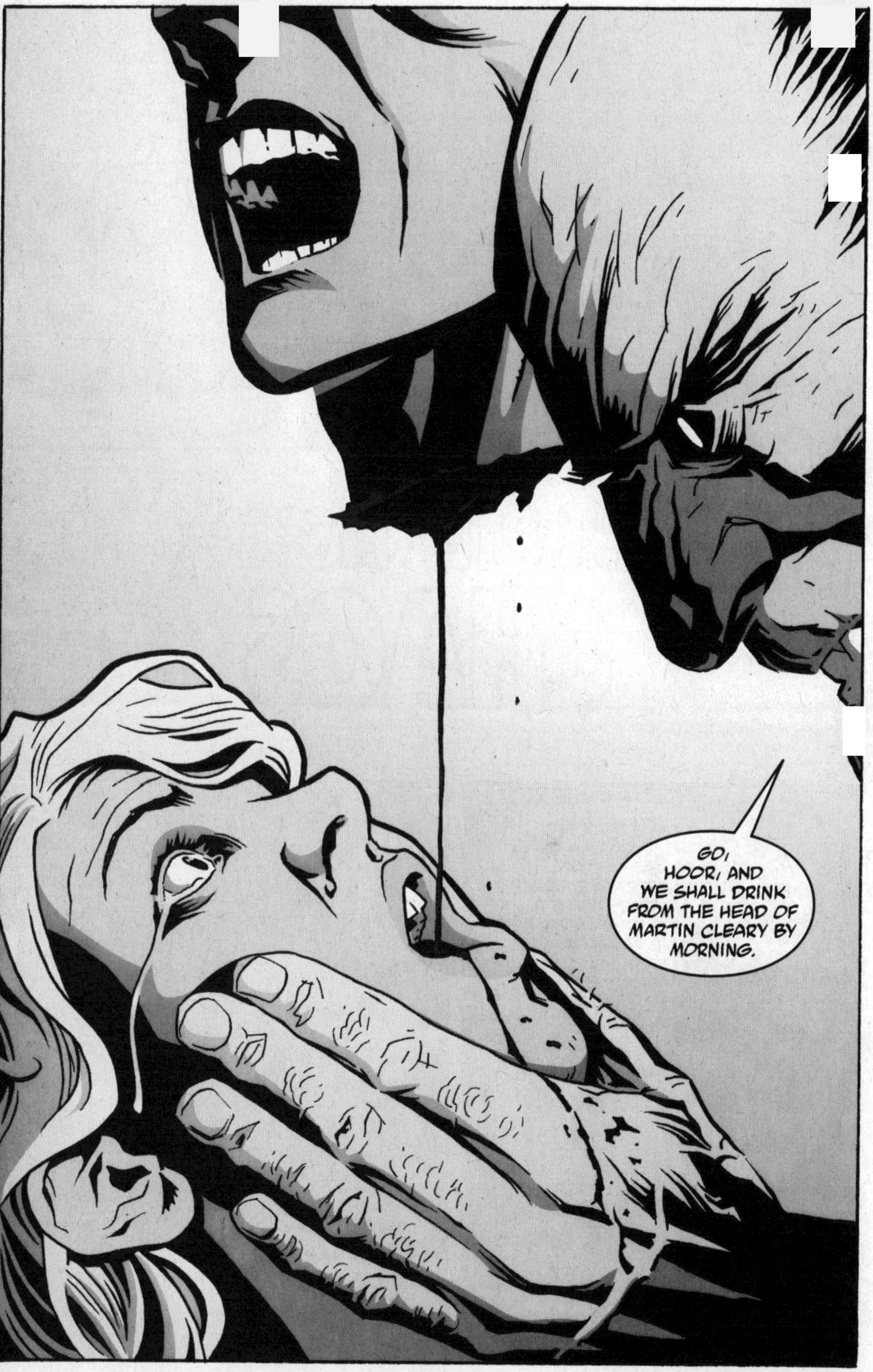
GO, HOOR, AND WE SHALL DRINK FROM THE HEAD OF MARTIN CLEARY BY MORNING.

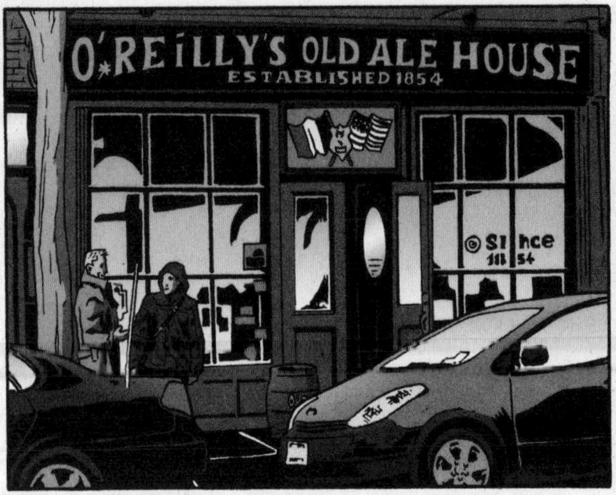
O'REILLY'S OLD ALE HOUSE
ESTABLISHED 1854
SINCE 1854

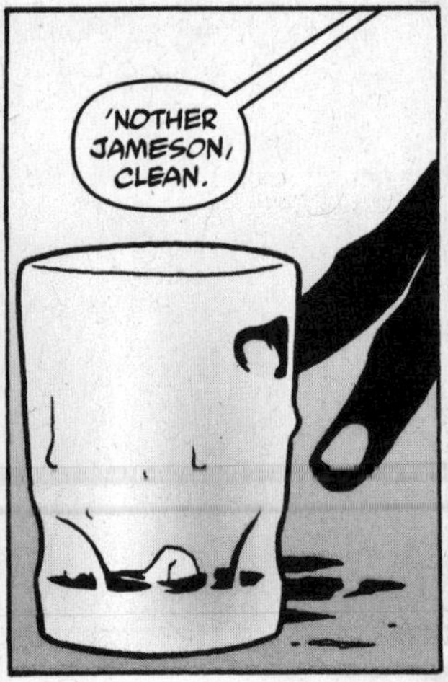
'NOTHER JAMESON, CLEAN.

CHAPTER EIGHT: CHAOS

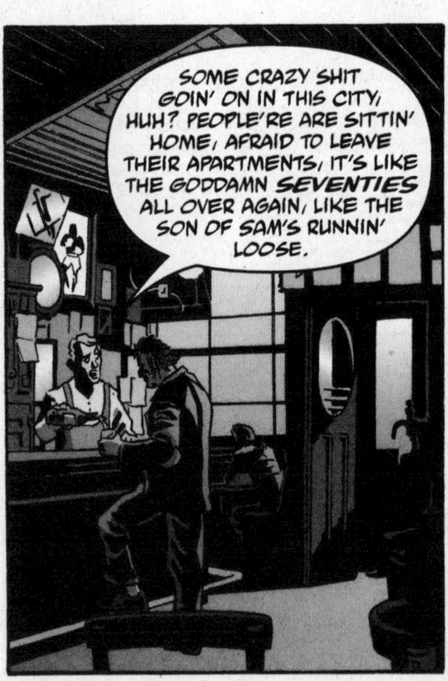
SOME CRAZY SHIT GOIN' ON IN THIS CITY, HUH? PEOPLE'RE ARE SITTIN' HOME, AFRAID TO LEAVE THEIR APARTMENTS, IT'S LIKE THE GODDAMN *SEVENTIES* ALL OVER AGAIN, LIKE THE SON OF SAM'S RUNNIN' LOOSE.

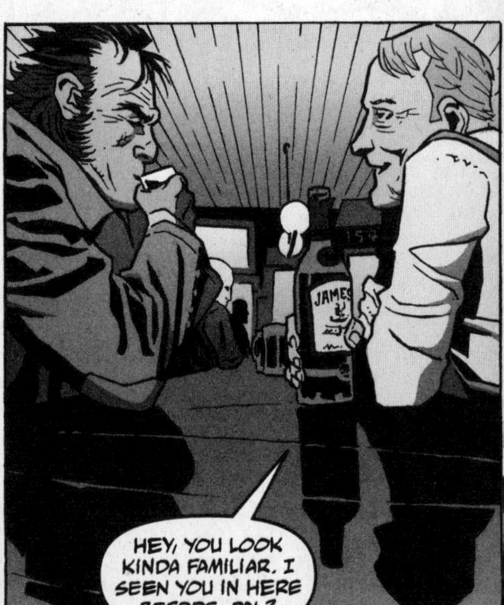
HEY, YOU LOOK KINDA FAMILIAR. I SEEN YOU IN HERE BEFORE, PAL?

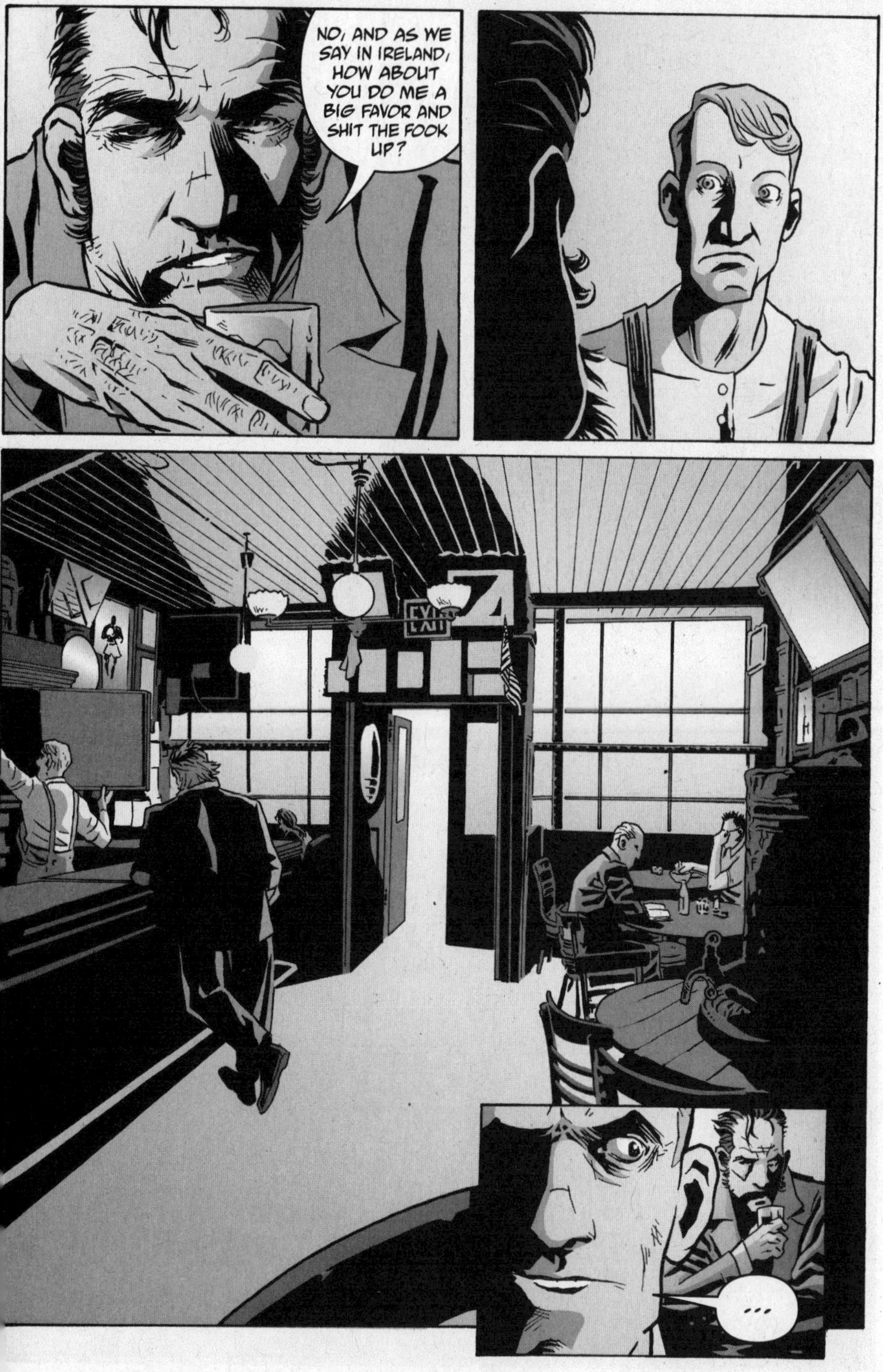
NO, AND AS WE SAY IN IRELAND, HOW ABOUT YOU DO ME A BIG FAVOR AND SHIT THE FOOK UP?
EXIT
...

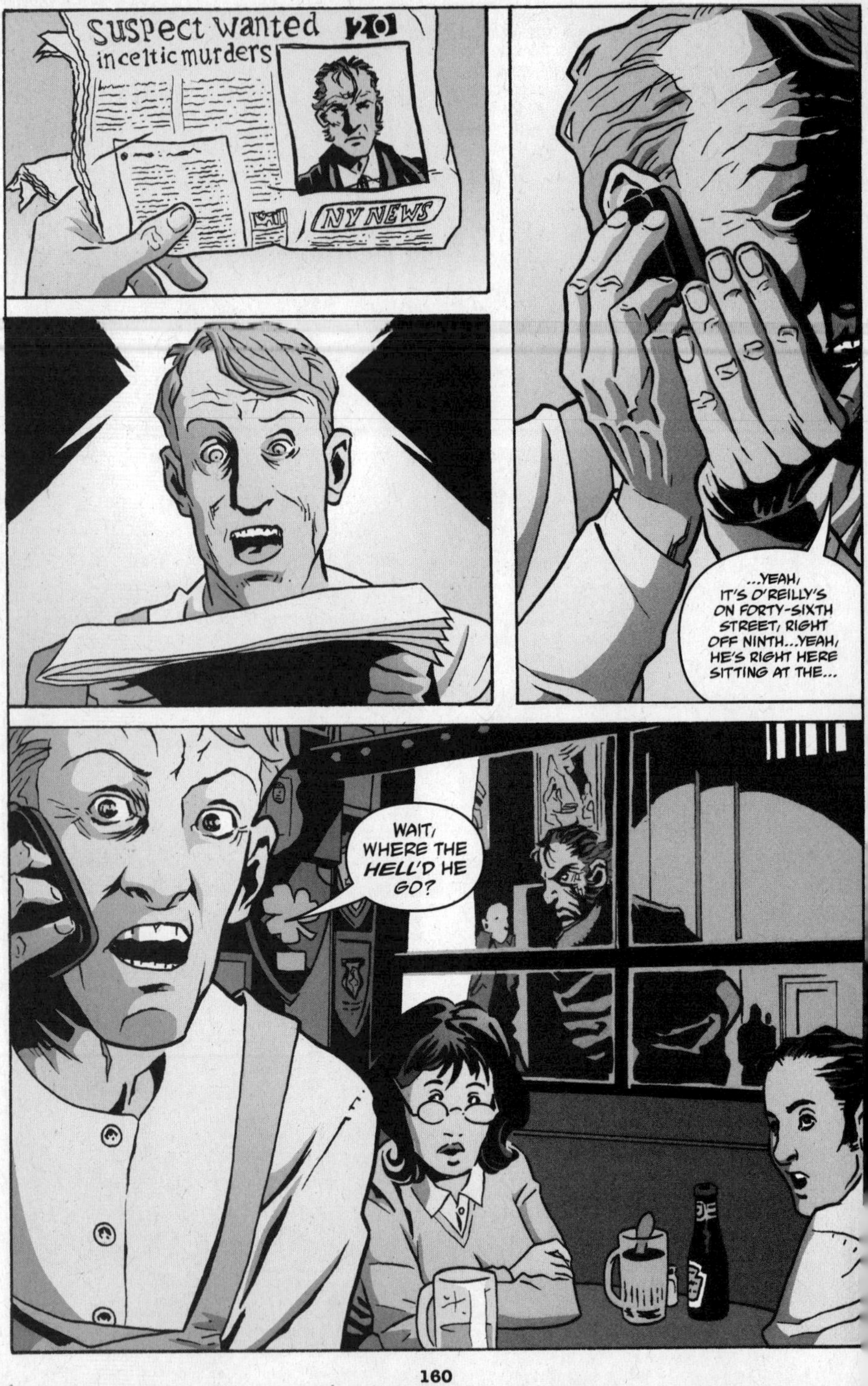
Suspect wanted in celtic murders
NY NEWS
...YEAH, IT'S O'REILLY'S ON FORTY-SIXTH STREET, RIGHT OFF NINTH...YEAH, HE'S RIGHT HERE SITTING AT THE...
WAIT, WHERE THE *HELL*'D HE GO?

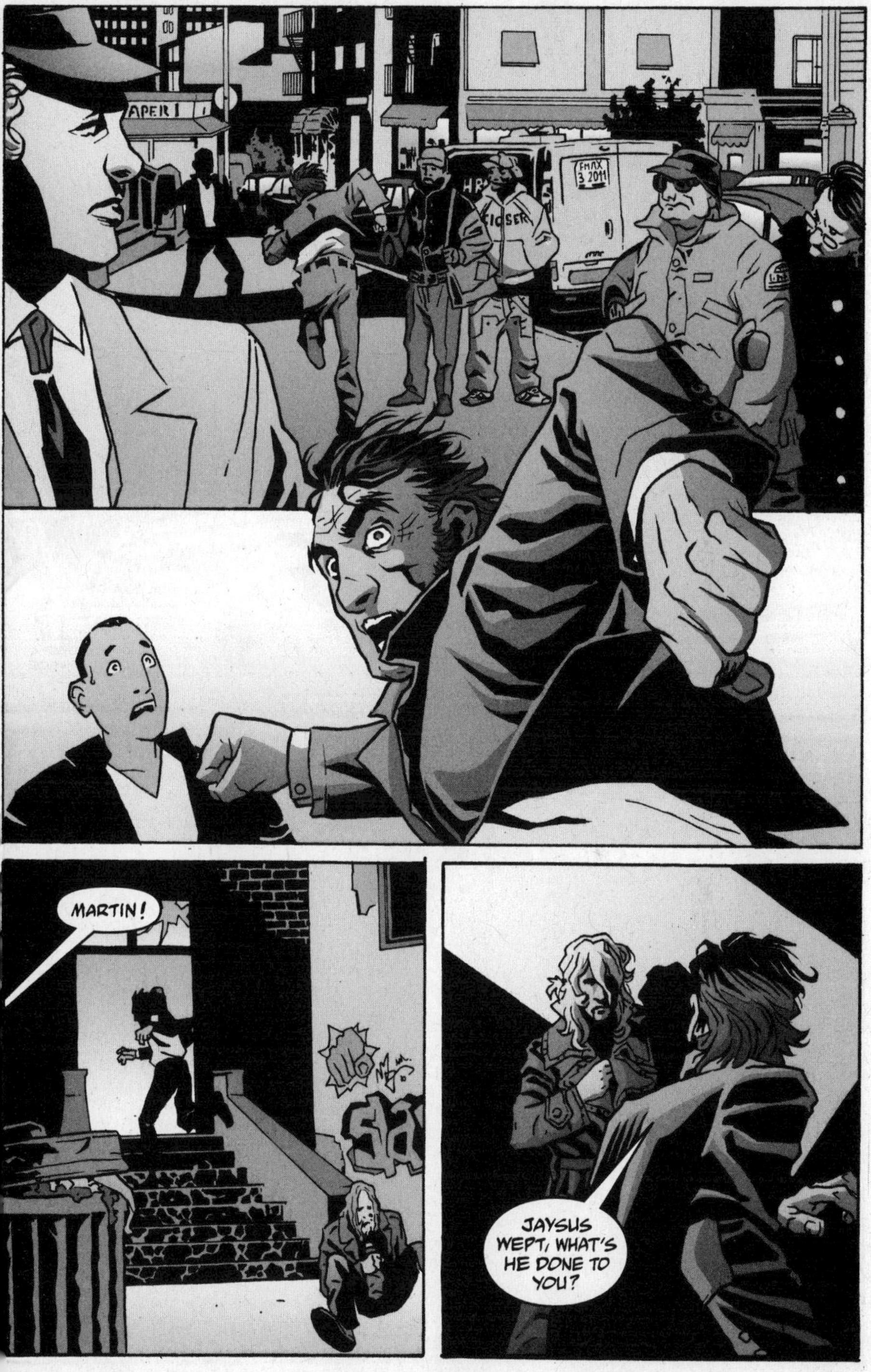
MARTIN!
JAYSUS WEPT, WHAT'S HE DONE TO YOU?

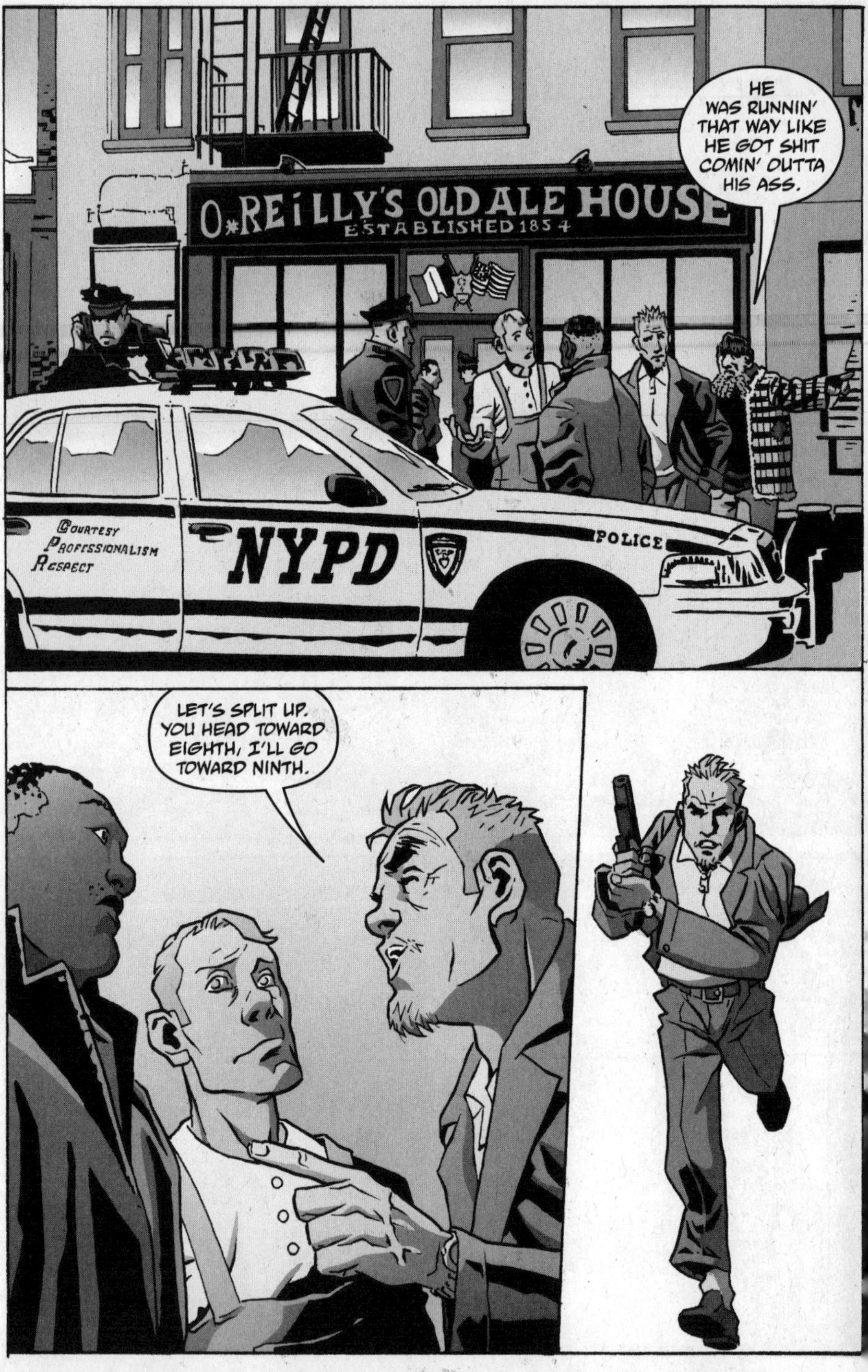
O'REILLY'S OLD ALE HOUSE
ESTABLISHED 1854
HE WAS RUNNIN' THAT WAY LIKE HE GOT SHIT COMIN' OUTTA HIS ASS.
COURTESY PROFESSIONALISM RESPECT
NYPD
POLICE
LET'S SPLIT UP. YOU HEAD TOWARD EIGHTH, I'LL GO TOWARD NINTH.

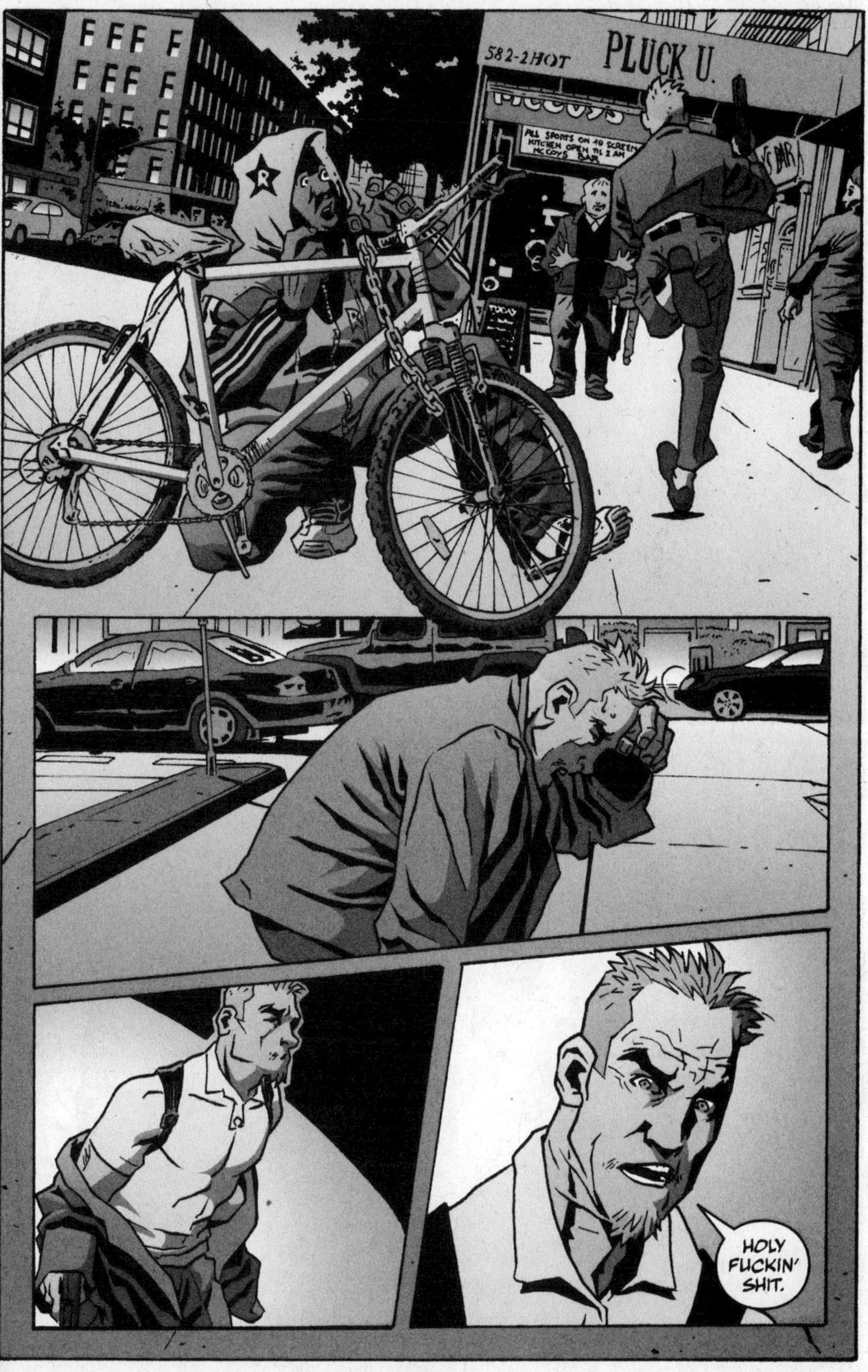
582-2HOT
PLUCK U.
ALL SPORTS ON 40 SCREENS
KITCHEN OPEN TIL 2 AM
McCOYS BAR
TODAY
HOLY FUCKIN' SHIT.

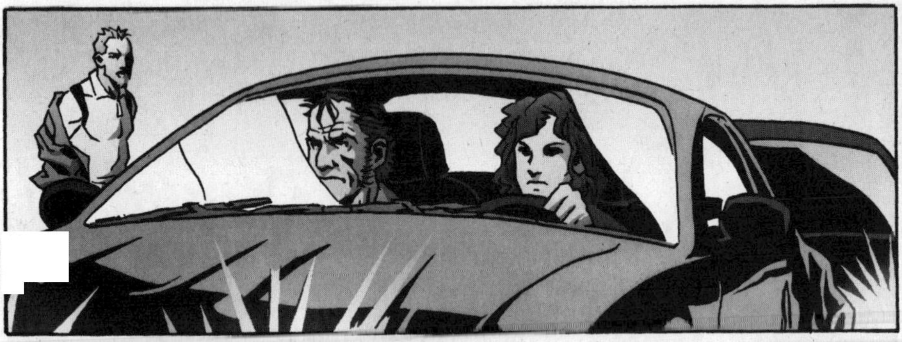

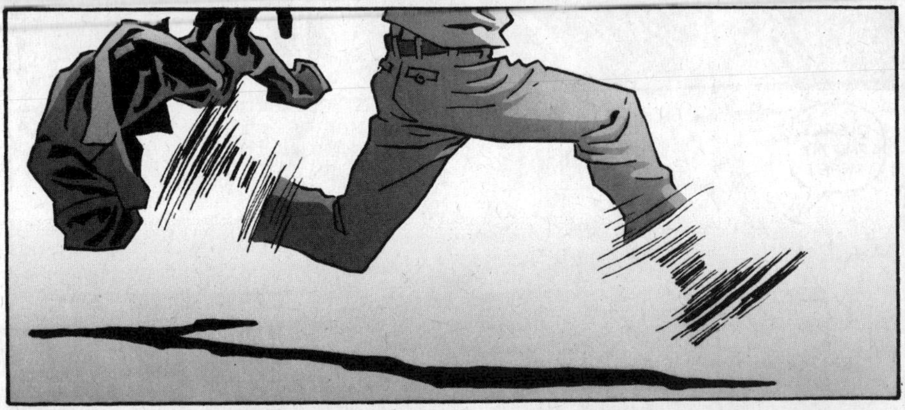

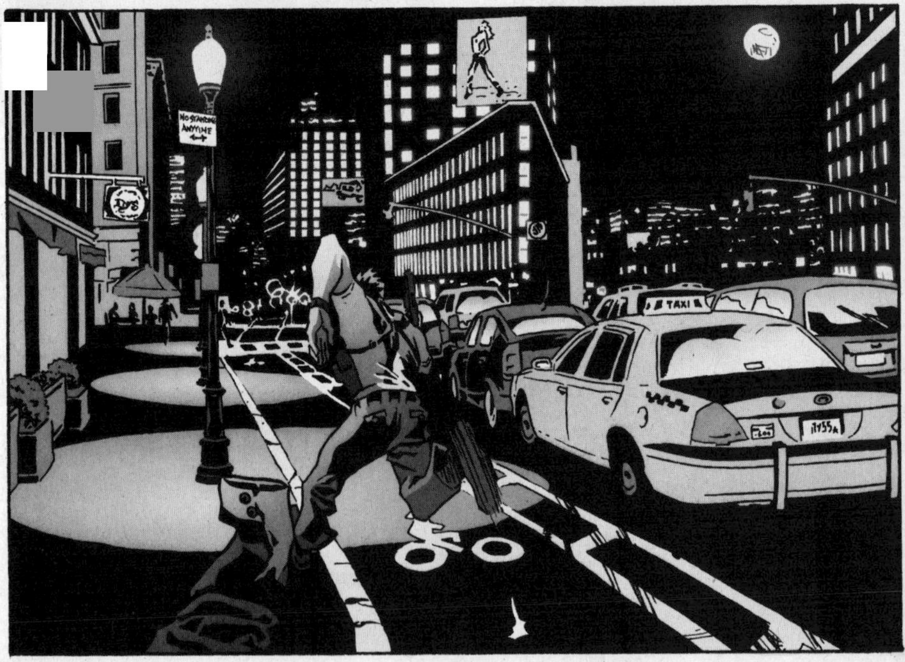
NO STANDING ANYTIME
TAXI

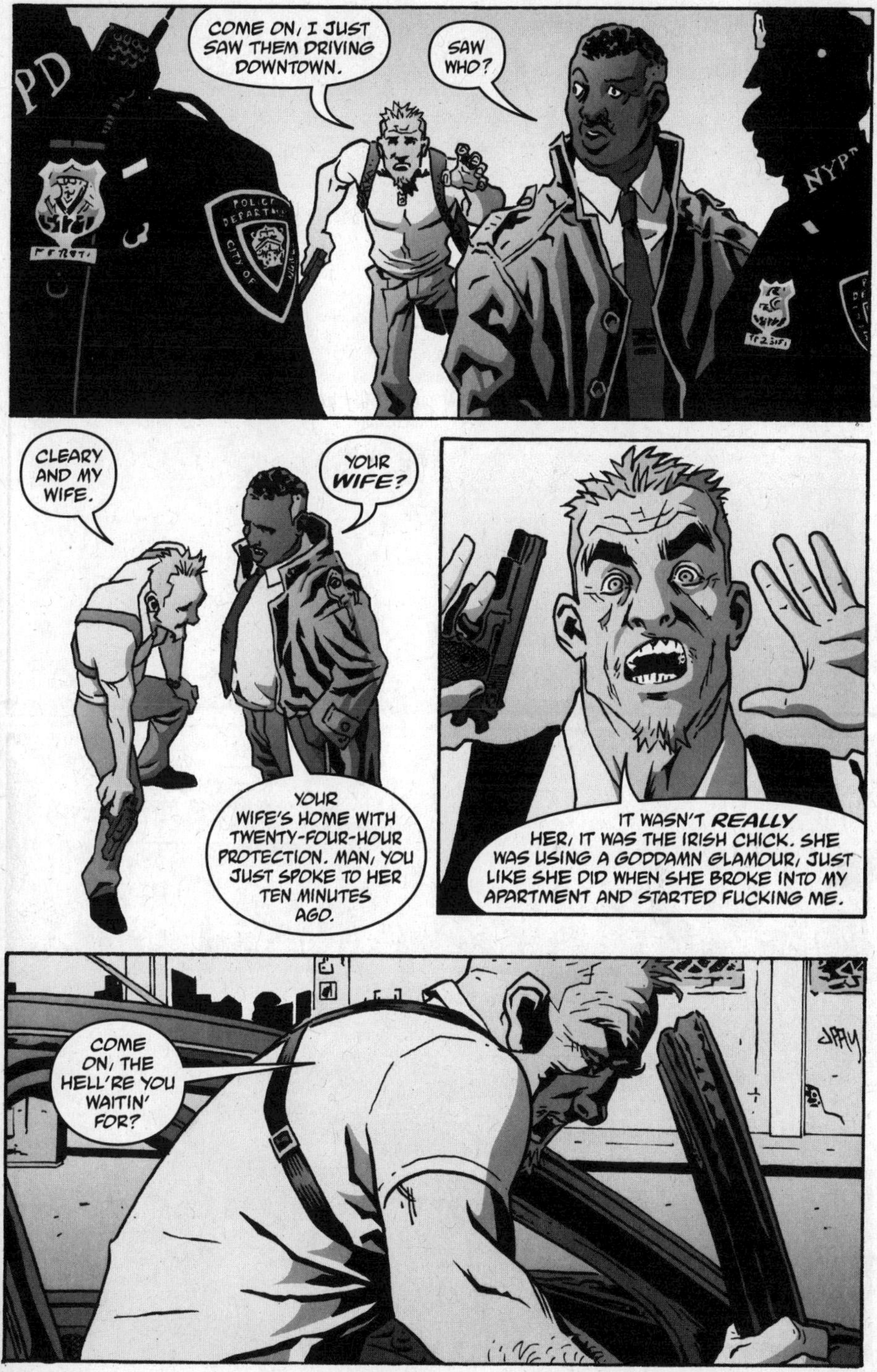
COME ON, I JUST SAW THEM DRIVING DOWNTOWN.
SAW WHO?
CLEARY AND MY WIFE.
YOUR *WIFE?*
YOUR WIFE'S HOME WITH TWENTY-FOUR-HOUR PROTECTION. MAN, YOU JUST SPOKE TO HER TEN MINUTES AGO.
IT WASN'T ***REALLY*** HER, IT WAS THE IRISH CHICK. SHE WAS USING A GODDAMN GLAMOUR, JUST LIKE SHE DID WHEN SHE BROKE INTO MY APARTMENT AND STARTED FUCKING ME.
COME ON, THE HELL'RE YOU WAITIN' FOR?

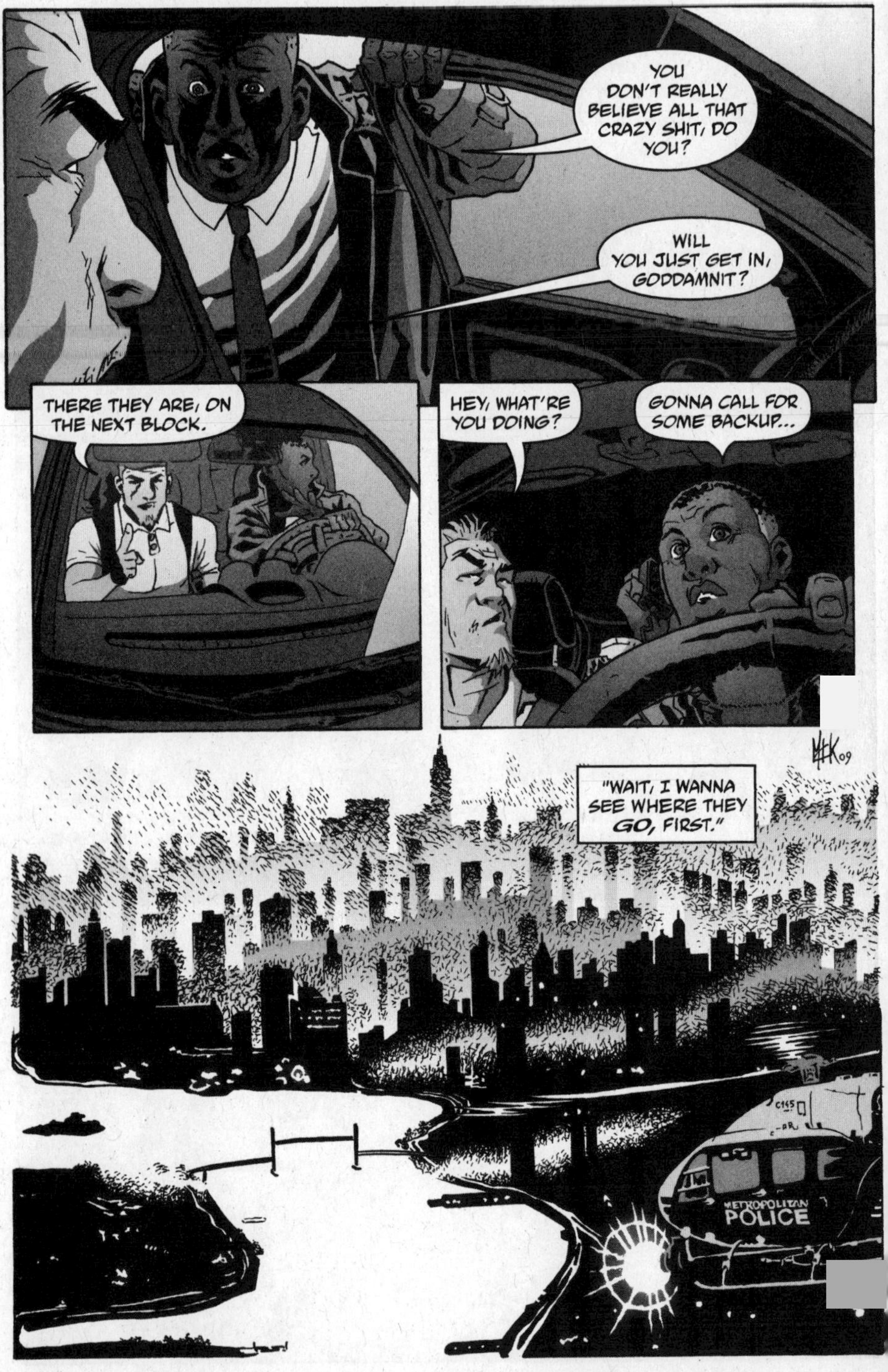
YOU DON'T REALLY BELIEVE ALL THAT CRAZY SHIT, DO YOU?
WILL YOU JUST GET IN, GODDAMNIT?
THERE THEY ARE, ON THE NEXT BLOCK.
HEY, WHAT'RE YOU DOING?
GONNA CALL FOR SOME BACKUP...
"WAIT, I WANNA SEE WHERE THEY GO, FIRST."
METROPOLITAN
POLICE

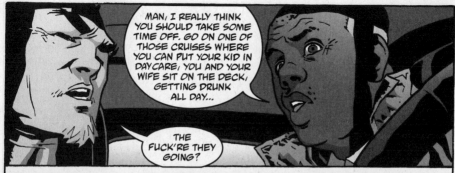

MAN, I REALLY THINK YOU SHOULD TAKE SOME TIME OFF. GO ON ONE OF THOSE CRUISES WHERE YOU CAN PUT YOUR KID IN DAYCARE, YOU AND YOUR WIFE SIT ON THE DECK, GETTING DRUNK ALL DAY...

THE FUCK'RE THEY GOING?

MAYBE WE SHOULD CALL FOR THAT BACKUP NOW?

NOT YET.

WHAT THE HELL?

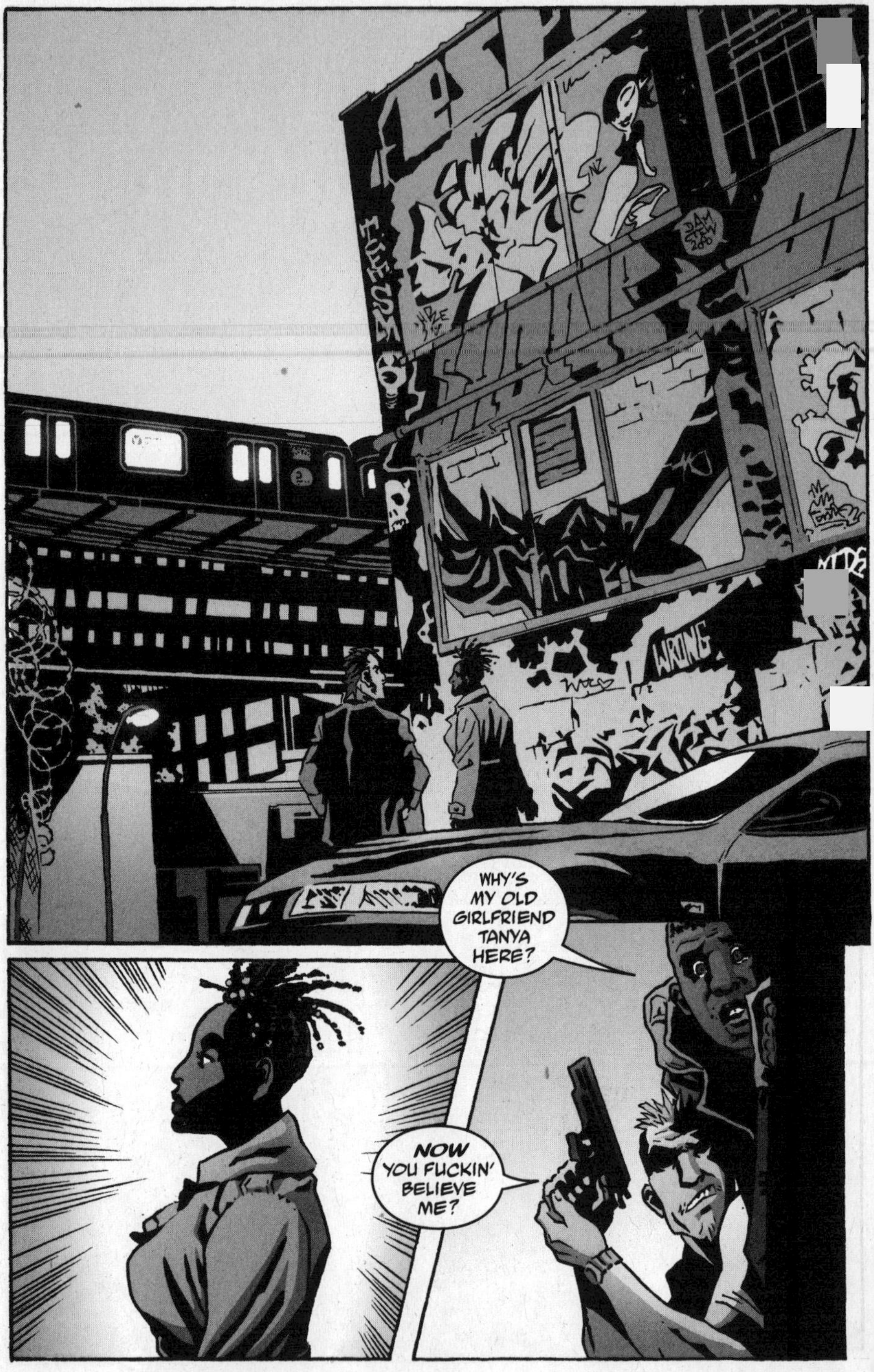
WRONG
WHY'S MY OLD GIRLFRIEND TANYA HERE?
NOW YOU FUCKIN' BELIEVE ME?

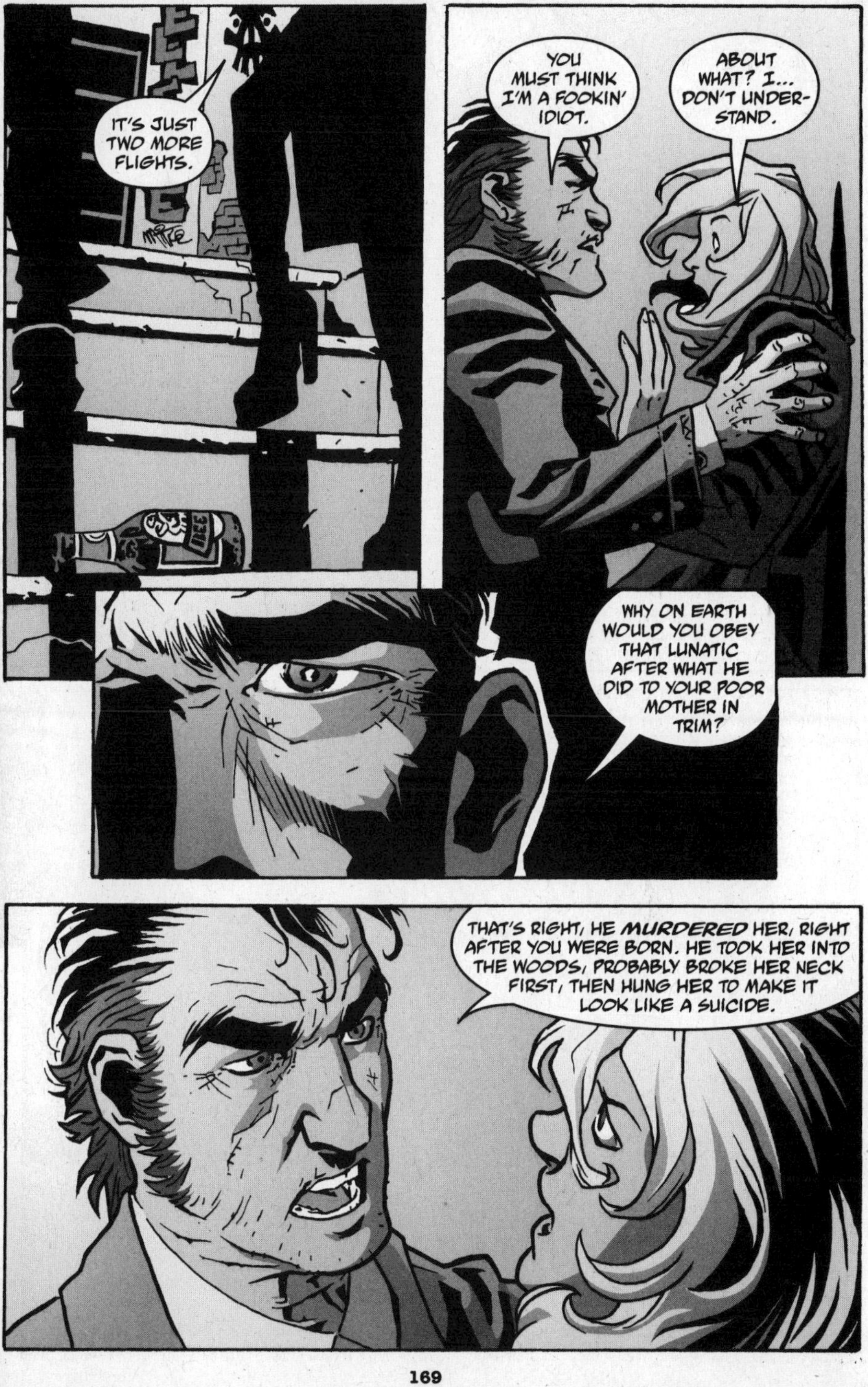
IT'S JUST TWO MORE FLIGHTS.
YOU MUST THINK I'M A FOOKIN' IDIOT.
ABOUT WHAT? I... DON'T UNDER-STAND.
WHY ON EARTH WOULD YOU OBEY THAT LUNATIC AFTER WHAT HE DID TO YOUR POOR MOTHER IN TRIM?
THAT'S RIGHT, HE *MURDERED* HER, RIGHT AFTER YOU WERE BORN. HE TOOK HER INTO THE WOODS, PROBABLY BROKE HER NECK FIRST, THEN HUNG HER TO MAKE IT LOOK LIKE A SUICIDE.

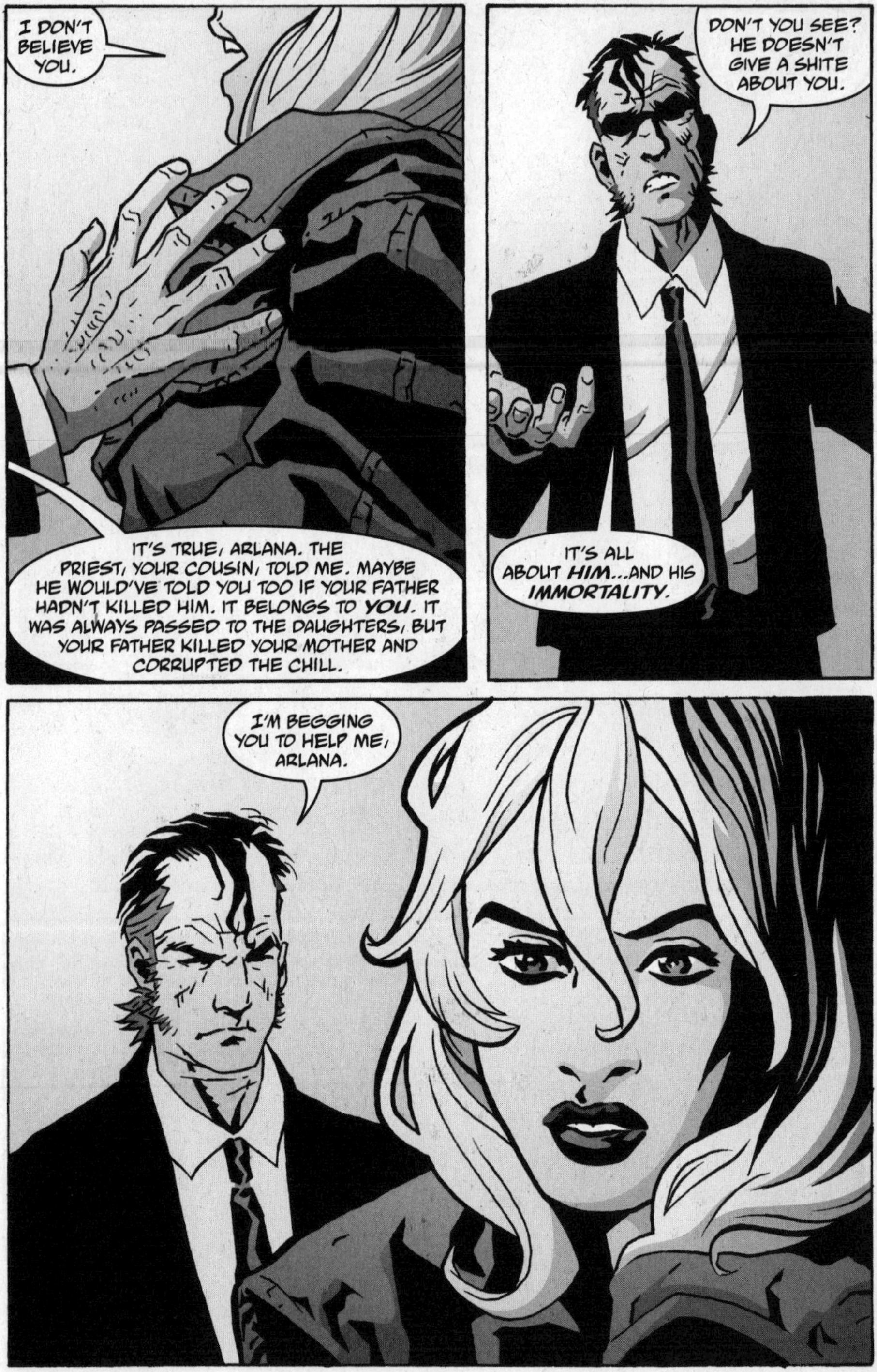
I DON'T BELIEVE YOU.
IT'S TRUE, ARLANA. THE PRIEST, YOUR COUSIN, TOLD ME. MAYBE HE WOULD'VE TOLD YOU TOO IF YOUR FATHER HADN'T KILLED HIM. IT BELONGS TO *YOU*. IT WAS ALWAYS PASSED TO THE DAUGHTERS, BUT YOUR FATHER KILLED YOUR MOTHER AND CORRUPTED THE CHILL.
DON'T YOU SEE? HE DOESN'T GIVE A SHITE ABOUT YOU.
IT'S ALL ABOUT *HIM*...AND HIS *IMMORTALITY*.
I'M BEGGING YOU TO HELP ME, ARLANA.

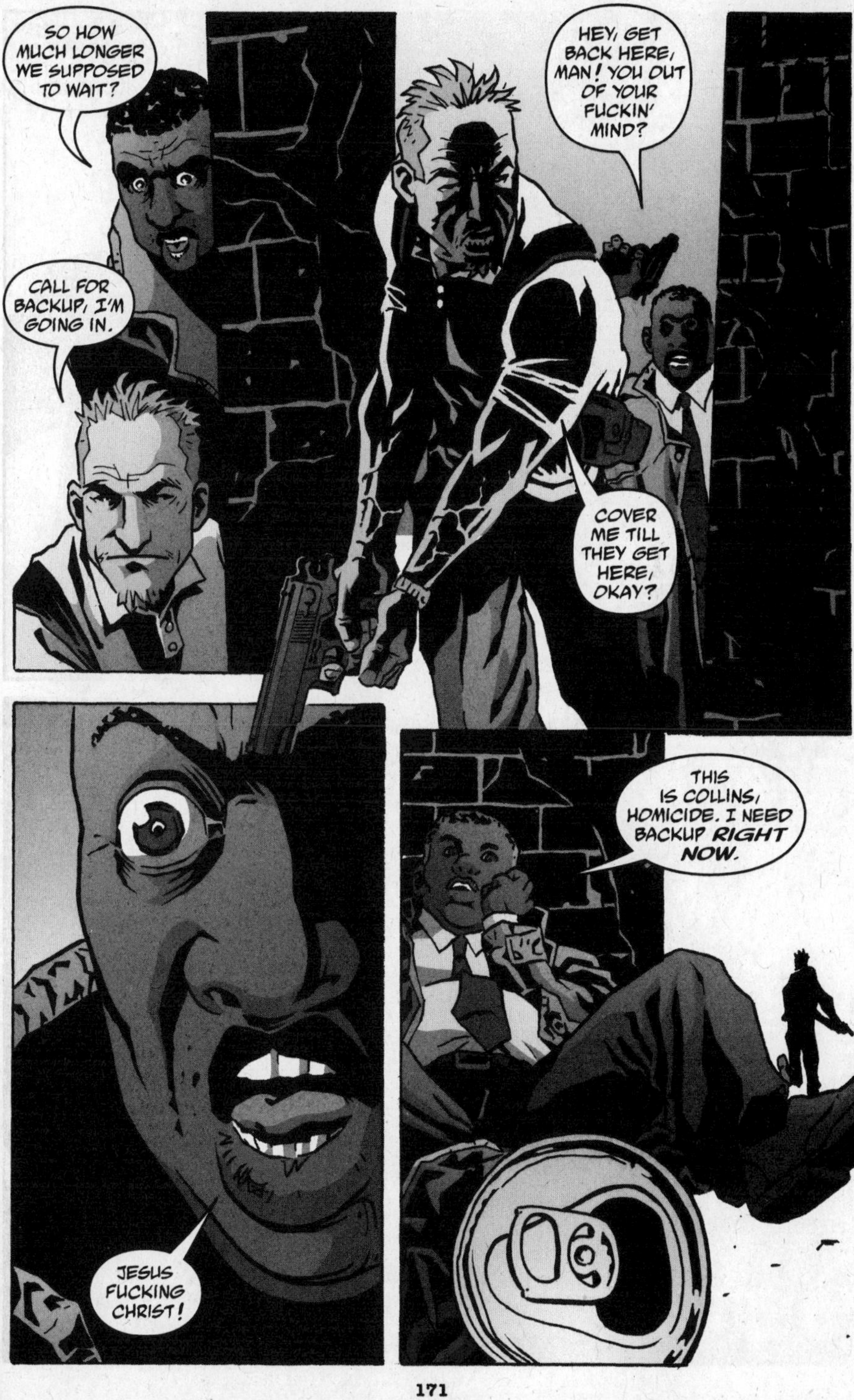
SO HOW MUCH LONGER WE SUPPOSED TO WAIT?
CALL FOR BACKUP, I'M GOING IN.
HEY, GET BACK HERE, MAN! YOU OUT OF YOUR FUCKIN' MIND?
COVER ME TILL THEY GET HERE, OKAY?
JESUS FUCKING CHRIST!
THIS IS COLLINS, HOMICIDE. I NEED BACKUP RIGHT NOW.

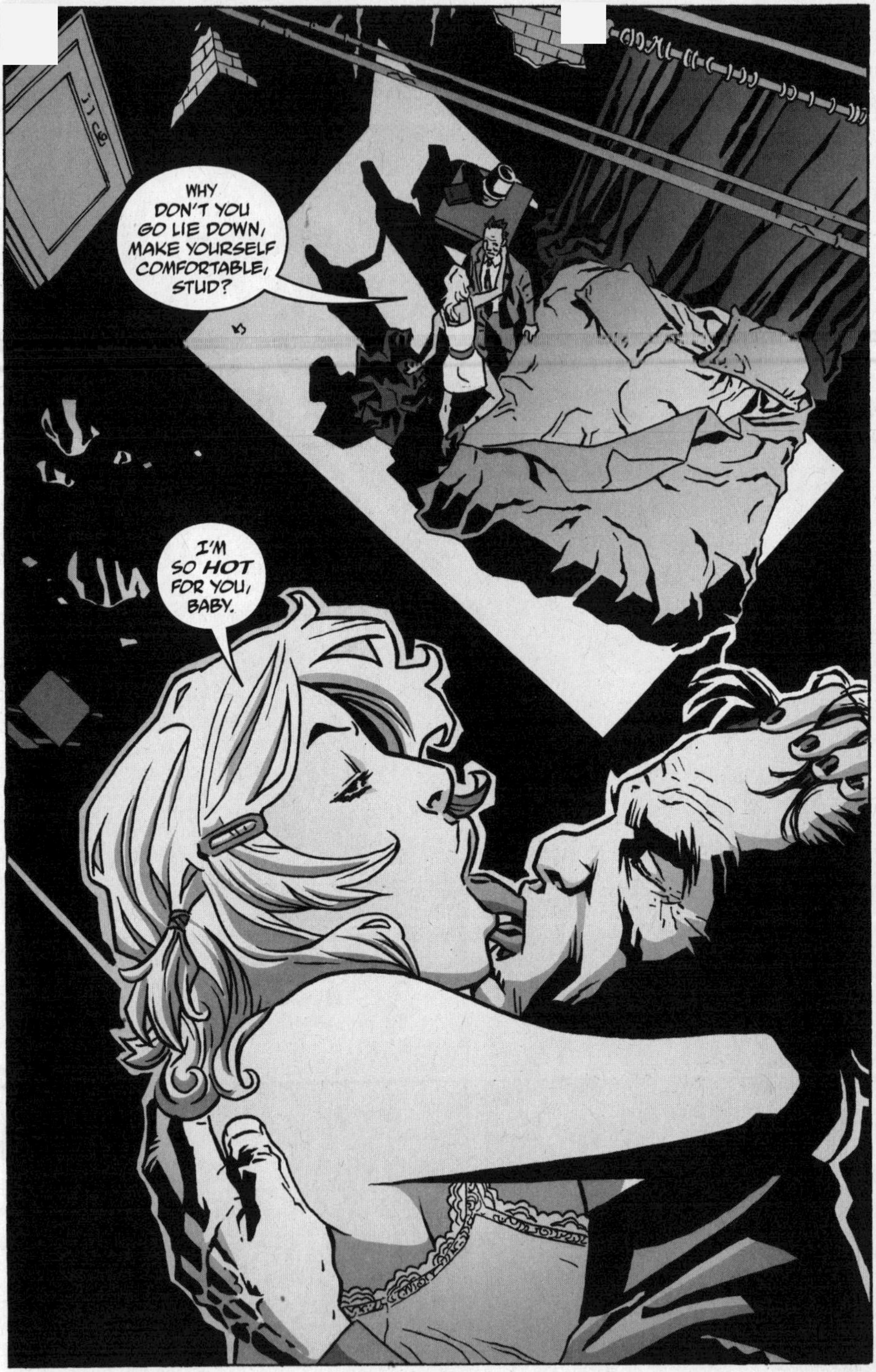
WHY DON'T YOU GO LIE DOWN, MAKE YOURSELF COMFORTABLE, STUD?
I'M SO **HOT** FOR YOU, BABY.

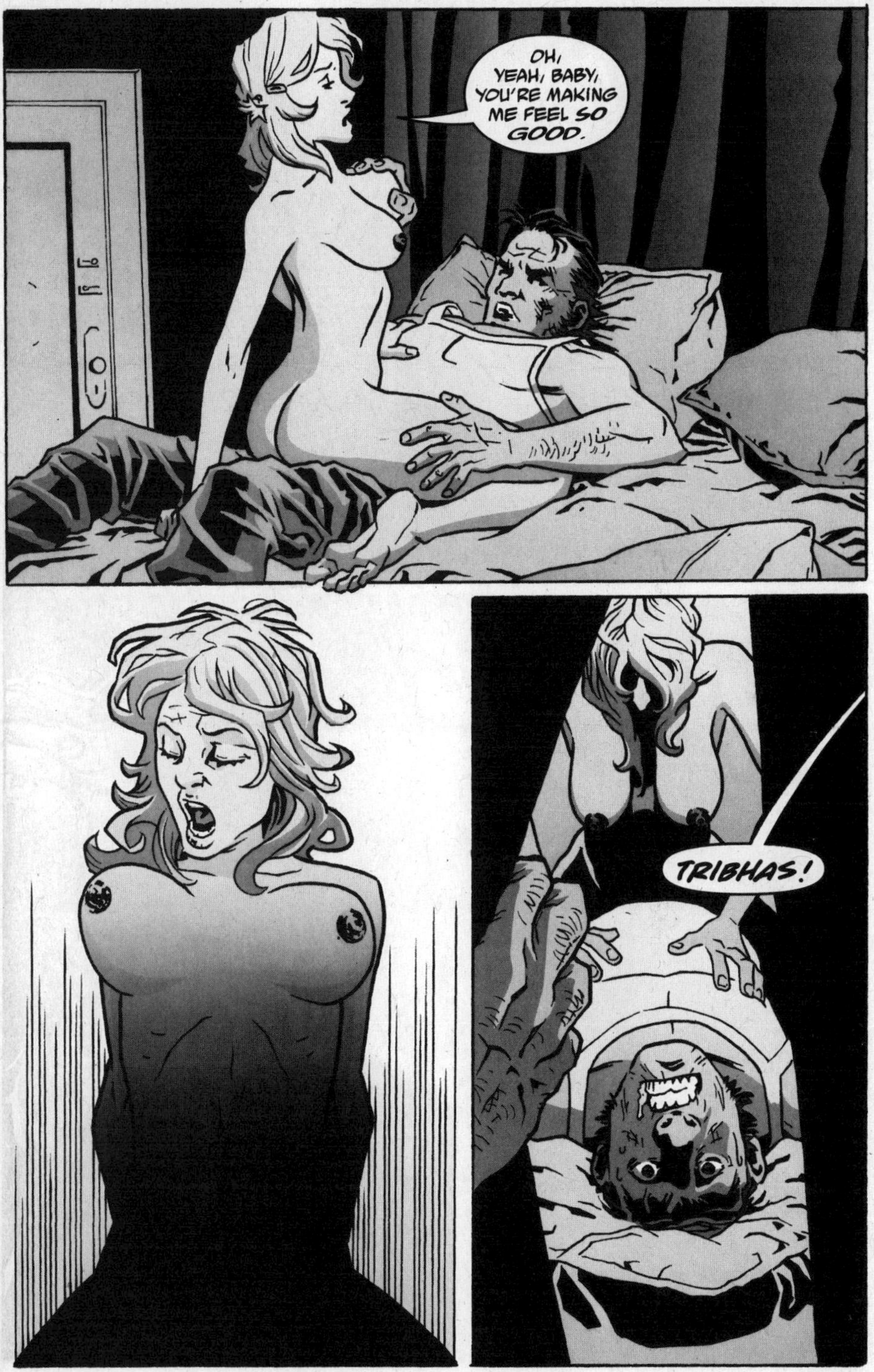
OH, YEAH, BABY, YOU'RE MAKING ME FEEL SO GOOD.
TRIBHAS!

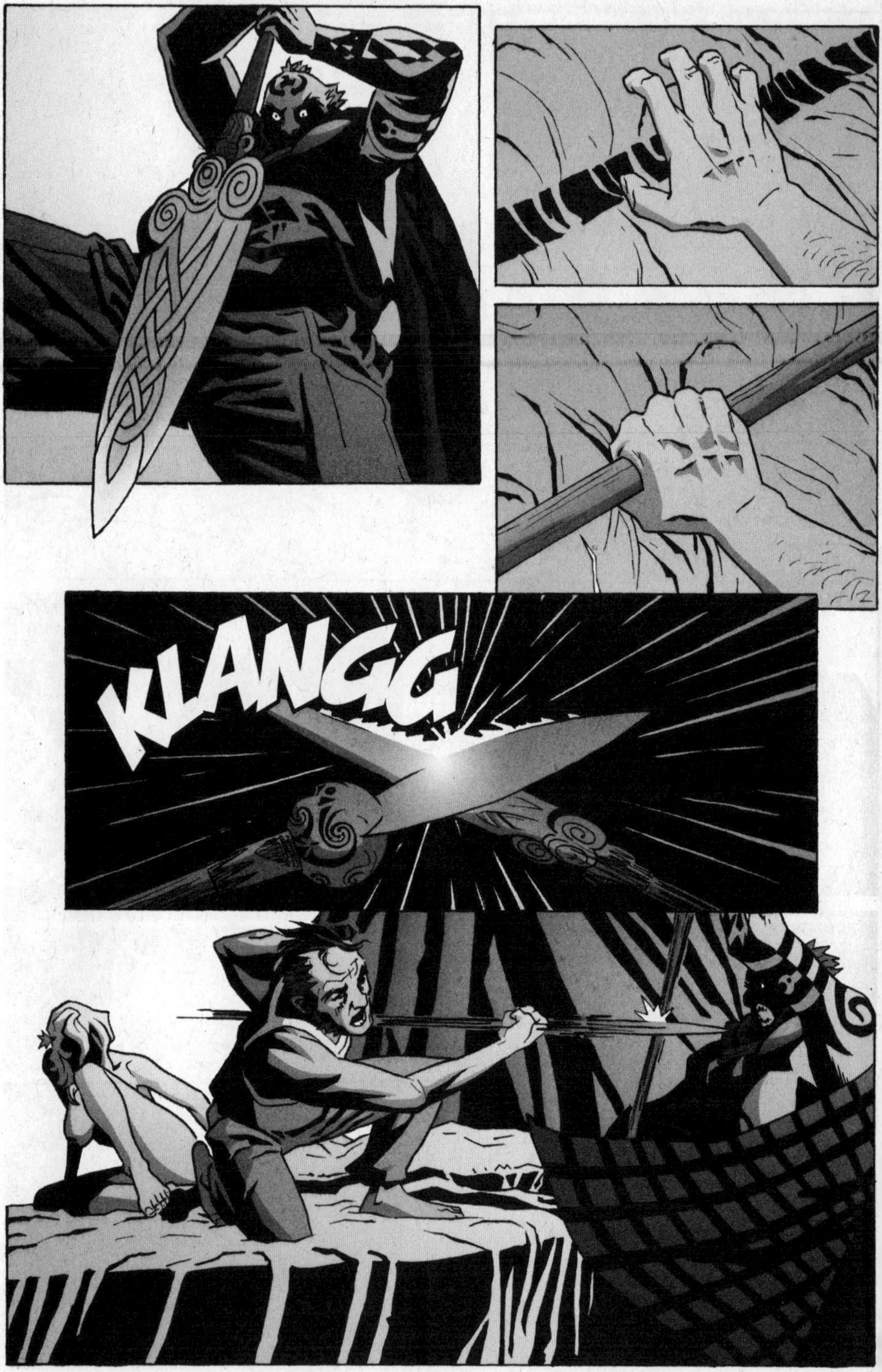
KLANGG

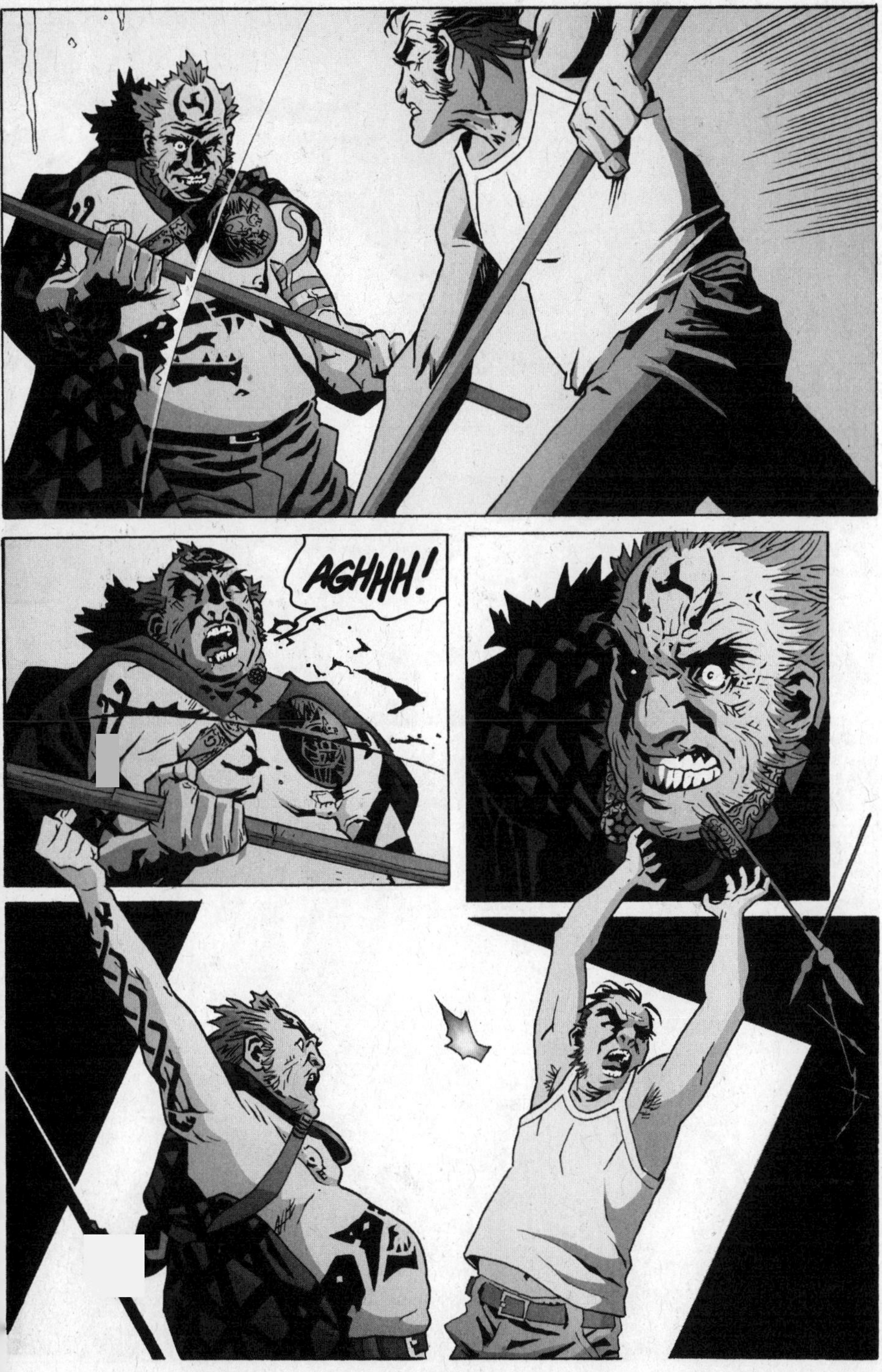
AGHHH!

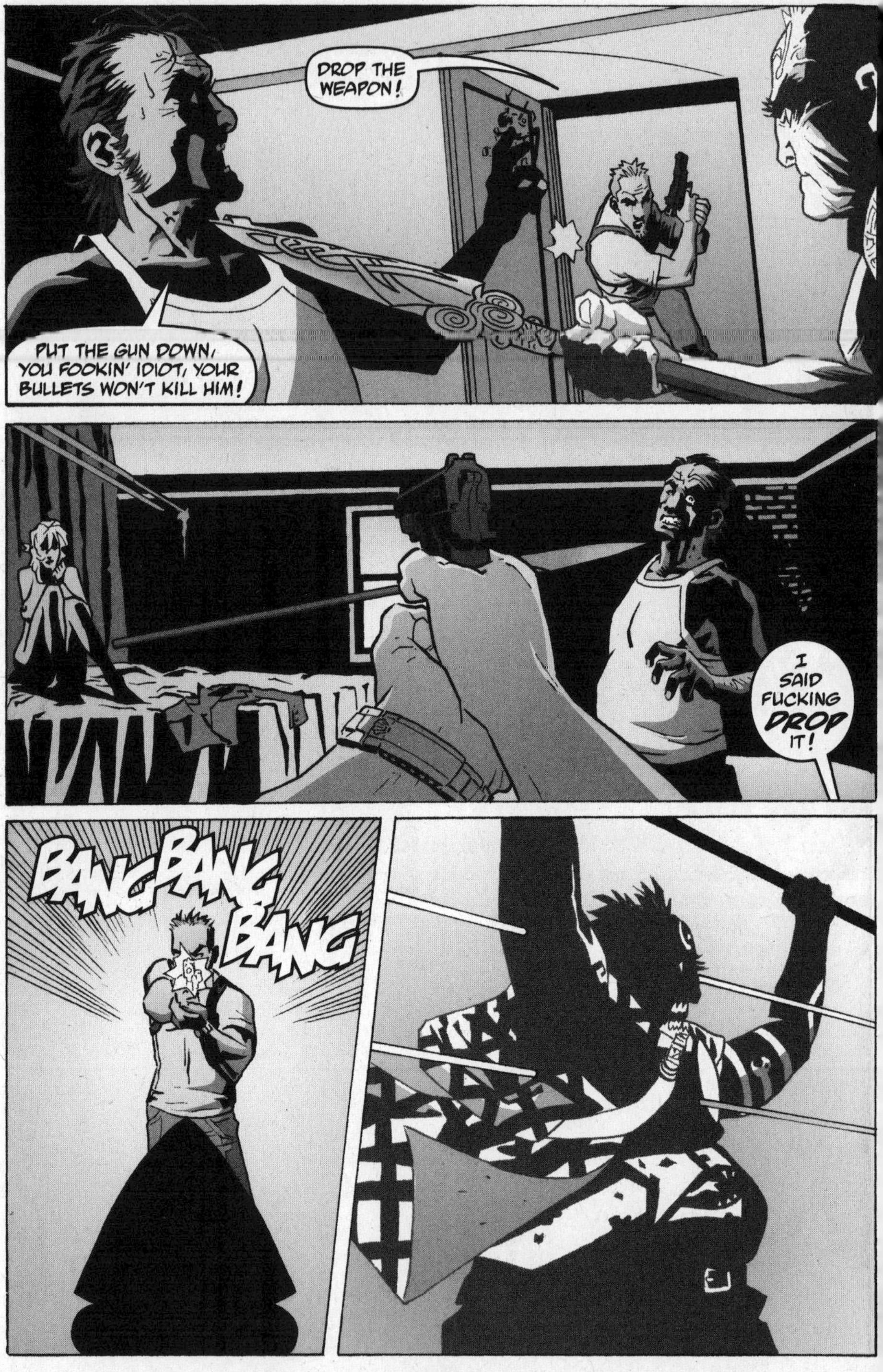
DROP THE WEAPON!
PUT THE GUN DOWN, YOU FOOKIN' IDIOT, YOUR BULLETS WON'T KILL HIM!
I SAID FUCKING DROP IT!
BANG BANG BANG

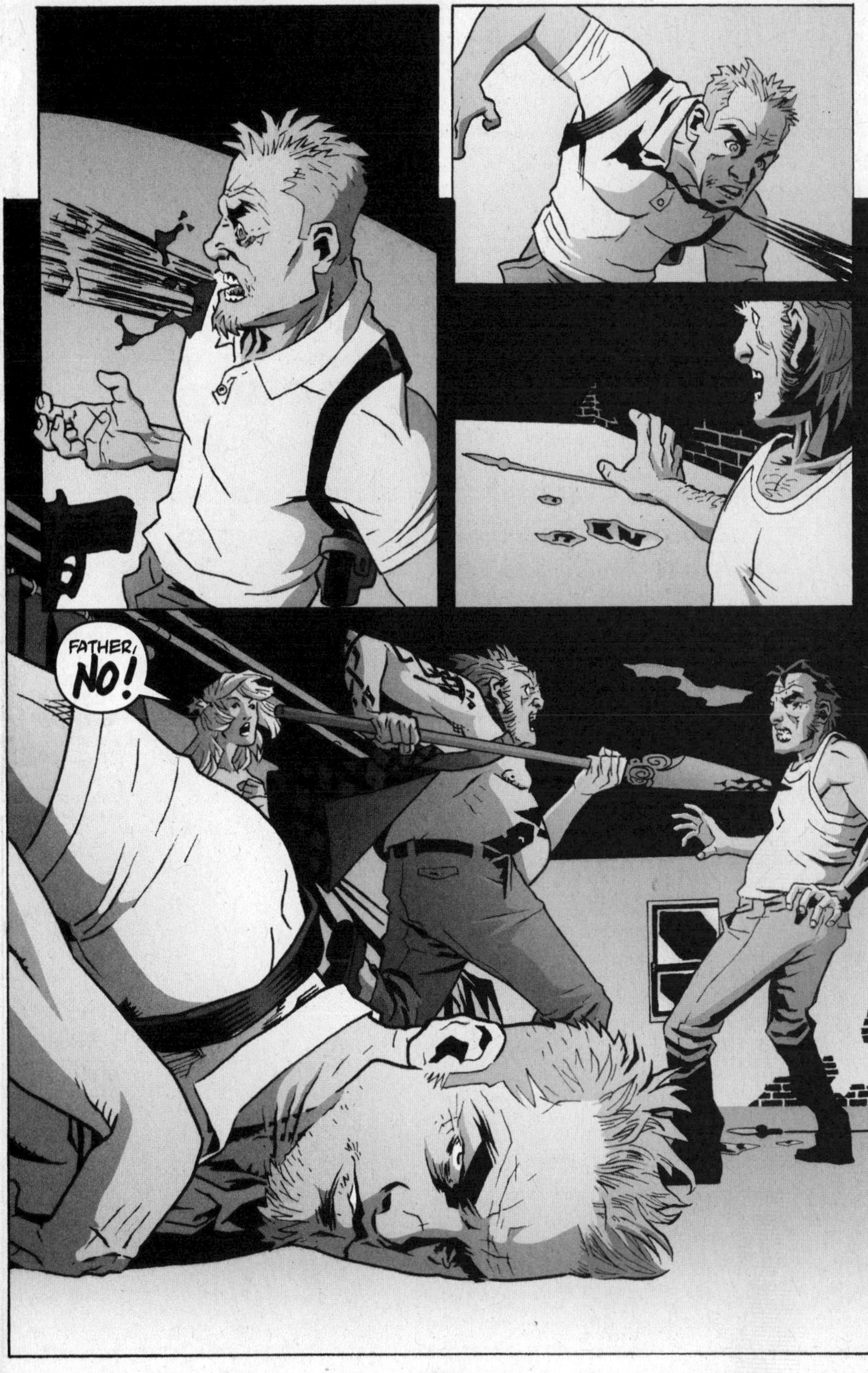
FATHER, NO!

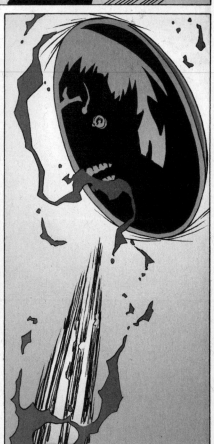

DOMUN!

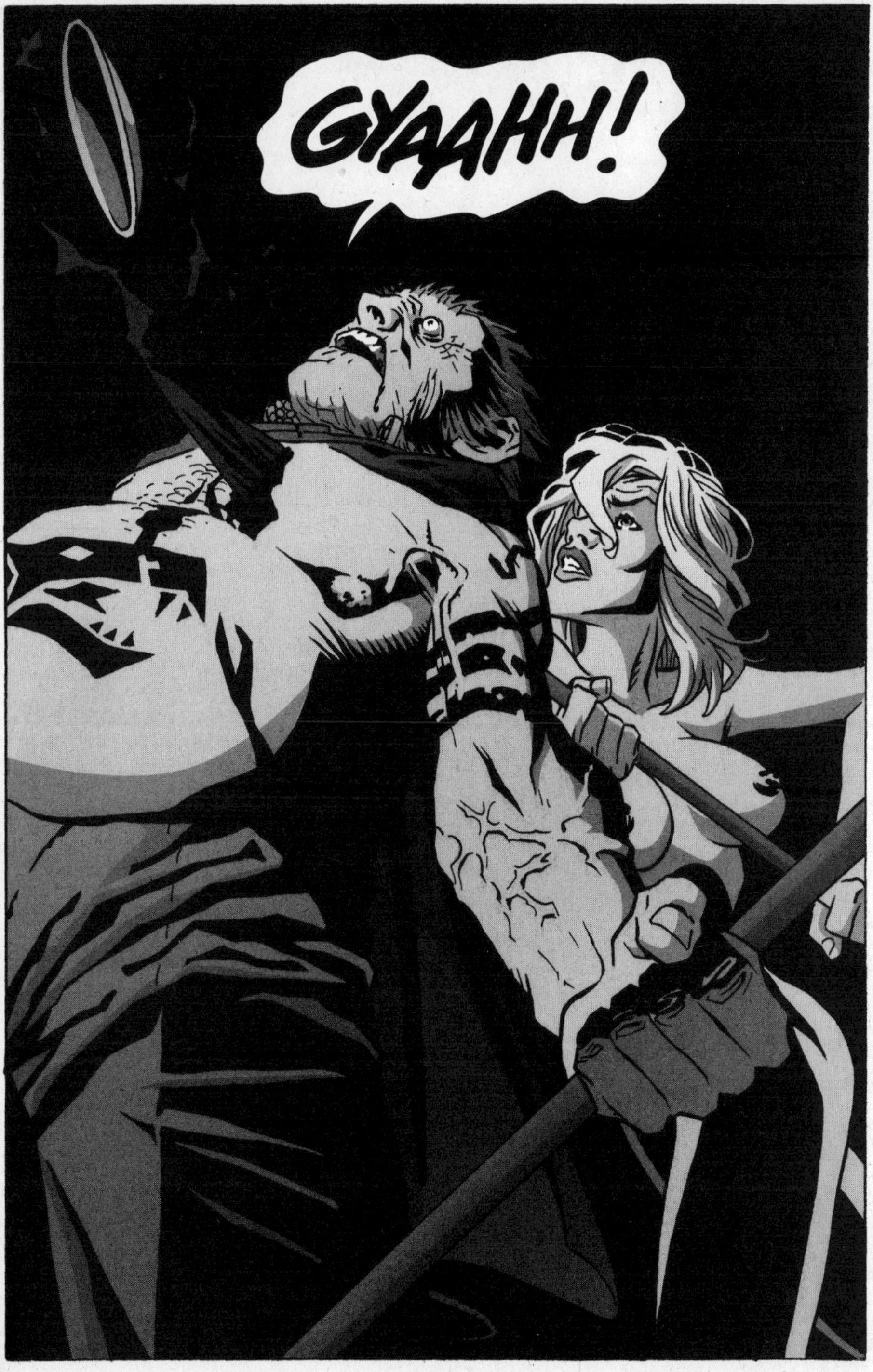
GYAAHH!

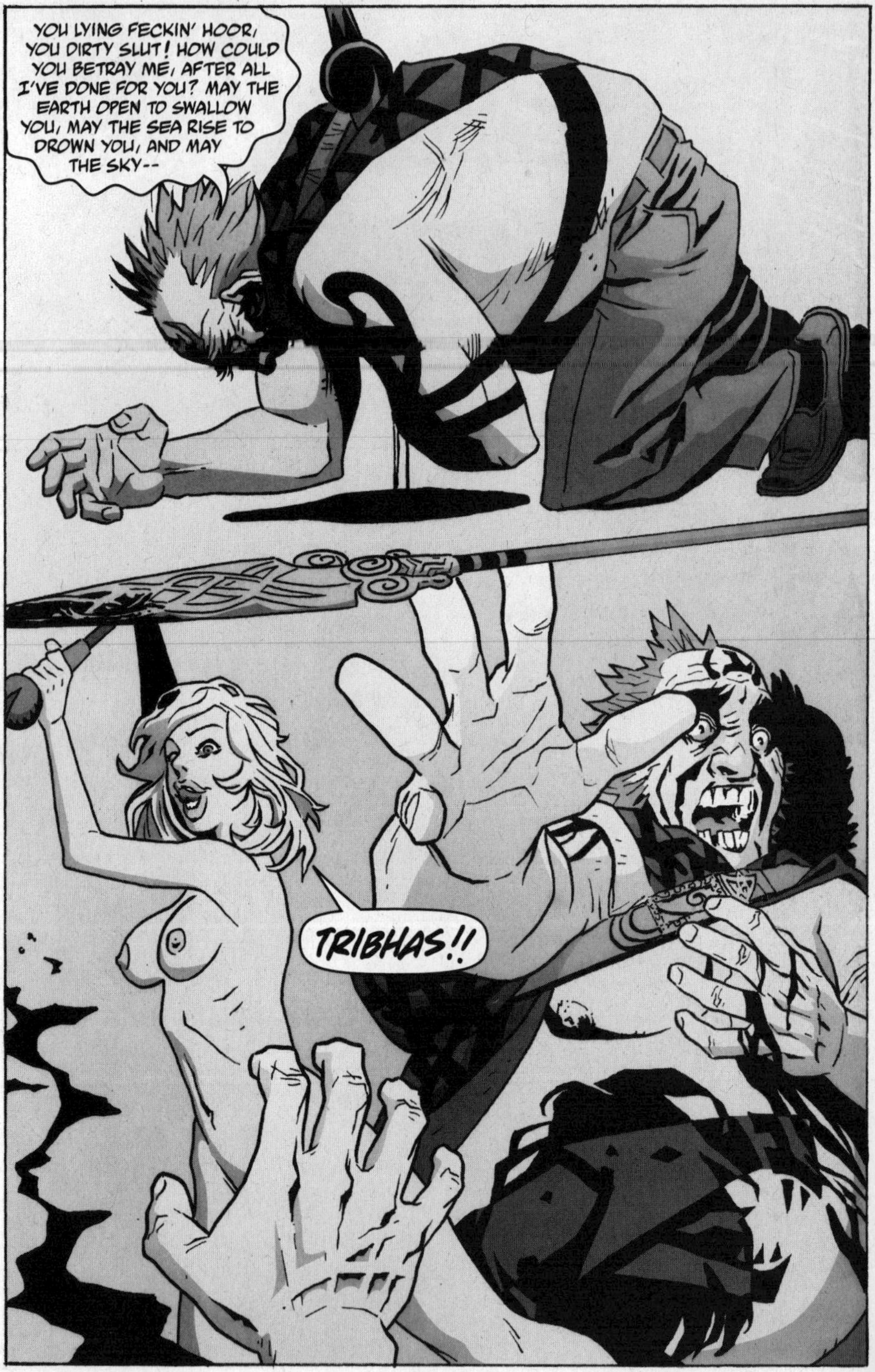
YOU LYING FECKIN' HOOR, YOU DIRTY SLUT! HOW COULD YOU BETRAY ME, AFTER ALL I'VE DONE FOR YOU? MAY THE EARTH OPEN TO SWALLOW YOU, MAY THE SEA RISE TO DROWN YOU, AND MAY THE SKY--
TRIBHAS!!

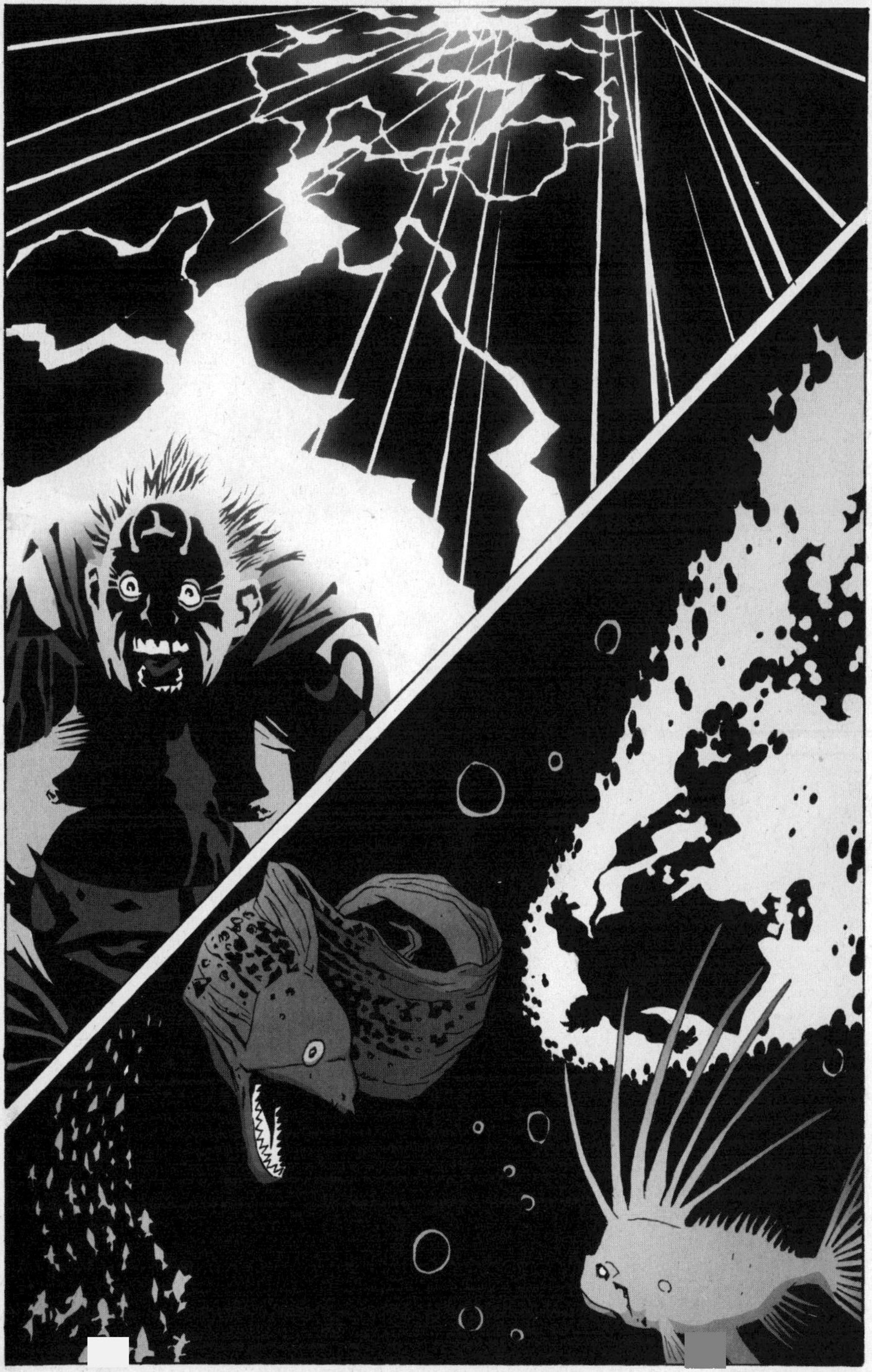

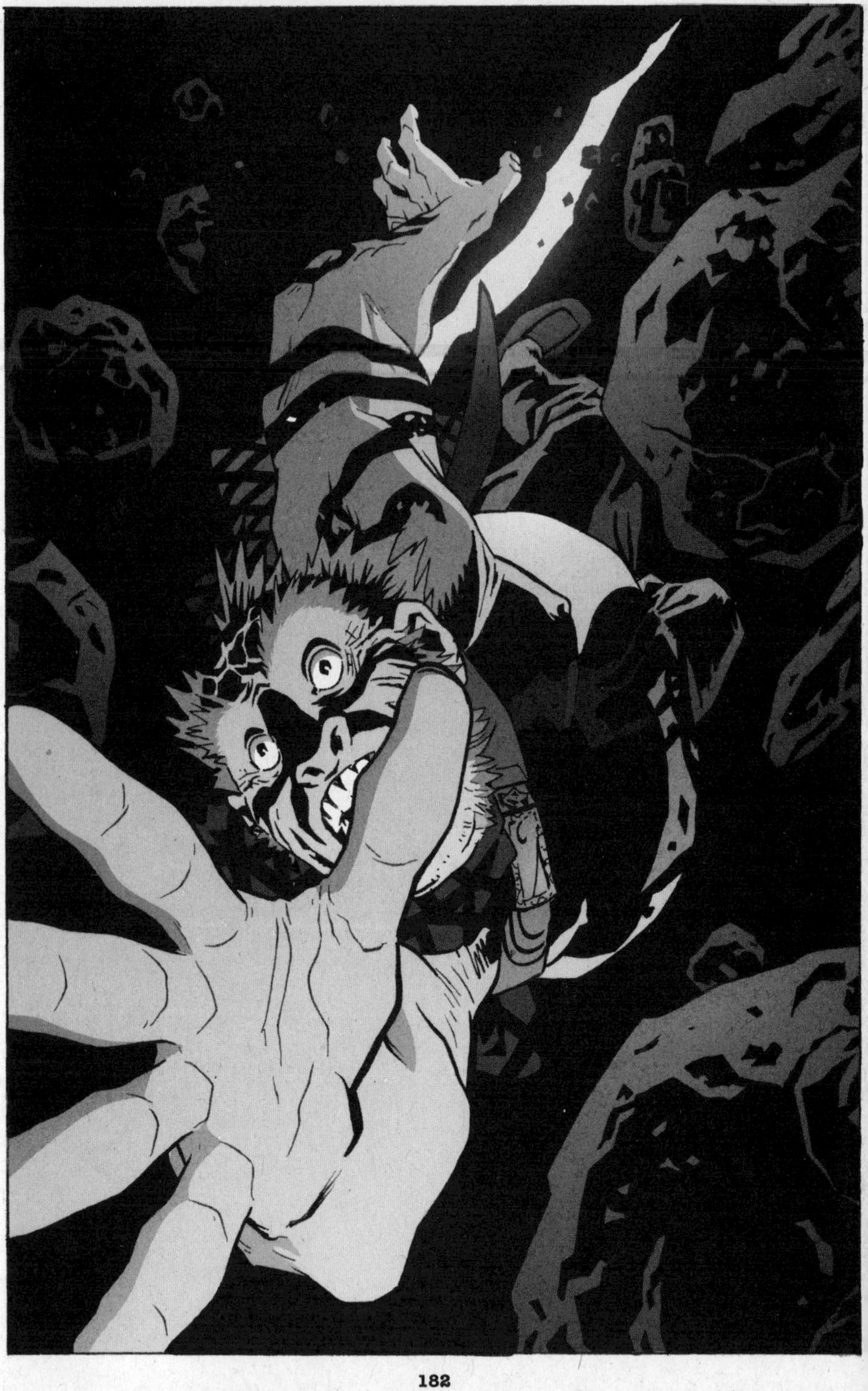

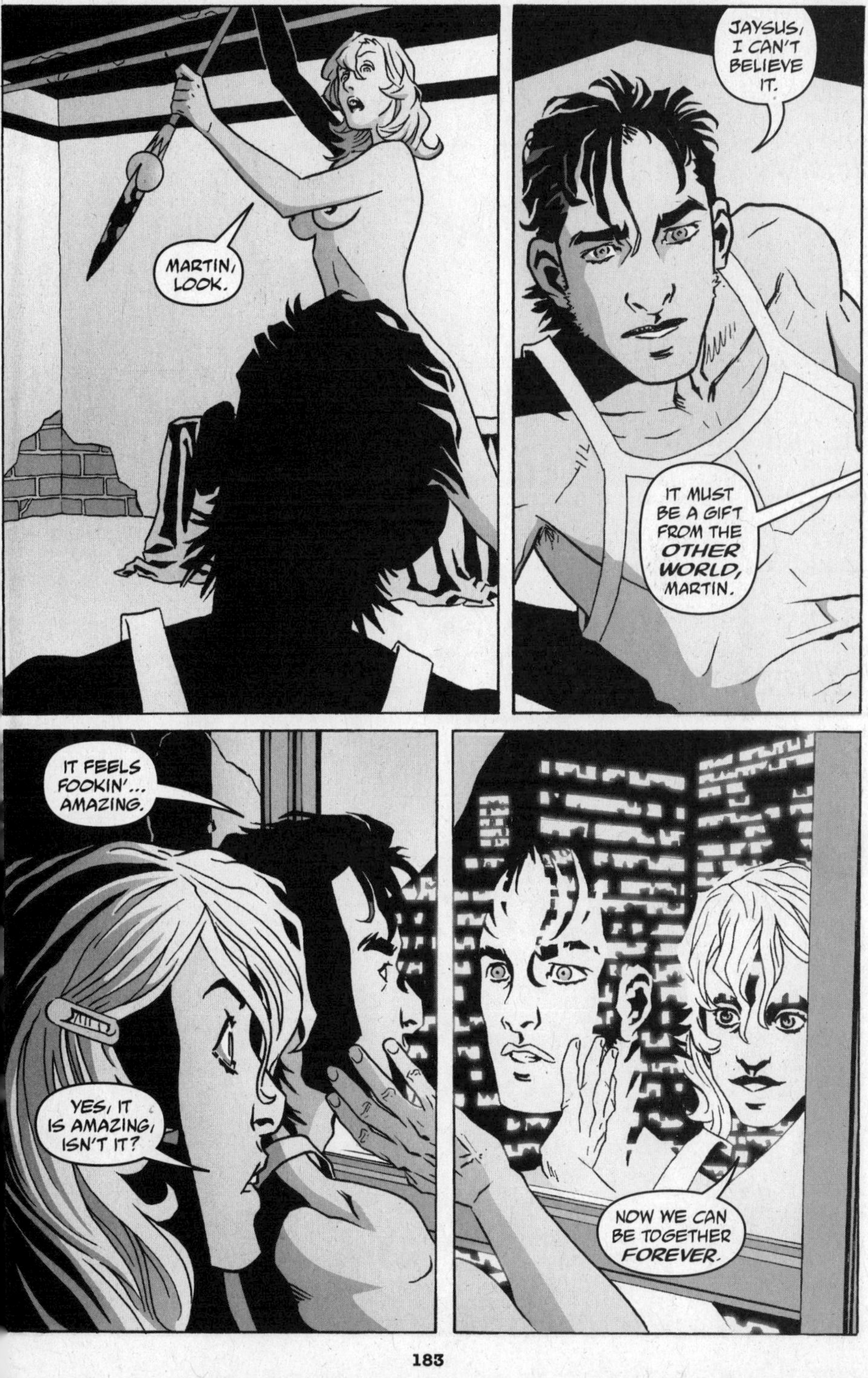
MARTIN, LOOK.
JAYSUS, I CAN'T BELIEVE IT.
IT MUST BE A GIFT FROM THE *OTHER WORLD,* MARTIN.
IT FEELS FOOKIN'... AMAZING.
YES, IT IS AMAZING, ISN'T IT?
NOW WE CAN BE TOGETHER *FOREVER.*

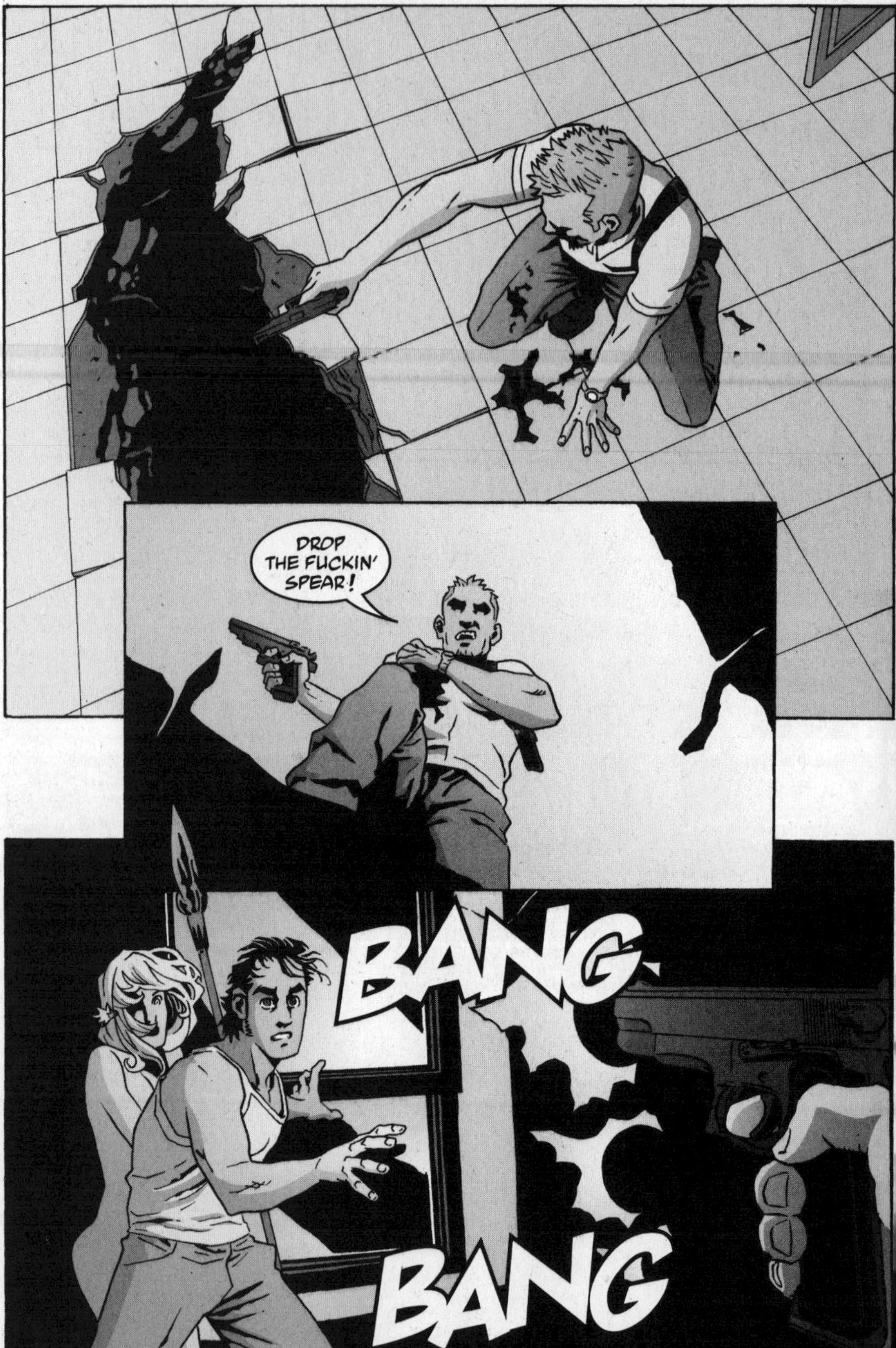
DROP THE FUCKIN' SPEAR!
BANG
BANG

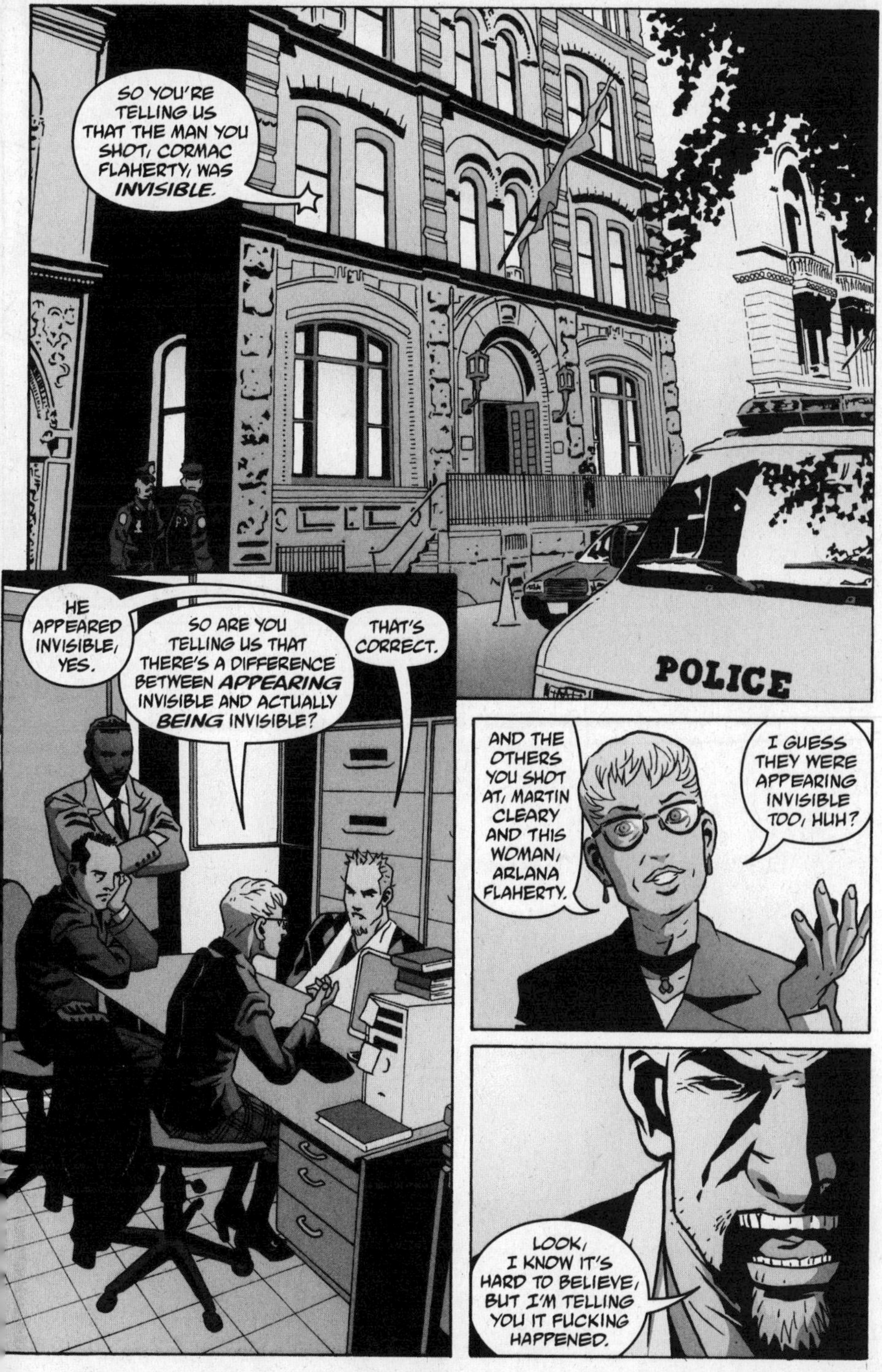
SO YOU'RE TELLING US THAT THE MAN YOU SHOT, CORMAC FLAHERTY, WAS INVISIBLE.
POLICE
HE APPEARED INVISIBLE, YES.
SO ARE YOU TELLING US THAT THERE'S A DIFFERENCE BETWEEN APPEARING INVISIBLE AND ACTUALLY BEING INVISIBLE?
THAT'S CORRECT.
AND THE OTHERS YOU SHOT AT, MARTIN CLEARY AND THIS WOMAN, ARLANA FLAHERTY.
I GUESS THEY WERE APPEARING INVISIBLE TOO, HUH?
LOOK, I KNOW IT'S HARD TO BELIEVE, BUT I'M TELLING YOU IT FUCKING HAPPENED.

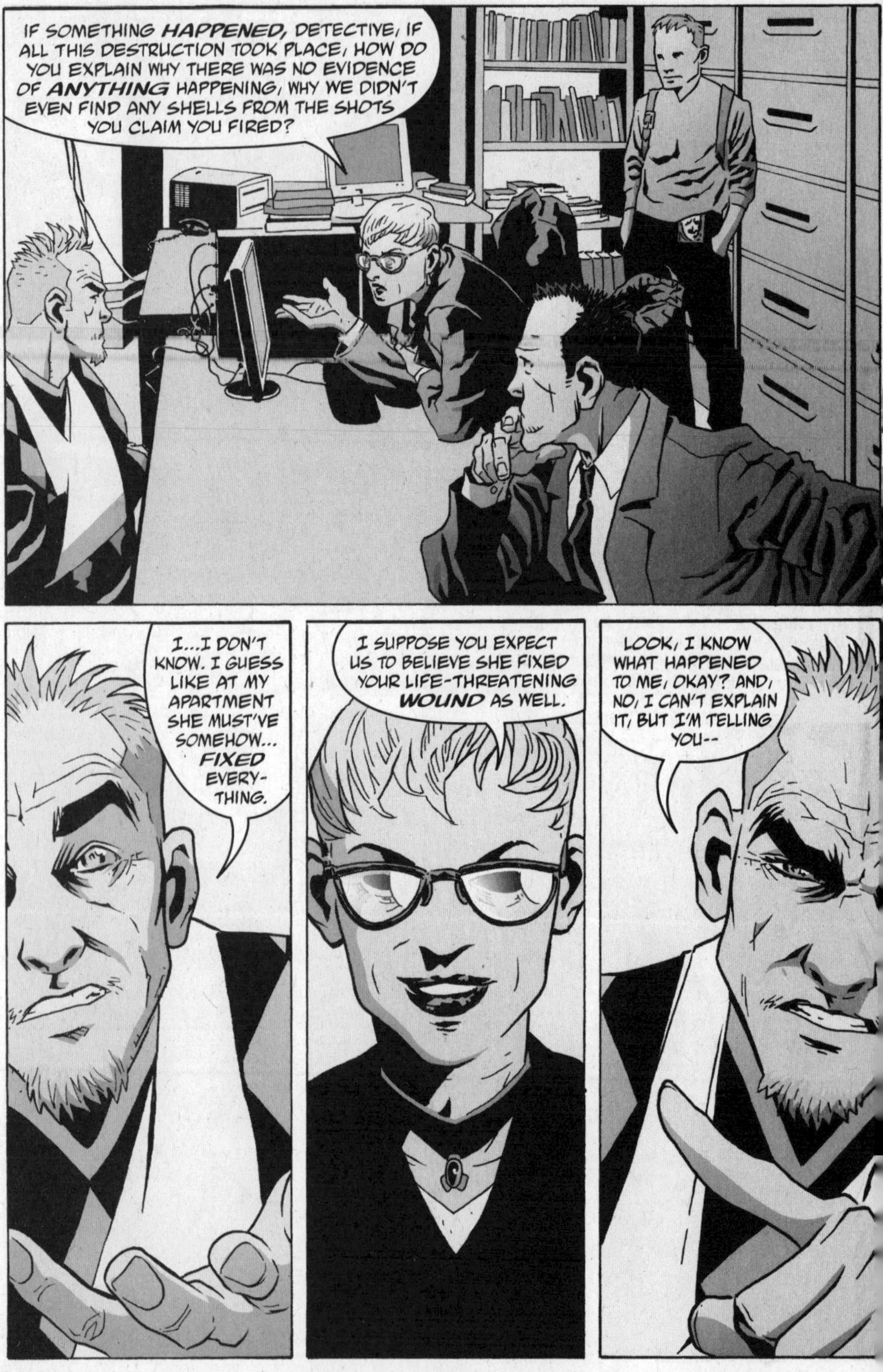
IF SOMETHING HAPPENED, DETECTIVE, IF ALL THIS DESTRUCTION TOOK PLACE, HOW DO YOU EXPLAIN WHY THERE WAS NO EVIDENCE OF ANYTHING HAPPENING, WHY WE DIDN'T EVEN FIND ANY SHELLS FROM THE SHOTS YOU CLAIM YOU FIRED?
I...I DON'T KNOW. I GUESS LIKE AT MY APARTMENT SHE MUST'VE SOMEHOW... FIXED EVERY-THING.
I SUPPOSE YOU EXPECT US TO BELIEVE SHE FIXED YOUR LIFE-THREATENING WOUND AS WELL.
LOOK, I KNOW WHAT HAPPENED TO ME, OKAY? AND, NO, I CAN'T EXPLAIN IT, BUT I'M TELLING YOU--

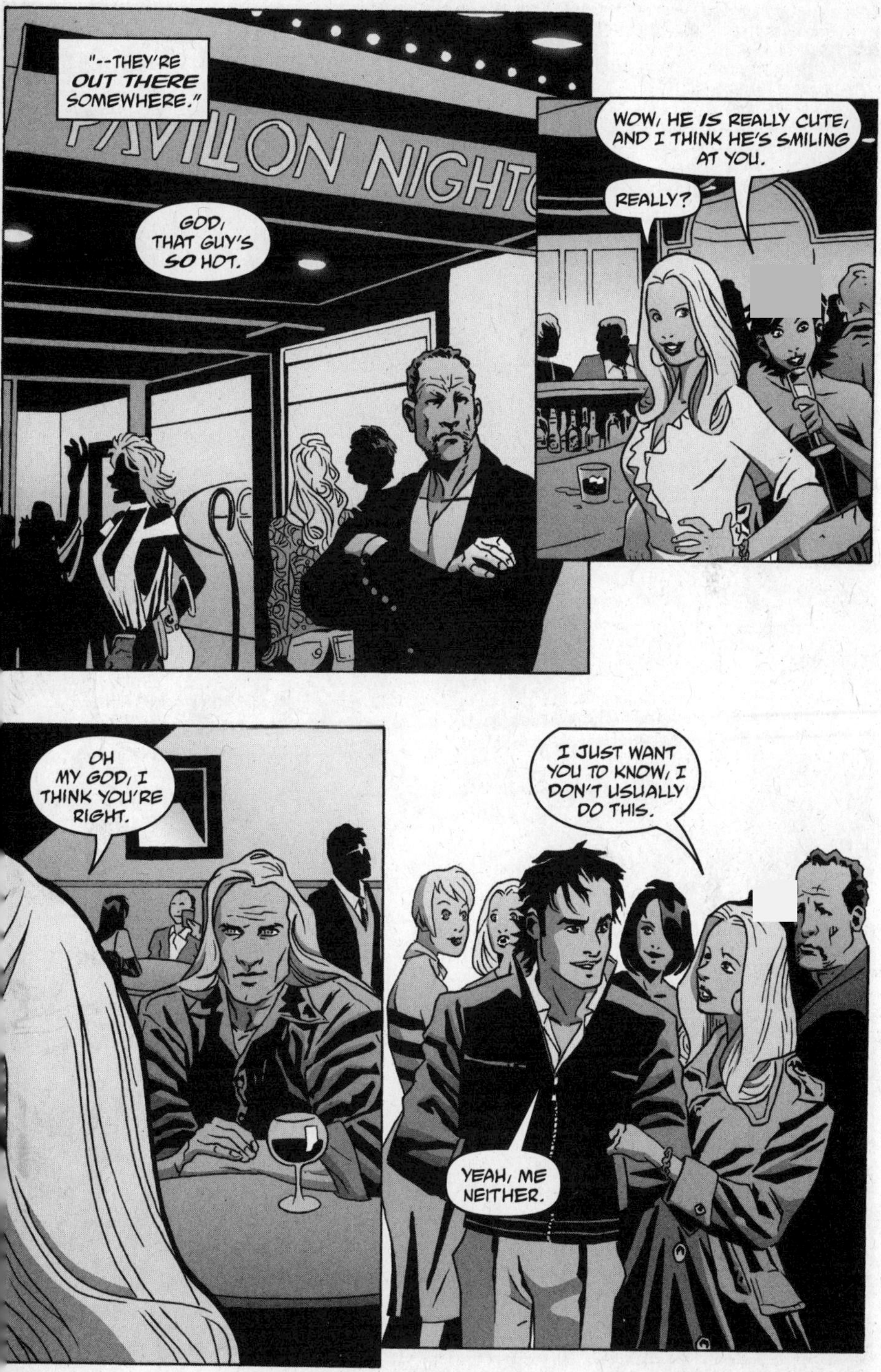
"--THEY'RE OUT THERE SOMEWHERE."
PAVILLON NIGHT
GOD, THAT GUY'S SO HOT.
WOW, HE IS REALLY CUTE, AND I THINK HE'S SMILING AT YOU.
REALLY?
OH MY GOD, I THINK YOU'RE RIGHT.
I JUST WANT YOU TO KNOW, I DON'T USUALLY DO THIS.
YEAH, ME NEITHER.

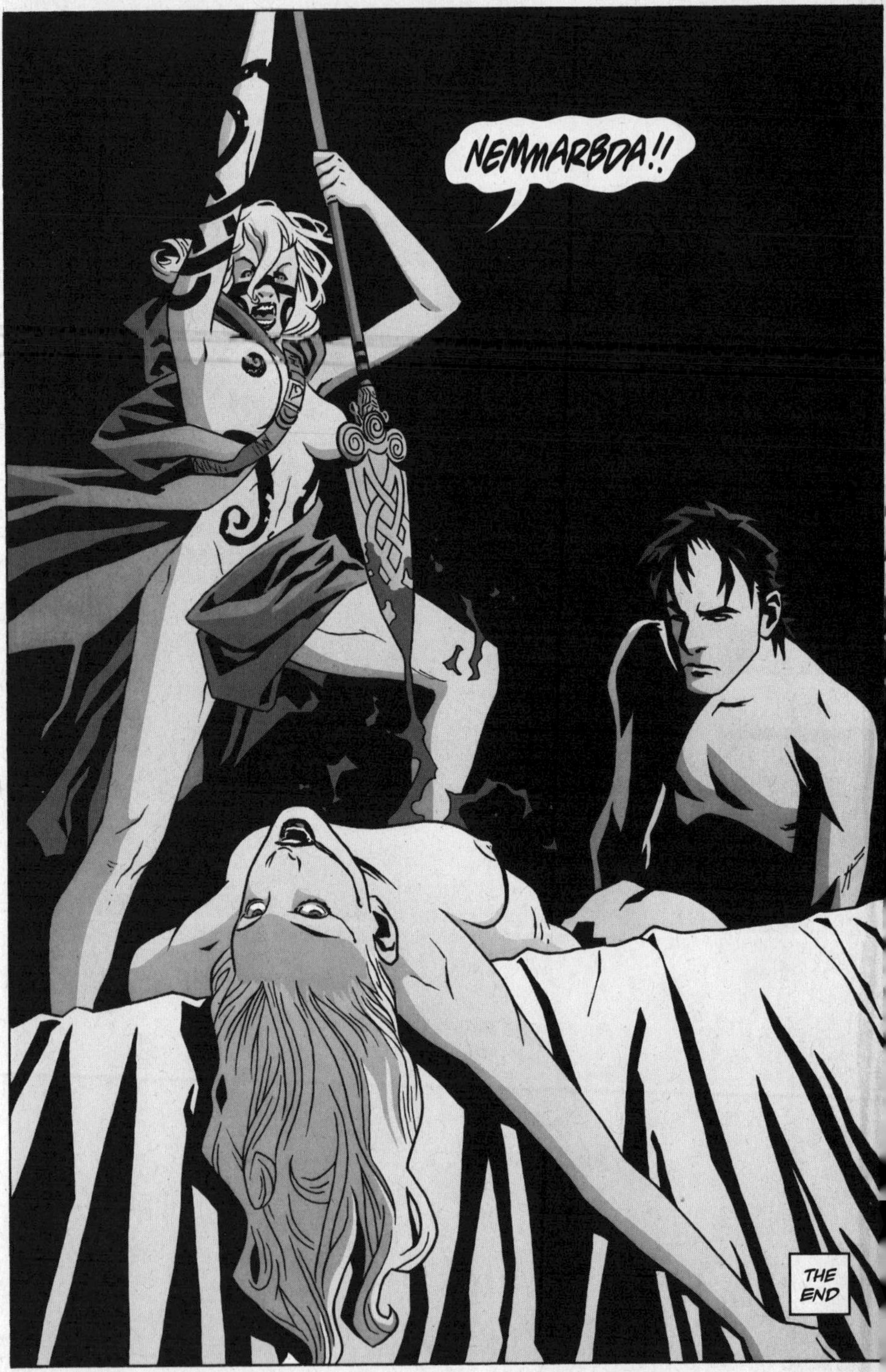
NEMMARBDA!!
THE END

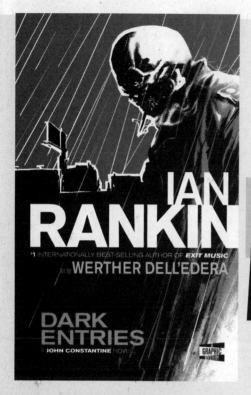

MORE VERTIGO CRIME

AZZARELLO
NEW YORK TIMES BEST-SELLING AUTHOR OF JOKER
FILTHY RICH

FILTHY RICH
AVAILABLE NOW

Written by **BRIAN AZZARELLO**
(Best-selling author of 100 BULLETS and JOKER)

Art by **VICTOR SANTOS**

Richard "Junk" Junkin has always lived on the wrong side of trouble... A former pro football star whose career was cut short by injury (and a nasty gambling problem), Junk now spends his nights playing bodyguard to his boss' unbelievably sexy daughter, Victoria. Before long, Junk finds that she wants a lapdog and not a chaperone, someone who's going to do all of her *dirty* work.

PETER MILLIGAN
JAMES ROMBERGER
THE BRONX KILL
VERTIGO CRIME

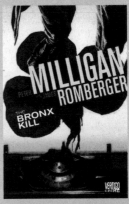

THE BRONX KILL
MARCH 2010

Written by **PETER MILLIGAN**
(GREEK STREET)

Art by **JAMES ROMBERGER**

A struggling writer is investigating his Irish cop roots for his next novel. When he returns home from a research trip, his wife is missing and finding her will lead him to a dark secret buried deep in his family's past.

AREA 10
CHRISTOS N. GAGE
CHRIS SAMNE

AREA 10
APRIL 2010

Written by **CHRISTOS N. GAGE**
(*Law & Order: SVU*)

Art by **CHRIS SAMNEE**

When a detective – tracking a serial killer who decapitates his victims – receives a bizarre head injury himself, he suspects a connection between his own fate and the killer's fascination with Trepanation – the ancient art of skull drilling.

VERTIGO CRIME